Reading Hemingway's *To Have and Have Not*

READING HEMINGWAY SERIES
MARK CIRINO, EDITOR

ROBERT W. LEWIS, FOUNDING EDITOR

Reading Hemingway's *The Sun Also Rises*
  H. R. Stoneback

Reading Hemingway's *Men Without Women*
  Joseph M. Flora

Reading Hemingway's *Across the River and into the Trees*
  Mark Cirino

Reading Hemingway's *To Have and Have Not*
  Kirk Curnutt

Reading Hemingway's *To Have and Have Not*

GLOSSARY AND COMMENTARY

Kirk Curnutt

The Kent State University Press

KENT, OHIO

© 2017 by The Kent State University Press, Kent, Ohio 44242
All rights reserved
Library of Congress Catalog Card Number 2016007527
ISBN 978-1-60635-271-7
Manufactured in the United States of America

Library of Congress Cataloging-in-Publication Data
Names: Curnutt, Kirk, 1964- author.
Title: Reading Hemingway's To have and have not : glossary and commentary / Kirk Curnutt.
Description: Kent, Ohio : Kent State University Press, 2016. | Series: Reading Hemingway | Includes bibliographical references and index.
Identifiers: LCCN 2016007527 (print) | LCCN 2016019122 (ebook) | ISBN 9781606352717 (pbk. : alk. paper) | ISBN 9781631012440 (ePub) | ISBN 9781631012457 (ePDF)
Subjects: LCSH: Hemingway, Ernest, 1899-1961. To have and have not.
Classification: LCC PS3515.E37 T624 2016 (print) | LCC PS3515.E37 (ebook) | DDC 813/.52--dc23
LC record available at https://lccn.loc.gov/2016007527

21 20 19 18 17   5 4 3 2 1

This book is for
Zayd Malik Curnutt
(b. Feb. 25, 2016)
Happiest of travels

"I was all fucked up when I wrote it and threw away about 100,000 words which was better than most of what [I] left in."
—Ernest Hemingway to Lillian Ross on *To Have and Have Not*, 2 July 1948 (*SL* 648)

CONTENTS

Preface and Acknowledgments   ix
An Introduction to *To Have and Have Not*   xvii
Abbreviations for the Works of Ernest Hemingway Used in This Book   lv
Series Note   lvii
Reading *To Have and Have Not*
    Front Matter   3
    Part One: Harry Morgan (Spring)   12
        Chapter 1   14
        Chapter 2   45
        Chapter 3   54
        Chapter 4   57
        Chapter 5   64
    Part Two: Harry Morgan (Fall)   66
        Chapter 6   67
        Chapter 7   69
        Chapter 8   77
    Part Three: Harry Morgan (Winter)   81
        Chapter 9   82
        Chapter 10   98
        Chapter 11   100
        Chapter 12   102
        Chapter 13   106
        Chapter 14   111
        Chapter 15   114
        Chapter 16   133
        Chapter 17   137
        Chapter 18   143
        Chapter 19   152
        Chapter 20   153
        Chapter 21   156
        Chapter 22   161
        Chapter 23   183
        Chapter 24   186
        Chapter 25   198
        Chapter 26   201
Appendix A: Manuscripts   205
Appendix B: A Comparison of the Original Draft of *To Have and Have Not* and the Published Version   208
Appendix C: Focalization and Technique: The Narratology of *To Have and Have Not*   214
Appendix D: Tense Shifts   220
Appendix E: Adaptations of *To Have and Have Not*   223
Appendix F: Correspondence Regarding the 1938 "Banning" of *To Have and Have Not* in Detroit, Michigan   226
Works Cited   232
Index   244

PREFACE AND ACKNOWLEDGMENTS

I still remember what a sock to the jaw the passage was.

In the fall of 1991 I was a stereotypically monastic graduate student preparing to embark upon a dissertation on the American short story. One chapter already outlined was to analyze "Hills Like White Elephants" (1927). At the time, this was Ernest Hemingway's most au courant story, having been plucked from relative obscurity in the late 1980s to become a favorite of classroom anthologies. This had happened because "Hills" not only addressed gender issues, but, unlike previous mainstays such as "The Short Happy Life of Francis Macomber" (1936), it sympathized with the female perspective, thereby providing a welcome rebuttal to Hemingway's reputation for misogyny. Already steeped in the critical history of "Hills"—and perhaps not a little bored with arid stories of expatriate alienation—I decided in the name of completism to familiarize myself with obscurer entries in my cockroach-nibbled copy of *The Complete Short Stories of Ernest Hemingway* (1987). The first neglected piece I flipped to was "One Trip Across" (1934), mainly because the title reminded me of a 1929 F. Scott Fitzgerald story I adored called "One Trip Abroad." I knew that few Hemingway critics even considered "Trip" a short story, because it subsequently reappeared as the opening section of the 1937 novel *To Have and Have Not*. On these grounds, a leading scholar named Paul Smith excluded it from his invaluable reference book *A Reader's Guide to the Short Stories of Ernest Hemingway* (1989), and in those days Paul Smith was my last word on Hemingway stories. I also knew "Trip" had originally appeared in the pages of the high-circulation magazine *Cosmopolitan*, advertised as a "complete short novel." Needing a break from contemplating the 150 years separating Washington Irving from Raymond Carver, I actually welcomed the genre confusion. I figured a more obscure, harder-to-categorize Hemingway work would lend me some personal space to articulate my tastes to myself, far from the madding pressure of inherited critical wisdom.

Right away, I knew something was up. This was a very different Hemingway than classics such as "Big Two-Hearted River" (1925) and "A Clean, Well-Lighted Place" (1933) had accustomed me to. Those stories are somber, quasi-philosophical meditations on the possibilities for design, reason, and control in a world of chaotic despair. By page 3 of "One Trip Across," gunfire had erupted, and bad guys' heads were getting blown off. Although a long episode did seem ethically grounded in the same sportsman's expertise as "River," the main character, Harry Morgan, was nowhere near as sympathetic as Nick Adams, the Hemingway alter ego whose coming-of-age experiences are traced through several other oft-studied stories. In fact, my initial response was that Morgan was so unlikable I didn't understand what Hemingway was doing. "One Trip Across" had neither the sensitivity nor the poignancy that I—a sensitive, poignancy-prone young bookworm—found compelling enough in his work to want to study it. Only one word could describe this tale of Cuban smuggling. Several years would pass before I peeked outside the churchly confines of my academic humanism to embrace it:

This was *hardboiled* Hemingway.

The passage that stopped my reading cold appeared on page 405 of *The Complete Short Stories*. It occurs when Morgan snaps the neck of the nefarious Mr. Sing, the smuggler who hires him to traffic a dozen Chinese nationals from Cuba to Key West:

> I got his arm around behind him and came up on it but I brought it too far because I felt it go. When it went he made a funny little noise and came forward, me holding him throat and all, and bit me on the shoulder. But when I felt the arm go I dropped it. It wasn't any good to him any more and I took him by the throat with both hands, and brother, that Mr. Sing would flop just like a fish, true, his loose arm flailing, but I got him forward onto his knees and had both thumbs well in behind his talk box and I bent the whole thing back until she cracked. Don't think you can't hear it crack, either. (*CSS* 405, *THHN* 53–54)

Something about that "crack" made me close the book. I couldn't finish the story. Hardly a wallflower, I wasn't repulsed by the killing so much as I was embarrassed by the flippant, smart-aleck tone. Here was prose that chuckled over its own capacity to depict brutality. This wasn't the shell-shocked detachment of World War I soldiers in Hemingway's classic collection *In Our Time*. As I had been taught, the experience of bloodshed depicted in that 1925 short-story debut so overwhelms the capacity to comprehend death and destruction that protagonists can only witness it with a "spectatorial attitude" (Cowley, *Exile's Return* 47). "One Trip Across," by contrast, exuded sadistic glee in snapping bone. Here, in one image, I believed I had stumbled upon irrevocable proof of what most of us beginning Hemingway scholars fervently wanted to refute: the conventional wisdom that the author was so obsessed with violence that he lost all capacity for nuance and compassion.

The morning after I broke off my reading, I happened to stroll through Louisiana State University's quad with my dissertation director, and I confessed how hard I blanched at the murder scene. "Oh, yes," grimaced the estimable J. Gerald Kennedy. "That's not my Hemingway." The judgment was good enough for me. I made a point of ignoring "One Trip Across" and any other work that tried to chokehold the reader.

Fast-forward more than a decade. In 2002 the then-president of the Ernest Hemingway Foundation and Society, Scott Donaldson, asked my dear friend Gail Sinclair and me to codirect the Eleventh Biennial Hemingway Conference, which the society's board had voted to hold in Key West. Our first task was to familiarize ourselves with the works Hemingway produced during his years in the legendary island city. Naturally, *To Have and Have Not* topped that list. During our first scouting trip to the Conch Republic, I confessed to Gail that the prospect didn't thrill me. When she asked why, I admitted to bailing on "One Trip Across" because of the murder scene. "That's not my Hemingway," I declared, pretending the phrase was mine. Gail made a great point: if aficionados steered clear of any Hemingway that didn't personally appeal to us, we would end up knowing only a skewed portion of the author's corpus. Perhaps it was the sangria, but I could not deny the logic. For the price of a key-lime pie slice, I bribed Gail into walking over to the (now defunct) Bargain Books on Truman Avenue for an appropriately salt-warped, wind-worn used copy. That night, after a hearty Cuban dinner, I stayed up late in my hotel room and read the novel, straight through.

This time the experience could not have been more different.

As a literary critic long intrigued by reception theory, I believe firmly that the books we read are products of the people we are at the time we read them. In my twenties, I worked overtime as I prepared for my profession to exhibit a high seriousness that was both aesthetic and political. A "good read" for me meant a text that was formally intricate. It should be full of symbols, motifs, and themes ripe for the explicating, and it should uphold the moral agenda I wanted to advocate in my scholarship—empathy, idealism, inclusiveness, and diversity. Not until I was in my mid- to late thirties and relatively secure in my career (hello tenure!) did I reconnect with reading pleasures that seemed more private, if not immature. Among these were my love of suspense, action, crime, violence, and gore, and that dirtiest martini of all, eroticism. Thrills, chills, and raunch: hardly the stuff one revels in when trying to impress the editors of *College Literature*, *Style*, the *Journal of Modern Literature*, and other scholarly outlets. Of course, in the early 1990s I had no shortage of friends and colleagues working on pulp fiction. My most enduring crush at the time happened to be a leading sci-fi scholar who published on *Attack of the 50 Foot Woman*. Members of my cohort wrote dissertations on lesbian sexploitation novels and dime-mag detective heroes. Regardless of subject matter, I didn't sense their approach was any less "serious" than mine. They spoke of ideology instead of narratology, which was my passion, but they didn't explore questions of enjoyment, which was far too tangled up in personal response for novice scholars to broach with the objectivity that earning our PhDs demanded. Looking back twenty-five years, I can honestly say I stopped reading "One Trip Across" not because I was offended but because I was out to repress my susceptibility to the tawdrier, visceral appeal of entertainment. Reading *To Have and Have Not* that night in Key West convinced me it was high time to embrace it.

Believe it or not, entertainment is not a word often associated with Hemingway, despite his omnipresence as a popular-culture icon. Clearly, this is not because his work is not entertaining. Fans and scholars alike would probably agree that, compared to the more esoteric writings of James Joyce or Gertrude Stein, his writing is more entertaining than that of many modernist contemporaries—at least if we define entertainment as the satisfaction that comes from the immediacy of pleasure. Yet, however accessible Hemingway's body of work, the culture still approaches him as a "serious" writer, as one whose themes reflect important humanist concerns. The snootier among us may label him *midcult*, to use Dwight Macdonald's famous term for middlebrow art that aspires to highbrow appreciation, but rarely is he spoken of as a masscult phenomenon. This is because to read him for the devices associated with the mass-market crowd-pleaser—"the formula, the built-in reaction, the lack of any standard except popularity," as Macdonald grumbled (37)—is to deny him the standard of individual accomplishment that remains the sine qua non of art. I believe if one were to extract Macdonald's condescending language from his reading of *The Old Man and the Sea*, he has a pretty good explanation for that book's blockbuster sales in 1952–54. The "fake biblical prose," the "Universal Significance" of the elemental, allegorical characters, and the "drone of the pastiche parable" all assured middlebrow readers in the early years of the Cold War that Western democratic values could endure the Atomic Age (40).[1] One could perform a similar exercise of "de-condescension" on Maxwell Perkins's surprisingly arch comment to F. Scott Fitzgerald that Hemingway pursued "the stamp of bourgeois approval" by crafting *For Whom the Bell Tolls* for the Book of the Month Club audience (Fitzgerald, *Dear Scott/Dear Max* 266), or Fitzgerald's own insistence that his rival's 1940 novel exhibited "all the profundity" of that great middle-class crowd-pleaser of the day, Daphne du Maurier's *Rebecca* (1938) (*Notebooks* 335). Yet few if any commentators have challenged the elitism in such remarks. Rather than explore the satisfactions of midcult and masscult reading, the critical agenda has been to ensure Hemingway's stature among the high cult.

To be more specific, I don't believe we have sufficiently analyzed the formula within Hemingway's crime fiction the same way studies such as Geoffrey O'Brien's *Hardboiled America: Lurid Paperbacks and the Masters of Noir* (1981, expanded 1997) and novelist Megan Abbott's *The Street Was Mine: White Masculinity and Urban Space in Hardboiled Fiction and Film Noir* (2002) delineate those within Dashiell Hammett, Raymond Chandler, Chester Himes, Jim Thompson, and many other pulp writers. Consider "The Killers" (1927), the most famous of several Hemingway short stories that could, with some elasticity of genre definition, be called noir. (Others include "The Gambler, the Nun, and the Radio," "Today Is Friday," "A Pursuit Race," and the sequel to "One Trip Across," "The Tradesman's Return"—that is, part 2 of *To Have and Have Not*). Although Don Siegel's 1964 in-name-only adaptation of Hemingway's tale of hit men pursuing a broken-down boxer is considered a film-noir classic, few scholars have done more with the story itself than to acknowledge its general affinities with crime fiction. The reason may be that generations of us cut our literary teeth on Cleanth Brooks and Robert Penn Warren's classic reading of "The Killers" in *Understanding Fiction* (1946, and updated for decades). Although Brooks and Warren make casual reference to elements of the story being "something you read about in a thriller," they do so to argue that Hemingway "charges" those familiar tableaux with aesthetic significance, *elevating* them from mere conventions of popular fiction into essential touchstones of the story's literary theme (317–18).[2] That Brooks and Warren define this theme as "the discovery of evil" further underscores their insistence on distinguishing the text from genre fiction: for formalist critics, youth's fall from innocence was *the* quintessential literary plotline. Yet I often wonder if had we grown up reading analyses such as Robert C. Meredith and John Dennis Fitzgerald's *The Professional Story Writer and His Art* (1963) our approach would be so insistently literary. Meredith and Fitzgerald's now-forgotten quasi-textbook assesses variations on basic plots and dramatis personae throughout popular fiction, showing how formula accommodates variety for authors hoping to sell stories to mass-market magazines. For the authors, the titular hit men and the doomed boxer Ole Andreson, not Nick Adams, are what make "The Killers" effective fiction, for these stock characters illustrate how "the almost thoroughly dehumanized caricature or the slightly less dehumanized stereotype may nonetheless be utilized to tell a gripping story" (233). Had we been taught from *The Professional Story Writer* alongside *Understanding Fiction,* would we be more inclined to talk about "The Killers" as servicing the same hardboiled fantasies dished out weekly in *Black Mask, Detective Story Magazine, Spicy Detective,* and other era pulps? Would I personally have been more prepared as a grad student to appreciate how Mr. Sing's murder is as viscerally gripping as the gruesome moment in Hammett's *Red Harvest* (1929) when gangster Reno Starkey, taking four bullets to the torso, must lean forward in his folding chair to keep his guts from literally spilling as he spills them metaphorically in a dying declaration to the Continental Op (140)?

I ask such questions for a very conflicted reason. While I cannot argue with a straight face that *To Have and Have Not* is a good book, I still enjoy the hell out of it. And I do so for the same reasons I can boast of enjoying W. R. Burnett's *Little Caesar* (1929); Paul Cain's *Fast One* (1932); Jim Thompson's *The Getaway* (1958); Sam Peckinpah's 1972 movie version of the latter with Steve McQueen and Ali McGraw; Armitage Trail's *Scarface* (1932) and every film version it has inspired, from Howard Hawks's censor-defying shoot-'em-up to Brian DePalma's 1983 cocaine-and-chainsaw-fest, on up to Tracy Letts's squalid play *Killer Joe* (1993) and its recent William Friedkin film incarnation (2012). On a basic level, I get a kick out of these efforts because every instinct within me says I shouldn't. They make me feel cheap and skeezy, and they let me indulge my cynicism toward my fellow man. They let me pretend that an afternoon in a dive bar is more redeeming than a morning at church. In catering to these illusions, my hardboiled predilections provide a release from the doldrums of routine and responsibility, a rush of blood to an otherwise well-regulated circulatory system. O'Brien has a nice phrase for the appeal of bloody, lurid noir: it excites a "subversive longing for all that is not nice" (11). In this regard, I find myself attached to *To Have and Have Not* for one simple reason. It lets me believe, contrary to my training, that not every Hemingway novel need be as noble as *The Old Man and the Sea*.

I say all this by way of apology for what the present volume is not. A book of glosses such as this typically has two functions. On the pragmatic front, it explains the references and allusions in a work so readers who do not recognize them can make basic sense of the text. More qualitatively, explicating pivotal passages makes the case for literary worth by demonstrating that the work's texture is intricate. As Brooks and Warren put it, to both understand and evaluate a piece of fiction, we must assess "the skill with which the theme has been assimilated" into its "detailed structure" (317). By explicating, we make a case for craft as embodied by unity and form—something that, admittedly, is harder to do for a book whose own author felt lacked his standard exhibition of literary skill. In commenting on the novel, then, I want to make clear that my aim is not to rehabilitate it. I do suggest that there are underappreciated moments of character development and theme iterating that make for a more "detailed structure" than critics have credited it with. Overall, however, my goal is not to insist that *To Have and Have Not* is better than its reputation insists. Even compared to second-tier pulp efforts by Hammett, James M. Cain, or Horace McCoy, it is a sloppy mess. Nevertheless, the novel does resonate with fascinating background and inspiration, much of which fails to attract attention just because it is considered such an unholy dud. Some of these details are biographical, illustrating how Hemingway fictionalized real-life events and acquaintances. Others are historical, exploring the conditions that created the story's Florida Straits milieu. Many are also intertextual, demonstrating the consistency of reference throughout the author's works. Whatever their type, these details are examined in order to confirm that even when an overall work isn't particularly admirable, its nuts and bolts can prove interesting components indeed.

For the opportunity to write this book, I want to thank Joyce Harrison, Mary Young, Will Underwood, and the team at Kent State University Press, including my wonderful copyeditor, Erin Holman. My friend and colleague Mark Cirino has done an excellent job managing the Reading Hemingway series for the press; I'm grateful to Mark for the many deadlines he has allowed me to renegotiate and for his good humor over the past several years as I have teased him about whether *To Have and Have Not* is a better or worse book than *Across the River and into the Trees*, which is his contribution to the series. I'm further indebted to the late, eminent Hemingway scholar Robert W. Lewis, the original editor of these Reading Hemingway guides, who entertained my prospectus and encouraged Kent to sign me.

A number of other Hemingway folks have likewise inspired and supported me over the years: Sara A. Kosiba, Scott Donaldson, J. Gerald Kennedy, Jackson R. Bryer, James Nagel, Susan F. Beegel, Sandra Spanier, Linda Patterson Miller, Suzanne del Gizzo, Debra Moddelmog, Miriam Mandel, our current Hemingway Society president, H. R. ("Stoney") Stoneback (author of the series entry on *The Sun Also Rises*), Linda Wagner-Martin, Alex Vernon, and my collaborator and cherished friend Gail Sinclair. James Plath has always been generous in encouraging scholarship on Hemingway in Key West, after serving for many years as the academic coordinator of the island's Hemingway Days Festival. For their help with Key West history and background, I wish to acknowledge several people who made the Conch Republic such a great site for research. Tom Hambright, who curates the Florida History Room at the Monroe County Public Library, let me take up residence for a week to scroll through two decades of the *Key West Citizen*. Douglas "Dink" Bruce, the son of Hemingway handyman Toby Bruce and Key West's much adored founder of the Florida Room, Betty Bruce, lent me fascinating pictures and entertained my questions with good humor—all while hosting me and my son, Kip, for happy hour on the deck at Louie's. Brewster Chamberlin was exceedingly generous in lending me his painstakingly researched Hemingway chronology, which has since been published as *The Hemingway Log: A Chronology of His Life and Times* (2015). Brewster and his delightful wife, Lynn-Marie, kindly took in this wayward stranger one Thanksgiving spent on the island. Before her retirement in 2012, Claudia Pennington at the Key West Art and History Museum was invaluable in helping me track down information on the WPA artists "stationed" in the Keys in the 1930s; her successor, Michael F. Gieda, and museum curator Cori Convertito likewise entertained multiple inquiries from me. Nor can I fail to acknowledge my friend at Immanuel Presbyterian Church in Montgomery, Alabama, Frances Sutton. Quite serendipitously, I discovered that Frances grew up on Fleming Street in Key West and that her elementary school teacher was Lorine Thompson, confidante to Pauline Pfeiffer and wife to Hemingway's close friend Charles, the inspiration for "Karl" in *Green Hills of Africa*. It's a small world.

I also thank my mother, Beverly Curnutt, who has become quite a regular at Hemingway Society conferences over the years, for giving me the gift of books as a child.

Finally, to two Hemingway friends who served as readers for this book, Robert W. Trogdon and Carl P. Eby:

I'll be seeing you boys soon at Sloppy Joe's.

NOTES

1. In a recent article, Thomas Gordon Perrin takes the opposite tack, arguing that *The Old Man and the Sea* reflects an anxious response to two competing modes of symbolism within modernism: the allegorical, hieroglyphic form of the linguistic device (popularized by Freud as a "dream language") that ensured a 1:1 correspondence between figure and thing; and the more romantic, imagistic mode that resisted logic by encompassing contradiction and disunity. Hemingway's reliance on the former, Perrin argues, makes the 1952 novella susceptible to being denounced as middlebrow; in a word, Hemingway's symbolism simplifies rather than problematizes interpretation, as illustrated by the use of the motif "too far out," which throughout the novel does not *literally* cause Santiago to lose his fish to sharks but instead is reiterated to dramatize Santiago's hubris: "The fact that Santiago's phrase 'I went too far out' makes no sense when read as a factual statement about fishing foregrounds its allegorical significance as a statement about hubris. The failure of Hemingway's impressionism makes it hard for readers not to see the novella as functioning allegorically and thus makes the novella a middlebrow text" (162).

2. Thus, as simple a word choice as substituting "towel" for "gag" in a sentence describing Nick Adams's reaction to being—well—gagged reflects the author's conscientious effort to treat his materials artistically. According to the formalist critics, by writing "He had never had a towel in his mouth before," Hemingway makes "that cliché of the thriller" (tying up a victim) "come true" (Brooks and Warren 317) by defamiliarizing its expression and dramatizing the utter terror of it, which Nick cannot suppress, no matter how hard he tries to "swagger it off" like a noir hero would (CSS 137). At all points, the aim of "The Killers" is to "emphasize . . . that the unreal clichés of horror have a reality" (318) so the reader can appreciate Nick's initiation into the evil of the world.

AN INTRODUCTION TO
TO HAVE AND HAVE NOT

Among the seven novels Ernest Hemingway published in his lifetime, *To Have and Have Not* counts as one of two abject failures. Four of the seven are certified American classics. The individual reputations of *The Sun Also Rises* (1926), *A Farewell to Arms* (1929), *For Whom the Bell Tolls* (1940), and *The Old Man and the Sea* (1952) may rise or fall as literary tastes change from decade to decade, yet all were critical and commercial successes at their times of publication, and no serious argument can be made that any one of them is less than a triumph of form, style, and moral vision. A fifth full-length fictional narrative, *The Torrents of Spring* (1926), is the oddball of the group.[1] Sometimes categorized as a satire instead of a novel, it is deemed a negligible effort, in part because its author never took it seriously: it was written to sever Hemingway from a mentor to whom early on he was too often compared (Sherwood Anderson) and to free him from a publisher he detested (Boni & Liveright) to join one he admired (Charles Scribner's Sons). Between the stellar reputation of the Big Four and the innocuous peculiarity of this toss-off, then, *To Have and Have Not* vies with *Across the River and into the Trees* (1950) for the ignominious honor of THE WORST. Which book deserves the title largely depends upon a reader's individual taste.

A good case can be made that even if *To Have and Have Not* is the bigger failure, it is still the more interesting read. A lion-in-winter love story that examines aging and mortality, *Across the River and into the Trees* is plodding and sentimental, saturnine in its acceptance that time defeats even the most decorated of heroes. It is a novel that, surprisingly enough for a man of Hemingway's iconic robustness, endorses going gently into that dark night, a whimper instead of a bang. *To Have and Have Not*, by contrast, is a relentless 262-page pummeling. The story of a charter-boat captain, Harry Morgan, struggling to survive the Depression on the economically ravaged island of Key West, it includes shootouts and fistfights, smugglers, rumrunners, and revolutionaries, adulterers and addled soldiers, and even the first uncensored appearance in Hemingway fiction of the *F* word. To cite another term in it that pops up repeatedly, it is a novel almost singularly obsessed with proving it has *cojones*. And yet, paradoxically, it is also recognized for "present[ing] an intriguing collection of female characters"—perhaps even Hemingway's *most* intriguing women (Tyler 57).

Between *To Have and Have Not* and *Across the River and into the Trees*, the latter is certainly far more unified and cohesive, with the form of the earlier novel a blatant hodgepodge of two previously published short stories with a long third section tacked to its end.[2] That a substantial portion of this final section was hastily amputated before publication only magnifies the feeling that the book, like its hero after page 87, is missing a limb.[3] And yet, despite the fractured structure, Harry Morgan's story still feels fresher and more invigorating than that of Colonel Richard Cantwell, the protagonist of *Across the River*. This is not simply because of the dowdy pace of the later novel. *Across the River* revisits tropes integral to the Hemingway legend, most obviously the code of heroism that insists that grace under pressure is the truest gauge of morality. Yet this familiar theme is not presented in revivifying fashion. Too often, the book reads like a geriatric *A Farewell to Arms*, with even the ultimate litmus test of personal valor, war, a distant memory.

To Have and Have Not, however, finds the author engaging two contemporaneous genres that infuse it with energies unique to his corpus. One of these is the proletarian novel that rose to the literary fore in the early 1930s as a response to the economic collapse of the Depression. Aggressively partisan and overtly reform-oriented, this type of fiction claimed to do away with aesthetics, which for politically minded writers represented a willful escape from class inequities and labor exploitation—"the hell of finance capitalism," as Delmore Schwartz put it in his review (qtd. in Meyers, *Critical Heritage* 255). The other genre is the violent hardboiled fiction that emerged in the 1920s and which reveled in tough-talking heroes, femme fatales, and hyperrealistic brutality. Hemingway's terse prose style had encouraged the development of this popular mode, with short stories such as "The Killers" (*MWW,* 1927) inspiring Carroll John Daly, Dashiell Hammett, Raymond Chandler, and other practitioners to amplify suspense through exchanges of stylized dialogue that rattle like bursts from a Tommy gun. As one critic noted at the time, *To Have and Have Not* reads like "glorified pulp" (qtd. in Stephens 167). He meant that as an insult, but it need not be interpreted as one. More than any other Hemingway novel, *To Have and Have Not* finds the writer plying literary techniques to popular-culture materials in ways that blur the line between "high" and "low" culture.

The pop-culture resonance of the novel is further substantiated by the afterlife it has enjoyed. Tellingly, for decades *Across the River and into the Trees* was the one Hemingway novel aside from *The Torrents of Spring* that Hollywood had never bothered to film. Only now, sixty-five years after its publication, is a movie version entering the preproduction stage. By contrast, *To Have and Have Not* has inspired not one but *three* different movies. These range from Howard Hawks's very liberal 1944 adaptation (the first screen pairing of Humphrey Bogart and Lauren Bacall, and cowritten by William Faulkner) to the much more faithful John Garfield / Patricia Neal vehicle *The Breaking Point* (1951) to future *Dirty Harry* director Don Siegel's decidedly B-grade *The Gun Runners* (1958), whose promotional material advertised it as "HEMINGWAY-HOT ADVENTURE!" (See appendix E on these adaptations.) *Across the River*'s most enduring legacy, meanwhile, is to have inspired the classic E. B. White *New Yorker* parody "Across the Street and into the Grill." This most famous of Hemingway takeoffs has been anthologized so often one is tempted to claim more people have read it than the novel at which it pokes fun.[4]

Finally, there is the matter of setting. *Across the River* takes place in the country that many would claim rivals France for the most influential geography to shape its author's sensibility. As an eighteen-year-old Red Cross ambulance driver, Hemingway had been wounded in Italy. Both that particular locale—just outside Fossalta, along the Piave River—and associated sites of recuperation (Milan, Stresa) recur throughout his most compelling war fiction, from *A Farewell to Arms*, "In Another Country" (*MWW*, 1927), "Now I Lay Me" (*MWW*, 1927), and "A Way You'll Never Be" (*WTN*, 1933). Several *Across the River* passages do hint at Hemingway's brilliant talent for crystallizing images of landscape. Yet, overall the stiltedness of the style and the pervasive aura of attenuation combine to sap this trademark strength of its characteristic surety. To this reader, whole patches of the narrative pass with Italian vistas rendered with an atypical blandness, as if the author's eyes were failing as quickly as those of Colonel Cantwell.

To Have and Have Not, in contrast, feels nearly febrile from the swelter of its tropical setting. With a violent opening scene in Havana, several episodes cast on the waters of the Gulf Stream, and gritty, often grotesque glimpses of Depression-era Key West, the novel amplifies the reputation of the Florida Straits as a humid nexus of piracy, roguery, and political intrigue. Certainly, more artistically satisfying novels have been born from the combustible combination of ethnicities, climate, and economic opportunism represented by the slim ninety-mile waterway separating Cuba and Key West. One thinks of Graham Greene's *Our Man in Havana* (1958), Thomas McGuane's *Ninety-two in the Shade* (1973), Thomas Sanchez's *Mile Zero* (1989), *King Bongo* (2003), and *American Tropic* (2013), as well as Leonardo Padura's marvelous Lieutenant Mario Conde mysteries.[5] For better or worse, though, *To Have and Have Not* is the title that leaps to mind when one attempts to name the work that has set the template for modern-day Gulf of Mexico intrigue.

The novel itself can only take partial credit for this influence. Its stature has equally to do with how the two cities depicted in it claim its author, which is another way that the book's legacy differs from that of *Across the River*. In the fifty years since Fidel Castro seized control of the country, Communist Cuba has effectively nationalized Hemingway, making landmarks of heritage and pride out of any site associated with his presence there from the early 1930s to the 1959 revolution (Beidler 108–09). This includes, most obviously, his Cuban home, the Finca Vigía, and his cabin cruiser, *Pilar*, both of which remain in the government's possession despite gentle diplomatic efforts to return them to the author's estate.[6] Yet many other locations that Hemingway merely frequented are emblazoned with his name and/or image. The Hotel Ambos Mundos, where he stayed throughout 1930s—and where he wrote the bulk of *For Whom the Bell Tolls*—offers tours of his room, 511, featuring "a roped-off bed, an antique dresser, photographs, and a few of Hemingway's books, locked in a china hutch," along with a period typewriter stationed to show off the view that inspired him to work (Hemingway and Brennan, *Hemingway in Cuba* 127). His preferred watering hole, the Floridita, serves Papa Dobles (double-dosed daiquiris), which tourists can enjoy while contemplating his cordoned-off barstool (Greene 75–78). Also named in his honor is a marina not far from the Jaimanitas suburb that was home to Jane Mason (1909–1981), the putative mistress skewered in *To Have and Have Not*. The Hemingway Marina often confuses tourists, who assume he docked *Pilar* there—he preferred the San Francisco Wharf nearer to downtown, as does Harry Morgan—but the lack of actual association hasn't stopped the facility from appropriating both the name and the legend. The marina is home to the annual Hemingway Fishing Tournament, sponsored by the Hemingway Yacht Club, while the nearest hotel is called The Old Man and the Sea.

At least Havana can claim that its exploitation of Hemingway has a political purpose. In Key West the motives are strictly commercial. The Hemingway House and Museum at 907 Whitehead Street, where Hemingway and his second wife, Pauline Pfeiffer (1896–1951), lived from 1931 until their marriage dissolved in 1939, has long bragged of being the island's most famous tourist attraction; one only wishes it would devote equal energy to fact-checking the legends it proliferates to entertain tourists. The Casa Antigua at 314 Simonton Street advertises itself as Hemingway's first residence, while two popular saloons, Sloppy Joe's and Captain Tony's, duke it out for recognition as his preferred place to drink and carouse. (Captain Tony's sits at the site on Greene Street where Sloppy Joe's was located before moving to its current Duval Street location in 1937; a sign on Captain Tony's western facade boasts "THE HEMINGWAY YEARS SPENT HERE 1933–1937"—illustrated with a rendering of Hemingway circa 1960).

For all of these reasons then, *To Have and Have Not* inspires interest that endures long after the reader has acknowledged its formal failures. This guide aims to aid understanding of the text by glossing specific passages through a combination of biographical, historical, and thematic analysis. Before embarking on the project, though, some preliminary questions of value arise. Is a line-by-line explication of a "bad" book really a productive use of time? However educational and diverting travels to Key West and Havana might be, isn't scholarly initiative better served unraveling the intricacies of the classic novels and stories? In the larger context of authorial reputation and standing, aren't close readings of a failed work counterproductive? Don't they risk drawing undue attention to weaknesses instead of accomplishments? And while few scholars would argue that the purpose of criticism is to panegyrize the positive, isn't a central if uncelebrated goal of interpretation to assure readers that a text is a rewarding read? That a novel pays off in enjoyment the scrupulous work necessary to analyze it?

A basic answer is that this volume belongs to a series dedicated to providing comprehensive commentary on Hemingway's works. In this regard, *To Have and Have Not* is included for completism's sake. But that is a perfunctory justification at best. I would argue that the novel's reputation as a failure has severely impeded appreciation of the many elements within it that are both interesting and, in at least a few cases, aesthetically compelling. Not the least of these is Hemingway's prowess with action and suspense, which is as much a product of his celebrated skill for eliminating "scrollwork" and "ornament" in his prose as his reputation for imagistic precision and symbolism (*MF* 12). Another is the experimentation with narrative perspective and storytelling style in general that makes *To Have and Have Not* Hemingway's most technically intricate novel. Nor have many of the book's motifs—those aforementioned cojones—been contextualized in terms of other Hemingway works to explain their thematic contribution to the novel. Moreover, while *To Have and Have Not* has inspired an excellent trickle of criticism over the decades, various rivulets of debate have only occasionally been pooled into a reservoir of discussion. To date, only two edited collections—Toni D. Knott's *One Man Alone: Hemingway and* To Have and Have Not (1999) and Gail Sinclair's and my *Key West Hemingway: A Reassessment* (2009)—have analyzed the novel in any extended depth. As a result, several useful insights remain too far-flung in autonomously published essays for even dedicated Hemingway aficionados to have charted them all. A book such as this, then, offers an opportunity to centralize extant criticism by comparing and contrasting crosscurrents of opinion.

Additionally, a reader's guide can challenge truisms about the roman à clef aspect of the novel. As with most Hemingway texts, interest in *To Have and Have Not* often focuses on the real-life inspiration for various characters and locations that make cameo appearances. Hardly a reference out there fails to mention how the author vented his ire at fellow novelist John Dos Passos (1896–1970) by mocking him as the facetious proletarian writer Richard Gordon, or how he expressed more ambiguous resentment at Jane Mason by portraying her as the voracious "rich bitch" Helène Bradley. The ostensible flaying of these former friends is often cited as the reason Hemingway lopped off the later fourth of the manuscript—the potential for libel was simply too great. Yet our understanding of how or even why the author chose to skewer compatriots is based on conventional wisdom instead of fresh inquiry. In some cases, that wisdom is even erroneous. Among the minor characters who fill out the novel, Hemingway mocks a couple named Laughton as endemic of the boorish vulgarity of the tourist class that invaded Key West after 1934. Since Carlos Baker's 1969 biography, *Ernest Hemingway: A Life Story,* the model for the pair has been identified as a "Mr. and Mrs. Jack Coles." This is thanks to an April 1936 letter to Dos Passos in which Hemingway's mockery anticipates the couple's satirizing in the novel (*SL* 447). Just who the Coleses were and how they were acquainted with Hemingway's circle has inspired little research. Subsequent biographers have simply embroidered upon Baker's reference to describe them as "friends of Dos Passos" for no other reason than that their names appear in a letter addressed to him. In fact, evidence suggests that Hemingway was referring instead to sometime acquaintance John Cheney Cowles (1894–1972) and that the single, troublesome *w* distinguishing the two names disappeared from his typing for reasons unknown. In the original *To Have and Have Not* manuscript, Laughton is alternately named "Boles" and "Bowles." (Cowles is pronounced *Coles*). As if that internal evidence weren't suggestive enough, two letters from Cowles in the Hemingway Collection at the John F. Kennedy Library in Boston, Massachusetts, suggest that the two men had a confrontation in July 1936 as Hemingway drafted the novel. A full detailing of this evidence can be found on pages 119–22, but for now suffice it to say such evidence is indicative of how many nuggets of textual background remain to mine.

The Cowles/Bowles connection suggests an even greater justification for annotating *To Have and Have Not*. Beyond commenting that the "Haves" originally played a far larger role in the plot than they do in the final published version, few critics have discussed the mass of drafts, discarded scenes, deleted passages, and insertions that Hemingway toiled over in 1936–37. What the late biographer Michael S. Reynolds told Toni D. Knott in the mid-1990s remains true twenty years later: the manuscript of *To Have and Have Not* "is the most neglected of the Hemingway texts" (Knott 228). While an excellent if obscure 1985 master's thesis by Sarah Finch Brown does survey the book's transformation, a complete inventory of the cut portions has heretofore remained unpublished. By no means does the present volume sell itself as a traditional textual study; a thorough catalogue of emendations will have to wait for a scholarly edition. Yet throughout this guide I do describe changes both major and minor to the manuscript, convinced that to appreciate fully what the novel "has" we must know what it once "had."

Before turning to the glosses then, I want provide detailed background by narrating the book's composition, publication, and reception history.

The beginnings of *To Have and Have Not* date to late September / early October 1933 during a burst of work in Madrid, Spain.[7] Having proofed his third full-length short story collection—the poorly received *Winner Take Nothing*, published that same fall—Hemingway agreed to edit the English version of a florid Spanish novel called *Currito de la Cruz* by Alejandro Pérez Lugín, which his bullfighter friend/factotum Sidney Franklin (1903–1976) translated into *Shadows of the Sun* (1934). As Hemingway reported on 16 October to his mother-in-law, Mary Pfeiffer, "The day I finished that [I] was so sick of trash that [I] decided to write a story to rinse my mouth out and started one that ran to over 100 pages of manuscript" (*SL* 397).

That same day he wrote almost identical words to Jane Mason: "I thought I would rinse my mouth out [after editing Franklin] and started a little story and the bastard got longer and longer and longer until just finished it three days ago—about 15,000 words." Comparing his depiction of "Habana" to that of "Hogsheimer"—aka Joseph Hergesheimer (1880–1954), whose writing often dealt with Cuba and whom Hemingway had previously chided as a "garter snapper" (*SAR* 43)—he noted his story had "plenty action. On land and on sea." He also made sure to add, "No you're not in it Madame" (Unpublished correspondence 1). Within three short years, this claim would prove ironic, when he conceived the character of Hélène Bradley. As both letters attest, Hemingway felt invigorated by the propulsive plot of a charter-boat fisherman who tangles with Cuban revolutionaries, witnesses a shootout, gets ripped off by a shifty tourist, and finally kills a Chinese trafficker in a decidedly antiheroic double-cross involving human smuggling. "It is almost entirely action," Hemingway enthused to his wife's mother. "It is exactly the story that this present book needs i.e. Winner Take Nothing. But it will be as well or better in another book. You can't very well put a story that you know will sell like hotcakes in a book called Winner Take Nothing" (*SL* 397).

Titling the potboiler "One Trip Across," Hemingway completed his editing by 27 October while waiting in Paris to embark on a two-month African safari. The revisions were minor, involving mostly syntactical tinkering with the opening bloodbath at the Café de la Perla de San Francisco and the penciling in of a flippant racial epithet that decades later would inspire great condemnation of his racism: "Some nigger" (8:4–5). According to biographer Carlos Baker, Hemingway's friend Solita Solano (1888–1975) agreed to type the manuscript for submission (*A Life* 247).[8] The question marks that dot the typescript are likely hers; the handwriting is feminine, and it seems doubtful that anyone in Hemingway's immediate camp would query either his nautical terminology ("soundings") or his Key West slang ("Conch").

Sometime in late November, Solano forwarded the story to *Cosmopolitan,* one of the top middlebrow fiction markets in the United States, which emphasized a variety of genres that appealed equally to men and women. (In this way, the publication could not have differed more from its most famous incarnation, initiated in 1965 by the late Helen Gurley Brown, as an oracle for sexually liberated women.) The manuscript barely arrived in New York before the magazine offered $5,500 for it, a record story sum for the writer, which corresponds to roughly $88,000 today. Hemingway hadn't even had to place "One Trip Across" in a book before the hotcakes were in high demand.

The decision to submit to *Cosmopolitan* reflects its author's evolving sense of literary identity. Only a few years earlier, in 1928, Hemingway had declined an invitation to serialize *A Farewell to Arms* in this very venue, a profitable centerpiece of the empire of media baron William Randolph Hearst (1863–1951). Although Hemingway lamented the loss of the windfall this opportunity represented, he feared *Cosmopolitan*'s nearly 2 million subscribers were not the right audience for his often explicit novel of war and love. No such qualms were suffered a short time later when he sold his first Gulf of Mexico story, "After the Storm" (1931), to editor Ray Long. *Cosmopolitan* paid a handsome $2,700 for this short monologue of a salvager who discovers a dead body while stripping a sunken ship of its booty.[9] Inspired by a story recounted by his Key West fishing guide, Captain Edward "Bra" Saunders (1876–1949), "After the Storm" nicely amalgamates Hemingway's habitual preoccupation with death with elements of the popular action-adventure story, including an exotic setting and a hint of piracy. (Greek competitors run the unnamed narrator from the salvage site.)

As lucrative as "After the Storm" was, Hemingway was likely surprised in January 1934 by *Cosmopolitan*'s generous offer for "One Trip Across." The windfall was a bright spot in an otherwise disappointing new year. After only two weeks on the Serengeti Plain, Hemingway had to be airlifted back to nearby Nairobi after catching a debilitating bout of amoebic dysentery. It was while recuperating at the New Stanley Hotel that he first learned of the bid for the story from a pair of month-old cables just then catching up to him. $5,500 was a risky investment for *Cosmopolitan,* which had recently undergone a radical, Depression-mandated belt-tightening. Whereas the slick had once enjoyed a lavish $74,000-a-month editorial budget (the equivalent of more than $1 million today), it now had to make due with roughly 40 percent of that—a cost-cutting measure that had forced it to relinquish many marquee names (Fannie Hurst) in favor of lesser-knowns. (The other victim of this austerity plan was Ray Long himself, who was replaced by Harry Pane Burton. By 1936, Burton would travel directly to Key West to negotiate with Hemingway.) Clearly, *Cosmopolitan* recognized a gem when it saw one and heavily promoted the issue. As junior editor Burton MacBride informed Hemingway that May, "We got a lot of swell comments on your 'One Trip Across'" (Unpublished correspondence 1).

Some of those swell comments were delivered directly to the author. Many friends and colleagues recognized what Hemingway had in his letter to his mother-in-law: the gunplay and criminal intrigue of "One Trip Across"—its "pure action"—had jolted his writing out of the dour stagnancy that drained many *Winner Take Nothing* stories of energy. Hemingway's editor at Scribner's, Maxwell Perkins (1884–1947), appreciated the riveting force upon reading the story in manuscript. In a congratulatory letter dated 7 February 1934, he praised the story while making clear his lukewarm regard for the collection: "['One Trip Across'] is one of your big stories,—takes two or three days to shake it off. There are four stories in *Winner Take Nothing* that are anyhow as fine in their own ways, but this is one of those spectacular stories which everybody will feel to full effect. I am mighty glad that you wrote it, and I'll bet there will be a lot of talk about it" (Bruccoli, *Sons* 174). F. Scott Fitzgerald (1896–1940) wasn't quite so subtle. Irritated by a letter in which Hemingway condescendingly critiqued his long-delayed *Tender Is the Night* (which appeared that same April), Fitzgerald seized upon Hemingway's admission that *Winner* was weak: "Because I'm going egoist on you in a moment, I want to say that just exactly what you suggested, that the edition [addition, that is] of that Chinamen-running story in the *Cosmopolitan* would have given Winner Take Nothing the weight that it needed was in my head too" (*Life in Letters* 262). Another reader, Arnold Samuelson (1912–1980) of Minnesota, was so exhilarated by the story that he hopped the rails to Key West intending to learn at the feet of the master. "I read your story 'One Trip Across' and I liked it so much I came down to have a talk with you," the eager young man declared upon rapping at the door of 907 Whitehead Street (4). Samuelson spent the rest of 1934 working as the *Pilar*'s unofficial boat guard, an experience he recounts in his posthumously published memoir, *With Hemingway: A Year in Key West and Cuba* (1984).

Yet if "One Trip Across" demonstrated that action could enliven the grimness that lately bogged down Hemingway's writing, a question remains: why did he wait another two years before committing to a Harry Morgan novel?

Perhaps the construction of the story was too immaculate for its own good, and he couldn't imagine a way to expand the plot from 12,000 words to the 50,000-plus necessary to fill out a book. (On its cover, *Cosmopolitan* advertised the story as one of two "short" *and* "complete" novels that the issue contained.) An even more obvious answer is that his mind was elsewhere. The same month "One Trip Across" hit newsstands, Hemingway returned to the United States via Europe from his African safari, his 3 April 1934 arrival in New York on the SS *Paris* covered by several of the city's daily newspapers.[10] Before heading home to Key West, he arranged to purchase the *Pilar*, delivered in early May to Miami, where he and Bra Saunders took possession to pilot the cabin cruiser to its new home in the abandoned Naval Station Key West submarine basin. The summer was spent breaking in the boat, with extended trips to Havana. But if Hemingway's heart was on the Gulf, his head remained on the Serengeti. From May to November he labored over *Green Hills of Africa*, a nonfiction account of his safari that proved a critical and commercial failure when published in October 1935. By this point, public pining for a Hemingway novel had grown palpable. Six years had elapsed since *A Farewell to Arms*, and coming on the heels of not only a disappointing story collection but the bullfighting treatise that preceded it (*Death in the Afternoon*, 1932), a hunting travelogue could only seem another misstep. *Cosmopolitan* dispatched Burton MacBride to Key West to read *Green Hills* in manuscript, rejecting it with an unambiguous insistence it would only consider a novel. ("Better luck next time," wrote Harry Burton [Unpublished correspondence 1].) Critics, meanwhile, complained of Hemingway squandering his talent by writing "rubbishy" articles for *Esquire*, a men's magazine that since mid-1933 had paid him $250 a month to pontificate on sport fishing, travel, and the literary life. Edmund Wilson (1895–1972) diagnosed why Hemingway's nonfiction paled in comparison to the genre that made him famous: "In his fiction, the conflicting elements of his personality, the emotional situations which obsess him, are externalized and objectified; and the result is an art which is severe, intense and deeply serious. But as soon as he talks in his own person, he seems to lose all his capacity for self-criticism and is likely to become fatuous or maudlin" (qtd. in Meyers, *Critical Heritage* 218). Although he couldn't say it as bluntly as Wilson, Perkins felt the same way. "The public regards you as a novelist," he wrote when his star author demanded to know why *Green Hills* failed. "This [book] they took as an interlude" (*TOTTC* 238).

Perhaps because Hemingway's return to fiction was so heavily anticipated, his second Harry Morgan story failed to pack quite the same punch as "One Trip Across." "The Tradesman's Return" appeared in the February 1936 issue of *Esquire*, and instead of human trafficking it centered on rum-running, something of a passé topic, given that Prohibition had been repealed two years earlier. As the story opens, Harry and his current mate, Wesley, return to Key West wounded after an ambush by Cuban authorities. While the mate lies blubbering and blaming his captain for his injuries ("Take it easy, the man says. . . . Take it easy. Take what easy? Take dyin' like a dog easy? You got me here. Get me out" [73:18–20]), Harry struggles to dump his cargo before the Coast Guard can intercept them, despite a bullet rendering his right arm useless. With the shootout occurring offstage this time, the focus falls upon how differently each man responds to his pain. When an ashamed Wesley apologizes at story's end for failing to help his boss, Harry comments, "Ain't no nigger any good when he's shot," before facing his own crippled future with the stoic humor the mate lacks: "I hope they can fix that arm. . . . I got a lot of use for that arm" (87:1–2).

Manuscript evidence suggests that "The Tradesman's Return" wasn't conceived as effortlessly as Harry Morgan's debut was. The Hemingway Collection at the John F. Kennedy Library houses a fifteen-page handwritten fragment that appears a preliminary attempt at this second installment (See MS 31, item 206, folder 18). Only here, as in "One Trip Across," the setting is Cuba instead of Key West, with the military police boarding Harry's boat to seize his black-market supply of cigarettes, razor blades, and matches. Instead of a shootout, Harry is arrested, and Wesley spends an entire month awaiting his release on the impounded boat. The draft crackles with witty tough-guy wisecracks but lacks compelling conflict; without the men filled full of lead and fearing for their lives, the stakes of the raid don't seem very consequential. The major benefit of the draft was that Hemingway could address in his own mind the question Wesley poses in the final version: "Why they run liquor now? . . . Prohibition's over. Why they keep up a traffic like that? Whyn't they bring the liquor in on the ferry" (70:16–18). As Harry explains in this abandoned draft, smugglers could run bootleg goods in and out of Mariel because for six months the city had become a "fixed port," meaning boats could come and go without customs declarations.[11] Rumrunners could thus load Cuban liquor that was stronger and cheaper than spirits then available in the States. Because it wasn't taxed, it was also more profitable. Mariel's open border was a historical fluke, arising out of the chaotic aftermath of Cuban dictator Gerardo Machado's toppling in August 1933 (shortly after the timeframe of "One Trip Across"). As unusual as it was, however, the export situation didn't contribute as centrally to the story's overall theme as the Cuban revolution did in Harry's first adventure, this time serving as mere backdrop.

The same is not true of the American political context depicted in "The Tradesman's Return." The story may lack the rip-roaring action of "One Trip Across," but it introduced a new militancy into Hemingway's fiction that would become the core rhetorical stance of *To Have and Have Not*. As a wounded Harry heaves his liquor cargo into the ocean, another boat, carrying a pompous New Deal bureaucrat who brags of being "one of the three most important men in the United States today" (80:8–10), crosses his path. The claim may be a delusion, but perhaps the man would take comfort in knowing that the story's working title, "White Man, Black Man, Alphabet Man," reveals he was conceived as its third most important *character*. ("Alphabet Man" refers to the common slang term *alphabet agency*, which mocked the abbreviations by which laboriously named government bureaucracies were popularly referred—for example, WPA for the Works Project Administration.) Realizing that Harry is a bootlegger, the bureaucrat flushes with visions of J. Edgar Hoover–style fame and orders his charter captain, Willie Adams, to pull alongside so he can make a citizen's arrest. As Harry's friend and a fellow working man, Captain Willie carries no truck with this "stool from Washington" and lectures him and his obsequious assistant on proletarian struggles: "[Harry's] got a family and he's got to eat and feed them. Who the hell do you eat off of with people working here in Key West for the government for six dollars and a half a week?" (81:13–16) (Like the hero of "After the Storm," Captain Willie is based on Bra Saunders.) As the old salt insists, the Depression forced good Conchs to break the law because the law wasn't saving them from starvation.

Captain Willie's dressing-down of the functionary made it clear that Hemingway was no fan of either President Franklin Delano Roosevelt (1882–1945) or his administration. The ire came from at least two sources. In the summer of 1934, Hemingway was stunned by the state of Florida's decision to cede management of his adopted city to the newly created Key West Administration, an offshoot of the state branch of the Federal Emergency Relief Administration (FERA), Roosevelt's initial clearinghouse for economic intervention. The KWA was the brainchild of FERA's top man in the state, Julius F. Stone Jr. (1902–1967), who became known across the island as the "Key West Kingfisher" for his imperious, Huey Long–like style of leadership. Under Stone's rule, the city attempted to resuscitate itself from a crippling financial crisis by reinventing itself as a tourist haven. The side effect, however, was to homogenize the native culture and raise the cost of living until native Conchs began to fear they couldn't afford their own homes. Amid Stone's various edicts and laws, Hemingway was personally affronted when the KWA listed 907 Whitehead Street as a tourist attraction on a pamphlet promoting island attractions.[12] Months before "The Tradesman's Return," he had written a satirical account for *Esquire* of the invasive hordes now rapping at his front door. Gawking at the famous author with the same curiosity they have for the turtle kraals, these visitors prove hilariously uninformed about his actual writing. Read side by side, "The Sights of Whitehead Street" (*BL* 192–204) and "The Tradesman's Return" lament the loss of Key West to outsiders whose ignorance of its history and tradition isn't compensated by the money they bring—mainly because that revenue wasn't trickling down to the working locals who most needed it.

The second source of Hemingway's disgust with the Roosevelt administration involved a natural disaster that also afflicted the downtrodden. On 2 September 1935, the most powerful hurricane ever to make landfall in the United States tore across the Matecumbe Keys, obliterating the area surrounding the city of Islamorada. Hemingway was acquainted with at least one casualty: local fisherman Joe Lowe had inspired the character of Eddy Marshall, Harry Morgan's drunken mate in "One Trip Across." Among the other 408 victims were 259 World War I veterans whom FERA had sent to the area the previous fall to help build a leg of the Overseas Highway then limited to ferry service. According to many outraged editorials, the veterans could have been saved; bureaucratic bumbling had delayed an evacuation train from Miami that should have safely transported them to Key West before the storm made land. With his natural empathy for soldiers, Hemingway was convinced FERA's ineptitude constituted manslaughter, and he penned a ferocious attack on the Roosevelt administration that accused it of intentionally abandoning the men to their fate.

Appearing in the 17 September 1935 issue of the leftist magazine *New Masses*, "Who Murdered the Vets?" announced this charge with a provocative title selected by its editor over Hemingway's more abstract "Panic." That Hemingway had dismissed ideological publications such as *New Masses* in his *Esquire* essays and in *Green Hills of Africa* seemed to herald a shift in political engagement. As Scott Donaldson writes, "the literary left regarded 'Who Murdered the Vets?' as an unmistakable sign that Hemingway had seen the light and was ready to join in the crusade against capitalism" (*Fitzgerald and Hemingway* 376). An *Esquire* reader happening upon "The Tradesman's Return" in early 1936 would have likely interpreted Captain Willie's rant as further proof of this newfound commitment to the "crusade." As Hemingway embarked on writing a third Harry Morgan episode, protestations against both capitalism and the New Deal would grow louder and more aggressive.

Manuscript evidence hints that the confrontation between Captain Willie and the Alphabet Man wasn't conceived until well into the drafting process. At first, Hemingway narrated the story from Harry's first-person point of view, as he'd done in both "One Trip Across" and his discarded Mariel sketch (see MS 30, item 204, folder 6). Seventeen handwritten pages in, however, he went back and scratched out the *I*s to switch to the more objective, externalized third-person perspective. Noting similar patterns of revision in *For Whom the Bell Tolls* and several short stories, Genevieve Hily-Mane has argued that Hemingway frequently vacillated on point of view because he struggled with "establishing distance between the author and the imaginary character the author changes into—the narrator" (37). Yet in "The Tradesman's Return" the decision probably owed more to story structure than to any tendency to over-identify with his protagonists. Allowing the Alphabet Man to gasconade on his importance to the New Deal meant shifting the scene from Harry's boat to Captain Willie's. That cutting away in turn precluded use of the first person for the simple reason that Harry could not report on a confrontation he wasn't physically present to witness. When the time came to stitch "One Trip Across" and "The Tradesman's Return" together into a novel, Hemingway would not bother revising the narrative perspective of either story. Instead, inconsistency would become a deliberate tactic, with first-person chapters juxtaposed against third-person ones until the point of view grew every bit as jumpy as the plot.

Precisely when this "stitching" process began is unclear. "The Tradesman's Return" was mailed to *Esquire* by 10 December 1935, but not until the last week of January 1936 could Hemingway report to his mother-in-law that he was engaged "in a rush of work (on a new book)" (*SL* 433). Whether he meant a novel or a new collection of short fiction is uncertain. On his desk were several promising stories in various states of completion, including two of his absolute best, "The Snows of Kilimanjaro" and "The Short Happy Life of Francis Macomber," both of which were finished that spring and featured in magazines by fall. In a 5 April letter to *Esquire* editor Arnold Gingrich, Hemingway mentions that *Cosmopolitan*'s Harry Burton had recently visited Key West to "get stories and bid on the novel." This suggests the author toiled over both projects simultaneously, a point reinforced by a subsequent comment in which he references a "long story which is getting plenty longer" while noting an imminent departure for Cuba because "am in the novel to where I needed to be over there again for something" (*SL* 441). Naturally enough, "One Trip Across" and "The Tradesman's Return" were slated for inclusion in the novel—at least until Hemingway decided the quality of his new stories was so strong he wanted to strike while the creative iron was hot. In a 9 April letter to Maxwell Perkins, he lists "Trip" and "Tradesman" alongside the working titles for "Snows" and "Macomber" as material he might include in either a career-spanning compilation or a collection of entirely new stories he aimed to publish that fall.[13] As difficult as imagining *To Have and Have Not* without Mr. Sing or the Alphabet Man is, Hemingway was convinced that Harry Morgan's third adventure could sustain a book of its own. Not until July would he renege on that idea. As he explained to Perkins, "Gingrich was down here and I showed him the 30,000 words I had done on the Key West–Havana novel of which One Trip Across and The Tradesman's Return were part. I had taken these for the book of stories and he seemed to think that was crazy" (*SL* 447). Gingrich was so "steamed up" over the narrative's prospects that he made his star contributor promise to hold off writing any new stories until the novel was done. Hemingway was quick to recognize the benefit of the advice. If he could come up with a few "new and unnamed" stories to replace "Trip" and "Tradesman" in the prospective collection of his short fiction, he could give his critics "both barrels" with "2 [back-to-back] books instead of one." All the better, too, that the first barrel would be "that thing all the pricks love—a novel" (*SL* 448–49).

The letter to Perkins goes on to suggest Hemingway was in solid command of the theme and scope of his new Harry Morgan material. The novel would contrast Key West and Havana while examining the "inter-relation" of their cultures. Two themes would predominate: "The decline of the individual" and "the mechanics of revolution and what it does to the people engaged in it." While the plot would trace Harry's fall as "Key West goes down around him," it would also follow "the story of a shipment of dynamite and all of the consequences that happened from it." As if this weren't enough, he promised Perkins "a hell of a lot more that I won't inflict on you," though he couldn't resist at least one teaser: "Also have the hurricane and the vets in it" (*SL* 448).

As epic as the description sounded, the letter did not begin to convey the breadth of ideas Hemingway outlined to himself. The manuscript of *To Have and Have Not* contains a single sheet that suggests he envisioned the novel as a three-tiered work. (The sheet is filed as the final page of MS 31, item 211, folder 24.) Understandably enough, the first level is characterological, focusing on Harry Morgan and the theme of defeated individualism. The second concerns the contrast between Key West and Havana and details issues of setting. Perhaps most intriguing is the third, which would expose the evolution of institutional mechanisms of control that impinge human liberty. These would include "The Rise of the Army" and "The Rise of the Bureaucracy" and even extend the narrative's reach to the question of national character with "The Decline of the Spaniard"—presumably, the decline of Spanish heritage in post–Treaty of Paris Cuba as the country struggled with its hard-won sovereignty. As Michael S. Reynolds notes, the diagram represents "an ambitious, complicated plan, a *War and Peace* in miniature" (*1930s* 233). Within the various tiers, Hemingway also listed specific historical events he intended to dramatize. These include not only the fall of President Gerardo Machado but the 4 September 1933 "Sergeants' Revolt" that elevated future dictator Fulgencio Batista (1901–1973) to the head of the Cuban army. Hemingway also intended to discuss the 29 September 1933 attempt by Cuban Communists to commemorate martyred hero Julio Antonio Mella (1903–1929), whose ashes had just been allowed back into the country from Mexico, where the exiled revolutionary was assassinated on 10 January 1929 upon Machado's orders. The 10 November 1933 siege of Havana's Atarés Fortress, where some eighty members of the reactionary ABC party were mowed down by Batista's troops after a poorly planned coup attempt, was also slated for the book. As if these news items weren't enough, Hemingway identified personal friends he planned to incorporate into the narrative, including two frequent *Pilar* guests, painters Antonio Gattorno (1904–1980) and Luis Alfredo Lopez Mendez (1901–1996).

The schema is so dense that one doubts even Tolstoy could have managed the intricacy. There is little evidence to suggest Hemingway consulted the sheet as he wrote, for nowhere in his drafts are these events specifically dramatized. Instead, this third section traces Harry Morgan's moral quandary when he is approached to ferry a quartet of Cuban revolutionaries to Havana (thus reversing the trajectory of "One Trip Across"). Harry is broke and unable to earn a living any other way, for since "Tradesman" he has lost his wounded arm to amputation and his boat to the Coast Guard. The captain thus consents to the plan, despite his antipathy for the crooked lawyer brokering the deal, Robert "Bee-lips" Simmons. Harry also knows why the revolutionaries are in Key West: they plan to rob the First State Trust and Savings Bank to fund their activities back home. To help him with the getaway, Harry recruits yet another mate, Albert Tracy, of Conch descent. (No mention is made of Wesley from "Tradesman.") After a great deal of debate about class inequities and the failure of the New Deal to alleviate the suffering of the poor, Albert agrees. The bank robbery goes disastrously wrong, however, and the mate is machine-gunned to death before the boat Harry borrows for the trip can leave the dock. Once at sea, Harry manages to kill three of the revolutionaries but is mortally wounded by the fourth. As he lies dying, the defeated hero ponders the futility of challenging the economic chain of being: "I guess it was nuts all along. I guess I bit off more than I could chew. I shouldn't have tried it. . . . It must be an unlucky business. Some unlucky business. I guess what a man like me ought to do is run something like a filling station. Hell, I couldn't run no filling station" (174:28–175:2). The writing throughout these scenes is predictably muscular and rippled with hardboiled repartee, especially in the exchanges between Harry and Bee-lips. If the bank robbery fails to quite crackle with the same vivacity as the opening shootout in "One Trip Across," the moments leading up to Harry's attack on his captors demonstrate that Hemingway had lost none of his flair for suspense.

Had he stopped here and fleshed out the grotesque atmosphere of impoverished Key West in a revision, Hemingway could have produced a worthy capstone to a Harry Morgan triptych. But his interests weren't solely with proletarian struggles. He also wanted to contrast the desperation of the poor to the excesses of the rich that had been streaming into his city since the Julius F. Stone / KWA takeover of 1934.[14] Already in chapter 15 he had introduced an unpleasant couple, the Bowleses (later changed to the Laughtons), and a somewhat more tolerable professor, John MacWalsey, who annoy the locals at Freddy's Bar, a thinly veiled version of Joe "Josie" Russell's Sloppy Joe's Bar. Beginning with chapter 19 (marked as the beginning of part 4 in the draft), he shifted focus to introduce an array of well-to-dos whose affectations and petty senses of self-importance reveal their blindness to social inequity. Foremost among these "haves" is a parasitic figure who makes his living off both sides of the class conflict. As a proletarian writer who campaigns against capitalism while socializing with the rich, Richard Gordon is meant to embody the hypocrisy Hemingway attributed to the politically motivated authors he bashed in *Green Hills of Africa* and assorted *Esquire* essays. Gordon is convinced the bank robbery has the makings of a new novel and decides to examine Harry's tragic role in it by shadowing the investigation led by Key West's sheriff, Roger Johnson. Yet a chance glimpse of the captain's frantic wife, Marie Morgan, reveals the writer's complete misunderstanding of working-class people. In the buildup to the bank robbery, Hemingway took great pains to depict the Morgans as a loving, committed couple, regardless of their pronounced lack of polish and gentility. Gordon, by contrast, can only imagine how "her husband when he came home at night hated her, hated the way she had coarsened and grown heavy, was repelled by her bleached hair, her too big breasts, her lack of sympathy with his work as an organizer" (177:3–7). As Hemingway makes clear, Gordon's problem is that he can only view characters as types instead of individuals and imposes class assumptions on dimensioned, dignified people. As deluded as he is, however, the writer is by no means a despicable character. Thanks to Hemingway's satiric intent, Gordon comes off more hapless than vile, a fool instead of a villain. Throughout the draft, he is subjected to insults from so many different characters that readers may be forgiven if they begin to feel sorry for him.

Such is not the case with the novel's other major antagonist, Helène Bradley. Even in manuscript, the femme fatale of *To Have and Have Not* appears only in a single episode, a tour-de-force party scene set at a transposed version of Grant and Jane Mason's Jaimanitas estate. Still, in her brief appearance, Mrs. Bradley is memorably viperous and calculating. Coaxing Richard Gordon upstairs for a tryst only minutes after their first meeting, she proceeds to slap his face when he suffers a humiliating bout of performance anxiety as her husband, Tommy, walks in on them in flagrante delicto. The design behind Helène's character could hardly be more transparent: Hemingway extrapolates a rather predictable condemnation of her promiscuity into a rather predictable condemnation of the dubiety of the rich. Nevertheless, without even realizing it, he managed to create a villainess who defies his era's stereotypes of feminine susceptibility to the romance plot. In Hammett's paradigm-setting *The Maltese Falcon* (1930), a prototypical femme fatale such as Brigid O'Shaughnessy is undone by her desire for love, not by her amorality. Never as hardboiled as any "real" man with whom she might tangle, such as Sam Spade, Brigid finds her criminal scheme foiled by her sentimental vulnerability. Helène Bradley suffers no such debility; she seduces Gordon not because she is sexually attracted to him but because she "collects" authors as carnal complements to the display of first editions she showcases in her boudoir. Unlike Brett Ashley in *The Sun Also Rises,* she is more than happy to be "one of these bitches that ruin children" (*SAR* 243). At the same time, while she may be a man-eater, Hélène isn't derided as a "mannish" shrew as are other women in the novel, including Mrs. Bowles / Laughton and Dorothy Hollis, the philandering wife of an alcoholic Hollywood director who shares her yacht bed with "a professional son-in-law of the very rich" (241:9–10). In her all-too-short cameo, Hélène radiates a rapacity that is unapologetically and unconquerably female, making her a fascinating foil to Marie Morgan, who is equally willful but draws her strength from her perfect partnership with Harry. In her calculating eroticism, Mrs. Bradley also provides an interesting counterpart to other Hemingway heroines such as *A Farewell to Arms*'s Catherine Barkley or *For Whom the Bell Tolls*'s Maria, for whom sexuality is a wound from which they struggle to recuperate. Given her uniqueness, it is unfortunate that Hemingway restricted Hélène to this single episode and more unfortunate still that her appearance in the published version of *To Have and Have Not* is whittled down to a mere flashback.

It is also unfortunate that libel anxieties caused Hemingway to cut the entire party scene, for the thirty-page set piece is a marvel of staging. In terms of technique, "An Afternoon at the Bradleys" parallels the cinematic tracking shot in which the camera eye moves from subject to subject for an extended period of time without a jump cut.[15] In the hands of an Orson Welles, Alfred Hitchcock, Stanley Kubrick, or Martin Scorsese, the continuous motion a tracking shot conveys can create a powerful sense of both sweep and fluidity. Through such a device, the narrative vantage passes among characters who lack the omniscience the device grants the viewer. In a similar fashion, Hemingway's lens pans among guests to dramatize the petty jealousies and resentments of this social stratum, most of them involving envy of Hélène's shameless, all-consuming behavior. Between Richard Gordon, a gossipy pair of (predictably stereotyped) gay painters, Mr. Tagaruchi and Mr. Stevens, and one ex-lover who only realizes he is an ex the minute he sees Mrs. Bradley beeline for her new bedroom acquisition, the centerpiece of the scene is a dialogue between Tommy Bradley and Rodney "Roddy" Simpson. Mr. Bradley is a Hemingway stand-in but for one odd trait: he is curiously indifferent to his wife's promiscuity. Indeed, the globetrotter seems almost grateful for other men to take Hélène off his hands. Yet at no point is the contented cuckold portrayed as effeminate or emasculated; he simply doesn't like his wife very much. As Roddy notes, he spends most of his time abroad as a big-game hunter so he won't have to abide the woman, who in Tommy's own judgment "has the taste of a magpie or packrat." As for Simpson, he begins the scene as a rather jaded observer of the beau monde ("The class you and I belong to is dead without knowing it") only to prove himself a committed revolutionary when he beseeches his buccaneering host to help smuggle a load of dynamite to Communist rebels in Cuba.

Between Roddy's extremes, the two men spend their time autopsying the Lost Generation, with Hemingway uncharitably diagnosing the moral failings of fellow authors who either succumbed to alcoholism or committed suicide. In addition to Black Sun Press founder Harry Crosby (1898–1929) and poet Hart Crane (1899–1932), F. Scott Fitzgerald comes in for particular abuse; he is dismissed under his own name for "jumping right from youth to senility" and under the transparent allonym John MacKenzie for turning into a Hollywood hack who talks about studio chieftain Irving Thalberg instead of Dostoevsky. (Fitzgerald was so intrigued by Thalberg he made the Hollywood studio chief the hero of two important works, the 1932 short story "Crazy Sunday" and the incomplete and posthumously published *The Last Tycoon* [1941].) Among the writers Tommy and Roddy ridicule, none is criticized more harshly than Hemingway himself. Referred to as the "Old Slob"—a Papa nickname in this period—the writer is derided for falling away from his craft and failing his art. When Tommy asks whether Hemingway even writes anymore, Roddy replies, "Well, opinions vary on that." Hemingway's reference to himself makes for one of the most unexpected metafictional moments in his entire corpus.

As crackerjack as the party scene was, the manuscript's fourth part was far from flawless. Most glaringly, patterns of repetition blurred the distinctiveness of both scenes and characters. Hemingway no sooner concludes Tommy and Roddy's dialogue about the dynamite than his next chapter cuts to the Key West yacht basin, where the tracking-shot-style device was reemployed to survey *a second* cross-section of upper-class inanity. In the published novel, a bizarre barroom vignette featuring the drunken, damaged veterans doomed to perish in the 1935 Labor Day hurricane would prove one of the book's most memorable scenes. In manuscript, however, the episode seemed to repeat an earlier moment from chapter 21 when two inebriated Marine flyers indulge in surreal wordplay as they taunt Sheriff Johnson for failing to capture the bank robbers. The flyers' vaudevillian back-and-forth is also the driving motor of Tommy and Roddy's elaborate exchanges, which occur not only in the Bradley party and yacht club scenes but also in a breakfast tête-à-tête, where, over "a small kipper and a large vomit" (MS 31, item 204, folder 11, page 397), the game hunter is finally persuaded to carry the dynamite across the Gulf.

Despite part 4's prevalent sense of duplication, Hemingway remained capable of staging his "mechanics of revolution" theme in startling, brilliant ways. An unnumbered chapter titled "Interlude (in Cuba)" may be the single-most arresting piece of his prose yet to make it into print. In the voice of a weary Cuban revolutionary, Hemingway explores the moral ambiguity of terrorism.[16] On the one hand, freedom fighters who resort to anarchistic violence to overthrow tyrants risk perpetuating their oppressors' bloodshed. On the other hand, those who abide the rules of war doom themselves to disadvantage: "When someone has you by the throat and is choking you," the voice demands, "do you defend yourself by the rules of boxing? No. So that is one necessity for dynamite." The monologue amplifies an earlier conversation Harry Morgan has with the youngest of the bank robbers, Emilio, shortly before the surprise attack that will leave them both dead. "We have to raise money now for the fight," insists the revolutionary, justifying the bank robbery and Albert Tracy's murder. "To do that we have to use means that later we would never use. Also we have to use people we would not employ later. But the end is worth the means" (166:17–21). As if wizened by Emilio and Harry's pointless deaths, the voice in the interlude puts far less faith in this truism, even if the speaker can't imagine any other alternative to the dynamite. "There is no hope in terrorism," he finally concedes. "It is a noise you make when you are hopeless." As Sarah Finch Brown insists of this narrator, "Throughout the chapter, his judgments are humane and considered and apparently justified and truthful" (40). As befits the topic of armed revolt, his judgments are also profoundly serious.

Unfortunately, the same can't be said for the manuscript's final chapter, in which Tommy Bradley describes in first-person narration his efforts to deliver the dynamite to the revolutionary's coconspirators. If the tone of the Cuban interlude is tragic, here it turns ironic and flippant, with the game hunter rolling his rhetorical eyes at the self-serving interests of the various ideologies vying for political power. "He was a Trotskyite," Mr. Bradley says of Richard Gordon, whom Roddy has convinced Tommy to carry along as his mate. "A Trotskyite I gathered is a sort of high church communist of some sort whose books don't sell due to the machinations of a number of lads whose names I didn't retain but all of whom, it seems, are utterly frightful. . . . I had no idea these boys hated each other so healthily." Not surprisingly, Gordon proves useless for much beyond inspiring this sort of tedious derision, of which there is much. Tommy even mocks his passenger's fuddy-duddy sexuality, embarrassing the writer by claiming that in Spanish paired mountain formations are known as "tits" and a peak is called "just what you'd think." In keeping with Tommy's attitude, the trip proves a woeful failure. As Bradley and Gordon linger along the Cuban coast awaiting word from Roddy's Communist contacts, they are swept up in a squall likely inspired by a 28 May 1936 storm that for fourteen terrifying hours caught Hemingway returning to Key West alone in the *Pilar*. Tommy's expertise in navigating the violent blow again underscores the lack of character differentiation throughout the draft: by the time the married playboy is squatting over his engine throwing out technical terms such as "stuffing box" and "grease cups," his voice is virtually indistinguishable from the narration that describes Harry Morgan performing similar tasks as he prepares to kill his terrorist captors.[17] Once the storm lifts, Tommy and Richard Gordon have little choice but to return to Key West with their cargo, much to Roddy Simpson's exasperation—and the reader's inevitable sense of anticlimax. For Tommy, the aborted mission is a comic misadventure that symbolizes the ultimate futility of political action. No matter how passionately man attempts to right the world, he insists, Mother Nature proves a "good old ambushing bitch" who upends the most noble of intentions, and for no other reason than she finds it humorous.

As if to hammer that point home, Hemingway ends the manuscript with a denouement in which Tommy Bradley discovers his boat has sunk in the Key West yacht basin. The near-disastrous crossing so weakened her seams that when the same storm that nearly cost him and Gordon their lives hit the island the vessel could not stay afloat even within feet of land. For Tommy, the only possible response to such absurdity is to laugh, a reaction guaranteed to irk those who don't share his philosophy of wry detachment: "Helène didn't think that was comic at all," he chuckles in the final line of the draft.

As this overview suggests, the manuscript version of the final quarter of *To Have and Have Not* differs greatly from the printed version. When and why the "haves" portion was cut remains steeped in both generalization and ambiguity. The only way Hemingway's 11 July 1936 claim to Perkins to have completed thirty thousand words even approaches being possible is if he included in that word count "One Trip Across" and "The Tradesman's Return," which combined run to roughly two-thirds of that total.[18] Even completing the first twelve thousand words or so of part 3 by this early date is admirable, considering a crowded social calendar that found Hemingway fishing with various circles in Havana from 26 April to 27 May and in Bimini from 4 June to 18 July (Chamberlin 166–69).

As they often had since 1928, Ernest and Pauline drove west for a leisurely autumn reprieve from the tropical heat, leaving Key West on 30 July 1936 and arriving at the Nordquist L-Bar-T Ranch in Wyoming on 10 August. Ten weeks of *almost* uninterrupted concentration allowed Hemingway to buckle down and plow headlong into the narrative. Only the occasional antelope hunt or fishing expedition interfered with his work schedule, enabling him to produce, by his own count, some 352 pages of manuscript before his return south. As Carlos Baker reports, early in this period, when a fellow Bimini fishing enthusiast, Tom Shevlin, decided to vacation in the area, Hemingway invited him to read over the manuscript: "Knowing his friend's sensitivity to adverse criticism, Tom reluctantly agreed. He admired Harry Morgan's prowess, but was not at all impressed by Ernest's portrait of Richard Gordon. . . . Nor did he care for the scenes involving the drunken CCC veterans in Freddy's Bar." In a harbinger of the critical reception to come, Shevlin let his friend know (albeit gently) that the novel was "lousy," so upsetting Hemingway that, in Baker's words, he "angrily pitched the manuscript out of the window into a bank of early snow. Both men stubbornly waited for three wordless days . . . [before] Ernest apologized for his loss of temper" (*A Life* 293).

If Hemingway felt deterred by the negative response, he hid it well. To various friends he sent glowing reports of how well the storyline was coming together. On 26 September alone, he insisted to both Archibald MacLeish and Maxwell Perkins that the heavy lifting was done. "All that remains now is to perform the unperformable miracle you have to always do at the end," he told MacLeish (*SL* 453). "Hope to finish my draft this month i.e. October," he assured Perkins (454). Yet by 27 October, when the Hemingways left Wyoming, Tommy Bradley's boat was not yet on the bottom of the Key West yacht basin. Indeed, if his 8 November claim to Perkins that he was "on page 354" is accurate, he was only then within the novel's knottiest, most experimental section, chapter 24, a long, nightmarish tour of the sins and vice that the "haves" stow below the decks of their moral entitlement.[19] "[The novel] seems to get longer," the author conceded to his editor, before attempting to persuade them both he labored upon an epic. "Anyhow a long one is a better one now isnt it? Doesnt your Mr. Wolfe write very long books and Mrs. Gone With the Wind too? Tell me if am misinformed" (qtd. in Trogdon, *Lousy Racket* 175).

Despite the blithe tone, Hemingway was frustrated by the spiraling narrative, for he was eager to wrap up "this sonof a bitching novel" to devote his attention to the very sort of political cause that Tommy Bradley would have mocked. In July 1936, right-wing generals in his beloved Spain initiated a military revolt against the country's leftist republican government. Eventually commanded by future dictator Francisco Franco (1892–1975), the attempted coup d'état evolved into a protracted civil war that encapsulated global tensions between Fascism and Communism. As early as his 26 September letter to Perkins, Hemingway announced his intention to tour the battle lines, provided the fight for control of Spain didn't end before his book could. Two months later, shortly after Franco's attempt to seize Madrid failed and the two sides faced off along a bloody urban front, the North American Newspaper Alliance (NANA) made Hemingway a lucrative offer to cover the war for anywhere between $500 and $1,000 per contribution, an invitation that made finishing the novel as much of a financial as artistic imperative. "I've *got* to go to Spain," he insisted to Perkins in a 15 December letter (Unpublished correspondence). And while he immediately qualified that urgency by claiming "there's no great hurry," his mind was on events abroad as he offered to fund travel for volunteers to fight for the Loyalists and donated money to the American Friends of Spanish Democracy's medical bureau (Vernon 12–13).

The distractions became even greater in late December, when Hemingway met a rising literary star in Sloppy Joe's Bar for whom he would quickly upend his life. By most accounts, the affair that led to Martha Gellhorn (1908–1998) becoming the third Mrs. Hemingway did not become physical until the subsequent March; nevertheless, the pair enjoyed an instant attraction. Within mere weeks, Gellhorn was boasting of Hemingway's charms to her friend and advocate Eleanor Roosevelt—no small irony, given the author's adamant dislike of the presidency of Mrs. Roosevelt's husband. Sometime between 2 January 1937, when Ernest wired Perkins to report he had finally finished a first draft, and 9 January, when she left Key West, Hemingway allowed Gellhorn to read the manuscript. Not surprisingly, her response was far more favorable than Tom Shevlin's had been. As a newcomer to his circle, she wasn't distracted by his derisive depiction of Dos Passos and Jane Mason and could appreciate the book's more technical aspects, including the taut dialogue, which left her "weak with envy and wonder" (qtd. in Moorehead 104).

If only the same had been true of other confidants. Writer Matthew Josephson—then known for *The Robber Barons* (1934), his leftist indictment of the Gilded Age, but today remembered more for his memoir *Life among the Surrealists* (1962)—later, in his *Infidel in the Temple: A Memoir of the Nineteen-Thirties* (1967), recalled Hemingway asking for a manuscript critique in January 1937: "I found the two parts of the novel did not gibe, and were even incongruous in tone.... With some embarrassment I expressed my reservations about the second half of the novel, but spoke with enthusiasm about the opening scenes at Havana and the descriptions of sea journeys. Hemingway received these observations with good grace, though I sensed he was unhappy about them" (421).

Summoned to Key West the following month to assess whether the book was libelous, Arnold Gingrich offered similar hesitations. In particular, he objected to the depiction of Heléne Bradley and encouraged the author to mute the constant denunciation of the character. What Hemingway didn't know—though he undoubtedly suspected—was that Gingrich and Jane Mason were romantically involved, having been introduced by Ernest and Pauline during the preceding summer's fishing holiday in Bimini. Thirty years later, Gingrich would pen a humorous account of what a "sticky wicket" this meeting was for him, describing with generous self-deprecation his attempts to outline the grounds Mason might have for suing, without revealing that "my interest in [her] might not be altogether academic" ("Scott, Ernest, and Whoever" 322). In 1937, the situation didn't seem so funny. The *Esquire* founder was married to his first wife at the time, and even if Heléne's real-life inspiration wasn't litigiously inclined, any gossipy public interest Jane Mason might attract because of the novel had the very real potential of exposing him as an adulterer. Upon leaving Key West, Gingrich scribbled a panicked letter to his lover, trying to cushion the shock of her portrait. Dated 8 February, the missive didn't become public knowledge until 1999, the centennial of Hemingway's birth, when Mason's granddaughter, W. W. Norton editor Alane Salierno Mason, described discovering it and other Hemingway-related keepsakes in an abandoned family trunk.

> Dear Jane:
>
> I just got back from Key West and I hasten to tell you my side before you hear it from Papa and Pauline.
>
> I probably made a mess of things with my usual exquisite tact but one character in Ernest's new book seemed to me to have six recognizable characteristics of yours and I took it upon myself to suggest that these be eliminated, since the character's other characteristics combined to spell bitch in capital letters in all civilized language. I called it a "vicious portrait" and immediately regretted that unfortunate choice of word because Ernest immediately and plausibly pointed out that it wasn't a *portrait* of you or anybody, and where the hell would *I* get the idea that it was, etc. etc.

Well, please, for Christ's sake, believe that my intentions were of the best, and don't doghouse me, no matter *what* he says I said, until I have a chance to explain to you my side of the thing.

It's quite possible, as he stormily insisted, that you would have liked the character immensely and that you wouldn't have asked for the changes that I said ought to be made. I couldn't believe, though, that you would have been flattered by the personal resemblances, as he also seemed sure.

(Unpublished correspondence 1–2)

Mason's response, if it survives, has not been made public, but Gingrich's follow-up, included among the papers Alane Salierno Mason donated to the Kennedy Library, implies she was deeply upset, for Gingrich apologizes for even telling her about the novel. Mason's reaction seems to have inspired a new fear in "the Mennonite," as Hemingway nicknamed his Michigan-born, Chicago-based editor. Instead of fretting about Papa discovering the affair, Gingrich worries that Mason will "upset the old apple cart" by making an issue over the fictional portrait, thereby costing them both Hemingway's friendship—not to mention the publisher a famous name on his magazine covers. "He would not only decide I am a louse (for telling you anything at all about a script that I read, after all, in confidence)," Gingrich laments, "but he would probably get his back up and decide that he would be damned if he would make the change that I asked for and that he agreed to" (Unpublished correspondence). In the end, Jane Mason took her lover's advice and declined to confront the author. As a result, their friendship ended with a whimper instead of a bang. Nine months after *To Have and Have Not* hit bookstores, Mason telegrammed Hemingway best wishes for a happy thirty-ninth birthday. The note is cordial but oceans away from the flirtatious, clubby tone of previous correspondence, with nary a mention of the novel. The lack of reaction may have disappointed Hemingway. Around this time the writer began telling friends an elaborate story in which Mason took revenge for his throwing her over for Martha Gellhorn by hiring away *Pilar*'s resident pilot, Carlos Gutiérrez, to captain her yacht.[20]

Just because Gingrich's advice about Heléne Bradley's potentially libelous depiction was biased didn't mean it was unsound. Nevertheless, Hemingway's immediate worry wasn't legal liability. The real issue was quality, for already he was sensing that reader reaction might veer more toward the ambivalence of Matthew Josephson and Tom Shevlin than Gellhorn's enthusiasm. Shortly before his February meeting with Gingrich, Hemingway offered *Cosmopolitan* the opportunity to excerpt the as-of-yet unnamed narrative. In New York in late January to sign his NANA contract, he received word from Harry Burton that the magazine didn't find Harry's encounter with the Cuban revolutionaries as formally satisfying as the smuggling adventure in "One Trip Across." "I find that it is not going to be so simple to lift the bank robbery episode out of the novel as it was the case of 'One

Trip Across,'" Burton wrote in a short note. "That, being the start of the novel, was a complete unit with the characters introduced and with a beginning and end. In the case of this other episode, however, it is a little different." Still, Burton offered to let his editorial staff tinker with the excerpt, "cutting detail that would be extraneous in the case of magazine presentation" and adding "some other slight passages" in hopes of "mak[ing] a very good magazine story out of it" (Unpublished correspondence). A few weeks later, the editor dispatched a more enthusiastic telegram to Whitehead Street, asking for ten thousand words to lead the next issue, but the offer was only for $3,500—$2,000 less than "One Trip Across" had earned three years earlier and $4,000 less than Burton had offered the previous spring during a personal visit to Key West to woo the writer (SL 411).

Although Hemingway would try to leverage Burton's offer against Gingrich to squeeze money out of *Esquire*, no evidence suggests he seriously considered rewriting for *Cosmopolitan*. (He certainly would never have allowed the magazine to rewrite for him.) Instead, as he told Perkins on 18 February, he was "principally trying to better The Bradley part" while "putting in more of the town too" before he was expected in Spain at the end of the month. Promising to leave a "publishable draft" in Paris because "I can work on the book on the boat" as he sailed to Europe, he noted this version was only tentative and that he planned to revise further after his NANA duties wrapped up in May (Outgoing correspondence). As Robert Trogdon notes, at this point Perkins had yet to read anything beyond the interpolated "One Trip Across" and "The Tradesman's Return" chapters, and Hemingway was working overtime not to convey his own doubts about whether his third and fourth parts lived up to them (*Lousy Racket* 177). Twice in the letter, he insists he needs to let the manuscript lie "to get a proper perspective on it" and "to get that detached eye I need for rewriting," but that this concern is *his* perfectionism talking, not qualms expressed by others. "Moe Speiser read it and liked it very much," he assures his editor, referring to the lawyer who also consulted him on the libel concern. "I told him how much I wanted to try to strengthen a part of it . . . which incidentally he did not think needed strengthening." The letter also makes clear that the revision plan didn't as of yet entail lopping off part 4. Trying to ease Perkins's concerns about production deadlines, Hemingway says, "You [already] know the length," a reference to their autumn exchange over the book's five-hundred-page handwritten bulk, which his editor had insisted was not an issue for Scribner's (Unpublished correspondence). A glimpse at the manuscript begs the question of how exactly "The Bradley part" was "strengthen[ed]" during this window of time. Differences between the handwritten manuscript, the typescript, and the setting copy (MS 30 item 204 and MS 32 items 212 and 213) are minimal, containing no major structural additions or deletions, merely occasional line edits. Hemingway seems to have been trying to persuade Perkins that the novel was still a priority.

In truth, it wasn't. Most of January and February 1937 were consumed with his accelerating activism on behalf of the Spanish Loyalists. As the newly named chairman of the American Friends of Spanish Democracy's ambulance corps fundraising committee, Hemingway helped arrange the shipping of $30,000 worth of supplies to the front. He also joined two fellow writers, Dos Passos and Archibald MacLeish (1892–1982), in an enterprise entitled Contemporary Historians, Ltd., set up by filmmaker Joris Ivens (1898–1989) to fund a pro-Loyalist documentary. Soon enough Hemingway agreed to write the script for the propaganda effort, eventually entitled *The Spanish Earth*. All this was in addition to secretive correspondence with Gellhorn, with whom he may have caroused in New York the week before he departed for Europe on 27 February.

Once in Spain, distance from the manuscript did little to clarify its faults or mute signs of its failure. On 4 May, shortly after completing his NANA tour, Hemingway agreed to a rare public reading from his fiction for a fundraiser held at Sylvia Beach's Shakespeare & Co. bookshop in Paris. Since Carlos Baker's biography, critics have reported erroneously that he read the short story "Fathers and Sons" (from *Winner Take Nothing*), but the *New York Herald Tribune* account describes his text as "the bright, white pages of his as yet unpublished novel" (qtd. in Trogdon, *Literary Reference* 192). Indeed, the details that reporter Francis Smith cites leave little doubt *To Have and Have Not* was previewed at the event. Yet, "unpublished" is a misnomer, for by referencing "Mr. Sing and the twelve Chinks," Smith further reveals the section excerpted came from "One Trip Across" and *not* the newer 1936–37 material (qtd. in Trogdon, *Literary Reference* 193). While no one attending complained about Hemingway reading from a short story that was now three years old, his decision not to debut the bank robbery or the Bradley portion suggests a lack of confidence in them.

Upon docking back in New York on 18 May, Hemingway solicited Arnold Gingrich's advice on revision while offering *Esquire* the opportunity to publish an excerpt, probably the same bank robbery scene offered to *Cosmopolitan* in February. Sent the following day, Gingrich's reply was as blunt and withering as he ever proffered his star contributor:

SLEEPING OVER IT MY CONSIDERED OPINION IS THAT HARRY MORGAN AND THE VETS ARE AS OIL TO WATER WHEN FORCED BETWEEN SAME COVERS WITH GENERIC FEMALE STUDY AND THAT YOU SHOULD FOLLOW THE INSTINCT THAT TELLS YOU TO DISASSEMBLE THE JOB AND WASTE NOT JUICE ON ATTEMPTED REVISION THAT MIGHT BETTER BE EMPLOYED ON A NEW ONE THAT WOULD START FROM SCRATCH AND BE A SMASH STOP WHILE YOU ARE DUE FOR A NOVEL IT SHOULD BE A BETTER ONE THAN FAREWELL AND THIS ONE WOULDN'T BE. (Unpublished telegram)

What feedback—if any—Maxwell Perkins provided on the manuscript remains undocumented. It has been suggested that when the editor finally read the novel (probably during the week of Hemingway's return, as the writer remained in New York for several days) he may have politely reversed his earlier counsel and declared the book too long (Brown 20). There is no specific evidence for this, however. The lack of a written reaction is unfortunate, for it could clarify whether Scribner's was as anxious about Hemingway's vulnerability to a libel suit as he was. The firm should have been; the previous October a Brooklyn landlord, Marjorie Dorman, had taken the publisher to court over her thinly veiled portrait as "Mad Maude" Whittaker in Thomas Wolfe's short story "No Door," first published in *Scribner's Magazine* in 1933 and collected in *From Death to Morning* two years later. Rather than fight the nuisance suit, Scribner's settled. Although the publisher paid only a pittance of the $125,000 Dorman had demanded, the deal infuriated Wolfe and contributed to his exodus from Scribner's in early 1937. Perkins had groused to Hemingway at the time of the lawsuit about being deposed for the case, leading Ernest to warn, "On this book of mine we will have to put something air tight in the front to make absolutely sure no one identifies themselves with the characters. How was Tom caught?" (*SL* 455). He was probably worried less about Jane Mason than about her husband, Grant, whose seeming indifference to his wife's infatuations with other men was the source of Tommy Bradley's accommodating attitude toward Heléne's adultery.

By mid-1937, a greater concern than either Mason would have been John Dos Passos, whose friendship with Hemingway was irreparably breaking over the Spanish Civil War. Just a month before his May return to the States, Hemingway had learned that the Republican government had executed Dos Passos's friend and translator, José Robles (1897–1937), on a vague charge of treason. To Hemingway's detriment, the news caused him nary a whit of moral quandary; he merely assumed, on assurance from government sources, that the Loyalist colonel was guilty *of something*.[21] Dos Passos took deep offense at the callous way Hemingway broke the news of Robles's death to him during a foreign correspondents luncheon on 22 April. Less than three weeks later, the two quarreled on the platform of Paris's Gare Saint-Lazare train station. The argument centered upon Dos Passos's desire to go public with the story to criticize the Soviet-sanctioned crackdown against factional elements in the Spanish left that opposed the Republic's brand of Stalinist Communism. In Dos Passos–friendly accounts, Hemingway is often depicted as warning his fellow observer of the war "that unless Dos Passos changed his tune regarding what he thought he saw happening in Spain, the New York critics would crucify him" (Carr 372). Hemingway's position on Robles's death remains one of the more troublesome chapters in his political development. In the heat of the conflict, Dos Passos's qualms about the Republic could only strike Hemingway as further proof of the hypocrisy and trendiness for which he castigated his fictional Richard Gordon. Yet in depicting Gordon as a political dilettante, Hemingway had also indulged in petty personal asides that clouded the righteousness of his critique, including the accusation that Dos Passos reneged on debts and that his wife, Katy—a childhood friend of Ernest's—was a kleptomaniac. Although Dos Passos was unlikely to sue over such slights, Hemingway may have recognized that publishing them would stir gossip and distract from the real issue at hand: his belief, voiced by Gordon's spiteful wife, Helen, that Dos Passos was guilty of "changing [his] politics to suit the fashion" (186:21). Certainly, if Perkins knew of Hemingway and Dos Passos's estrangement in May 1937, with the Dorman/Wolfe debacle fresh in his mind, he would have advised against retaining these more gratuitous insults. The lack of any preserved exchange between editor and author about the book's revision again means we can only speculate.

With Scribner's deadline for completing the book less than a month away, Hemingway also had to confront an ideological dilemma that made the prospect of revision all the more daunting: the politics of the novel's final chapter were no longer his own. Specifically, the story of the thwarted dynamite run to Cuba—not to mention the ironic detachment with which Tommy Bradley narrates it—contradicted his own very public advocacy of Spanish Loyalists. As Donaldson notes, during his first foray to the Spanish Civil War Hemingway "converted from a presumably objective antiwar correspondent to a fervent supporter of the Republican cause" (*Fitzgerald and Hemingway* 381). In doing so, he effectively transformed himself from the apolitical Tommy Bradley into the partisan Roddy Simpson. The parallel isn't precise, for in the buildup to his departure for the war Hemingway didn't evince quite the mercenary adventurism that Bradley claims is his only reason for assisting in the fight to overthrow Batista. (Tommy boasts his participation won't transform him, à la Saul on the road to Tarsus, into a true believer.) Nevertheless, a rough equivalence does exist between Bradley's insistence to Simpson that he fights totalitarianism "to quiet you Christers who are always whining about me being so useless" and Hemingway's claim, as remembered by journalist George Seldes, that it took him journeying to Spain "before you liberal bastards would believe I was on your side" (qtd. in Baker, *A Life* 622). Both lines reflect what Alex Vernon describes as "Hemingway's sensitivity in the 1930s to criticism by other writers, that his writing did not engage the pressing social issues of their times" (14). This sensitivity may have only been a "secondary or even tertiary" reason for covering the Spanish Civil War, but what is striking is how irrelevant that anxiety would have been by May 1937. No longer could anyone whine about Hemingway being useless: the twelve NANA dispatches he sent during his first trip to the conflict are the work of a committed propagandist. (He would produce an additional nineteen, for a total of thirty-one, in his three subsequent tours of the war, in 1937–38.) As historians have complained, his coverage underplayed Loyalist defeats, fixated in gruesome detail on atrocities on the right while ignoring equally heinous abuses on the left (such as the Robles execution), and suppressed the close affiliation between the Kremlin and the Republic government while decrying Italian and German contributions to the fascist side. Whether this makes Hemingway a terrible journalist, as many critics allege, is a debate for another context. What is relevant is how utterly off-message Tommy Bradley's sardonic attitude toward political engagement must have sounded to a writer now on a crusade. Certainly, pro-Loyalist colleagues like Ivens would not have been amused by a novel whose concluding message is "I don't think you have to take [people] seriously." For the dynamite run to jibe with its author's political profile, Tommy Bradley *would* have to undergo a Saul-like conversion. There is no evidence Hemingway even considered this option, and for good reason: it would require a thorough overhaul of this long final chapter that his pressing deadline simply would not allow.

For reasons at once aesthetic, legal, and political, then, Hemingway repaired to Bimini in late May, having decided to cut his losses by severing rather than salvaging "the Bradley part." Even this wholesale hacking had to compete for his attention with other obligations. At least three days in early June were lost to a return trip to New York to deliver a blunt oration entitled "Fascism Is a Lie" at the second annual American Writers' Congress, an event staged at Carnegie Hall under the aegis of the Communist Party USA (Chamberlin 187). Additionally, Hemingway was preoccupied with *The Spanish Earth,* whose précis needed revision in preparation for a scheduled 8 July screening for President and Mrs. Roosevelt at the White House. Also in this same short window, he had agreed to write captions for a *Life Magazine* photo spread on the Spanish Civil War. All told, fewer than fourteen working days were available for revising the novel. It is doubtful that even that much time went into the effort before the amended typescript was delivered to Scribner's. This occurred circa 20 June, when the author traveled yet again to New York, this time to record the narration for the Ivens film.

No surprise: the time constraint resulted in a "rather malformed" novel (Gingrich, "Scott, Ernest, and Whoever" 323). To his credit, Arnold Gingrich not only described the book as such but accepted blame for having pressed Hemingway to cut the "generic female study." As the editor nevertheless complained, the final version remained "a little disillusioning, after believing for so long that [Hemingway] started every day's work by rereading everything that had been written up to that point and, as he put it, 'challenging every word's right to be there,' to find him chopping whole hunks out of a book and not bothering to put one damn word back in" (323). That disillusionment is especially apparent in the hasty way Richard Gordon and Hélène Bradley are now introduced into the storyline. Cutting scenes depicting Gordon at home with his wife meant Hemingway had to stitch the couple's initial appearance into an earlier scene in chapter 15 at Freddy's Bar with the Bowleses (now officially renamed the Laughtons). Doing so meant not only extending an already tedious interlude with unpleasant characters; it also meant revealing, rather ham-fistedly, that Helen Gordon is having an affair with Professor MacWalsey (141), a plot twist much more dramatically unveiled in the manuscript when Gordon happens upon the pair kissing on his living-room couch (See MS 32, item 212, folder 6, page 102). Similarly, the scene in which Tommy Bradley politely excuses himself after walking in on Gordon and Hélène Bradley making love is slipped into a later chapter, in which the Gordons end their miserable marriage. The insertion can't help but feel like a cut-and-paste job, given its newfound rendering as an italicized memory that appears unprompted. (Nor does it help that the technique recalls Hemingway's much defter use of italicized flashbacks in "The Snows of Kilimanjaro.") The cuts did trim at least some of the odd repetition plaguing the manuscript: without the vignette featuring the babbling Marine Corps flyers, the nightmarish episode with the Matecumbe veterans packs a much stronger punch. Yet with the twin tracking-shot scenes at the Bradley party and the yacht club now excised, the novel also lost proportion. Indeed, the "have nots" so swamp the "haves" that a reader may rightly wonder why Richard Gordon et alia were retained at all. As Gingrich would joke, "As the book appeared, the title applied about like the 'fifty-fifty' recipe for hamburger: one horse, one rabbit" ("Scott, Ernest, and Whoever" 323).

Yet Gingrich's complaint that Hemingway failed "to put one damn word back in" is not quite accurate. Revising did force him to produce a handful of new passages and scenes, among them two of the novel's best moments. Specifically, with the final Cuban crossing gone, the book needed a new ending. Initially, Hemingway pinned his hopes on chapter 26, a stream-of-consciousness elegy from Marie Morgan to her dead husband. In the original manuscript, this overt nod to the "Penelope" section of Joyce's *Ulysses* was lost in the rush of Tommy Bradley and Roddy Simpson's negotiations over the dynamite. Scuttling that plotline allowed Marie's Molly Bloom–styled monologue to emerge in relief, offering a lyrical "evocation of the powerful bond" between the Morgans that would stand as a poignant testament to the "memory of appreciative love" (Spilka, *Eight Lessons*, 220). This testimony would once again refute Richard Gordon's ignorance of working-class life while encouraging readers to empathize with Marie's loss and suffering.

Despite the monologue's literary potential, Hemingway struggled to find the right concluding note to the widow's reflections. Remembering Harry is such a private, internal act for Marie that extrapolating her memories into a class condition proved too great a challenge. As a result, Hemingway decided to shift the perspective outward by adding a three-paragraph coda in which his camera eye zooms past bicycling tourists and a squawking peacock to "the sea looking hard and new and blue in the winter light." Once there, the focus settles on a final image of two contrasting boats: "A large white yacht was coming into the harbor and seven miles out on the horizon you could see a tanker, small and neat in profile against the blue sea, hugging the reef as she made to the westward to keep from wasting fuel against the stream" (262:7–9). Here finally was an ending that played to Hemingway's descriptive strengths instead of indulging in Tommy Bradley's sarcasm. As with many of his panoramas, it depicts a vista whose precision of detail implies symbolic significance beneath its surface, floating like the bulk of an iceberg, sensed but unseen. Concluding on a literary note of ambiguity offered a fitting counterbalance to the book's proselytizing politics; if the tanker suggested some naturalistic moral about man striving to navigate and endure his environment, the specific point was left to readers to elaborate.

Not so the other significant passage Hemingway added. To ensure that his politics weren't misunderstood, he inserted a scene in which Harry Morgan delivers the novel's credo to Coast Guard officers who arrive too late to save his life:

> "Don't fool yourself," he said. The captain and the mate both bent over him. Now it was coming. "Like trying to pass cars on the top of hills. On that road in Cuba. On any road. Anywhere. Just like that. I mean how things are. The way that they been going. For a while yes sure all right. Maybe with luck. A man." He stopped. The captain shook his head at the mate again. Harry Morgan looked at him flatly. The captain wet Harry's lips again. They made a bloody mark on the towel.
>
> "A man," Harry Morgan said, looking at them both. "One man alone ain't got. No man alone now." He stopped. "No matter how a man alone ain't got no bloody fucking chance."
>
> He shut his eyes. It had taken him a long time to get it out and it had taken him all of his life to learn it. (225:6–22)

As Donaldson notes, Harry's dying declaration represents "something new in Hemingway's fiction—a change from concentration on the courage in defeat of the isolated protagonist to a statement that men, and particularly working-class men, needed to band together against inimical economic and political forces" (*Fitzgerald and Hemingway* 407). The line satisfied the demand in revolutionary literature for pithy apothegms that could mobilize readers to action. The intricacy of its syntax and its blunt profanity also gave it an artful flourish that elevated it above the genre's often flatfooted sloganeering. Indeed, in the appeal of reciting it, "one man alone" stands as not only the novel's most famous line but among the most famous in 1930s proletarian fiction. As a call to arms, it is perhaps second only to Tom Joad's "I'll be there" speech in John Steinbeck's *The Grapes of Wrath* (1939).[22]

As he cut the Bradley section that June, Hemingway worried that the novel was now too slender to stand on its own. To prevent complaints he shortchanged readers, he suggested packaging *Harry Morgan* (as he was temporarily calling it) in different sui generis forms. His initial thought was to beef up the table of contents by adding "The Snows of Kilimanjaro," "The Short Happy Life of Francis Macomber," and a third story, "The Capital of the World" (published in *Esquire* that same month). An even more radical plan was floated circa 10 June, when he described to Perkins the idea for a "new sort of book," a "living omnibus," that alongside the novel and stories would gather "Who Murdered the Vets?" "Fascism Is a Lie," and a selection of his NANA dispatches from Spain (*TOTTC* 250). Perkins was unenthusiastic about the "Fascism" speech, but he was partial to the Matecumbe and Madrid material, which he felt rose above the level of mere journalism. What most excited the editor, however, was that after six months of badgering Hemingway had finally come up with a title. *To Have and Have Not* was only one of three possibilities proposed in the letter (*The Various Arms* and *Return To The Wars* were his decidedly inferior alternatives), but Perkins commended it for encapsulating the current mood of political critique: "Certainly it fits the Vets in a literal fashion," the editor wrote, "and in some sense it fits everything that will be in the book. I would be in favor of sticking with it" (251). Unfortunately, Perkins misread the phrase. Much to Scribner's chagrin, the first circulars for its Fall 1937 list announced the book as *To Have and To Have Not* (Hanneman 41; Trogdon, *Lousy Racket* 181).

With the manuscript delivered only four months before the publication date, Perkins had little time for editing. As a result, the book's publication history lacks the memorable exchanges by which editor and author had debated censorable passages in previous novels, including *A Farewell to Arms*'s infamous use of the word *cocksucker*, which Scribner's wouldn't even allow Hemingway to amend to "c—s—r" (Trogdon, *Lousy Racket* 78). The absence of correspondence is disappointing, given inevitable curiosity over how Hemingway got away with saying *fuck* in a book for the first time. Whether Perkins simply consented to the profanity or Hemingway won him over arguing for it isn't known. Nor is it clear why he could use it in Harry Morgan's credo ("bloody fucking chance") while an earlier occurrence *is* bleeped out ("F—his revolution," thinks Harry, as Emilio explains his insurgent aims [168:5]). Most likely, Perkins recognized the obscenity was integral to the power of Harry's declaration and urged the company to let it pass. Whatever the real story, the expletive would prove controversial. The following year, Detroit authorities banned *To Have and Have Not* on obscenity grounds, causing its removal from bookstores and libraries (see appendix F). According to American Civil Liberties Union reports, it was the only book suppressed in the United States in 1938. Whether the *F* word was the real reason for the action remains debatable. Many free-speech advocates were convinced that the Detroit Council of Catholic Churches, the group pressing hardest for the ban and a staunch supporter of the Spanish Nationalists, intended it as retaliation for Hemingway's pro-Loyalist campaigning.

Hemingway received proofs of *To Have and Have Not* by mid-July 1937. Neither additions nor deletions were major. His galleys, stored at the Monroe County Library's Florida History Room in Key West, reveal that his most significant change was to add a refrain to Harry's fatal wounding in chapter 18: "Then he lay quietly and took it" (175:18)—a line that nicely tied in with a strange exclamation from a wounded vet named Jodi in the scene with the Matecumbe veterans at Freddy's Bar ("I can take it" [202:4]).

Rather than the text, the main concern throughout July was cover design. Waldo Peirce (1884–1970), a charter member of the group of pals, nicknamed the Mob, that since 1928 Hemingway had summoned to Key West for fishing and carousing, submitted two sketches to Scribner's. Perkins, a mutual friend, liked neither. Hemingway wrote Peirce on 27 July to express his dissatisfaction. Not only did the images picture Harry's boat as an old-fashioned tiller model (inspired by Bra Saunders's charter) instead of a modern cabin cruiser, but Harry looked like a caricature of a Conch. Hemingway's "fundamental squawk," he wrote, was that "any element of caricature" would undermine the tragedy of the story. Profusely apologetic, he figured he would end up with "some terribly lousy Scribner jacket" for declining artwork that was undoubtedly "better and truer and more valuable" than the novel itself (Unpublished correspondence). Peirce does not seem to have taken Hemingway up on his invitation to try a third sketch of a drifting boat and a tanker on the Gulf Stream, the latter of which Perkins believed was a picturesque necessity. Instead, the artist focused on a painting of Hemingway fishing. *Time Magazine* would feature the portrait on its 18 October cover. As for *To Have and Have Not,* true to Hemingway's fear, the eventual cover would prove "terribly lousy," bereft of any image at all and featuring only the title and author's name in large type against a bland tan backdrop. In keeping with the book's own reputation, it remains the worst of any of his novels' original jackets. Even the first printing of *Across the River and into the Trees* enjoyed a memorably bold, colorfully impressionistic cover.[23]

Hemingway's comment about Peirce's sketch being "much better and truer and more valuable" than the book captures his disregard for the novel by August 1937. Two months before its official publication, he returned for a second NANA tour of the Spanish Civil War, in effect abandoning *To Have and Have Not* to the wolves. To his surprise, the reception was not as harsh as it could have been. A handful of critics even praised the book extravagantly. Elliot Paul of the *Saturday Review of Literature* declared he preferred it to all other Hemingway novels, "style, subject matter, dialogue, all" (qtd. in Stephens 184).[24] *Time Magazine* promised readers "a more serious Hemingway" than they would find in his 1920s writing (177). At the other extreme, Delmore Schwartz in the *Southern Review* called it "a stupid and foolish book, a disgrace to a good writer, a book which never should have been printed" (qtd. in Meyers, *Critical Heritage* 251). Sinclair Lewis—not the most objective of commentators, given that he and Hemingway had exchanged insults in print for years—called it "a thin, screaming little book" that exposed "a senile weariness in the man who could have been the greatest novelist in America" (qtd. in Stephens 178). Most reviews were ambivalent. Alfred Kazin deemed *To Have and Have Not* "troubled, sketchy, feverishly brilliant and flat by turns, and only a little heartening" (qtd. in Meyers, *Critical Heritage* 229). Malcolm Cowley was equally exasperated, finding it "easy to read, impossible to lay down before it was finished, and very hard to review": "It contains some of the best writing he has even done," yet "as a whole it lacks unity and sureness of effect" (234).

If one quality of the novel won unmitigated praise, it was its suspense. Thus, even if Clifton Fadiman found it an overall disappointment, he could still declare that "no one now writing English can equal him in the tense narration of scenes of violence" (qtd. in Stephens 173). Edward Weeks in the *Atlantic Monthly* agreed: "Action is Hemingway's forte. He does it better than any other living American writer" (183). But if one single aspect of *To Have and Have Not* failed to impress critics, it was the "Haves" storyline. Weeks dismissed his "social satire" of "oversexed women and literary flabbies" as "exercises in cool contempt" and "too obvious to be wholly convincing" (183). Donald J. Adams in the *New York Times Book Review* considered Hemingway's take on the economics of the Depression "adolescent": "For all their being handpicked specimens, the yachtsmen and other parasites are simply the selfish rich who have existed in every age. They do not prove anything about the evils of economic royalism" (174). While praising Harry Morgan's depiction, the *Kansas City Star* lamented that its hardboiled power "is largely lost when the author breaks the thread of the narrative to drag in Richard Gordon, the novelist, and skip around the harbor for brief glimpses of yacht owners and their guests." The contrast between haves and have-nots "not only deprives his novel of unity, but fails to relate Harry Morgan to this environment, or to develop adequately that environment" (177).

Despite the mixed reviews, *To Have and Have Not* sold thirty-six thousand copies within its first six months, better than any Hemingway book since *A Farewell to Arms*. It peaked at number 5 on *Publisher's Weekly*'s monthly bestseller list for October, falling out of the Top Ten by January 1938 (Hanneman 41). To come anywhere near the six-figure sales of *Arms*, however, Hemingway would have to wait another three years until *For Whom the Bell Tolls*, the blockbuster that all but superannuated his Key West novel. In the meantime, he had to deal with the reaction of his adopted city. An interview given to the *Key West Citizen* in February 1938 suggests residents were not flattered by his portrait of the island: "Expressing concern at the local criticism of his latest novel, *To Have and Have Not*, Mr. Hemingway regretted that this is so and said, 'I am delighted to be back in Key West. It is my home and where my family is. My best friends are here. No one has more admiration for the town, and appreciation of its people, their friendliness, the fine life and wonderful fishing here than I have'" ("Hemingway Tells of War" 1).

Hollywood offered *To Have and Have Not* a more enthusiastic reception. Hemingway's hardboiled influence on writers is taken to almost laughable extremes in the synopsis that Warner Bros. employee A. E. Mackenzie dashed off for the studio while the book was still in galleys. Harry's three unnamed daughters are "young bitches at an age when they [are] liable to lay any one with the price of a movie they wanted to see badly enough," Marie a "whore," and Harry "the only man she ever found capable of subduing her physically": "By conventional standards the Morgans were scum; but in terms of their background and jungle surroundings they were a worthy family unit of 'have-nots.' One must do what is necessary to live in one's own world. Only sperm-less suckers try to kid themselves they're in another" (qtd. in Biesen 177). The possibly apocryphal story of how director Howard Hawks obtained the rights to the book would become a Tinseltown legend. As Hawks told Bruce Kawin in 1976, he and Hemingway were supposedly fishing in 1939 when the producer bet the writer he could make a great movie out of his "worst story." When Hemingway asked what Hawks might consider his worst, the producer didn't mince words: "That god damned bunch of junk called *To Have and To Have Not* [sic]" (Kawin 16). Making lemonade from this literary lemon forced Hawks and screenwriters William Faulkner and Jules Furthman to wholesale jettison the plot, setting, and economic themes. By October 1944, when the film made it to theaters after a protracted development process, the result bore little resemblance to the book. As Bogart and Bacall are concerned with smuggling Resistance members out of Vichy France during World War II, a more appropriate title would have been *Casablanca II*.

Given the reputation of *To Have and Have Not* as a "bunch of junk," a question lingers: would the original manuscript version have fared better with critics? If the opinion of notable Hemingway scholars such as Robert E. Fleming is any indication, the answer is a firm no. Citing Arnold Gingrich's remorse over urging Hemingway to delete part 4, Fleming is adamant: "Gingrich is wrong . . . about the 'mutilation' of the novel, as the cuts helped more than they harmed" ("Libel" 598). I would respectfully disagree and advocate for a "restored" edition along the lines of Seán Hemingway's version of *A Moveable Feast* (2009), which undid a number of fourth wife Mary Hemingway's editorial emendations to that luminous memoir while adding sketches not included in the 1964 original. At the very least, making the draft version of *To Have and Have Not* available would allow readers to make up their own minds about the value of the "Bradley part."

Until that happens—if it ever happens—we have the book as published in 1937. *To Have and Have Not* is that rare literary work whose influence on popular culture outstrips its intrinsic value. The glosses that follow do not aim to redeem the novel or singlehandedly discount negative reactions to it. Instead, we proceed from the basic idea that even a flawed book contains interesting and entertaining facts, history, narrative devices, and ideas, all meriting explication.

NOTES

1. Of course, before Hemingway's 1961 suicide, he also published three major volumes of short stories, *In Our Time* (1925), *Men Without Women* (1927), and *Winner Take Nothing* (1933); two books of nonfiction, *Death in the Afternoon* (1932) and *Green Hills of Africa* (1935); and even a play, published with a story compendium as *The Fifth Column and the First Forty-Nine Stories* (1938). I focus specifically on the seven novels here.

2. Even the author was aware the construction was ramshackle. As the epigraph to this study notes, Hemingway told *New Yorker* interviewer Lillian Ross that the hundred thousand words he "threw away" were "better than most of what [he] left in" (*SL* 648). For many years scholars looked to an unpublished working note Hemingway addressed to himself entitled "Novel—Have Reached Chap 20 Question," as proof of his compositional frustrations: "Question—what the hell is going to happen in this novel?" (MS 31, item 617, folder 34; see also Fleming *Face* 66). The note was actually not written in 1936–37, however, but dates back to 1927, when Hemingway was flustered by the manuscript he intended to call *A New Slain Knight*, sometimes referred to as "Jimmy Breen." Thanks to the negative reputation of his Key West novel, the scholars who catalogued Hemingway's papers assumed he must have been talking about *To Have and Have Not*.

3. In what may be the funniest single line ever written about the novel, William James Ryan describes it as a "book whose principal unity is in the binding" (329).

4. The essay originally appeared in the 14 October 1950 issue. It is most conveniently located in David Remnick and Henry Finder's *Fierce Pajamas: An Anthology of Humor Writing from the* New Yorker (2002), 10–13.

5. These include *Havana Red* (2005), *Havana Black* (2006), *Havana Blue* (2007), and *Havana Gold* (2008). The parenthetical dates refer to English translations; the original Spanish publication dates are 1991, 1994, 1997, and 1998.

6. How President Barack Obama's December 2014 proposal to lift the embargo with Cuba—strengthened by his March 2016 visit to the Communist nation (the first such visit by a sitting president since Calvin Coolidge in January 1928, before Hemingway ever stepped foot in the country)—will affect Hemingway studies obviously remains to be seen.

7. As Chamberlin notes (129), there is some discrepancy about exactly when Hemingway began "One Trip Across," thanks to Baker, who cites the date as April (*A Life* 607). Most critics, however, follow the dates outlined in the correspondence, which suggests a fall timeline.

8. Solano today is best remembered as the partner of *New Yorker* correspondent Janet "Genêt" Flanner (1892–1978) from 1921 to 1940. The manuscript of "One Trip Across" is located in MS 30, item 204, folders 1–5, pages 1–117, at the Ernest Hemingway Collection of the John F. Kennedy Library and Museum, Boston, Massachusetts.

9. This price is the equivalent of $47,776 in 2016 dollars. Hemingway asked for $5,000, but *Cosmopolitan* instead paid a penny a word, he reported.

10. Foreshadowing his parody of *Across the River and into the Trees* sixteen years later, E. B. White published a satirical poem, "The Law of the Jungle," mocking the press Hemingway's return generated.

11. This is the same harbor city of Mariel that would become notorious in 1980 when Fidel Castro allowed some 125,000 Cubans to relocate to the United States. The "Mariel Boatlift" ignited a political crisis in the United States because a small number of the emigrants—as small as 2 percent—were convicts and mental-health patients released from Cuban prisons and asylums.

12. Trogdon reprints the description of the Hemingway home from the hard-to-find *Key West in Transition: A Guide Book for Visitors* in his *Literary Reference* (149).

13. Working titles for "The Short Happy Life of Francis Macomber" include "The End of a Marriage," "A Marriage Has Been Terminated," and "Marriage Is a Dangerous Game," while the prospective title for "The Snows of Kilimanjaro" was "A Budding Friendship."

14. In an essay published before the *THHN* manuscripts were open to the public, John L. Cobb mistakenly described the "haves" scenes as "late additions [to the story], alterations that Hemingway made in the basic novel of Harry Morgan's struggles" (2). His wording implies that the Gordon/Bradley subplot was added after the Harry Morgan story was complete, when, in fact, Hemingway conceived of part 4 of the novel at the same time that he wrote about the bank robbery and Harry's death. Cobb's insistence that *To Have and Have Not* is a victim of "didactic revision" is not necessarily inaccurate, if the reader thinks the book suffers from Hemingway's attempt to emphasize his political activism in the June 1937 cuts that resulted in the published version a few months later.

15. See MS 32, item 212, folder 3, page 70. For a brief history of the tracking shot, see Romney, who notes two recent, highly praised examples: the 2014 HBO television series *True Detective* featured a six-minute tracking shot in one episode, while the film *Birdman*, also released in 2014, starring Michael Keaton and directed by Alejandro González Iñárritu, created the illusion of a single, 113-minute shot (emphasis on *illusion*). Of the many examples of the tracking shot Romney explores, one in particular seems relevant to Hemingway: "The jazziest arthouse mad tracking shot surely features in *I Am Cuba* (1964) by Soviet director Mikhail Kalatozov. In a three-minute evocation of a wild party in pre-revolutionary Havana, the camera descends through several reveler-crammed balconies, weaves between hordes of bathing beauties, then goes underwater in a swimming pool: a delirious advert for the joys of pre-Castro decadence."

16. Larry Grimes argues that the voice in this monologue belongs to Tommy Bradley (75). I disagree; neither the style nor the attitude bears any resemblance to the sarcastic adventurer. If this were Tommy as speaker, the ideology would be especially jarring, for in the next section in which he is definitely the first-person "I," his stand on revolution is the exact opposite of the political engagement argued for here.

17. I say similar despite one major glaring difference: the scene in which Harry works the engine of the *Queen Conch* is written in third person, while Tommy Bradley's chapter is scripted in first.

18. The question here is whether that figure *includes* the previously published stories (which together make up about eighteen thousand words of it) or if Hemingway was counting from the beginning of part 3.

19. See MS 31, item 204, folder 10, page 354.

20. Paul Hendrickson writes that Gutiérrez's "name has seemed to slip into the folds of Hemingway history," overshadowed by Gregorio Fuentes (1897–2002), who in his later years was a minor celebrity in Cuba, thanks to his relationship with Hemingway (422–23).

21. For a decidedly anti-Hemingway (and anti-left) view of the Robles incident, see Koch. For a more balanced perspective, see Donaldson, *Fitzgerald and Hemingway* 399–401 and 417–19.

22. For a comparison of *To Have and Have Not* and Steinbeck's other great proletarian novel, the underappreciated *In Dubious Battle*, see Pressman, who explores how both works muddy the distinction between individuality and political collectivism.

23. The covers of both *Across the River* in 1950 and *The Old Man and the Sea* two years later were the work of Adriana Ivancich (1930–1983). Hemingway grew obsessed with the

young Italian woman in the late 1940s, culminating in the idealized character of Renata in *Across the River*.

24. Paul's enthusiasm may reflect his fondness for mystery and crime novels, which he was shortly to begin publishing himself, beginning with 1939's *The Mysterious Mickey Finn Or, Murder at the Café du Dôme*. His most famous whodunit is *Murder on the Left Bank* (1951).

ABBREVIATIONS FOR THE WORKS OF ERNEST HEMINGWAY USED IN THIS BOOK

ARIT	*Across the River and into the Trees.* New York: Scribner's, 1950.
BL	*By-Line Ernest Hemingway: Selected Articles and Dispatches of Four Decades.* Edited by William White. New York: Scribner's, 1967.
CSS	*The Complete Short Stories of Ernest Hemingway: The Finca Vigía Edition.* New York: Scribner's, 1987.
DLT	*Dateline: Toronto: The Complete Toronto Star Dispatches, 1920–1924.* Edited by William White. New York: Scribner's, 1985.
DIA	*Death in the Afternoon.* New York: Scribner's, 1932.
FTA	*A Farewell to Arms.* New York: Scribner's, 1929.
FWBT	*For Whom the Bell Tolls.* New York: Scribner's, 1940.
GOE	*The Garden of Eden.* New York: Scribner's, 1986.
GHOA	*Green Hills of Africa.* New York: Scribner's, 1935.
IOT	*In Our Time.* 1925. New York: Scribner's, 1930.
IIS	*Islands in the Stream.* New York: Scribner's, 1970.
Letters 1	*The Letters of Ernest Hemingway.* Ed. Sandra Spanier et al. Vol. 1. 1907–1922. Cambridge: Cambridge University Press, 2011.
Letters 2	*The Letters of Ernest Hemingway.* Ed. Sandra Spanier et al. Vol. 2. 1923–1925. Cambridge: Cambridge University Press, 2013.
MF	*A Moveable Feast.* New York: Scribner's, 1964.
MF-RE	*A Moveable Feast: The Restored Edition.* Edited by Seán Hemingway. New York: Scribner's, 2009.
MWW	*Men Without Women.* New York: Scribner's, 1927.
NAS	*The Nick Adams Stories.* New York: Scribner's, 1972.
OMS	*The Old Man and the Sea.* New York: Scribner's, 1952.
TOTTC	*The Only Thing That Counts: The Ernest Hemingway–Maxwell Perkins Correspondence.* Edited by Matthew J. Bruccoli. New York: Simon & Schuster, 1996.
SAR	*The Sun Also Rises.* New York: Scribner's, 1926.
SL	*Ernest Hemingway: Selected Letters, 1917–1961.* Edited by Carlos Baker. New York: Scribner's, 1981.
TAFL	*True at First Light.* Edited by Patrick Hemingway. New York, Scribner's, 1999.

THHN	*To Have and Have Not.* New York: Scribner's, 1937.
TOS	*The Torrents of Spring.* New York: Scribner's, 1926.
TSTP	*Three Stories and Ten Poems.* Paris: Contact Editions, 1923.
UK	*Under Kilimanjaro.* Edited by Robert W. Lewis and Robert E. Fleming. Kent, OH: Kent State University Press, 2005.
WTN	*Winner Take Nothing.* New York: Scribner's, 1933.

SERIES NOTE

All page references in this volume are keyed to the page and line numbers of the Scribner Paperback Fiction edition of the novel, published by Simon & Schuster in 1996. Chapter 1 begins on page 3, and the final words of chapter 26 end on page 262. Line numbers begin with the first line of each page.

Annotations are given a page and line number, separated by a colon. A reference to the third line of page 17, for instance, would be 17:3. A reference to the first three lines of page 40 would be 40:1–3.

When citing, I have appropriated the standard abbreviations for Hemingway texts used by the *Hemingway Review*, in concert with the Hemingway Letters Project, available online at https://www.hemingwaysociety.org/abbreviations-works-ernest-hemingway.

Map of Havana 1930s with significant sites from "One Trip Across" keyed. Map by Katherine Rodman/TomKat Designs.

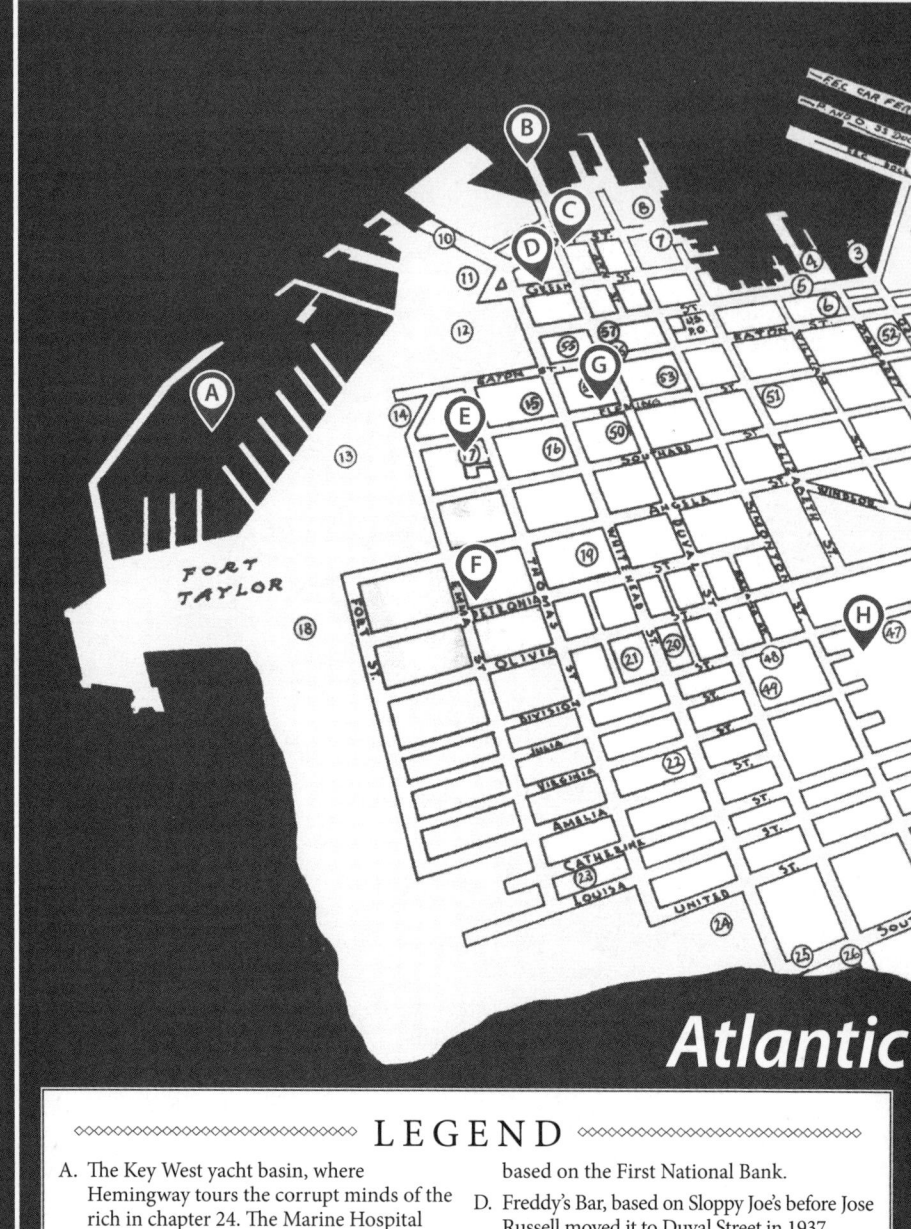

LEGEND

A. The Key West yacht basin, where Hemingway tours the corrupt minds of the rich in chapter 24. The Marine Hospital where Marie sees Harry's body is no. 14 on this map.

B. Porter Dock, where the Cuban revolutionaries murder Albert and kidnap Harry.

C. The site of the fictional First State Trust and Savings Bank that the revolutionaries rob, based on the First National Bank.

D. Freddy's Bar, based on Sloppy Joe's before Jose Russell moved it to Duval Street in 1937.

E. The Lilac Time, where Richard Gordon encounters Herbert Spellman. Site of the real-life Pena's Garden of Roses.

F. The Square Roof brothel that Richard Gordon passes during his drunken tour of Key West bars.

Map of Key West 1930s with significant sites from novel keyed. Map by Katherine Rodman/TomKat Designs.

GULF OF MEXICO

Ocean

G. The La Concha Hotel, tall enough at seven stories that Harry can spot it from his boat both coming and going from the island.

H. St. Mary Star of the Sea, Key West's major Catholic Church in the 1930s, which Richard Gordon walks past on his way to Old Town. Directly east of the church is the Convent of Mary Immaculate (no. 48).

I. The boulevard Harry and Albert travel to the Roberts' bar, based on Raul's Club (not shown here).

J. The Key West Cemetery and the general area of Conch Town Gordon walks through on his way to Freddy's Bar.

K. Division Street, referred to by its former name Rocky Road in the novel. Richard Gordon passes The Red House and Chica's on this route.

L. 1401 Pine Street, likely address of Richard and Helen Gordon's home given that John and Katy Dos Passos stayed here.

M. Garrison Bight, mentioned several times in the novel.

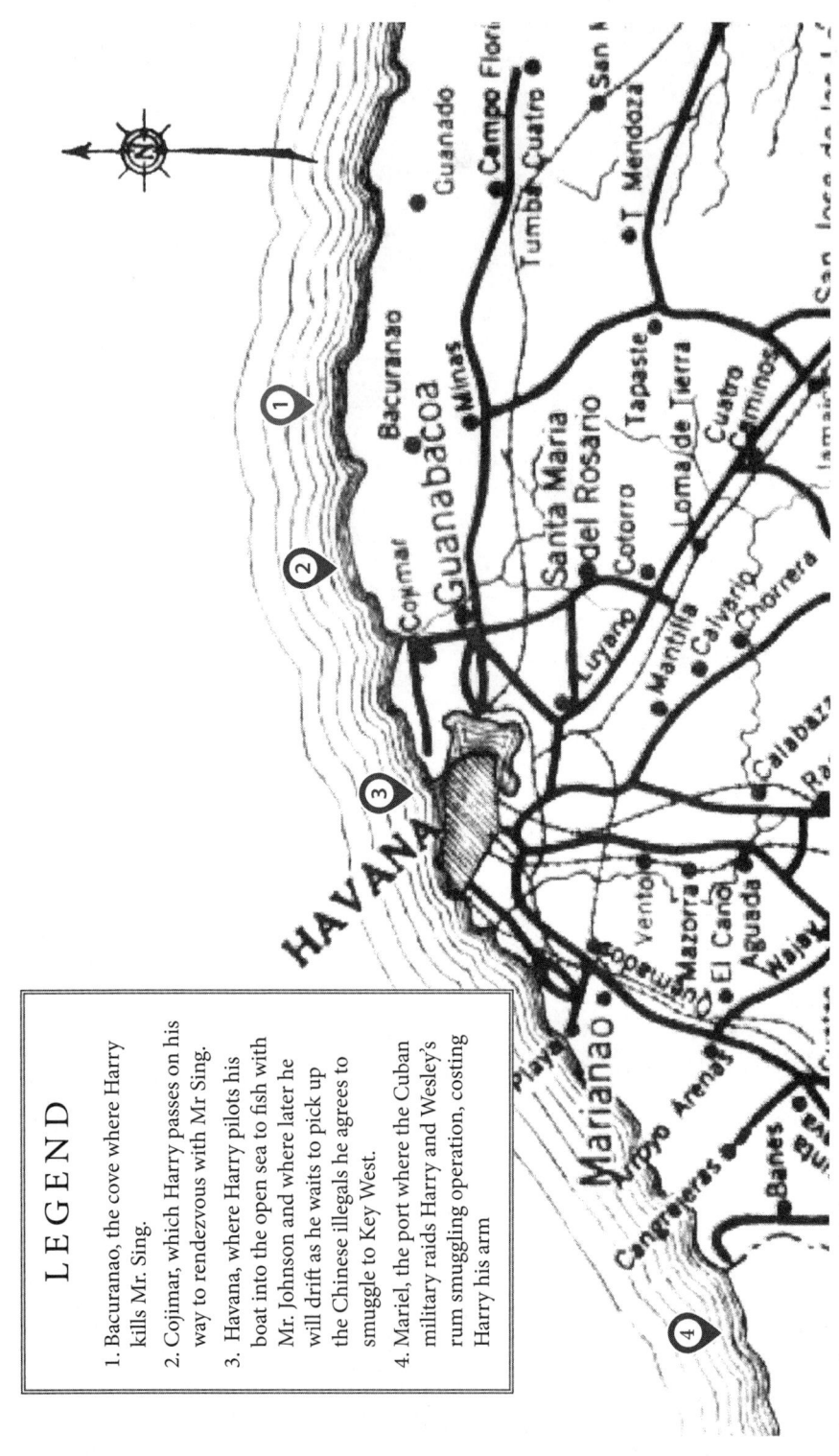

The northern coast of Cuba, where key events in parts 1 and 2 of *To Have and Have Not* occur. Map by Katherine Rodman/TomKat Designs.

Reading *To Have and Have Not*

FRONT MATTER

Title: As with most Hemingway works, the title *To Have and Have Not* was decided on only after much deliberation. In fact, Hemingway usually generated so many prospective titles for his works that an enterprising scholar could use the discarded alternatives to create a literary version of Trivial Pursuit to test colleagues' expertise. In manuscript, *The Sun Also Rises* had been called *Fiesta* (also the book's U.K. title); it might be known by such inertly biblical phrases as *River to the Sea, Two Lie Together*, or *The Old Leaven*, had its author not fallen for a much more sonorous line from the Book of Ecclesiastes. Three years later, in 1929, while completing his second novel, Hemingway composed a list of possible titles that included allusions to Goethe (*The Italian Journey*), Flaubert (*The Sentimental Education*), and Andrew Marvell (*World Enough and Time*) before committing to *A Farewell to Arms*, borrowed from a 1590 poem by George Peele. The process was no different for many of his best-remembered stories. Before deciding on "The Short Happy Life of Francis Macomber," Hemingway considered alternatives that were as overtly bitter as "The Short Happy Life" is ironic: "Marriage Is a Dangerous Game," "A Marriage Has Been Terminated," and "Through Darkest Marriage," a play on British explorer Henry Morton Stanley's *Through Darkest Africa* (1890).

So when Hemingway wrote Maxwell Perkins in June 1937 proposing *The Various Arms* or possibly even *Return To The Wars* for his next book, it was not unusual for him to include a caveat ("Can maybe do better" [*TOTTC* 250]). Perkins quickly wrote back to say he was smitten with the suggestion that had preceded these, one Hemingway had qualified with yet another marker of hesitation ("Temporarily"): "I have got to like the title 'To Have and to Have Not' very much," Perkins said. "I would be for sticking with it" (250–51). Given that Hemingway's letter is the one that outlines his "living omnibus" plan for a volume that would include fiction and nonfiction, it is not correct to say the title referred to the narrative itself at this stage. It was intended, rather, as the name of the entire miscellany. In his letter to Perkins, Hemingway listed his Key West potboiler alongside "The Snows of Kilimanjaro," "Who Murdered the Vets?" and several other texts as *Harry Morgan*—although this option, too, was also followed by a qualifying notation ("Temporary Title"). Had Perkins assented to it, the title *Harry Morgan* would have placed his rumrunner tale in the tradition of eponymous novels such as *Robinson Caruso, Daniel Deronda, David Copperfield,* and *Daisy Miller*—works in which a protagonist's developing character is the central thematic focus. As previously noted, Perkins feared that including the 1937 American Writers' Congress speech "Fascism Is a Lie" would give the book a hodgepodge feel, and eventually the suggestion of including either short stories or journalism was junked in favor of the novel alone. Yet the question of the title was not quite resolved.

A perceptive reader will recognize that Perkins misread Hemingway's letter. The author's proposed *To Have and Have Not* became *To Have and To Have Not* in the editor's eyes, a minor misprision but one that suggests, as A. Scott Berg notes, that proofreading was not a particular strength of Perkins's (20). The incorrect title made its way through the Scribner's sales department, even appearing on a mock-up cover used by salesmen in the field before it was caught and corrected. Even today, the error occasionally appears in scholarly texts and popular literary histories. *To Have and To Have Not* may just be Scribner's second most mistakenly cited title, after F. Scott Fitzgerald's *The Beautiful and Damned* (or *The Beautiful and the Damned,* as many call it).[1]

The thematic significance of the title is the most straightforward of any Hemingway novel this side of *The Old Man and the Sea*. In general, Hemingway preferred titles with more poetic resonance and thematic mystery. The relevance of the biblical phrase "the sun also rises" to Jake Barnes and Brett Ashley's story is fairly opaque unless one knows the letter in which, post-publication, the author explicated Ecclesiastes for Perkins; if one follows Hemingway's interpretation of the phrase ("The point of the book to me was that the earth abideth forever.... I didn't mean the book to be a hollow or bitter satire but a damn tragedy with the earth abiding forever as the hero" [*TOTTC* 51]), it also renders his plot ironic by suggesting that a lost generation is nothing new under the sun. *Men Without Women, A Farewell to Arms,* and *Winner Take Nothing* are more literal, but their narratives still contain enough subtle contradictions to complicate their import. It is often noted, for example, that one of the most analyzed stories in *Men Without Women*, "Hills Like White Elephants," sympathizes with its female protagonist, Jig, a fact that does not support the advertising line by which this 1927 collection of stories was publicized: "The softening feminine influence is absent—either through training, discipline, death, or situation" (qtd. in Meyers, *Critical Heritage* 105). With its metrical cadence, *To Have and Have Not* seems squarely to define the novel's excoriating contrast between the decadent rich and the noble working poor, between Richard Gordon the hypocritical novelist and Harry Morgan the mangled, martyred prole. Yet not all critics agree that the two halves of the title refer to the respective characters they appear to. Carlos Baker claims that the literal level is only the "economic meaning" and that a "reciprocal action" takes place if we view the title metaphorically in terms of morality:

As one of the *Have-Nots,* Harry Morgan must take desperate measures for survival, and his adversaries are those who *Have* money, power, prestige, and unearned privilege. Yet this is a novel, not a treatise in economics. John Ruskin, whose approach to economic problems always emphasized morality over money, once defined *having* as a power whose importance lay "not only in the quantity or nature of the thing possessed" but also, and more significantly, "in its suitableness to the person possessing it and in his vital power to use it." On these ultimately moral grounds, a reversed interpretation of the title suggests itself. Harry Morgan *has* a combination of social courage and personal integrity precisely suited to his character. The same qualities are notably absent among the leisure-class wastrels and other ne'er-do-wells by whom he is surrounded and with whom he is contrasted. He shows a "vital power" in putting his possessions to use. *To Have* what Harry has in the way of self-reliance, self-command, and self-knowledge is qualitatively superior, one would judge, to the strictly economic forms of having. (Baker, *Writer as Artist* 215–16)

Some readers may find this interpretation an overly ingenious effort at steepening the complexity of a narrative whose power lies in its surface punch. Ultimately, when it comes to purpose, the title *To Have and Have Not* has more in common with that of proletarian novels such as Agnes Smedley's *Daughter of the Earth* (1929), Jack Conroy's *The Disinherited* (1933), Clara Weatherwax's *Marching! Marching!* (1935), and Isidor Schneider's *From the Kingdom of Necessity* (1935) than to John Dos Passos's *The Big Money* (1936) or John Steinbeck's *The Grapes of Wrath* (1939): it eschews the figurative and allusive suggestiveness of the latter in favor of the buttonholing directness of a *roman à thèse*. In this way, the title *To Have and Have Not* was perfectly apiece with the aims of 1930s proletarian literature, which generally insisted that "literary" qualities of fiction (ambiguity, symbolism, allusion) interfered with the pragmatic aim of redressing social injustices. What Barbara Foley says of the aforementioned literal titles applies to Hemingway's: titles such as *Daughter of the Earth* and *The Disinherited* "propose that recognition of one's place in social relations entails the seizure of what is rightfully one's own: cognition produces action. Readers who identify with the [title] are thus positioned to undergo an education of their own. . . . The text is expressly didactic, teaching not the fixity of the bourgeois world, but its ripeness for revolution" (284).

Epigraph and Dedication: If listing potential titles for *To Have and Have Not* is typical of Hemingway's modus operandi, the book's lack of either an epigraph or a dedication is not. John Updike once described a good epigraph as a "mystical offering" that clues readers to a novel's themes while simultaneously steepening and enriching them (84). Certainly such is the ambiguity achieved in *The Sun Also Rises* when Hemingway juxtaposed what would become one of the most famous quotes in modernist literature—Gertrude Stein's admonition "You are all a lost generation"—to the passage from Ecclesiastes that provided the title. The Bible quotation balances the portentousness of Stein's estimation (which was not actually hers in the first place, but something she repeated from the owner of a French garage). As suggested above, the juxtaposition also imbues the text with irony, complicating readers' abilities to decide how we ought to feel about Hemingway's expatriate wastrels. Less ironic is the excerpt from John Donne's *Devotions upon Emergent Occasions* (1624) that lent *For Whom the Bell Tolls* its title. By insisting that "No Man is an Iland" and that "Any mans *death* diminishes *me*, because I am involved in *Mankinde*," Donne provided Hemingway a poetic image of political engagement, one that insisted that Robert Jordan's commitment to fighting Spanish Fascism should be the reader's moral fight as well because "every man is a peece of the *Continent*, a part of the *maine*" (98).

In other cases, epigraphs justify the books they introduce. *The Torrents of Spring* takes as its raison d'être a paragraph from Henry Fielding (1707–1754), author of the satire *Shamela* (1741) and the picaresque *The History of Tom Jones, a Foundling* (1749): "And perhaps there is one reason why a comic writer should of all others be the least excused for deviating from nature, since it may not be always so easy for a serious poet to meet with the great and the admirable; but life everywhere furnishes an accurate observer with the ridiculous" (i). Borrowed from Fielding's preface to *The History of the Adventures of Joseph Andrews, and His Friend Mr. Abraham Adams* (1742), the quote explains why a Hemingway then known for the dark, violent stories of *In Our Time* (1925) would take such a left turn into farce. Serious tragedy is rare, the passage insists, but comedy is the quintessential realism because absurdity is the condition of life. Most *Torrents* readers are likely to dismiss this hoity-toity rationale for a more obvious one. In quoting Fielding, Hemingway was proactively defending the book from charges that it was an appallingly ungracious attack on a friend and supporter. The writer mercilessly satirized in the novel, Sherwood Anderson, had helped launched Hemingway's career by reading his earliest stories, expanding his reading tastes, and encouraging his expatriation to Paris in December 1921—even writing letters of introduction to Ezra Pound and Gertrude Stein for him. Only six months before the satire's publication, Anderson was prominently featured on the cover of *In Our Time* in a blurb declaring, "Mr. Hemingway is young, strong, full of laughter, and he can write." *The Torrents of Spring* thus seemed quite a stick in the eye. Fielding is invoked as a warrant: just as the seventeenth-century satirist felt compelled to mock the frigid piety Samuel Richardson preached in *Pamela, or Virtue Rewarded* (1740), Hemingway implies he was obliged to go after Anderson for turning "phony" and sentimentalizing the modern psyche in the 1925 novel his farce ridicules, *Dark Laughter*. Readers have not been persuaded.

In one case, Hemingway resorted to the common authorial tactic of writing his own epigraph, though he didn't bother to attribute it to a fictional source, as Fitzgerald does in *The Great Gatsby* (1925), which cites a poem called "Then Wear the Gold Hat," credited to one "Thomas Parke D'Invilliers," a character in Fitzgerald's own debut novel *This Side of Paradise* (1920). Instead, Hemingway prefaces *Winner Take Nothing* with an anonymous passage: "Unlike all other forms of lutte or combat the conditions are that the winner shall take nothing; neither his ease, nor his pleasure, nor any notions of glory; nor, if he win far enough, shall there be any reward within himself" (iii). *To Have and Have Not* isn't his only book to lack an epigraph; *Death in the Afternoon* eschews the device, and *Green Hills of Africa* instead employs a brief forward that serves the same purpose of defining his intent, only more assertively: "The writer has attempted to write an absolutely true book to see whether the shape of a country and the pattern of a month's action can, if truly presented, compete with a work of the imagination" (vii). (*Across the River and into the Trees* also employs a note instead of an epigraph, this time discouraging readers from interpreting the book autobiographically.) Other novels simply do not require an encapsulating quote. For example, a literary device that sometimes strikes critics as "a little fussy" (Updike 84) or pretentious could interfere with the sparse, elemental tone of *The Old Man and the Sea,* which asks to be read as an allegory or fable.

If any Hemingway work could have benefitted from an epigraph, it is *To Have and Have Not*. A prefatory quote might have helped smooth over its patchwork appearance by highlighting strands of thematic continuity among its three sections. An epigraph could have also placed the story in a literary tradition whose own stature might have burnished its significance. Had Hemingway drawn a passage from Charles Dickens's *Hard Times* (1854) or Thomas Hardy's *Jude the Obscure* (1895), he could have drawn readers' attention to the long history of novels protesting poverty and labor exploitation. Or, conversely, he might have quoted a contemporary work about Cuba or Key West—whether fiction or nonfiction—to emphasize the importance of place and setting to the story. The possibilities are as broad as the book's touchstone topics: revolution, crime, political commitment, et cetera. Had he chosen to go the ironic route, he might have even cited a nemesis, whether President Franklin Delano Roosevelt or Julius F. Stone Jr., the New Deal bureaucrat mocked in part 2 of the novel. Yet the lack of a prefatory quotation contributes to the book's haphazard feel, the sense *To Have and Have Not* conveys that it is unfinished. Rather than intentional, the absence likely reflects Hemingway's haste to finish cutting and revising the novel in June 1937.

Initially, a dedication in a book may seem to have less literary significance than an epigraph. For most readers, it is simply a note of thanks to a partner, patron, or colleague who helped inspire or make the work possible. Yet according to narratologist Gerard Genette, dedications are never innocent; they affect our understanding of the text, just not as directly as epigraphs. As Genette insists, "The dedication is always a matter of demonstration, ostentation, exhibition; it proclaims a relationship, whether intellectual or personal, actual or symbolic, and this proclamation is always at the service of the work, as a reason for elevating the work's standing or as a theme for commentary" (135).

The most famous literary dedication to "elevate" a work is arguably T. S. Eliot's message of thanks to Ezra Pound for editing *The Waste Land* into its final form: "For Ezra Pound / il miglior fabbro" (1922, though the dedication did not appear in print until 1925). By crediting Pound as "the better craftsman," Eliot publicly commemorated his colleague's role as the modernist movement's big brother, "always a good friend and . . . always doing things for people," as Hemingway would recall (*MF* 107). Yet on a more obscure level, the dedication has thematic value that only specialists recognize, for it marks Eliot's subtle assertion of his own literary identity. "Il miglior fabbro" alludes to a quote from Dante's *Purgatorio* on the obscure twelfth-century Arnaut Daniel, whom Pound had trumpeted as the quintessential poet in *The Spirit of Romance* (1910), an opinion Eliot did not share. Given Eliot's identification with Dante (of whom Pound disapproved), many Eliot scholars read the dedication as recognizing Pound as the better technician but not the better judge of poetic talent. This competitive undercurrent is not recognized widely outside of Eliot criticism, however. As a result, contemporary writers often borrow the dedication without understanding that calling a peer the "better craftsman" might not be an unmitigated compliment. In rare instances, the mitigation may prove doubly ironic. When Donna Tartt published her debut bestseller, *The Secret History* (1992), she cited the dedication to recognize her friend and fellow Bennington College alumnus Bret Easton Ellis, who had helped her land the agent who sold her book for a hefty six-figure advance. Yet anyone who reads *Less Than Zero* (1985) or *The Rules of Attraction* (1987) alongside *The Secret History* is unlikely to consider Ellis better than Tartt at *any* aspect of fiction, craft or otherwise. As Tartt's reputation continues to ascend, with critically praised Dickensian epics such as *The Goldfinch* (2013), Ellis has become better known for his social media feuds than his writing. Today, the dedication almost seems laughable.

Peer appreciation is only one tradition of literary dedication. For every Herman Melville who exuberantly hails Nathaniel Hawthorne as his professional role model in *Moby-Dick,* many more authors credit their personal muses for inspiration. The longer-running the relationship, the more creative the writer must get in finding new ways of thanking the same person in book after book. By the time of *The Great Gatsby,* for example, F. Scott Fitzgerald had already dedicated his first short story collection, *Flappers and Philosophers* (1920), to his wife, Zelda, so for his third novel, he wrote, "Once Again / to Zelda" (iv). For many Scott and Zelda fans, the dedication encapsulates the bond that kept the couple coming back to each other's best and worst tendencies. The metrical elegance and symmetry of the line also strikes readers as irresistibly musical. No less than Gertrude Stein wrote Fitzgerald a letter of congratulation, stating, "I like the melody of your dedication and it shows that you have a background of beauty and tenderness and that is a comfort" (qtd. in Fitzgerald, *Crack-Up* 308). *Gatsby*'s dedication is so widely adored that when Marlene Wagman-Geller needed a title for her 2008 survey of the real-life stories behind famous literary dedications, she borrowed it. Her explanation summarizes the function a memorable dedication serves: "I discovered [in it] that what precedes the opening line of a novel can serve as a crystal ball as to what is to follow the turning of the pages" (3).

Compared to those of Eliot, Fitzgerald, and most others discussed in Wagman-Geller's study, Hemingway's dedications may strike readers as rather plain, more like simple nameplates than the prophecies of plot implied by "crystal ball." At best, his dedications seem to support the biographical truism that he associated each book with the current woman in his life. *Three Stories and Ten Poems* and *In Our Time* are both dedicated to first wife Hadley Richardson. (*The Sun Also Rises* is co-dedicated to her as well.) *Death in the Afternoon* is dedicated to Hadley's successor, Pauline Pfeiffer, *For Whom the Bell Tolls* to his third wife, Martha Gellhorn.[2] *Across the River and into the Trees* belongs to the fourth and final Mrs. Hemingway, Mary Welsh.[3] None of these dedications is personally revealing; in none of them does Hemingway append a message or quote to signal the significance of the tribute. Each simply reads "To—."

For Mark Spilka, the appearance of unimportance is misleading. "Hemingway's dedications offer a rich field of speculation," he argues in *Hemingway's Quarrel with Androgyny* (1990). "*The Sun Also Rises,* in which he predicts the end of his first marriage, was dedicated to Hadley. *A Farewell to Arms,* in which he mourns the loss of Hadley, was dedicated, not to his second wife, Pauline, but to her rich uncle Gus," who generously supported the couple during their 1927–1940 marriage. "The book he would dedicate to Pauline was *Death in the Afternoon,*" hardly a romantic gesture, given that this bullfighting treatise is "a study in the ritual proving of manhood," not a love story (*Quarrel* 223). In Spilka's view, Hemingway's dedications reflect passive-aggressive tendencies that made it difficult for him to maintain intimate relationships. A nonmarital example of this trait is his dedication of *Winner Take Nothing* to "A. MacLeish." When poet Archibald MacLeish made the mistake of asking what he had done to deserve such an honor, Ernest snapped, "What makes you think you're A. MacLeish?" (Donaldson, *MacLeish* 248). MacLeish's wife, after all, was named Ada, and some critics have speculated that the deliberate ambiguity was Hemingway's way of emasculating a potential literary rival.

One need not confine oneself to Spilka's thesis to see deeper resonances in other dedications. When Hemingway co-dedicated *The Sun Also Rises* to his two-year-old son, John Hadley Nicanor Hemingway, he underscored the point of his Ecclesiastes epigraph that the sun would rise on the next generation, no matter how lost his own might feel. His most ironic and cleverest dedication appears in *The Torrents of Spring,* which commemorates two Menken/Menckens who had absolutely nothing in common except for the writer's loathing: the right-wing Red scare agitator Solomon Stanwood Menken and literary icon Henry Louis Mencken, whose main sin was to have rejected several Hemingway submissions to his magazine the *American Mercury*. Despite these examples, other dedications are straightforwardly earnest and defy the desire for detecting a mixed message, much less covert hostility. *Green Hills of Africa* is dedicated to Key West pals Charles Thompson and James "Sully" Sullivan, while *The Old Man and the Sea* recognizes Hemingway's late editor, Maxwell Perkins, and his publisher, Charles Scribner III, for supporting the writer's work over the decades.

To Have and Have Not is the one book in Hemingway's lifetime to lack a dedication.[4] Whether the author simply forgot, in his haste, to finish the novel or whether he was too embarrassed to inscribe it to anyone is unknown. Either way, it is difficult to see this break from tradition as anything but another sign of the book's slighting. What potential dedicatee might have given Harry Morgan's story an elevating aura of demonstration, exhibition, or even ostentation?

One option lay in a copy hand-inscribed to Joe "Josie Grunts" Russell, the Sloppy Joe's Bar owner who is the model for the novel's Freddy Wallace:

To Joe Russell
who was my professor in the
sociological studies which
resulted in this little economic
treatise.
—Ernest Hemingway

This dedication was too personal for Hemingway ever to print for public consumption.[5] Nevertheless, it stands as an insightfully wry moment of self-deprecation that reveals a great deal about how he saw both himself and his novel. Had it been part of the book, the inscription might have prepared readers for a novel that is indeed more concerned, at least outwardly, with sociology and economics than literary polish. It could have also offered readers a winking admission that Hemingway's relationship to the Key West proletariat was far closer to Richard Gordon's than Harry Morgan's.

But if readers of *To Have and Have Not* are deprived of "welcoming" paratexts such as epigraphs and dedications, they did for decades enter the text confronting a more defensive, alienating "Note" placed in their stead. This was Hemingway's legal disclaimer designed to indemnify him against libel suits:

In view of the recent tendency to identify characters in fiction with real people, it seems proper to state that there are no real people in the volume; both the characters and their names are fictitious. If the name of any living person has been used, the use was purely accidental.

The claim is truer in letter than spirit, but it likely would have served its purpose and protected Hemingway, had John Dos Passos, Jane Mason, Grant Mason, or any other Key West acquaintance taken him to court. That protection came at a cost, however. Until the 1980s, when Scribner's finally deleted it from editions of the novel, the disclaimer began the book projecting a condescending, abrasive tone that nothing in the hardboiled narrative that followed softens or mollifies. One might go so far as to suggest that the declaration fails the central function that Genette argues paratexts should serve. As "thresholds," epigraphs, dedications, and prefatory notes inevitably function as zones of transmission, for they are overt indications to readers that the writer is passing the book along to them. In the overlapping space between text and context, the printed page *ought* to enable "a better reception for the [work] and a more pertinent reading of it (more pertinent, of course, in the eyes of the author and his allies)" (1). The key phrase is "better reception." Coupled with the lack of an epigraph and dedication, the tone of *To Have and Have Not*'s original disclaimer can put readers on the defensive, suggesting that the text is a hostile environment they should negotiate guardedly.

NOTES

1. *The Green Hills of Africa* [sic] is a close third. Among many instances, see Grant 179.
2. *For Whom the Bell Tolls* is the only Hemingway dedication Wagman-Geller discusses; see 77–82.
3. The irony is that *Across the River and into the Trees* doesn't celebrate Hemingway's fourth marriage but fictionalizes his infatuation with an eighteen-year-old Italian girl, Adriana Ivancich, in the late 1940s.
4. The initial, privately printed version of *In Our Time*, known in lowercase form, as *in our time* (1924), is dedicated to three friends/supporters who played pivotal roles in Hemingway's literary emergence: "to robert mcalmon and william bird publishers of the city of paris and to captain edward dorman-smith m.c, of his majesty's fifth fusiliers this book is respectfully dedicated" *(iot* i). McAlmon ran Contact Editions, which published *Three Stories and Ten Poems* in 1923, while Bill Bird published *in our time*. Dorman-Smith, nicknamed "Chink," was a British soldier Hemingway met in Italy during World War I. Dorman-Smith's accent inspired the British inflections in many of *in our time*'s interchapters.
5. I am indebted to Benjamin "Dink" Bruce, son of Toby and Betty Bruce, for providing me a photograph of the inscription given to him by Joe "Josie" Russell's descendants. See photo gallery, this volume.

PART ONE

Harry Morgan (Spring)

As previously noted (see pages xxii–xxv), part 1 of *To Have and Have Not* appeared under the title "One Trip Across" in *Cosmopolitan* April 1934: 20–23, 108–22. The five chapter breaks that divide the novel's opening adventure do not correspond to the magazine's section breaks. (The version of "One Trip" printed in 1987's *The Collected Short Stories of Ernest Hemingway: The Finca Vigía Edition* does away with breaks completely.) MS 31, item 211, folder 23 in the Hemingway Collection at the Kennedy Library includes a set of "tear sheets" from *Cosmopolitan* on which Hemingway first determined the breaks that would appear in *To Have and Have Not*.[1] In both manuscript and proof, the novel's chapter divisions were originally designated by Roman numerals until Hemingway decided that he disliked their unadorned look: "Why not name it Chapter One instead of I—much better," he wrote on page one of the galleys held today at the Monroe County Library in Key West.

Each of *To Have and Have Not*'s three parts is titled "Harry Morgan," with a different season added in parentheses to designate the time of the action. Part 1 is "(*Spring*)," with internal evidence establishing that the year is 1933. With the exception of *The Torrents of Spring*, Hemingway was not in the habit of titling the interdivisions of his novels, preferring to designate them simply as "Part One" or "Book One." The use of Harry's name on the title page of all three parts is both unusual and redundant. The eponym neither enhances the theme by serving as a motif nor conveys a sense of narrative structure by juxtaposing different elements of its organizational design (as the seasonal markers in the parentheses do). One might further suggest that by part 3 the title is not even accurate, considering that the narrative point of view roves through a variety of ancillary characters, including Richard Gordon. The use of the name for a section title is most likely a vestige of the author's June 1937 "omnibus" plan, which proposed that a novel called *Harry Morgan* would appear in a book called *To Have and Have Not* alongside unrelated stories, war dispatches, political editorials, and speeches (*TOTTC* 250).

NOTE

1. Tear sheets are torn pages from a magazine. It was not uncommon for short-story writers in this period to pencil or pen revisions onto tear sheets of their published work. Typesetters then used these as setting copy for a forthcoming collection instead of working from a newly produced typescript. Presumably because the tear sheets had already been proofread as a magazine went to press, there was less chance of perpetuating typos and errata in the new proofs.

CHAPTER ONE

At twenty-six pages, the opening chapter is the second longest of the novel's twenty-six component pieces. Only chapter 22, which runs thirty pages, exceeds it in length. (At twenty-four pages, chapter 18 is a close third.) The action begins at Havana's Pearl of San Francisco Café with a tense meeting between Harry Morgan and three revolutionaries who want to hire the American charter-boat captain to smuggle them to Key West. Harry no sooner refuses than the revolutionaries are killed in a gruesome shoot-out with government thugs. The captain escapes the melee and returns to the San Francisco wharf where his boat is docked. There he joins his mate, Eddy Marshall, and their customer, Mr. Johnson, in his third week of fishing on the Gulf Stream, running up a large tab, at $35 per day. The core of the chapter centers on the tourist's ineptitude at deep-sea fishing. After failing to land two separate marlin, Johnson loses Harry's rod and reel overboard to a third fish and then objects to covering the cost. When the boat returns to Havana, the tourist stiffs Harry Morgan on his $900 bill, leaving the captain with few options. As Harry tells his local errand boy, Frankie, he will now have to smuggle cargo back to the States, and the cargo will have to be human.

3:1 **You:** The first word of the novel is an excellent example of how Hemingway interpolated his audience into his prose. In its use of *you*, *To Have and Have Not* begins ambiguously, somewhere between second-person narration and the authorial tactic of directly addressing readers. Second-person narration involves using *you* as a substitute for either first- or third-person points of view, both of which are more conventional. In other words, the second-person pronoun is the name given to the protagonist of a narrative, as in the opening line of a 2008 *New Yorker* story by Wells Tower entitled "Leopard," which was subsequently included in Tower's debut collection, *Everything Ravaged, Everything Burned* (2009): "You have not slept well. Don't open your eyes. Stick out your tongue. Search for the little sore above your upper lip. Pray that it healed in the night" (111). Yet, unlike "Leopard," *To Have and Have Not* almost immediately abandons the pronoun for Harry Morgan's first-person *I*, which is maintained for the rest of part 1. *You* is therefore not a participant in the plot.

The speed with which the device is abandoned suggests Hemingway employs the opposing narrative strategy associated with the second-person pronoun, the direct address to readers. Here the *you* is not a formal character but a dramatization of the "narratee," the audience to whom the story is told. A famous example of an opening direct address employing *you* is J. D. Salinger's *The Catcher in the Rye* (1951): "If you really want to hear about it, the first thing you'll probably want to know is where I was born, and what my lousy childhood was like, and how my parents were occupied and all before they had me, and all that David Copperfield kind of crap, but I don't feel like going into it, if you want to know the truth" (3). Holden Caulfield's stance toward *you* is defensive, if not passive-aggressive, his tone suggesting he imagines his audience as a quasi-authority figure, perhaps a therapist at the mental hospital where he implies he is staying; he certainly does not imagine *you* as a sympathetic listener. Even so, the *you* to whom Holden speaks is never a physical presence, merely the recipient of the boy's asides. In *To Have and Have Not*, it soon becomes clear that this is close but *still* not Hemingway's approach, either. Once Harry Morgan reveals himself as the narrator, only occasionally will he invoke *you* (see, for example, 6:9, in describing one of the terrorists Harry meets with: "the same sort of good-looking kid. You know, slim, good clothes, and shiny hair"). This infrequency of address, coupled with their relatively benign tone, suggests that the relationship between narrator and narratee is not a crucial index to the hero's character, as it is in Holden's case.

The difference between second-person narration and direct addresses is not always clear-cut. A work famous for its extended invocation of second person, Italo Calvino's *If on a winter's night a traveler* (1979, trans. 1982), begins with a sentence that defines *you* as both character *and* narratee: "You are about to begin reading Italo Calvino's new novel, *If on a winter's night a traveler*. Relax. Concentrate. Dispel every thought. Let the world around you fade" (3). Despite the imperative voice, Calvino is not using *you* in the same manner that Wells Tower does in "Leopard." Once past its opening chapter, *If on a winter's night a traveler* addresses the reader instead of dramatizing him as a main character. *You* might be caught up in the action of reading, but only rarely in the action of the plot. The story is about *you* only in the sense that Calvino returns repeatedly to the reader's reaction, enumerating the distractions that interrupt his concentration and the disappointments with the text that may prevent him from thoroughly immersing himself in the writer's fictional world.

If *To Have and Have Not* opens with a direct address but fails to use the technique consistently enough for the narrator-narratee relationship to serve a consistent function, what is the purpose? Essentially, *you* is best understood as a conversational gambit. It immerses readers in the scene, kicking off the action in a far more dramatic fashion than an objective description of setting would. Imagine for a moment if *To Have and Have Not* simply began, "Most mornings in Havana bums sleep against the side of the buildings until ice trucks come by with ice for the bars." The *you* makes the opening more compelling by involving the reader. Moreover, the second-person invocation defines the narratee as Hemingway's ideal reader—he is someone who knows "how it is there" in Havana, who has seen "the bums still asleep against the walls of the buildings" before "the ice wagons come by with ice for the bars" (1:2–4). This point is reinforced by the fact that this opening sentence is not an assertion but an interrogative. And not just any question, either, but a *rhetorical* one: "You know how it is, right?" The reader is thus encouraged to visualize the scene, even as Hemingway qualifies it in subsequent sentences by noting that on this particular day only one beggar occupies the square.

These distinctions might seem negligible, were Hemingway's use of *you* throughout his career not so fascinating for the range of effects it granted him. Instances of the second person can be traced as far back as his early, pre-expatriate journalism days: "Have you a coming Corot, a modern Millet, a potential Paul Potter or a Toronto Titian temporarily adding whatever the new art adds to your home?" begins his debut contribution to the *Toronto Star Weekly* on 15 February 1920 (*BL* 3). Far more magisterially, *you* appears as late as the posthumously published *A Moveable Feast* (1964), where it universalizes Hemingway's memories so the reader can picture him- or herself wandering the romantic streets of Paris in search of literary fame: "You got very hungry when you did not eat enough in Paris because all the bakery shops had such good things in the windows and people ate outside at tables on the sidewalk so that you saw and smelled food" (*MF* 69).

To be sure, not all of Hemingway's invocations of *you* are so genial. Especially in his *Esquire* columns of 1933–36, he could prove downright belligerent when addressing his audience. "Out in the Stream: A Cuban Letter," his debut article for the magazine, enumerates his observations on migratory fish patterns in the Gulf, only to end with an overt challenge: "Now you prove me wrong," he taunts the reader (*BL* 158). This closing line seems wholly out of place in an essay that otherwise presents itself as a scientific exercise; it suggests how intolerant Hemingway was of even the possibility of readers questioning his authority. In other *Esquire* essays, he sarcastically addresses his audience as "gentlemen," "boys," and "gents," imagining readers specifically as those dissenting critics who deflated his literary reputation in the 1930s. Yet more often—and more felicitously—he uses the second person to *personalize* the structure of address, allowing his audience to identify with the experiences described, as in the innumerable instances when Robert Jordan in *For Whom the Bell Tolls* speaks to himself in second person: "You went into [this war] knowing what you were fighting for. You were fighting against exactly what you were doing and being forced into doing to have any chance of winning" (162).

The frequency with which Hemingway invites his reader into his writing by using *you* should qualify his reputation as a "camera-eye" modernist, one whose narrative perspective was rigorously objective, like a lens.[1] In some famous instances

("The Killers"), he did excise signs of his storytelling presence, but in many others he experimented with self-reflexive markers that hint at a narrative exchange between narrators and readers.

Combined, the opening *you*, the interrogative, and the imagery of Havana's bum-filled squares are responsible for an interesting paradox that surrounds *To Have and Have Not:* while the novel is considered an overall failure, its kick-off paragraph is among Hemingway's most celebrated beginnings. Subsequent practitioners of noir sometimes even begin their own novels with homages to the opening sentence. Daniel Woodrell's *Tomato Red* (1998) begins, "You're no angel, you know how this stuff happens" (3) while the author of this readers' guide kicked off his *Dixie Noir* (2009) with "You know how it is when you drop a guy who thought he had the drop on you" (9). In his 2006 study, *101 Best Scenes Ever Written: A Romp through Literature for Writers and Readers,* Barnaby Conrad analyzes *To Have and Have Not*'s opening as an example of effective suspense (17–19), and it is often also reprinted in creative-writing and discourse-analysis textbooks where it is studied as a model of an effective "hook." In a 1996 interview, the late author and teacher Albert Murray (1916–2013) describes how he encouraged students to study the entire first paragraph, noting how it avoids tropical clichés: "I would ask my students, 'Did you see the palm trees?' He didn't even mention them, but with the rest of the description, you'd see them. I read Hemingway and thought, this is it. This is art" (*Conversations* 138). Arguably, only two other opening lines of Hemingway's are more arresting: those of "In Another Country" ("In the fall the war was always there, but we did not go to it any more" [CSS 206]) and *A Farewell to Arms* ("In the late summer of that year we lived in a house in a village that looked across the river and the plain to the mountains" [FTA 3]).

3:2 **Havana:** The capital of Cuba, often called the "Paris of the Antilles" or the "Casablanca of the Caribbean" for its rich and usually exoticized cultural history. Founded in the early sixteenth century by Spanish explorers, the city served as an outpost for European forays to and from the New World until the country obtained its independence in 1898 after a protracted, bloody struggle that encompassed three separate wars (1868–78, 1879–80, 1895–98).

Hemingway first glimpsed Havana in 1928 on his "American homecoming," his return to the United States after more than six years of living in Europe (save for a four-month spell in late 1923 / early 1924 in Toronto). The stay was a mere two-day layover, barely long enough to switch from his transatlantic steamer to a quick boat to Key West. Travels would keep him from truly discovering the city for a few years; until then, Havana simply served as the site where Hemingway would catch passage to Europe.

His first extended stay began in April 1932. What was to have been a ten-day charter turned into two months as he fished aboard Joe "Josie" Russell's boat, the *Anita*.

During this trip Hemingway began staying at the Hotel Ambos Mundos, his home base in Cuba until the decade's end when he and third wife, Martha Gellhorn, relocated to the Finca Vigía outside the small village of San Francisco de Paulo.

More than his 1932 stay, his 1933 return trip is the one that inspired "One Trip Across." That May in Havana, having again chartered the *Anita* for two months, Hemingway met photographer Walker Evans (1903–1975), who was on assignment from J. P. Lippincott to photograph the city for journalist Carleton Beals's *The Crime of Cuba,* a soon-to-be-published exposé on the country's grave political situation. President Gerardo Machado (1871–1939), in power since 1925, ruled with a despotic brutality that in turn roiled opposing forces, factions of whom responded with terrorist tactics. The result was an ever-mounting body count that required the diplomatic intervention of Franklin D. Roosevelt's special envoy to Cuba, Sumner Welles (1892–1961), who engineered an end to Machado's reign that August. Although *To Have and Have Not* is never specific about this political history, it is the backdrop against which this opening chapter is set, and thus central to appreciating the depiction of Havana.

It would be an exaggeration to credit Evans with awakening Hemingway's awareness of Cuban politics. Before the *Anita* embarked that spring, Hemingway had written Maxwell Perkins requesting a letter certifying that "Ernest Hemingway is at work on a book dealing with the migratory fish of the Gulf Stream, their habits and capture with special reference to the fishing in Cuban Waters from a sporting standpoint. . . . I wish you could get somebody from the State Department stating the same thing." As he noted, "In a time of revolution, [the letters] might keep me from getting shot" (*TOTTC* 184–85). Yet he and Evans certainly discussed the violence and upheaval in Havana. Hemingway was also aware of the photographer's project, for he later claimed Evans asked him to secret a set of prints back to the States aboard the *Anita.* As Ernest recollected of his two weeks with the future coauthor of *Let Us Now Praise Famous Men,* "We were both working against Machado at the time" (qtd. in Mellow, *Walker Evans* 180). As most biographies agree, this is an exaggeration. No evidence suggests Hemingway was involved in any political activism in Havana, in either 1932 or 1933. For many years, it was uncertain whether he had even ferried prints as he claimed. In the early 2000s, Benjamin "Dink" Bruce, the son of Hemingway's Key West handyman, Toby Bruce, discovered a set of photographs among boxes Hemingway had abandoned in Key West after the 1930s. The images were from negatives already housed in Evans's own archive at the Metropolitan Museum of Art in New York and published in *Walker Evans: Cuba* (2001), raising questions about their origins. After the prints were authenticated, Bruce and Claudia Pennington, then executive director of the Key West Art and Historical Society, surmised that Evans printed the photos in Havana for Ernest to smuggle home in case Machado's men seized his own negatives when he tried to leave the country. When the negatives indeed made it safely to American shores, Evans had no need for Hemingway's copies, and the set was apparently forgotten. Proof of this theory was not substantiated until Bruce discovered among the Key West materials a letter from Evans to Ernest setting up an appointment to hand over the prints—along with a request to borrow money Hemingway had previously offered the struggling artist. According to Bruce, Evans's envelope reads "loaned $25" in Hemingway's handwriting (Carlson).

3:5 **Pearl of San Francisco Café:** Or "Café de la Perla de San Francisco" in Spanish. A real-life café in the 1930s located behind the Old Havana seaport across from the Plaza de San Francisco, which in this paragraph is the "square" Hemingway references. In *Hemingway in Cuba* (1984), Norberto Fuentes writes that the Pearl was owned by one Antonio Rodriguez, also known as "Kaiser Guillermo," who died in 1951 not knowing "that Hemingway had been a frequent customer at his establishment, and least of all that his [café] had appeared in one of his novels. Because of [Rodriguez's] indifference to literature, he lost a good chance of capitalizing" on the association—a mistake not made by many other owners of bars and restaurants Hemingway patronized (94–95). Unlike Hemingway's most famous Havana haunt, the Floridita, the Pearl of San Francisco no longer exists. Many travelogues to contemporary Cuba feature expeditions to find the exact site where the café stood until 1953, when it was torn down. Dave Schaefer's *Sailing to Hemingway's Cuba* (2000) describes a walking tour with a local named Manuel, who identifies the location for him: "The building that had replaced [the Pearl] looked much older than 1953. It is made of stone and has five tall arched portals, behind which are ten stairs leading to five tall wooden doors. The first floor looks like a commercial building, but the stories have balconies and tall French doors leading onto them, suggesting residences" (180).

3:7–8 **a drink out of the fountain:** The Fuente de los Leones, or the Fountain of Lions (Estrada, *Havana* 168), carved by the Italian sculptor Giuseppe Gaginni in 1836. The tourist attraction remains a popular landmark in fiction set in Havana. The titular hero of Thomas Sanchez's *King Bongo* (2003) passes by these "slouching white-marbled beasts" that are "gathered around a gurgling waterspout" (268).

4:13–14 **All this will not last . . . I don't care who is president here:** "All this" means the violence exploding throughout Cuba in 1933, while "president" refers specifically to Machado, known to supporters as "El Supremo" but derided behind his back as a "tropical Mussolini." Machado was actually a popular head of state during what should have been his single four-year team. In 1929, he rewrote the Cuban constitution and named himself to a second, now six-year term. As the Depression deflated the price of sugar and bled dry the Cuban tourism market, Machado responded to growing unrest by clamping down on opposition newspapers and rounding up dissenters. By the time Hemingway began staying in Havana, stories of the despot's abuses had grown macabre: he was said to feed his enemies to sharks.[2]

4:20 *lenguas largas:* Literally, "long tongue." This term for an informant appears to be Hemingway's corruption of the term *lenguilargos,* used by anti-Machado revolutionaries, as in, "'El ABC dará este muerte a todos los lenguilargos" (see 4:24 entry). Pancho, the character who introduces the term, takes great offense when he misinterprets Harry Morgan's insistence that he doesn't "carry anything to the states that can talk." If his subsequent comment to his fellow radical is any indication ("He said we would talk" [4:29]), Pancho believes Harry insults him by accusing him of being a potential stool pigeon and traitor to the cause.

4:24 Do you know what we do with them? Harry soon makes it clear he knows exactly what Pancho and his pals do to traitors: "I'm sure you've cut plenty people's throats" (5:19–20). Original readers would not have needed this clue to guess what happened to pro-Machado informants; American newspapers covered the violence in Cuba in great detail.

Walker Evans biographer James R. Mellow (also the author of a valuable 1992 life of Hemingway) has traced a probable source for Harry's knowledge of what fate awaits a *lenguas largas.* During his assignment, Evans collected "atrocity photographs," probably passed to him from both pro- and anti-Machado journalists. Two of these appear in *The Crime of Cuba,* one documenting the death of Juan Mariano González Rubiero, a seventeen-year-old victim of the *ley de fuga* (law of the fugitive), whereby Machado opponents were shot to death under the pretext of fleeing the police. In reality, Rubiero and others were let out of police cars on isolated roads and told to run for their lives. The other borrowed photograph in Beals's book features another victim—a young black man—"laid out with a coiled rope and a sinister knife." According to Mellow, neither of these is as graphic as the most shocking photo Evans obtained from his sources:

> But the most gruesome photo he acquired was that of a stool pigeon named Manuel Cepero, a victim of an [anti-Machado] reprisal. Months before the arrival of either Hemingway or Evans, Cepero had made the mistake of warning one of Machado's most notorious henchmen, Major Arsenio Ortiz—guilty of wholesale atrocities, murders, and mutilations—that an assassination attempt would be made against him. Ortiz, forewarned, managed to kill his assailant. But Cepero was found a few nights later with his throat cut, his tongue and ears cut off, and a sign reading: 'El ABC dará este muerte a todos los lenguilargos'.... 'Death to all big mouths.'" (*Walker Evans* 181–82)

El ABC refers to the ABC Revolutionary Society, the most prominent anti-Machado opposition group, in part because it had embarked on a well-publicized program of assassination and terrorism to bring down the regime. (The name *ABC* was not an acronym but alphabetic letters.) Mellow argues that the ABC's murder of Cepero "almost certainly" inspired this passage in *To Have and Have Not,* implying (though not stating) that Evans showed Hemingway the photograph of the young man's body. In recent years, the Cepero photograph has been included in the traveling exhibition "Ernest Hemingway and Walker Evans: Three Weeks in Cuba, 1933." Harry Morgan will specifically describe a similar photograph at the end of chapter 2 (39:16–19).

5:5 **Can Chinamen talk?** Pancho seems to make this comment out of nowhere. The line foreshadows the later appearance of Mr. Sing, the Chinese smuggler/villain. It also insinuates, whether Hemingway intended it or not, that the three ABC members believe Harry Morgan has smuggled Chinese illegals to the States in the past. Harry's reply ("They can talk but I can't understand them") is another fine example of the tough-guy sense of humor throughout the book.

5:18 **Don't be so tough early in the morning:** A line as evocative of the hardboiled tradition as any other in *To Have and Have Not.* Variations of it appear throughout detective and mystery fiction of the 1920s and 1930s, with private dicks and crooks coming up with ever inventive ways of telling each other not to "get tough." In *Death in the Afternoon,* Hemingway mentions that then-wife Pauline read Dashiell Hammett's *The Dain Curse* (1929) to him when his eyes hurt, substituting "the word umpty-umped for the words killed, cut the throat of, blew the brains out of, spattered around the room, and so on" (*DIA* 181).

6:2–6:8 **They were good-looking young fellows . . . they spoke the kind of English Cubans with money speak:** For Hemingway's original audience, this paragraph would have offered the most obvious clue that Pancho and his fellow revolutionaries were members of the ABC Revolutionary Society. The group's membership is estimated at thirty to forty thousand, though hard numbers are not certain, because the ABC was a cell organization whose constituents were unknown even to its leadership. Although it advocated agrarian reform, social justice, and strict controls on foreign ownership, the ABC leaned far more to the political right than the left. Members were assumed to be upper-middle class, educated, and young. As Cuban historian Jaime Suchlicki explains,

> Led by several Cuban intellectuals who were Harvard graduates, the ABC undermined Machado's position through sabotage and terrorist actions, and in December 1932 published a manifesto in Havana criticizing the underlying structure of Cuban society and outlining a detailed program of economic and political reforms. Although the means to achieve their political economic program were not clear, the ABC called for the elimination of large land holdings, nationalization of public services, limitations on land acquisitions by U.S. companies, and producers' cooperatives as well as political liberty and social justice. (91–92)

Despite their penchant for secrecy, the group did have public spokesmen. Its most visible leaders were Carlos Saladrigas Zayas (1900–1956), who served as prime minister of Cuba from 1940 to 1942 and was a member of the Batista regime toppled by Castro in 1959; Joaquín Martínez Sanz (exact dates unknown); and Jorge Mañach (1898–1961).

Yet not all critics agree that these "Cubans with money" are members of the rightist *abcederos*. In a recent translation of a central chapter of her *Cuba y Hemingway en el gran rio azul* (1981, originally translated 1994), Cuban scholar Mary Cruz argues that the revolutionaries are "most likely from the Directorio Estudiantil, the [leftist] student organization that, together with blue-collar workers, led the movement against the Machado regime" ("Selection" 92). She writes that the men's lack of hats, which Harry notes at 6:3, is telling: "Ever since Cubans had gone hatless in a show of solidarity with a hat makers' strike, the gesture had come to signal defiance, especially among young people" (92). Cruz does not discuss the Evans photo, which traces the lenguilargos motif specifically to the ABC. In the end, whether these revolutionaries are right- or left-wing may not matter. As one historian explains, "Many individuals moved from one group to another, and the ABC would sometimes work with the Directorio Estudiantil" (Gott 134).

The two paragraphs between 6:1 and 6:11 are among the most heavily revised of the original "One Trip Across" manuscript. After drafting the story in 1933, Hemingway added several details and phrases, among these the reference to the revolutionaries' clothes, including their missing hats, as well their English and the sentence, "You know, slim, good clothes, and shiny hair" (6:9–10; see MS 30, item 204, folder 1, pages 3–5).

6:16 I heard the gun going: This shootout scene is not typical of how Machado's secret police would have dispatched an ABC cell. Rather than mow down opposition groups, the *porra* (literally, the *bludgeon*) preferred to arrest members and then torture them. Scholars often claim that the gun battle here was inspired by a 4 August 1933 incident in which Hemingway's wife, Pauline, and sister-in-law, Jinny Pfeiffer, witnessed a *porra* attack. Hemingway claimed he was in the Pearl of San Francisco Café when it broke out. In a letter to Maxwell Perkins dated 10 August, he invokes the situation while defending himself against Gertrude Stein's caricature of him as "yellow" in *The Autobiography of Alice B. Toklas* (1933), excerpts of which were then appearing in the *Atlantic Monthly*. As Hemingway insisted to Perkins, "Saw everything that happened—No not everything—but what one person could see—keeping in the streets when supposed to be fatal and with my customary fragility or whatever G. Stein called it had no marks—Pauline and Jinny both fired on in the streets—good etc cut off for 3 days—" (*TOTTC* 196). A highly novelized account of the episode appears in Hilary Hemingway and Carlene Brennen's *Hemingway in Cuba* (2003) (8–10).

Hemingway's rendering of the ambush is also atypical of how he portrayed violence. Absent from the affray is the element of spectatorial detachment that had appeared in his depictions of carnage since the first mature stage of his writing. Beginning in 1923 with the brief vignettes that would later serve as "interchapters" in *In Our Time* (1925), his characteristic strategy was to limn shocking sights with only a minimum of emotional reaction. The result is not simply photographic precision; implicit in the style as well is the awe incumbent with witnessing graphic spectacles. Thus, Hemingway's early portrait of a bullfight: "They whack-whacked the white horse on the legs and he kneed himself up. The picador twisted the stirrups straight and pulled and hauled up into the saddle. The horse's entrails hung down in a blue bunch and swung backward and forward as he began to canter, the *monos* whacking him on the back of his legs with the rods" (*CSS* 127). The details Hemingway includes in his Havana shoot-out do seem similarly grotesque in specificity. He mentions bottles exploding along the café's showcase wall (6:15), an ice-wagon horse caught in the crossfire "plunging his head off" in terror (7:2), and the "buckshot marks" left by the *porrista*'s shotgun on the sidewalk "like silver splatters" (7:13). Yet, one element present in *To Have and Have Not* that is not found in *In Our Time* is the sarcastic commentary that gives the gore a sardonic edge. Pancho becomes "old Pancho" when he looses his bravado and shoots back desperately and wildly at his attackers (7:17, 7:28), while the most vicious of Machado's killers earns a punch line when he blows off the side of the revolutionary's head with a shotgun: "Some nigger" (8:4–5), a line Hemingway penciled into his typescript of "One Trip Across" in 1933. Hemingway even plays Harry's reaction to the violence for a joke: "I took a quick [drink] out of the first bottle I saw open and I couldn't tell you yet what it was" (8:6–7).

These glib, flippant interjections owe much to the hardboiled crime tradition, where ironic wisecracking is a trademark of tough-guy narration. As Frank Krutnik writes, "In many private detective [and noir] stories, language is wielded as a weapon, and is often more a measure of the hero's prowess than the use of guns and other more tangible aids to violence" (28). In this case, the comment dramatizes the narrative attempt to distance the threat of violence with commentary that frames it as an eye-rolling absurdity rather than an imminent danger. For Harry Morgan as a character, the acerbic attitude is one of the few available means of control in a hostile economic environment that otherwise disempowers individuals.

For Hemingway the writer, the flippancy has a slightly different purpose. While still part of the stylistic armature of masculinity, it also injects a strain of black humor into the narration that in turn becomes the dominant device of reader entertainment as it punctuates paragraphs with pseudo-vaudevillian one-liners.[3] There are two dangers inherent in the reliance on this device. The first is artistic, one risked by any stylistic trait that threatens to devolve through overuse into a tic: the deadpan rejoinders begin popping up for their own sake, becoming catchphrases rather than ideological substitutes for prowess. This is what might be called the "Dirty Harry Syndrome" (or "the Schwarzenegger Syndrome") in which the gag line must grow consecutively more ridiculous in order to remain memorable (from

"You've got to ask yourself one question: 'Do I feel lucky?' Well, *do ya,* punk?" to "Go ahead, make my day" and from "I'll be back" to "Hasta la vista, baby"). The second danger is ethical. The more absurd the punch line, the more cartoonish the narration becomes, its comedic callousness costing the narration any sense of empathy and humaneness.

Once again, Dashiell Hammett is usually credited with making the mordant tone a mainstay of crime fiction. Detective tales such as Carroll John Daly's "Knights of the Open Palm" (1923)—generally credited as the first hardboiled story—might be violent, but the main character, Race Williams, was quicker with his gun than his ripostes. Thus, a standard volley of bullets in a Williams adventure such as *The Snarl of the Beast* (1927) radiates an aura of earnestness that today can seem almost naïve in its braggadocio: "For an ordinary man to get a bullet through his hat as he walked home at night would be something to talk about for years. Now, with me; just the price of a new hat—nothing more. The only surprise would be for the lad who fired the gun. He and his relatives would come in for a slow ride, with a shovelful of dirt at the end of it" (1). As Hammett began developing his Continental Op character, he bracketed moments of violence with quips and zingers that became integral to the narrative voice of the American detective. Hammett's detectives weren't always the ones firing the wit. One of the funniest moments in *Red Harvest* occurs when the Op asks a bystander who filled a murder victim full of lead: "Somebody with a gun," the stranger answers (Hammett 4).

Perhaps because of the acerbic tone of Harry's narration, not all critics agree that the violence of the *porra* attack is compelling. In *Deadly Musings: Violence and Verbal Form in American Fiction* (1993), Michael Kowalewski criticizes the scene for its "self-consciously slovenly prose," "uninspired narration" and descriptive "triviality," and lack of "realistic force" (132). Fair enough. But his judgment overlooks just how inventive Hemingway's syntax is, in particular with its clauses conjoined by "and" to convey speed and pace: "The [*porrista*] with the Tommy gun got his face almost into the street and gave the back of the wagon a burst from underneath and sure enough one came down, falling toward the sidewalk with his head against the curb" (7:4–8).

6:21 Thompson gun: If the shoot-out scene is atypical of Machado tactics, the weaponry of choice is not. The Thompson submachine gun—better known, thanks to gangster argot, as the *Tommy gun*—was first developed in 1919 by John T. Thompson (1860–1940). As a lieutenant colonel in the United States Army, Thompson served as chief ordnance officer for the Spanish-American War, proving so adept at managing munitions transportation into Cuba that he eventually became the then-youngest officer to make full colonel. During World War I, by then retired from military service, Thompson cofounded his own manufacturing firm, the Auto-Ordnance Company, and set to work developing a "trench broom," a one-man machine gun whose rapid firing could clear a trench. He did not obtain a patent until 1920, however, by which time the army had no need for the "Annihilator," as its first iteration was dubbed. With a $200 price tag, the submachine gun was too expensive for mass-market sales, so Auto-Ordnance marketed it largely to police departments. It soon found favor not with law enforcement but with gangsters, especially after the St. Valentine's Day Massacre of 1929.

To counter the negative publicity associated with the weapon, Auto-Ordnance stopped marketing to the private sector and in the early 1930s focused instead on governments, both domestic and foreign. Thompson's only qualification was that customers be "constituted governments"—legitimate ones, in other words. One early foreign customer was the Machado regime (Yenne 112). Much like Hemingway's description of the shoot-out, accounts of the 1933 Cuban conflict inevitably slip into onomatopoeia to describe the trademark sound of the Tommy gun's automatic spray. An 18 July 1932 *Time Magazine* article describing an assassination attempt on the chief of Machado's secret police, Miguel Calvo, is typical: "As Captain Calvo rode down the broad Malećon with two Havana policeman one day last week, a submachine suddenly began to spat-spat. The two policemen were instantly killed. Captain Calvo was rushed to a hospital, died with 36 slugs in his body. The submachine gunners escaped unidentified" (112).

Hemingway's contemporaneous association with the Tommy gun is itself notorious. In May 1935, while fishing in Bimini, he was given a Tommy gun by Bill Leeds Jr., a millionaire yachtsman who used the weapon to fend off sharks who would devour an angler's catch before it could be landed. John Dos Passos, present on the scene, would offer a mocking account of Hemingway's covetousness of the weapon in his 1968 memoir, *The Best Times,* creating a stereotype of a firepower-mad Papa that would endure for decades: "The Old Master . . . [had] been trying all sorts of expedients over the rum collinses to get Leeds to part with his submachine gun. He kept suggesting that they match for it or that they cut a hand of poker for it or shoot at a target for it. I believe he even offered to buy it" (234). As Hemingway's correspondence became public in the 1980s, his own words seemed to substantiate the caricature of his trigger-happiness. "Tell Patrick I have a Thompson Sub Machine gun and we shoot sharks with it," he wrote Sara Murphy in July 1935, hoping to lift the spirits of her ailing oldest child, who would pass from tuberculosis two years later. "Shot 27 in two weeks. All over ten feet long. As soon as they put their heads out we give them a burst" (*SL* 416). Similarly, photographs of Hemingway wielding his new weapon have been used to document his supposed bloodlust. One pictures him aiming directly at the camera; another, one oft-reprinted, shows him seemingly passed out on the *Pilar* with the weapon resting on his chest, a drink in one hand and his oldest son, John Hadley Nicanor Hemingway ("Bumby"), at his feet.

So pervasive is the image of Hemingway and his Tommy gun that careless historians sometimes project it into another famous shooting incident. As Hemingway's June 1935 *Esquire* essay, "On Being Shot Again: A Gulf Stream Letter," describes, the author inadvertently wounded himself aboard the *Pilar* when a bullet ricocheted off a railing and its splintered fragments punctured his leg (*BL* 198–204). That incident took place on 7 April, however, a solid month before Leeds gave Hemingway the Tommy gun. The weapon that fired the bullet came from a .22 Colt Woodsman pistol. A far less flattering incident that *did* involve Hemingway's submachine gun concerns a subsequent *Esquire* piece, July 1935's "The President Vanquishes: A Bimini Letter," which describes a day of Bimini fishing when painter friend Henry "Mike" Strater hooked a thousand-pound black marlin (23, 167). (Strater is the titular president, which was his nickname in Hemingway's circles because he headed the Maine Tuna Club.) As Strater struggled to reel in what observers recognized right away as a prized catch, Hemingway blasted congregating sharks with his Tommy gun, exacerbating the feeding frenzy by bloodying the water. "The President Vanquishes" does not tell this part of the story—a "lie of omission," according to Paul Hendrickson, that forever dampened the friendship between Strater and Hemingway (299).

6:28–29 **Tropical beer . . . Cunard bar:** Tropical Beer, or "Cerveza La Tropical," is Cuba's oldest beer, first brewed in Havana in 1888 by the Blanco Herrera family on the site of an ice plant that lent the company its name: the Nueva Fabrica de Hielo (new ice factory). Beginning in 1930, the company's president, Julio Blanco Herrera, established the brand as a major Cuban presence, building a baseball stadium adjacent to the family beer garden that hosted both international and American exhibition games. Castro nationalized Nueva Fabrica in 1960, and the label disappeared outside of Cuba, reappearing only in 1998 under the aegis of a new firm located in Coral Gables, Florida.

The Cunard Bar was a higher-end drinking establishment located in proximity to the Pearl of San Francisco Café, aimed mainly at tourists traveling the Cunard cruise line, whose ships docked at the same San Francisco wharf where Hemingway docked. At the time of Norberto Fuentes's *Hemingway in Cuba,* the building housed an auto repair shop (95).

7:21 **the big Luger:** Pancho's weapon is a semiautomatic pistol manufactured by the Deutsche Waffen und Munitionsfabriken (DWM) corporation of Germany beginning in 1900. Miriam B. Mandel describes the gun's genesis: "In 1898, [George] Luger [1849–1923] invented a semiautomatic hand weapon which had a toggle-joint breech mechanism; on recoil after firing, this mechanism would open to receive a new cartridge from the magazine in its grip" (182). Despite its rapid-fire capabilities, a Luger was no match for either the Tommy gun or the sawed-off shotgun wielded by the *porristas.*

8:5 **Some nigger:** Of the twenty-nine instances of *nigger* in chapter 1 alone, because of its deadpan tone this is perhaps the most troubling. It reminds one of Mark Twain's most notorious use of the epithet (some 215 instances) in *Adventures of Huckleberry Finn* (1884). When Huck returns home late from a Mississippi River jaunt due to a blown cylinder head his Aunt Sally asks if anyone was hurt by the accident. "No'm," the boy replies. "Killed a nigger" (352). Just as Huck implies that African Americans are not counted as people, Harry Morgan seems to emphasize this *machadista*'s innate sadism by having him blow "the side of [Pancho's] head off" as the terrorist sits on his rump bleeding from a Tommy gun blast to the stomach. In Toni Morrison's words, "in this slaughter the blacks are singled out as the most gratuitously violent and savage" (74).

Not all critics view the line as exclusively racist, however. The same Albert Murray who encouraged writing students to study the opening paragraph of *To Have and Have Not* explained the passage thus: "When Harry, watching the Negro empty a submachine gun and switch to a shotgun under fire, says, 'Some nigger,' he is expressing his (and no doubt Hemingway's) profound appreciation for any man, whoever he may be, who can perform under pressure with grace and style" (*Blue Devils* 212).

While the epithet is inarguably offensive, there is a sociological explanation for depicting the triggerman as black, although in the end, the explanation turns out to arise more from assumption than fact. Machado was rumored to have stocked the *porra* with disenfranchised Afro-Cubans, supposedly because their resentment of the racism within the middle and upper classes would encourage their brutality. Hemingway would have been aware of this widespread perception and likely inclined to accept it as fact, even though, as an observer for the *Afro-American* newspaper noted at the time, "Most of the pictures of *porristas* which appear in the papers are white in spite of assurances given me by many persons of both races that most of them were colored" (qtd. in Guidry 53). In the tumultuous aftermath of Machado's unseating, known *porristas* were singled out for retribution, with stories of mob violence against them filling the papers for weeks. One unlucky minion, the deputy of the reviled *machadista* Major Arsenio Ortiz (a man so ruthless his nickname was the "Jackal of Oriente"), was lynched and his corpse dragged through the streets. (Ortiz managed to escape into exile.) This political violence segued into racial violence by feeding off the perception that Afro-Cubans in general were ardent supporters of Machado. By September 1933, the ABC morphed into an explicitly supremacist organization by insisting that only repression of Afro-Cubans could prevent blacks from militarizing in the spirit of *porra* violence. The Ku Klux Klan Kubano likewise emerged to spread rumors of a "Negro menace" and a "Negro uprising," specifically calling for a "War on the Negro" (Guidry 560). In reality, Afro-Cubans were proportionally no greater *machadistas* than any other ethnic segment of the Cuban population. Hemingway's machine-gun wielding killer, however, is the stereotype of the black *porrista* that persisted during the Revolution of 1933—a stereotype that the constant use of *nigger* would have perpetuated rather than subverted.

8:10–14 I went clean around the outside of the square . . . through the gate and out onto the dock: As Harry slips out the back of the Pearl of San Francisco, he makes his way to the nearby San Francisco wharf, where—not coincidentally—Josie Russell's *Anita* docked throughout the summer of 1932 and 1933. The wharf would remain Hemingway's chosen dock after he procured the *Pilar* the following summer.

In the manuscript, Hemingway was not immediately clear about how to segue Harry from the shoot-out to the succeeding charter-fishing scene. This paragraph originally ended with him editorializing on the incident ("That town was in a hell of a shape all right") before heading *back* to the Pearl after two hours and "a couple of drinks" to steady his nerves. Not two minutes into his return, another café patron is propositioning the captain. "Only this time," Harry says, "it was something else" (MS 30, item 204, folder 1, page 5). Whether this means a booze run, or Mr. Sing's illegals, or even an offer from a prostitute is unclear. Hemingway excised this paragraph before he could specify and instead introduced Mr. Johnson.

8:17 Eddy: Although at 3:4 Harry refers to *we,* not until Mr. Johnson asks, "Where's Eddy?" do we have any idea that anyone accompanied him to the Pearl to meet with the ABC cell, for Eddy neither speaks nor is mentioned by name in the shoot-out scene.

Harry Morgan's mate was based upon Joe Lowe (1887–1935), a Key West fisherman who worked for Joe Russell on the *Anita* during the summers of 1932 and 1933. Lowe was among the casualties of the 1935 Labor Day hurricane, when the sponger he was then employed on, the *Gilbert,* was wrecked at the Matecumbe ferry slip. According to contemporary reports, Lowe was one of four crewmembers who abandoned the boat to seek shelter on the key's railroad tracks. He and another man, Felipe Perdomo, were unable to keep grip on the rails when the storm surge hit (Knowles 196). Hemingway would write to Maxwell Perkins shortly after the disaster claiming to have recognized Lowe's drowned body as he arrived at Lower Matecumbe to help with disaster assistance (*SL* 423).

9:14 What sort of a day will it be? It may seem rather ludicrous that Harry's client, Mr. Johnson, would be indifferent enough to the morning's violence to ask about fishing prospects so quickly on the heels of asking Eddy what he saw in the café, but his detachment is exactly the point. Johnson is the novel's first "have," providing readers the first glimpse of a character whose wealth grants a privileged distance from the woes of the oppressed. From a broader perspective, he also represents a stock character found throughout Hemingway: that of the detached tourist who has little interest in the land in which he journeys. In this regard, Mr. Johnson is not unlike Brett Ashley and Mike Campbell in *The Sun Also Rises*. As Keven Maier writes, the modern era saw "an emergent distinction between traveler and tourist," one that "helped develop hinges on what counts as an authentic experience and on how much work is required to achieve it" (66). From the beginning of his career,

Hemingway frequently posited this dichotomy in his fiction in order to bolster both his own authenticity as a globetrotter and his literary authority to depict foreign cultures. *To Have and Have Not* is no different than *The Sun Also Rises* in this regard. Just as Brett and Mike define by contrast Jake Barnes's status as an "aficionado," someone "who is passionate" enough about local customs to learn their traditions (*SAR* 105), as opposed to a passing tourist, so, too, Mr. Johnson is essential to Hemingway's ability to depict Harry Morgan as having firsthand knowledge of Cuban culture and a working relationship with Havana's harbor population. The contrast is so well executed, in fact, that it is often overlooked that Harry *is* a traveler, no matter if he is working while in Cuba.

The best critique of tourism in extant criticism of the novel is Adam Pridemore's relatively obscure article in the 2006 proceedings of the Florida College English Association, "Decolonizing the Native Conch in Ernest Hemingway's *To Have and Have Not*: Harry Morgan as a Cautionary Tale against Tourism." Applying the work of postcolonial studies godfather Frantz Fanon to the story, Pridemore demonstrates how the characters reflect the three stages of colonization at the hands of Key West's tourism industry: first, the "embrace of the master culture"; second, expressions of passive nostalgia for the oppressed culture that "focuses on the dead remnants of the colonized culture's past"; and, finally, a rebellious push for "a new language of freedom, a language against the colonizer" that frees the oppressed from dominance (94–95). Harry represents this last stage, his willingness to break the law serving as his effort "to stop the colonization process in its attempt to deprive him of his livelihood" (97). For Pridemore, the novel is a profound protest against "the overwhelming sense of centralization that our nation's unique brand of neocolonialism" imposes, especially in the behavior of tourists (98).

Mr. Johnson's tourism is historically intriguing as well against the backdrop of the Cuban Revolution of 1933. As anti-Machado protests turned bloody in the early 1930s—coupled with the onset of the Depression—the casual tourism that Mr. Johnson represents became relatively uncommon. Traveling to Cuba was simply unsafe and unaffordable for many of the ninety thousand American tourists who had flocked there only a few years earlier during the record-breaking winter tourism season of 1926–27 (Skwiot 99). To be sure, plenty of Americans remained in Cuba during the 1933 revolution, but they tended to have business connections to the country and to own land there, such as Jane Mason's husband and the novel's Tommy Bradley, G. Grant Mason, who worked in the aviation industry from the couple's estate in Jaimanitas.

9:18 **this bird:** Those familiar with Hemingway's propensity for British slang in *The Sun Also Rises* and *A Farewell to Arms* might find this colloquialism confusing, given that it usually refers to a young, sexually attractive woman. Harry uses the term in the relatively newer sense of the word describing someone as an old, odd, or "queer bird," a meaning that, according to the *OED*, arose in the mid-nineteenth century. However commonplace a slang expression, Hemingway likely took literary justification for using it from hardboiled fiction, where it is part of the tough-guy idiom. Dashiell Hammett's characters use *this bird* constantly. See, for example, *The Dain Curse,* which Hemingway owned, in which a San Francisco cop, Pat Reddy, refers to a corpse as "this bird" (Hammett 154).

9:18–9:23 **fishing the stream . . . thirty-five dollars a day:** The "stream" refers, of course, to the Gulf Stream, the warm-water ocean current that whirls through the narrow passage between the Florida Straits and Cuba. The "world's largest river," as it is sometimes called, begins in the Gulf of Mexico and once past the Straits flows swiftly northward along the eastern coast of the United States to Newfoundland before dispersing toward Europe. From there it circles clockwise back, creating a ten thousand-mile loop. The stream is distinguished by its striking indigo hue, which contrasts to the normal green-gray of the Atlantic Ocean. Credit for its discovery is given to Ponce de Leon, who documented its existence as early as the sixteenth century. Its name comes from none other than Benjamin Franklin.

After 1928 Hemingway wrote frequently about the Gulf Stream. The subtitles of at least two *Esquire* columns set those particular essays within it, while several others that take place in Cuba and Key West give insight into his intrigue with it. The most notable among these 1933–36 articles is "On the Blue Water: A Gulf Stream Letter" (April 1936), in which he describes the stream as "the last wild country" and "the last unexploited country": "Once you are out of sight of land and of the other boats you are more alone than you can ever be hunting and the sea is the same as it has been since before men ever went on it in boats" (*BL* 237). As evidence of the primeval battle between man and environment, he recounts the story of a Cabañas fisherman who spent two days hooking a giant marlin, only to have sharks devour it after he lashed it to the side of his skiff—a story later developed into *The Old Man and the Sea. Green Hills of Africa* also includes an oft-analyzed lyrical excursion on the Gulf Stream in which Hemingway mediates on its timelessness, noting that it will endure long after "the palm fronds of our victories, the worn light bulbs of our discoveries, and the empty condoms of our great loves" (108). Of equal interest is a later essay, "The Great Blue River" (*Holiday,* July 1949), which begins with a list of all the pleasures Hemingway declines to recite when asked why he lives in Cuba, culminating with the one he is willing to share: "You tell them the reason you live in Cuba is the great, deep blue river, three quarters of a mile to a mile deep and sixty to eighty miles across, that you can reach in thirty minutes from the door of your farmhouse, riding through beautiful country to get to it, that has, when the river is right, the finest fishing I have ever known" (*BL* 356—and apropos of the first entry in this reader's guide, notice the use of *you* here as well).

As a charter-boat captain, Harry Morgan works in a sector of the Key West economy that was only about thirty years old in this period. Fishermen began taking paying customers on trips at the turn of the century as an alternative to the moribund sponging industry, then in its final years. Yet sport fishing in the Keys did not truly take off until the early 1910s. That was when the Long Key Fishing Camp opened on the site of the work camp of the recently completed Long Key Viaduct, the first leg of the Key West extension of Henry Flagler's monumentally ambitious Florida East Coast Railway. Sportsmen quickly descended on the camp, its popularity spurred by the presence of prolific pulp novelist Zane Grey (1872–1939). As the president of the Long Key Fishing Club, Grey became the face of Keys fishing; his nonfiction collection *Tales of Fishes* (1919) includes an essay entitled "Gulf Stream Fishing" (88–106) whose description of the minutiae of angling for sailfish and bonefish anticipates Hemingway's writing (though Grey lacks his lyricism). *Tales* also includes a confrontation with a barracuda that looks forward to the battles with marauding sharks in the *Esquire* essays, *The Old Man and the Sea*, and *Islands in the Stream* (103).

Hemingway learned the charter-fishing business from several locals who, though not necessarily models for Harry Morgan, nonetheless provided the expertise necessary to make his main protagonist a credible character. Upon arriving in the Keys in 1928, he engaged the services of Captain Eddie "Bra" Saunders, a crusty fifty-two-year-old Bahamian immigrant, and his half-brother/mate, Berge, to serve as his guides.[4] In 1932 and 1933, it was Joe "Josie" Russell who carried him to Cuba on the *Anita* for several months of fishing. Equally important was Charles Thompson, the local marina and bait-shop owner (among other business interests) who accompanied Hemingway on his 1934 safari, appearing as "Karl" in *Green Hills of Africa*. That name comes from Charles's brother Karl, who appears in *To Have and Have Not* as Sheriff Roger Johnson.

10:3 **twenty-eight cents a gallon:** Adjusted for inflation, the cost of gas is comparable to $5.11 a gallon in 2016 dollars. By contrast, the average price of gas in 2015 (the last year for which information is available), $2.40, would translate to only thirteen cents per gallon in 1933, slightly lower than 1933's national average of eighteen cents.

10:17 **plugged:** Here Hemingway idiomatically uses the preferred hardboiled term for shooting someone as a synonym for uptight.

10:22 **this nigger . . . comes down the dock:** This sentence marks the first of many tense shifts that will prove an idiosyncratic stylistic tic throughout the novel's first third. (These are listed in appendix D.) Such tense shifts are common in oral storytelling but far rarer in written narration. When employed in print in this manner, the aim is usually to create the illusion of a conversational exchange, as if a storyteller were speaking to a live audience. Hemingway also seems to shift tense at random moments to foster an atmosphere of immediacy, imbuing the action with a "nowness" that makes it more vivid than the past tense does. What Blanca Schorcht says about the effect of similar random shifts in Leslie Marmon Silko's *Ceremony* (1977) applies here: a shift "causes the reader to take notice as well as respond to the storytelling session. It is as if the reader is suddenly drawn back into the storytelling performance. He or she is never allowed to slide back complacently into the time and space of the novel.... The abrupt shifts in tense remind the reader of the differences between a world that theorizes itself through story, and other worlds of experience. The tense shifts simultaneously draw the reader into [a] storied reality and also make the reader aware of the stories' power to *create* reality" (124). At a very basic level, the shifts remind us that Harry is narrating the story of his Cuban misadventure to us.

Although Toni Morrison briefly discusses the depiction of the Afro-Cuban *porrista* in the shoot-out scene at the Pearl, she comments more on this unnamed fisherman who baits hooks on Harry's charter boat: "The black man is not only nameless for five chapters, he is not even hired, just someone 'we had getting bait'—a kind of trained response, not an agent possessing a job" (70). Morrison explores the odd lengths Hemingway must go to keep from granting this character any agency whatsoever, focusing in particular on an awkward passage at 13:18–19 in which the narrative voice ties itself into a syntactical knot to deny him authority as a fishing expert.

Morrison's analysis is the best-known critique of racism in *To Have and Have Not,* but it should be noted that she does not question whether Hemingway's canonical status should be challenged because of it. For that argument, the reader should seek out a more obscure essay, Charli g Valdez's "Racing *To Have and Have Not*": "While [Morrison] disavows asking or answering if Hemingway is a racist or if his novel is a racist cultural artefact," Valdez argues that "Hemingway reveals not only his characters' racist obsessions, but his own. [The novel] is rife with racist perspectives and epithets that defy literary conventions of the time"—an argument that, although Hemingway fans may not like it, bears some truth, even though Valdez offers no supporting evidence from contemporaneous authors of this assertion (124). Valdez effectively complements Morrison's reading of the novel's objectification of its black characters through an extended comparison to Howard Hawks's 1944 film adaption, which, despite avoiding Hemingway's conspicuous use of *nigger* and naming black characters, still does not humanize them adequately.

That Hemingway chose not to name the black fisherman is somewhat surprising, for the character was likely based on a real-life acquaintance known as Jig who worked intermittently on the *Anita* in 1932. Jig appears in that year's *Anita* logs, sometimes described as sleeping at the wheel; more importantly, he is visible in a rare film from that season's fishing expedition now housed in the Hemingway Collection at the Kennedy Library. Known as *The Fishing Voyage of the Good Ship Anita,* the fifteen-minute, black-and-white home movie was shot by Raymond White, the half-brother of Hemingway's aunt Arabella, wife of the late uncle, Tyler Hemingway, who had helped Hemingway obtain his cub reporter job at the *Kansas City Star* in 1917–18. The story of the discovery of this footage and its preservation at the Kennedy Library is told in Joseph Sigman's unpublished essay "*The Fishing Voyage of the Good Ship Anita:* A Recently Discovered Film of Hemingway in 1932," presented at the First International Hemingway Conference in Madrid, Spain in June 1984. A copy of Professor Sigman's paper is held in the Hemingway Collection's vertical file, box 010.

11:20 **on a rumba:** A rumba brings to mind ballroom dances of the sort taught at Arthur Murray or Fred Astaire franchises alongside the cha-cha, mambo, and the pasodoble. The steps and pace of ballroom rumbas are actually derived more from the bolero-son than the much more frantic, sexually assertive dance steps that bear the term among rural Afro-Cubans even today. For better or worse, those distinctions tend to be lost as the word has become a synecdoche for any sensual Latin American expression of the body. Hemingway is equating the Cuban mate's drunken gestures with these generic dance moves.

11:23 **the smacks . . . fish cars:** *Smack* describes any cutter-styled fishing vessel. The term *well smack* refers to fishing boats with large internal holding compartments built below deck to keep catches alive until they reach market. Especially for smaller smacks, storage is external, usually in the form of buoyed containers either anchored nearby or attached with a rope. Smacks tend to appear in Hemingway as picturesque devices connoting an artisanal as opposed to commercial approach to living off the sea. See "Marlin Off the Morro: A Cuban Letter" (*BL* 138) and *Islands in the Stream* (246).

11:24 **Cabañas:** Better known as "La Cabaña" or by its full name, Fortaleza de San Carlos de la Cabaña, the Fort of Saint Charles is a military fortress built on the eastern side of the bay inlet into Havana. Construction began in 1763 shortly after the British returned Havana to Spain in exchange for Florida after seizing the island the previous year. The fort shares a promontory with Morro Castle (see 11:26).

11:26 **the Morro:** Officially known as Castillo de los Tres Reyes Magos del Morro, Morro Castle sits at a slight northwestern proximity to La Cabaña on the same two-hundred-foot-tall hilltop overlooking Havana from the east. El Morro actually predates its neighbor by nearly two hundred years, having been constructed in 1589 to guard the city from invaders. (It was largely because the British were able to foil the castle's defense of Havana harbor in 1762 that La Cabaña was constructed the following year, after Cuba was returned to Spain.) As one of Havana's most recognizable landmarks, the castle appears frequently in Cuban travelogues both pre- and post-Hemingway. During his early days as a dime novelist, Upton Sinclair (1878–1968) set one of his Clif the Naval Cadet adventures here without having ever stepped foot in Cuba (*A Prisoner of Morro; or, In the Hands of the Enemy*, 1898). If El Morro is slightly more famous than La Cabaña, it is because of visibility. Because it sits to the north of its companion, it is immediately visible as one approaches the city, whereas the younger installation is visible only from within the bay. Since Harry Morgan's boat is heading out to sea, he passes La Cabaña first.

11:29 **almost to soundings:** *Sounding* is the nautical term for measuring the depth of a body of water. For centuries, this was done with a simple weighted line. The accuracy of the measure was often unreliable, because sailors could not guarantee that the line hung plumb from the boat and not an angle due to currents or even the tug of a vessel's movement. As a result, echo systems were developed to give more accurate readings. Nevertheless, in the 1930s, it was still common for noncommercial boaters to use line sounding, as Hemingway did. *In soundings* refers to water less than a hundred fathoms deep (six hundred feet) where the line is employable. For the Gulf Stream to be "in almost to soundings" means it runs into relatively shallow waters. According to "Marlin Off the Morro: A Cuban Letter," the depth near the Morro was twenty fathoms (120 feet) (*BL* 138).

Hemingway sometimes used *sounding* as a metaphor, as in "Banal Story" (1925): "And what of our daughters who must make their own Soundings. Nancy Hawthorne is obliged to make her own Soundings in the sea of life. Bravely and soundly she faces the problems which come to every girl of eighteen" (*CSS* 274). As George Monteiro shows, here Hemingway parodies a now-forgotten novel called *Soundings* by Arthur Hamilton Gibbs (1888–1964), the type of overwrought reading recommended by the object of his ire, the magazine *The Forum* (143). In a more serious, reflective vein, the term appears in a quote in A. E. Hotchner's *Papa Hemingway* (1966). In it, Hemingway recounts how "The Snows of Kilimanjaro" was inspired by an unnamed society maven's 1934 offer to finance an African safari as long as she could accompany the author: "I had given a lot of thought to her and the offer and how it might be if I accepted an offer like that. What it might do to a character like me whose failings I know and have taken many soundings on. Never wrote so directly about myself as in that story" (161–62). (In *Hemingway's Boat*, Paul Hendrickson identifies the woman as Helen Hay Whitney [77–82].)

12:5 **Lindbergh crossing the Atlantic:** At the age of twenty-five, Charles Lindbergh (1902–1974) made history on 20–21 May 1927 as the first man to cross from the United States to Europe in a solo, nonstop airplane ride. By the time he attempted the journey, six noted aviators had already perished pursuing the $25,000 Orteig Prize, which New York hotelier Raymond Orteig (1870–1939) had been offering since 1919. The key to Lindbergh's success was his custom-built, streamlined single-engine monoplane, the *Spirit of St. Louis,* whose cockpit was so cramped the pilot could not stretch his legs. Upon arriving at Paris's Le Bourget Field from Long Island, Lindbergh was hailed as a hero, a prominence he used to promote air travel for both tourism and mail delivery. Five years after his historic accomplishment, he garnered an entirely different and unfortunate sort of renown when his eighteen-month-old toddler, Charles Jr., was kidnapped in a crime that became a media sensation. After two months, the child was found dead of a skull fracture. Eventually, Richard Bruno Hauptmann (1899–1936) was tried, convicted, and executed for the murder, though questions about his guilt have persisted since his arrest.

Lindbergh is mentioned in Hemingway's accounts of his 1953–54 safari, posthumously published in truncated form as *True at First Light* (1999) and then in its original manuscript's fuller length as *Under Kilimanjaro* (2005). Here the writer describes reading the aviator's Pulitzer Prize–winning memoir of his journey, *The Spirit of St. Louis* (1953) (*TAFL* 163, 175; *UK* 197, 209, 236). (Lindbergh had previously told the story in *We* [1927].) Leo Braudy's history of fame, *The Frenzy of Renown: Fame and Its History* (1986), begins with a fascinating chapter comparing Hemingway's and Lindbergh's iconicities (19–29).

12:16 **the Hardy reel:** The House of Hardy is the brand name of a British sporting goods manufacturer founded in 1872. Its line of angling tackle was considered premium product in Hemingway's time; he owned a six-inch Zane Grey reel, named after the eminent angler-author. Although, as the plot reveals, a Hardy reel and rod would constitute an expensive outlay for a struggling charter-boat captain such as Harry Morgan, his affluent clientele would expect high-end equipment on a rig.

12:22 **Keep the rod butt in the socket on the chair:** Harry's instruction serves as a subtle bit of foreshadowing. Because Johnson fails to secure the rod, the expensive equipment ends up going overboard when the marlin strikes the boat's bait line. This line is indicative of how, in Paul Hendrickson's words, "'One Trip Across' could be read almost as much for its marlin instructions as for its taut drama" (213).

13:1 **goofy:** Harry's rant about how little the majority of his customers know about the art and technique of fishing is typical of Hemingway's disdain for the novice, the non-aficionado, of any sport. From this moment until 22:29, when Harry returns the boat to the dock, Hemingway constantly reminds readers of what an amateur and poor sportsman Mr. Johnson is. *Goofy* seems an oddly childish if not bland word choice for a writer as devoted to le bon mot as Hemingway. Nevertheless, it appears throughout his writing in the *To Have and Have Not* era. See, for example, his 1933 letter to Arnold Gingrich, in which he speaks of Gertrude Stein going "professionally goofy" (*SL* 384), or his April 1936 *Esquire* essay, "On the Blue Water: A Gulf Stream Letter," in which he describes an elephant hunter going "goofy" for sport fishing

(*BL* 237). The hunter referenced here is likely Bror von Blixen-Finecke (1886–1946), best remembered today as the husband of Karen Blixen (penname Isak Dinesen) of *Out of Africa* fame. Movie lovers invariably associate von Blixen with Austrian actor Klaus Maria Brandauer, who portrayed him in the 1985 Academy Award–winning film adaption by Sidney Pollack, in which Robert Redford plays the philandering Denys Finch Hatton, von Blixen's foil for his wife's affections. (Blixen is portrayed by Meryl Streep.) Hemingway befriended von Blixen long after his divorce from Karen; by the mid-1930s when the two men socialized in Africa and Bimini, von Blixen was married to his third wife, Eva Dickson (1905–1938), a legendary aviatrix. Along with Hemingway's hunting guide Philip Percival, von Blixen partially inspired the character of Robert Wilson in "The Short Happy Life of Francis Macomber." Paul Hendrickson writes about the friendship of Hemingway and von Blixen in *Hemingway's Boat*, although he does not connect the big game hunter to "On the Blue Water." Instead, he notes that von Blixen is cited by name in the July 1934 *Esquire* essay "Notes on Dangerous Game: The Third Tanganyika Letter" (*SL* 167–71) and explores rumors perpetuated by Henry "Mike" Strater that Hemingway and Eva had an affair in 1935 (294–97).

13:18–19 The nigger was still taking her out and I looked and saw he had seen a patch of flying fish: Toni Morrison seizes upon the odd construction "saw he had seen" as indicative of how Hemingway suppressed the presence of African American characters, keeping them voiceless and diminishing their expertise: "'Saw he had seen' is improbable in syntax, sense, and tense but, like other choices available to Hemingway, it is risked to avoid a speaking black. . . . A better, more graceful choice would be to have the black man cry out at the sighting. But the logic of the narrative's discrimination prevents a verbal initiative of importance to Harry's business coming from this nameless, sexless, nationless Africanist presence. . . . What would have been the cost, I wonder, of humanizing, gendering, this character at the opening of the novel?" (73).

14:9–12 You party-boat captains: Johnson's term seems strikingly contemporary until one distinguishes between what a "party boat" meant then and now. The tourist does not use the term referring to anything comparable to what we today would call a "booze cruise," a short, captained jaunt around a waterway where the main purpose is to drink and socialize for a sort of floating happy hour. Instead, a *party boat* was any charter that accommodated multiple parties or groups of people. Some in the industry still use the description as a synonym for a fishing charter, often to the confusion of tourists more interested in the partying than in the sport. Johnson's complaint that whether or not the fish strike Harry will "take the money just the same" is a jab at the professionalism of the charter-fishing industry, implying that the captains cheat clients by making excuses for the scarcity of fish.

14:22 **to troll:** In deep-sea fishing, trolling occurs when a boat moves at a relatively low speed so the bait lines don't merely sit in the water but are dragged, effectively bringing the bait to the fish.

16:1 **a little drag:** A drag is a mechanical device on a fishing reel that applies pressure to the spool to create resistance on the dispersal of the line. Working the drag is a major technique of sports fishing; by screwing down the drag, the fisherman "brakes" the catch's ability to run with the line. By alternately tightening and loosening the drag, one tires the fish by forcing him to fight against the tautness of the line. As Hemingway demonstrates, Johnson is clueless when it comes to working the mechanism. When the tourist snags a "brown buggar" of a marlin (16:6), Harry has to repeatedly instruct him on its usage (12:24, 16:1–6, 16:16, 16:18–19, 17:7, 17:15), and even then it is because Johnson over-tightens the drag that the line snaps and the first catch escapes: "I felt his drag. He had screwed it down tight. You couldn't pull out any line. It had to break" (17:28–29). C. B. McCully notes in *The Language of Fly-Fishing* (2000) that at one point the *OED* credited Hemingway with *inventing* the meaning of drag with the aforementioned line on 17:28–29, which is odd, "since the word is obviously older" (58).

16:9–10 **Sock him!. . . . Stick it into him:** Here Harry instructs Johnson on when to pull back on his rod to yank the hook deeper into the marlin's mouth. Johnson is equally oblivious when it comes to reading the line: he assumes because the line is slack the hook has failed to take.

17:10 **brother:** Harry suddenly addresses the reader to remind us of the storytelling situation in a way we haven't been since the novel's opening paragraph with its ambiguous *you*. This particular address was a narrative tic of Hemingway's throughout the 1930s. It begins with "After the Storm" ("Brother, that was some storm," *CSS* 233) and continues on through such *Esquire* essays as "Notes on the Next War: A Serious Topical Letter," where it is nearly always combative ("But you will die, brother, if you go to [war] long enough," *BL* 210). (Although Jake and Bill trade *brother*s in *The Sun Also Rises,* they direct it toward each other, not the reader [*SAR* 98]. The effect is therefore not the same.) Both in Hemingway and in hardboiled fiction, where it is equally prevalent, the *brother* address conveys a tone of condescension and aggression. Yet during the Depression the term also began to convey an appeal to collective action, signifying comradeship and mutual survival, giving its use a complex register. The term's currency during the economic collapse was no doubt increased by the popularity of "Brother, Can You Spare a Dime?" (1930), written by Edgar "Yip" Harburg (1896–1981) and Jay Gorney (1894–1990). *Brother* is used as a form of address eight times in the novel.

17:13 **keeping him on the quarter:** In boating lingo, "on the quarter" means roughly midway between the beam, the center of a boat, and its stern, or back. For a fisherman to keep his quarry "on the quarter" thus means keeping his line at a forty-five-degree angle between these two points.

17:18–19 **the pull of the belly of the line:** Presumably, refraction creates the illusion that the marlin remains hooked. As the eye follows a straight line into the water's surface, it will appear to angle out as light rays are bent by the change in speed they travel from air and water.

18:5–13 **If you don't give them line:** This passage is typical of the expertise that Hemingway narrators model when they must explain the art of a particular sport to a neophyte. The only Hemingway fiction that goes into more detail on the techniques of angling is *Islands in the Stream,* in which Thomas Hudson and Roger Davis direct Hudson's son David on how to reel in a thousand-pound swordfish in that novel's most famous episode. The scene is an even greater tour de force than Mr. Johnson's shorter encounter with his fish, running thirty pages (109–39). *Hemingway on Fishing,* edited by Nick Lyon (2002), excerpts the *Islands* episode, along with a pair of *Esquire* essays that flesh out Hemingway's how-to expertise with deep-sea fishing, "Marlin Off the Morro: A Cuban Letter" (Autumn 1933) and "Out in the Stream: A Cuban Letter" (August 1934), both of which also share details with the Mr. Johnson episode. He does not, however, include this scene from *To Have and Have Not.*

19:7–8 **Some Eddy:** This is the second appearance of this narrational tic using "some ___," after "some nigger" at 8:4–5. Coming eleven pages after its predecessor, the interjection may seem unobtrusive, yet it nevertheless hints at how Hemingway could overdo the repetition of these asides until his style seems mannered. It will appear a third time, at 28:13, in referencing the deadbeat tourist who leaves Harry high and dry in Cuba: "Some Mr. Johnson."

19:20–21 **a mill race:** A mill race refers to a current and/or the channel in which it flows as it moves toward the waterwheel of a mill.

19:23 **a feather squid:** A feather squid is a fishing lure outfitted with bright feathers that fan out like squid tentacles in the water to attract a catch. Hemingway also describes the device in "The Great Blue River": "Ordinarily, fishing out of Havana, we get a line out with a Japanese feather squid and a strip of pork rind on the hook, while we are still running out of the harbor. This is for tarpon, which feed around the fishing smacks anchored along the Morro Castle–Cabañas side of the channel, and for kingfish" (*BL* 356).

20:7–8 **a sloppy way to fish:** Holding the rod across his knees as Johnson does here is "sloppy" because the fisherman is not in position with one hand on the rod grip and the other on the reel spool, attentively awaiting a strike. Hemingway's most extended criticism of "sloppy" fishing is the introduction to S. Kip Farrington's *Atlantic Game Fishing* (1937), which Farrington later reprinted en toto in his *Fishing with Hemingway and Glassell* (1971). In the piece, Hemingway identifies several techniques that cheapen the sport: resting the rod on the gunwale "whenever the angler's back gets tired while the boatman plays the fish with the boat; 72-thread line, which when wet can tow a good size launch with the fish doing the towing; two handle-reels with a 1:1 ration which work like chair hoists" (9–10). Mr. Johnson does not commit the cardinal sin of deep-sea fishing, however: "I knew an American sportsman in Havana who found the easiest way to beat the existing records was to buy his marlin from the market fishermen and then bring them in and hang them at the Yacht Club. No one could compete with him" (13). In his posthumously published memoir of spending the 1934 marlin season with Hemingway, Arnold Samuelson tells a similar story of a "phony fisherman," nicknamed Principe, or "Prince of the Fisherman." After Hemingway unmasks him as a fraud, Principe disappears from Havana, "afraid that Hemingway would use the incident to brighten up one of his *Esquire* pieces" (114).

20:10 **that old cement factory:** The cement factory was a landmark along the Cuban coast near Cojimar opposite which Hemingway found marlin fishing especially advantageous, in part because the Gulf Stream came in close to shore between it and the village proper. As Mark P. Ott notes, references to the cement factory show up in the log book kept aboard the *Anita* during Hemingway's 1933 fishing expedition with Josie Russell. In particular, Hemingway would mention the landmark in an entry for 17 May describing how his line snagged on a rock while reeling in a marlin, eventually snapping and losing nearly a hundred yards of line. "Most punishment I ever took," Hemingway wrote in the log, anticipating the measure of exertion Harry and Mr. Johnson debate after Harry's tackle goes overboard. As Ott writes, "Re-creating the moment [in *To Have and Have Not*], Hemingway transformed his own loss of a striped marlin into Mr. Johnson's loss of a black marlin" (152). References to the cement factory also crop up in the 1934 log Hemingway kept aboard the *Pilar* (Miller, "Matrix" 114).

20:13 **a depth bomb:** A depth charge, as a depth bomb is commonly known, is an explosive device that detonates while submerged in a body of water. Its concussive pressure, if released near enough to the surface, can result in the type of magnificent eruption Hemingway describes here. The British Royal Navy developed depth charges during the Great War to combat marauding German U-boats; by the end of that conflict and on into World War II, they were mainstays of submarine warfare. Depth charges differ from mines in that they are not simply deposited in a waterway and left to explode from accidental contact. Instead, they are considered "smart" weapons, their effectiveness dependent on deliberate targeting. "Marlin Off the Morro: A Cuban Letter" uses the same image when it describes how a fish will "come from below and hit the bait with a smash like a bomb exploding in the water" (*BL* 140).

20:28 **being derricked:** As used here, *derrick* means simply to hoist up as if lifted by a boom crane. The word has an interesting etymology, deriving from the notorious seventeenth-century executioner Thomas Derrick, whose development of a pulley system to dispatch some of the three thousand victims that crossed his gallows earned him the honor of an eponym.

21:12–15 **The reel cost two hundred and fifty dollars:** $250 in 1933 dollars is equivalent to $4,560 in 2016—clearly a huge investment for a party-boat captain of Harry Morgan's modest means. Today, a high-end House of Hardy reel such as the Zane Ti, a titanium descendant of that first reel named after Zane Grey, retails for $8,000. Most steel Zane reels are priced in the $550 range.

21:16 **Just then Eddy slaps him on the back:** This is an example of the shifts into the present tense Hemingway employs in part 1 of the novel.

22:3 **Still fishing:** As opposed to trolling, still fishing involves allowing the bait to lie stationary in the water so the fish comes to it.

22:8–9 **If it isn't enjoyable, why do it?** Christian K. Messenger makes an important point when he notes that Mr. Johnson's dialogue about fishing for fun instead of "punishment" is indicative of his faulty sense of sportsmanship. His "whole concept of sport fishing for 'enjoyment' is incomprehensible to Harry and Eddy," writes Messenger. "Johnson's unwillingness to suffer for the fish is extended to cover his unwillingness to see the dilemma of people like Harry Morgan. Johnson avoids unnecessary punishment; he doesn't consider that sport. Harry Morgan knows how to take punishment and sees it as necessary to survival, even as he has a craftsman's respect for the motion of the rite itself. Punishment is part of any satisfactory effort, especially in desperate situations" (258).

22:21 **a highball:** A highball is a generic term for any number of alcoholic drinks that mix a base liquor with carbonated water or seltzer. There are several explanations for the name, but the most obvious is that it contains a shot and a half of spirits (the ball) in a tall glass. More colorfully, the name is said to come from the go-ahead signal nineteenth-century locomotive drivers gave each other when they hoisted a ball aloft in their hands.

23:16 **The nigger gets his ball of twine:** Another tense shift. See appendix D for a full listing of these.

26:2–3 **a Chink place:** Clearly, Hemingway's use of this racial slur is as troubling as the constant references to *nigger*. Unlike the Pearl, the Cunard, and Donovan's (see 26:8), the specific restaurant Harry visits goes unnamed. Chinese eateries abounded in 1930s Havana, serving an estimated population of twenty-five thousand immigrants. As Norberto Fuentes notes, the reference here is not to El Pacifico (95), which was Hemingway's preferred Chinese restaurant, located inland from the San Francisco plaza at 518 Calle San Nicolás in the small but vibrant Chinatown district. In *Michael Palin's Hemingway Adventure* (2000), the Monty Python comedian-turned-literary-footstep-follower describes El Pacifico as "a monumental barn of a place" (227). As of this writing, the restaurant still operates.

26:8 **Donovan's:** The third Havana watering hole Harry Morgan frequented, following the Pearl of San Francisco and the Cunard. Of the trio, Donovan's was by far the rowdiest and most colorful, attracting sailors and hookers. Josie Russell was particularly fond of it. According to legend, Donovan's opened in Havana shortly after Prohibition began in 1920, when its Irish owner painstakingly shipped his bar over from the United States and reassembled it.

26:11 **Frankie:** As the middleman between Harry and the Chinese smuggler, Mr. Sing, Frankie is a suitably shadowy presence in the opening section of the book. Hemingway tells us so little about him, aside from the fact he is mostly deaf, that ascertaining the simplest of facts about his background is a difficult task. As Mary Cruz suggests, "Frankie's English nickname and the way he speaks English make it rather difficult to ascertain whether he is a Cuban or a poorly educated American. . . . He seems stupid, but he is not. Perhaps his faulty way of speaking is due to poor education; perhaps a defense mechanism" ("Selection" 87). The latter seems likelier; at 28:24–34 Harry summarizes his relationship with Frankie, noting that the pair have known each other "since I first started to run" liquor from Cuba. That Frankie first helped Harry load and was a regular at the wharf "when I quit handling stuff and went partyboating and broke out this swordfishing in Cuba" suggests the man is indeed Cuban.

26:27 **We saw the plane go out:** In this period, Pan American Airways was the only carrier in the nascent airline passenger industry with a route between Key West and Cuba. The company, founded in 1927, operated sea planes in and out of the harbor. In the early 1930s, Hemingway was a friend of founding partner George Grant Mason (1904–1970), who will appear in part 3 of *To Have and Have Not* as the cuckolded husband of the sexually voracious femme fatale Helène Bradley (based on Mason's wife and putative Hemingway mistress, Jane Mason; see pages 129–31.

Through connections in banking circles, Mason had been instrumental in procuring funding for Pan Am's chief partner, Juan Trippe, and subsequently relocated to Cuba to manage the airline's Caribbean operations. In its first three months of existence, Pan Am's Key West–Cuba route was strictly a mail carrier. Passenger service began on 16 January 1928, a few months before Hemingway arrived in the Gulf. (A sign at 303 Whitehead Street in Key West still recognizes the site where its original office was located. Since 1991, the building has housed Kelly's Bar and Restaurant, owned by actress Kelly McGillis, the star of such 1980s hit movies as *Witness* and *Top Gun*.) A ticket to Havana in the late 1920s ran $50, the equivalent of $912 in 2016 dollars. Despite the high price, more than eleven hundred tickets were sold in 1928 alone—a testament to Cuba's lure as a destination for wealthy tourists before the Depression. To ensure Pan Am's monopoly on the route, Mason maintained close ties to Machado (as well as subsequent presidents) (Van Vleck 66–69). As the portrait of Tommy Bradley in the published version of the novel suggests (the manuscript version, again, is far more complicated), Hemingway found the Ivy League Grant effete. Nevertheless, in American aviation, Mason remains a notable name. Pan Am Airlines would dominate the airline industry for the next six decades. Its demise in late 1991 came about in no small part because the company's international visibility made it an appealing target for terrorists. On 21 December 1988, Pan Am Flight 103 from London to New York was the target of one such attack when a bomb was detonated as the plane passed over Lockerbie, Scotland. More than 270 people, including 11 Lockerbie residents, were killed. Although Pan Am had suffered massive debt since the mid-1970s, lawsuits arising from Flight 103's downing hastened the company's demise three years later.

27:1 **I sent Frankie up to the hotel to see if Johnson was there:** Although Hemingway does not specify where his customer stays while chartering Harry's boat, the proximity to the San Francisco wharf implies he means the Hotel Ambos Mundos, the writer's own preferred lodging in Havana.

27:34 **that gang that hangs around the dock:** Harry refers to rival party-boat captains and fishermen.

27:36 **Conchs:** A "Conch" is a term used to describe native Key Westers—thus, the island's nickname since the early 1980s, the "Conch Republic." The term originally possessed a far narrower meaning, referring to Bahamian immigrants who settled on the island at the height of the salvaging industry in the mid-nineteenth century. Hemingway seems to employ the more modern meaning. One unsolvable mystery of *To Have and Have Not* is whether Harry Morgan is properly a Conch. The locals certainly accept him as a native, though the reference to his former career as a policeman in Miami introduces the possibility that he moved to the island in adulthood.

28:3–13 All right, what was I going to do now? This entire paragraph is our first extended introduction to the various experimental forms of narration Hemingway employs throughout the novel. Gerald Prince's *A Dictionary of Narratology* defines the particular technique used here, interior monologue, as "the nonmediated presentation of a character's thoughts and impressions or perceptions." The term is not to be confused with a more readily bandied-about one, *stream of consciousness,* which expresses sensory impressions in a less orderly fashion. As Prince notes, a passage of interior monologue will "respect morphology and syntax," whereas stream of consciousness conveys "thought in its nascent stage, prior to any rational organization" (45).

28:4–6 you have to have money to buy the booze and besides there's no money in it any more: Rum-running is no longer a profitable option for Harry because the opening section of *To Have and Have Not* occurs after Franklin D. Roosevelt signed the Cullen-Harrison Act on 23 March 1933, which effectively ended Prohibition. (The Twenty-first Amendment that repealed the constitutional ban against alcohol sale and transportation was not ratified until 5 December of that year, however.)

28:8 starve a summer in that town: When "One Trip Across" was published, in 1934, Key West was in the midst of a debilitating economic crisis. Only fifty years earlier, the city had boasted the highest per-capita income in the United States; now the unemployment rate topped the staggering national average of 25 percent. The fall from prosperity was not simply a reflection of the Great Depression crippling the rest of the country. The island's problems had festered throughout the Florida land boom of the 1920s, with the lack of economic diversification contributing to a lowering of the per-capita income to a paltry $7 per month in 1934. To a certain extent, Key West had always entrusted its economic stability to a single industry, first salvaging, then sponging, and, after that, cigar-making. These markets were moribund by the outbreak of World War I, however. Military spending briefly took up the slack, but the army, navy, and coast guard all departed for mainland Florida by the mid-1920s. While city fathers courted manufacturing, half of the island's sixty-plus plants had either closed or relocated before Black Tuesday 1929 decimated the rest of the nation's financial health. Among the industries fleeing the island was pineapple canning, which suffered due to a tariff imposed on imported fruit from other countries, including Cuba. With more than 14,000 jobs disappearing in Key West during the 1920s and early 1930s, the population dwindled by a third, down from a high of 19,350 to 12,831 (Boulard 168–69). Of those who remained, an astonishing 5,000—nearly half—received public relief.

Surrounding Monroe County fared no better. In the 1920s the county bet its economic hopes on building the Overseas Highway, raising some $3 million through two separate bond issues in 1922 and 1926 so motorists might travel the 127-mile span between Key West and Miami in their own vehicles instead of relying on Henry Flagler's Florida East Coast Railway, which had operated in debt since its 1912 opening. (The 1922 bond issue raised $300,000, while the 1926 one topped it considerably, with a $2.5 million total [Kerstein 39].) The bonds burdened the county with an unserviceable debt, mainly because the expected tourist salvation failed to materialize after the highway opened on 25 January 1928. Travelers found it far easier to visit Cuba via steamship than to vacation in Key West, in part because the "highway" included a forty-mile ferry leg between Lower Matecumbe Key and No Name Key that added four to five hours to the supposedly speedy jaunt. That gap would not be bridged until 1938.

To capture the island's grave state when he arrived in 1928, Hemingway scholars often cite a letter to Maxwell Perkins: "There was a pencilled inscription derogatory to our fair city in the toilet at the station, and somebody had written under it—'if you don't like this town get out and stay out.' Somebody else had written under that 'Everybody has'" (*SL* 277).

Had Hemingway indulged his metafictional instincts in the published version of *To Have and Have Not* as he did its manuscript when he criticized his own reputation as the "Old Slob" (see page xxxiv), Harry Morgan might have acknowledged the author's own economic importance to the city at its nadir. Maureen Ogle only slightly exaggerates when she writes, "By early 1933 . . . about the only things keeping Key West afloat were the Hemingways' remodeling jobs [at 907 Whitehead Street], Ernest's bar tabs and fishing jaunts, and the yachtsetters who showed up hunting for fish or a piece of the growing Hemingway legend" (153).

28:9–10 clearance . . . the broker: Harry has already paid the equivalent of an exit tax to leave the harbor, adding to the amount Johnson has cheated him out of.

NOTES

1. For a discussion of this perception of Hemingway as regards "The Killers," see Chatman 168–69 and Lanser 269.

2. See Staten, who tells the story of the secretary general of the Confederación Nacional Obrera Cubana, who, a year after CNOC was founded in 1925 as Cuba's first national labor union, was thrown to the sharks by the *porra* (58).

3. For an analysis of the vaudevillian roots of wisecracking in "The Killers," see Berman 65–81.

4. Since Baker's biography, Berge Saunders's name has been spelled "Burge." According to Chamberlain, the man himself spelled it "Berge." See *Hemingway Log* 97n214.

CHAPTER TWO

This short chapter begins and ends at the Pearl of San Francisco Café, with a brief episode in between at the nearby boat docks. To help Harry make enough money to cover the losses from Mr. Johnson's unpaid bill—or enough just to make it home to Key West—Frankie introduces the down-on-his-luck captain to Mr. Sing, an affected Chinese smuggler with a taste for silk shirts and $100 Panama hats. The two negotiate an agreement for Harry to load twelve immigrants onto his boat for $1,200. Mr. Sing ominously implies he does not care whether the cargo makes it to Key West; he tells Harry to "embark" them for the Dry Tortugas, but when Harry points out lighthouse keepers could easily alert the Coast Guard to their whereabouts, the smuggler gives the captain the authority to "land" the illegals wherever he would like—meaning Mr. Sing invites Harry to dump them at sea. Mr. Sing makes all his money off the front end of the deal, after all. As Harry consents, readers begin to question his moral character, and the tension mounts as we wonder whether a Hemingway hero is capable of cold-bloodedly killing a dozen strangers.

As Harry prepares his boat for the trip, the "rummy" mate Eddy Marshall returns to the docks after a long debauch. Eddy expects a ride back to Key West, but Harry refuses, concerned that the drunkard could never keep his dealings with Mr. Sing secret. Harry eventually pays Eddy $5 from his advance for the smuggling operation to go away. Back at the Pearl, preparing his paperwork to leave Cuba, he is given an ominous photograph of a young Afro-Cuban with his throat cut. The threatening message is from the ABC, letting Harry Morgan know they suspect that he set up Pancho and his fellow revolutionaries for the preceding day's *porra* ambush.

30:4 **gallegos:** Technically, a Gallego refers to a native of Galicia in northern Spain. Thus, Hemingway's use of the term throughout *For Whom the Bell Tolls:* "These [rebels] at this post are Gallegos. I know that from hearing them talk this afternoon. They cannot desert because if they do their families will be shot. Gallegos are either very intelligent or very dumb and brutal" (211). As Miriam B. Mandel notes, "Galicians have migrated to the New World in such large numbers that in Latin America people of Spanish descent are sometimes called *gallegos* even if they or their ancestors came from a different section of Spain" (174). In this regard, it is tempting to suggest

Hemingway is simply referring to Cubans of Spanish descent lounging at the Pearl. However, a *gallego* in Cuba at this time was also a stock character of burlesque, a "caricature of a Spaniard, with a beret and a red sash around his prominent belly" (Estrada, *Welcome to Havana* 207), usually paired with a comedian in blackface. This common usage suggests Hemingway also stereotypes the Pearl's clientele as layabouts. While in Cuba in 1934, Hemingway employed a taxi driver nicknamed "the Gallego" (Samuelson 98–99). Among the clippings held at the John F. Kennedy Library is a 1933 article from the *Diario de la Marina* that features pictures of Hemingway with his "choferservicial," identified as Ignacio "El Gallego."

30:7 **Hatuey beer:** The main rival to Tropical Beer, Hatuey was introduced in the Cuban market in the late 1920s as a Bacardi brand marketed to American tourists. Bacardi, of course, dominated the rum market. The name Hatuey commemorates a sixteenth-century Indian chief who fought the Spanish, thereby earning distinction as the first Cuban national hero. He was burned at the stake on 2 February 1512. In "Marlin Off the Morro: A Cuban Letter," Hemingway names Hatuey "the best beer" to stock on a fishing trip (*BL* 138).

30:13–14 **Yellow stuff:** As much as the novel's freewheeling use of *nigger,* this dehumanizing reference to people of East Asian descent often shocks contemporary readers. The racism is best understood in the context of "yellow peril" rhetoric that proliferated from the late 1890s through World War II, peaking in the 1930s. The first great wave of Asian immigration began in the 1850s, driven partly by the Taiping Rebellion of 1850–64 in South China, in which a massive peasant uprising across seventeen separate provinces briefly challenged imperial rule. The Gold Rush was the other major lure for Chinese people to immigrate to the United States. The majority of the forty-one thousand immigrants who came to America in this period gathered in San Francisco, working either in mining or railroad construction. The presence of such a large influx created the "coolie" stereotype of the late nineteenth century, which proliferated largely as a means of justifying the confinement of East Asians to unskilled labor. The rhetoric of "yellow peril" intensified this racist response to immigrants by depicting them as an ethnic pollutant that imperiled the purity of Western culture with supposedly deviant inclinations, from anti-democratic imperial ambitions to opium smoking to the sexual defilement of white women. While the xenophobia first focused on the Chinese, it intensified against the Japanese after that nation's victory over the Russians in the Russo-Japanese War (1904–05). Filipinos, Samoans, and Hawaiians were likewise subject to yellow-peril racism.

Newspapers played a major role in stirring this anti-Asian hysteria, with those owned by William Randolph Hearst noted in particular for disseminating propaganda. Some critics go so far as to link the "yellow peril" to the tawdry "yellow journalism" tag associated with Hearst via the cartoon character the Yellow Kid, whose "vaguely Asian features . . . lampooned the yellow peril hysteria" (Milton 41). Most historians, however, attribute the phrase *yellow journalism* to the cheap yellow paper upon which Hearst's sensational newspapers were printed. Whatever the connection, other observers viewed the yellow peril as nothing more than a media panic propagated by yellow journalists, as witnessed by John Otway Percy Bland in 1912: "It is a poor bogey at best, this Yellow Peril, bred by ignorance out of a bad national conscience . . . yet a phantom that has served, and should serve again, many a politician's turn. The modern world fears, even while it seeks, these grisly phantoms that make its flesh creep, and in the Yellow Peril the fervent imagination of yellow journalists has found a perennial source of thrills and shudders" (407). Despite such attempts at debunking the "peril," the "bogey" of anti-Asian sentiment was hugely influential in shaping immigration policy. The 1882 Chinese Exclusion Act banned the immigration of Chinese laborers, allowing only educated professionals, including teachers and merchants. A decade later, the Geary Act required each naturalized immigrant to carry a resident permit. The culmination of Sinophobia was the 1924 National Origins Act, which outlawed Chinese immigration in toto. The law remained on the books for forty years. As for Japan, an informal 1907 agreement with the recent victors of the Russo-Japanese War prevented American legislation against immigration from that East Asian empire only when Japan agreed not to issue its citizens passports for travel to the United States. In return, the United States informally agreed to stop discriminatory practices against people of Japanese descent already living within its borders, particularly in California. The National Origins Act voided that agreement as well.

Not surprisingly, the "phantom" of the Asian Other seeped into the era's popular culture, often in ways not manifestly obvious. Admirers of Charlotte Perkins Gilman's feminist classic "The Yellow Wallpaper" (1892) are often disheartened to discover that the author's other works—whether her science-fiction novel, *Herland* (1915), her nonfiction, or her public speeches—are overtly xenophobic, promoting racist eugenics and depicting immigrants as diluting the Aryan essence of the American character. As critics have struggled to accept, Gilman's anti-Asian sentiments taint the meaning of her most famous story's dominant color, suggesting references to the "yellow smell" indeed invoke nativist fears to make readers' flesh creep (Doran 73–80). Other period texts hardly require a connotative reading to recognize the stereotypes invoked. By the 1920s, Yellow Peril imagery pervaded pulp fiction. Science fiction explored anxieties over Asian world domination with titles such as M. P. Shiel's *The Yellow Danger* (1898), H. P. Lovecraft's *The Horror at Red Hook* (1927), Arthur Banks's *The Invading Horde* (1927), and Philip Francis Nowlin's *Armageddon 2419* (1929), which introduced the time-traveling hero Buck Rogers. In crime fiction, Asians are often gang lords, drug peddlers, or, like

Hemingway's villain, human traffickers (see 30:15). At least two of Dashiell Hammett's oft-reprinted Continental Op stories employ these stereotypes: "The House on Turk Street" (1924) and "Dead Yellow Women" (1925).

No pulp writer exploited Yellow Peril anxiety more famously than Arthur Henry Sarsfield Ward (1883–1959). Under the penname Sax Rohmer, he created the Chinese master criminal Dr. Fu Manchu in 1912, producing three novels up through 1917 and then, after a break, an additional ten from 1931 to 1958. Invariably, the installments center upon Rising Tide plots for world domination foiled or at least stalled by the series' British crime-stoppers, the very Holmes-and-Watson–esque Denis Nayland Smith and Dr. Petrie. In the kickoff to the series, *The Insidious Fu Manchu* (known in the United Kingdom as *The Mystery of Fu Manchu*), the archvillain is explicitly described as "the yellow peril incarnate in one man" (26), the "advance-guard of a cogent yellow peril" (312), and "the genius of the yellow peril" (335). In his later years, Rohmer would defend himself against charges of racism, insisting that the Chinatown neighborhood within Limehouse, a district in London's East End where his novels were set, was populated at the turn of the century with Chinese who "knew no way of making a living other than by the criminal activities which had made China too hot for them. They brought their crimes with them" (qtd. in Van Ash and Rohmer 72). Despite Rohmer's insistence that he based his novels on this significant Chinese underworld, the earliest Fu Manchu books are hardly discreet in linking the evil doctor's criminal organization, the Si-Fan, to Yellow Peril hysteria over the supposed Asiatic takeover of the Western world. In the series' third entry, *The Hand of Fu Manchu,* Naylan Smith describes the intent of the cabal:

> "For Heaven's sake!" [Dr. Petrie] cried, "what is the Si-Fan?"
>
> "The greatest mystery of the mysterious East, Petrie. Think. You know, as I know, that a malignant being, Dr. Fu-Manchu, was for some time in England, engaged in 'paving the way' (I believe those words were my own) for nothing less than a giant Yellow Empire. That dream is what millions of Europeans and Americans term 'the Yellow Peril'! Very good. Such an empire needs must have—"
>
> "An emperor!" (17)

Fu Manchu became the prototype for an array of "Oriental" overlord villains, from Ming the Merciless in the Flash Gordon pulps to the Blue Scorpion, archenemy of Peter the Brazen, the brainchild of Loring Brent (i.e., George F. Wort). The Fu Manchu novels were not Rohmer's only attempt at cashing in on the Peril. His most famous non–Si-Fan thriller is *The Yellow Claw* (1915), whose Mr. King resembles *To Have and Have Not*'s Mr. Sing even more than Fu Manchu.

To Have and Have Not includes several racial stereotypes common to Yellow Peril rhetoric. In addition to using *Chink* twenty-seven times, Hemingway will refer derisively to the smell of Chinese people (55:2), call them "rat-eating aliens" (57:25), and allow Harry to worry without irony whether a bite from a Chinese man is poisonous (60:4–5).

30:15 **Mr. Sing:** The Yellow Peril overlord embodied by Rohmer's Fu Manchu and Mr. King was by no means the only Chinese villain to populate pulp fiction. The human trafficker/slave dealer was an equally common stock character, appearing even before Rohmer's early novels. One formative version is Hop Lee, the nemesis of detective Old King Brady, who, with his son, Young King Brady, starred in eighty-five adventures in the American magazine *Secret Service*. In "Hop Lee, the Chinese Slave Dealer" (1899), the Bradys crack a white-slavery ring in San Francisco's Chinatown. Early films such as D. W. Griffith's *The Fatal Hour* (1908) likewise exploited fears of miscegenation and rape by Chinese kidnappers.

30:19–22 **he talked like an Englishman and he was dressed in a white suit with a silk shirt and black tie and one of those hundred-and-twenty-five-dollar Panama hats:** In a discussion of Hammett's "The House on Turk Street," William F. Wu notes apropos of that story's villain, "a Chinese ringleader named Tai," that a Chinese character who speaks with "a cultured British accent" in Yellow Peril fiction "usually suggests a wealthy background in Hong Kong or Singapore." For Wu, the accent would "probably make [Tai's] ancestry Cantonese, which is further suggested by his description as . . . 'immaculately clothed in garments that were as British as his accent'" (185). Like Hammett, Hemingway supplies very little background about Mr. Sing, so it is impossible to make a similar leap about his ancestry. Nevertheless, it is fascinating to read the character against the backdrop of smuggling history to speculate about his backstory. According to Robert Chao Romero, between the early 1880s and 1917, when the United States entered the Great War, a fraternal organization of Chinese immigrants known as the Chinese Six Companies managed the smuggling of illegal immigrants through Mexico and Cuba into California and Florida. Although headquartered in San Francisco, the operation was managed in Havana through the Six Companies' "eastern chief," Chin Pinoy, who also worked as the Chinese agent for the Southern Pacific Railroad Company, the Morgan steamship line, and the Ward steamship line, which traveled from Tampico, Mexico, to New York (33–34). The Great War halted the Six Companies' smuggling endeavors, creating opportunities for local entrepreneurs. According to Elliot Young, the Havana chapter of the Chinese National League dominated smuggling operations in the 1920s, headed by its president, Lou Sat Yun, a Chinese immigrant who worked by the cultural borders of Cuban and Chinese communities after marrying a Cuban woman (261). Another prominent smuggler in the period was John Williams, who, although Jamaican, was according to legend, born in China (261).

Mr. Sing's English accent and flashy attire are both common components of the Chinese villain stereotype. While the similarities between Mr. Sing and Tai are notable, it is unlikely Hemingway ever read "The House on Turk Street," which was not collected in book form until 1966.

31:6–7 Hundred horse Kermath: Kermath Manufacturing of Detroit produced marine engines from the 1920s to the 1950s, their product line ranging from $400 to $550. Hemingway likely borrowed this boat detail from Joe "Josie" Russell's *Anita*, which, according to brother Leicester Hemingway (1915–1983), was propelled by a similar make and model: "With a reliable, medium-speed Kermath of a hundred horsepower, the *Anita* never did more than eight knots an hour, with her stern pulling low. But she trolled nicely" (118).

31:26 You don't speak Spanish? When Mr. Sing tells Harry to order Frankie to step away from the table so the two of them can speak in confidence, Harry directs his middleman to the bar with a thumb jerk instead of verbally addressing him in Spanish. Harry then asks Mr. Sing if he speaks Spanish, presumably wondering why the smuggler couldn't tell Frankie to get lost himself. Mr. Sing admits he is indeed fluent; in doing so, he effectively admits his command was a test to see if Harry would conspire against him with Frankie in Spanish. Hemingway lets this moment pass by without comment, embedding the suspense instead of overtly rendering it.

32:17–22 the Tortugas, Loggerhead Key: The Dry Tortugas are a cluster of small islands that lie roughly seventy miles west (and slightly north) of Key West. In Hemingway's time, eight islets existed. Today there are only seven, while three others disappeared as early as the 1870s. Because several of these coral landmasses rise only three or four feet above sea level, they are extremely vulnerable to shifting currents and erosion from hurricanes. The central islet is Garden Key, which houses the unfinished Civil War–era Fort Jefferson, today best remembered as the prison where Dr. Samuel Mudd (1833–1883) served his sentence for abetting John Wilkes Booth after Abraham Lincoln's assassination. Garden Key was the site of the Tortugas' first lighthouse, built in the mid-1820s. Due to the number of shipwrecks in the vicinity of the islets, another lighthouse was built in 1858 on nearby Loggerhead Key, roughly three miles west of Fort Jefferson. The Tortugas were originally named in 1513 by explorer Ponce de Leon, whose men feasted on the abundant sea turtles gathered among the islands. Sailors later added the "dry" appellation due to the lack of fresh water.

Hemingway knew the Tortugas well. In March 1930 he and several friends (Henry "Mike" Strater, Maxwell Perkins, John Herrmann, and Captain Edward "Bra" Saunders) were stranded on Garden Key for more than two weeks due to bad weather. The following year Hemingway made a subsequent trip with Herrmann, and they were stranded for five days. It was during the 1931 adventure that Hemingway first encountered Gregorio Fuentes (1897–2001), future first mate of the *Pilar* (Baker, *A Life* 220).

34:12 Bacuranao: Also known as Playa Bacuranao, this cove sits roughly fifteen miles east of Havana in a spot where the Rio Bacuranao enters the ocean; Hemingway gives a detailed description of it at 49:1–13. Here Harry notes that it was once a dock for loading sand and that a hurricane leveled the small town that once stood there, "except one house that some Gallegos built out of the shacks the hurricane blew down," used as a clubhouse "when they come out to swim and picnic" on Sundays.

35:18–19 Another one ship them before him. Somebody kill him: For some readers, Frankie's comment may imply that Mr. Sing killed his predecessor in the smuggling business. For others it may simply be an acknowledgment of the cutthroat violence of human piracy, a form of trafficking in which the life expectancy of even the crime lords is short. Either way, Harry's reply ("Somebody will kill Mr. Sing, too") foreshadows exactly what will happen on the fisherman's boat (see 53:27–54:3).

36:1 Hundred thousand Chinamen here. Only three Chinese women: Frankie's statistics are surely an exaggeration, but the Cuban government was nevertheless more inclined to enforce immigration strictures against Chinese women than men. The policy was long running. An 1861 census reports that out of 34,834 Chinese in Cuba, a mere 57 were women. Ten years later, the Chinese population expanded to 40,261, while the number of women rose only by 9—yes, 9—to 66 (De La Torre 229). In 1931, overall numbers fell to 24,445 Chinese, with 202 women—a far higher number, obviously, but hardly gender proportional.

36:8 Good business: Frankie's claim that smuggling Chinese into the United States from Cuba is a big industry raises the question of how common a practice it was. Mary Cruz says that in the 1930s operations such as Mr. Sing's were "as common as rum-running" ("Selection" 92), but that seems a hyperbolic claim. At the other extreme, in his *Grits and Grunts: Folkloric Key West* (2008) folklorist Stetson Kennedy includes a testimonial from a pseudonymous rumrunner called "Lalo Lopez" who claims the smuggling of Chinese from Havana was "bunk," at least in Key West: "There were some [Chinese] smuggled in from Havana, but they were landed up in the Keys—never at Key West. Most of the people smuggled in were Cubans, Spanish, Slovaks, and such stuff." At the same time "Lopez" admits he had heard stories of "guys . . . in Cuba collecting [immigrants'] pay in advance, and then landing them on the other side of Cuba!" (79–80), not unlike what Harry does to his cargo. Suffice it to say that statistics on immigrant smuggling are fleeting and most evidence is anecdotal. See, for example, Dorothy Stanhope's 30 November 1902 *New York Times* article, "Havana Boatmen Smuggle Chinese; Carry Them Across the Gulf to the Florida Coast," which tells an interesting story but offers little in the way of context (28).

36:22–23 **the broker . . . clear us:** Americans traveling in and out of Havana's ports had to declare both manifest and crew through the marina customs agent ("the broker").

37:3 **Standard Oil docks . . . twenty-eight cents a gallon:** The price is equivalent to $5.11 in 2016 dollars. The station was located at what were known as the Casablanca docks, directly across the Bay of Havana from the San Francisco Wharf.

37:13 **Hello, Harry:** This is the first time Harry's name is mentioned in the story. The delayed appearance raises questions about the varied points at which readers recognize that the narrator of part 1 is a man named "Harry Morgan." Some may bring external knowledge to the book (say, from a review, a scholarly analysis, or a biography of Hemingway), while others may pick it up from paratextual indicators such as the jacket copy or the eponymous section titles. Still others may have no idea that "I" is Harry until this point, thirty pages into the plot.

Cruz suggests that Hemingway may have chosen Harry's name "thinking of the homophone *hairy,* suggested by the Spanish expression *hombre de pelo en pecho* (hairy-chested man) applied to bold, daring, virile men" ("Selection" 90). As with much of the interpretation she offers in *Hemingway on the Great Blue River,* this reading seems forced. Philip Young speaks for most critics when he says the name references "Henry Morgan the pirate, who once ravaged the coasts off which Harry works, who like Harry was really hard, but brave and resourceful, too" (90). The most developed comparison between Harry and Sir Henry Morgan (circa 1635–1688) is Susan F. Beegel's essay, "Harry and the Pirates: The Romance and Reality of Piracy in Hemingway's *To Have and Have Not.*" As Beegel writes:

> Purportedly a gentlemen's son from Wales, the historic Henry Morgan made his way to the New World to join an expeditionary force against the Spanish in Hispaniola. Eventually basing himself in Port Royal, Jamaica, after England seized the island from Spain in 1655, Morgan created a small fleet manned by soldiers and sailors, deserters and runaway slaves, cutthroats and criminals. . . . His career depended on England's mood with respect to Spain—at one point he was arrested and carried to London for trial as a pirate; later he was released, knighted, and made lieutenant-governor of Jamaica. There he died of the combined effects of tropical fevers, dropsy, and alcoholism in 1688, leaving behind thousands of acres of sugar plantations, and his [wife] of twenty years, Dame Mary Elizabeth Morgan. . . . Sir Henry Morgan is arguably the most famous pirate in English history, and one aspect or another of his legend echoes in virtually every pirate

story penned, filmed, or painted since his time, including *To Have and Have Not*. When Hemingway chose to name his protagonist Harry Morgan, the allusion to the pirate tradition was less than subtle. (111–12)

37:27–28 **get plugged:** This interesting expression reappears in the novel at the beginning of chapter 13, at 118:16–17 as well. It clearly means "to get angry," or perhaps, more indelicately, "to get pissed." It seems to combine two slang meanings of *to plug*: the recent hardboiled expression for being shot ("getting plugged") and the sexual innuendo of penetration ("getting screwed").

38:18 **You know how you feel when you hit a drunk:** This second-person interpolation, which has no real plot purpose, harkens back to the opening sentence, reminding us again of Hemingway's habit of integrating the reader into the text.

39:15–19 **a close-up picture . . . lenguas largas:** This paragraph evokes the photograph James R. Mellow describes as one of the atrocity photos that Walker Evans collected while in Havana (see 4:24). Although Mellow cites *To Have and Have Not*, he does not, oddly enough, quote this passage, which seems fairly persuasive proof that Hemingway did indeed see the actual photo.

39:22 **gone with the con:** Slang for tuberculosis, as in "gone with the consumption." Through Frankie, the boy lets Harry know that the ABC believes he is responsible for the *porra* raid: "They think you told the police you were meeting those boys here that morning" (40:3–4).

CHAPTER THREE

Even shorter than its predecessor, this chapter intensifies the suspense by exploiting readers' growing anxiety regarding Harry Morgan's amorality. Already we have seen the captain passively consent to Mr. Sing's permission to dump the Chinese illegals at sea after stealing their money; now we wonder if the captain is willing to kill one of his own. Harry no sooner sets to sea to meet the smuggler than he discovers Eddy Marshall has stowed onto the boat. "Brother, you're in plenty of trouble," an exasperated Harry tells his mate. Going down below, the captain retrieves his pump-gun and a .30-30 Winchester; along with a .38 Special from his days as a Miami policeman, he is fully armed for whatever may happen. Despite his weaponry, he decides not to kill Eddy quite yet; he may need the kind of help that not even bullets can lend when his cargo loads.

41:15–16 **the National Hotel . . . the Capitol:** At the time "One Trip Across" was written, the Hotel Nacional de Cuba was barely three years old but already a favorite haunt of American movie stars, writers, and politicos—it was where Sumner Welles stayed as he negotiated the end of the Machado regime. Located in Havana's Vedado district, it is a prominent landmark along the coast because it sits on a bluff along the city's oceanfront esplanade, El Malecón. The Capitol, whose dome Harry sees, sits further inland along the Passeo de Prado. The building was also a new construction in this time period, having been completed in 1929 as part of Machado's ambitious national construction program. El Capitolio was modeled on the U.S. Capitol, designed to top its American counterpart in height by exactly one foot.

42:1–2 **Cojimar:** Located six miles east of Havana, Cojimar is a small fishing village, most famous today as the site from which Santiago in *The Old Man and the Sea* sets out on his adventure. Hemingway often docked the *Pilar* here during his Finca Vigía years. For decades after his death, literary tourists flocked to Cojimar to snap a picture of the boat's Cuban mate, Gregorio Fuentes, whom, according to legend, Hemingway first met when his "mob" was stranded on the Dry Tortugas (Chamberlin 107). Fuentes lived in the village until his death at 104 in January 2002.

42:5 **the lights of Baracoa:** The two references to Baracoa in Harry's trip (the other occurs in chapter 4 at 47:5) are problematic, since there are two sites in Cuba with this name. Hemingway undoubtedly refers to Playa Baracoa, located some thirty kilometers, or eighteen miles, west of Havana. A reference to this beach area appears in "Marlin Off the Morro: A Cuban Letter," his debut *Esquire* article, in a list of Havana fish markets with significant marlin catches during the 1933 season, including Jaruco, Cojimar, Jaimanitas, and Mariel (*BL* 139). The other Baracoa, meanwhile, is located all the way on the eastern edge of the island in the Guantánamo Province, home since 1903 to the United States' Guantanamo Naval Base and since January 2002 to the infamous Guantanamo Bay detention camp where anti-American insurgents deemed a significant terrorist threat are incarcerated. The first capital of Cuba, Baracoa sits more than nine hundred kilometers (six hundred miles) from Havana, clearly too great of a distance for Harry to see its lights while drifting toward Cojimar.

Hemingway's references to Playa Baracoa pose their own geographical problems, however. As Harry tells us, he first heads due north toward Key West (41:9) before he decides to drift to Bacuranao, some twelve miles east of Havana. Since Playa Baracoa is south of Havana's latitude on a descending crescent of the Cuban coast, it is doubtful Harry could see its lights past those of the Morro at the mouth of the Havana Bay.

42:24 **Do you know what he'd done?** Another interpolated address to the reader that recalls the novel's opening sentence by reminding us of the storytelling frame and integrating us in the action. Hemingway's use of these markers of address is curious, to say the least, considering we never have a sense of why, when, or to whom Harry Morgan is narrating this story. That is, we have no notion that at some point subsequent to the plot with Mr. Sing he told anyone about this Cuban adventure.

43:7 **Us Conchs:** Eddy's comment is the most specific suggestion in the novel that Harry Morgan is a native Key Wester, despite the forthcoming information that he was once a Miami cop. See 44:14–17.

43:10 **you're hot:** Harry tells Eddy he is drunk. The Oxford English Dictionary traces the usage to Shakespeare's *The Tempest* (1616), although it is merely implied when in Act IV Ariel describes Caliban and his henchmen to Prospero as "red-hot with drinking" (75). A more relevant usage appears in Jonathan Swift's *The Journal to Stella*, a compilation of sixty-five letters written to the author's confidante (and perhaps wife) Esther Johnson: "[I] am glad I am in bed; for else I should sit up till two, and drink till I was hot" (*Works* III.213). The phrase dates to a 1711 letter, although Swift's *Journal* itself wasn't posthumously published until 1766.

44:2–3 **the pump gun, the Winchester .30–30:** Harry's pump gun is likely based on the 12-gauge Winchester Hemingway purchased in 1928 and with which he hunted for upward of thirty years. It is by no means the most notorious firearm in either his fiction or his life. The honor for the former would have to go to the 6.5mm Mannlicher with which Margaret Macomber dispatches her husband, intentionally or not, in "The Short Happy Life of Francis Macomber" (*CSS* 28). In life Hemingway's most famous shotgun is, tragically, the weapon that ended his life on 2 July 1961. For many years, that weapon was thought to be a Boss shotgun; recently, that assumption has been challenged and an alternative—a Scott & Son Monte Carlo B—suggested (Calabi, Helsley, and Sanger 151–52). Although associated more with hunting than death in Hemingway's writing, his Model 12 pump shotgun appears in an array of works, including *True at First Light* and its fuller version, *Under Kilimanjaro* (*TAFL* 240, *UK* 391). Pump shotguns are also mainstays of crime fiction, both print and film, largely because of the uniquely physical action created by pulling the sliding foregrip to eject its spent shells (the "pumping").

The Winchester .30-30 is an unusual weapon in Hemingway's fiction; it is the rare example of a rifle that is not based on his personal armory. In *Hemingway's Guns: The Sporting Arms of Ernest Hemingway,* Silvio Calabi, Steve Helsley, and Roger Sanger cite a 1930 letter to Milford Baker in which the author confesses that it and a .22 caliber Marlin are the only two rifles he had then fired. As the three writers go on to note, "The Winchester is never mentioned again," overlooking its appearance in *To Have and Have Not.* "At the time [the Winchester .30-30] was an extremely popular deer rifle and may have been borrowed from a friend or his father. It would have been a lever-action, similar to the Marlin that Hemingway mentioned" (122).

44:14–17 the Smith and Wesson thirty-eight special I had when I was on the police force up in Miami: Harry's reference to Miami is the first significant detail we have about his background. Later, we will learn from dialogue between Harry and Marie that they used to travel to Miami to stay in hotels (114:11–12), but otherwise nothing more about his career in the city is revealed.

CHAPTER FOUR

The climactic chapter of part 1 finds the captain and his unwanted mate rendezvousing with Mr. Sing at the Bacuranao cove east of Havana. Drifting a mile from shore as they wait for the meeting, Harry tries to keep Eddy from getting too drunk to be useful by badgering the rummy about his lack of cojones. The bullying does little good, and Harry worries about Eddy turning trigger-happy as he grills his captain on how to work the boat's weapons. The pair makes contact with the smuggler, who carries the illegals, six at a time, in a small boat with a single oar. On the second trip, with all twelve Chinese people stowed in the charter's forward cabin, Harry jerks Mr. Sing out of his boat, ordering Eddy to speed away. With the smuggler flopping on the stern rollers, Harry first breaks Mr. Sing's arm and then crushes his "talk-box" (54:1). When Eddy asks why they had to kill the man, Harry says, "To keep from killing twelve other Chinks." After sinking the dead body, the pair carry the illegals to the next beach and order them to wade to shore. The chapter ends with Eddy taking a nap while Harry cleans the lone bite in his own shoulder Mr. Sing managed to administer before his neck was snapped.

46:5 **Rincōn and Baracoa:** El Rincon is a village east of Havana, most famous for its annual 17 December pilgrimage to Santuario de San Lazaro, or the Sanctuary of St. Lazarus, patron of the sick. More than a decade and a half after writing "One Trip Across," Hemingway suffered in Rincōn one of the peculiar injuries to which he was prone throughout his life. As the *Pilar* came into the channel to anchor, Gregorio Fuentes swung the boat as Hemingway climbed the ladder to the flying bridge, throwing Hemingway headfirst into the gaffes and opening a wound that took three stitches to close (Reynolds, *Final Years* 227).

As previously noted, the reference to Baracoa (see entry for 42:5) makes little sense here, since it is located on a latitude southwest of Havana. The directions can throw off readers as well. Hemingway's reference to passing Bacuranao *before* reaching Cojimar would suggest that he reversed these two landing points in his mind, since the latter is west of the former, meaning Harry Morgan would pass it on his way to Bacuranao. This seems highly unlikely, however. A better explanation is that Harry has turned his boat around since we last heard of his route, in chapter 3. During the course of the afternoon and into evening he has drifted east past Bacuranao and has now turned to head west, running his engine against the eastward flow of the current before cutting off the motor and drifting inland near Cojimar. He seems then to turn around once more and navigate back to Bacuranao for his meeting with Mr. Sing.

47:2–3 *cojones:* Perhaps the most loaded word in the novel. Used a half-dozen times, the Spanish term for testicles appears in *To Have and Have Not* on more occasions than in any other Hemingway text save *Death in the Afternoon,* the first work in English to use it (Morton 123), and *For Whom the Bell Tolls*—two works set in Spain, not coincidentally. Several additional indirect references to testicles make *To Have and Have Not* seem even more preoccupied with genital fortitude than Hemingway's bullfighting treatise or his Spanish Civil War novel. As Bernard DeVoto wryly commented, the novel is downright "gonadotropic," although another reviewer, Cyril Connelly, offered a "polite translation" of *cojones* for unsuspecting readers as "guts" (qtd. in Meyers, *Critical Heritage* 224, 226). Hemingway fans may even agree with Douglas Grant, who writes of *To Have and Have Not,* "Los cojones . . . the reader comes to feel that if Hemingway uses the word again he will throw it back in his teeth. And he will not have long to wait . . . *Los cojones!*" (175).

Original reviewers may have considered this testicular preoccupation an unfortunate symptom of Hemingway's tiresome machismo, in part due to poor timing. Only two months before *To Have and Have Not* was published, Hemingway was involved in a physical altercation with critic Max Eastman in the office of their mutual Scribner's editor, Maxwell Perkins. The tussle was highly publicized in the newspapers, with Hemingway bragging to the *New York Times* that he had slapped Eastman's face for negative comments made about *Death in the Afternoon* almost five years earlier. Hemingway was in particular irked by Eastman's suggestion that he lacked "the serene confidence that he is a full-sized man" and that he had created "a literary style . . . of wearing false hair on the chest" (qtd. in Meyers, *Critical Heritage* 176). As bystander Maxwell Perkins related the story to F. Scott Fitzgerald, "Ernest ripped open his shirt and exposed a chest which was certainly hairy enough for anybody" before "reach[ing] over and open[ing] Max's shirt, revealing a chest which was as bare as a bald man's head" (*Dear Scott/Dear Max* 239). Hemingway then swatted Eastman in the nose with a copy of his own book, recently published *Art and the Life of Action, with Other Essays.* Amid conflicting reports of who beat whom in the scuffle, Hemingway assured the journalist interviewing him at the scene of the battle that Eastman had "jumped at me like a woman—clawing, you know, with his open hands" (qtd. in Hemingway, *Conversations* 15) Hemingway did not seem concerned that the journalist's account would lightly mock him for his braggadocio.[1]

As cartoonish as Hemingway's fixation with masculinity can seem, it belies a fascinating psychological preoccupation. Sympathetic scholars trace his castration anxiety across the course of his career to ask what the source of the fixation with testicular vigor was. For many years, critics attributed it to his 8 July 1918 wounding at Fossalta di Piave, where according to a self-generated legend, Hemingway took more than 220 shrapnel wounds, including many to the groin. The number was correct, just not the placement. As James Nagel later reported, the uniform Hemingway wore at the time shows no visible tears above the knee (213). Moreover, throughout Hemingway's life, whenever the writer recounted his near-death experience on the Italian front, he tended to exaggerate the threat to the scrotal region. Thus his bizarre 1950 claim to F. Scott Fitzgerald's biographer, Arthur Mizener, that he had been "shot twice through the scrotum" (*SL* 694).

While many of Hemingway's characters are haunted by a fear of genital mutilation, at least one actually suffers from it. Jake Barnes in *The Sun Also Rises* has lost his penis to a freak aviation accident on the Italian front and cannot consummate his love for Brett Ashley. Although his testicles remain intact, he suffers from such a grievous injury that the liaison for the Italian Army jokingly told him in the hospital that he had "given more than [his] life" (25). The theme of emasculation is reiterated throughout the novel as well by references to steers at the San Fermin festival. In manuscript, Hemingway even had a character noting, "The bulls have no balls," which Scribner's forced him to change to "the bulls have no horns" (113). (The original reference was restored in the 1950s.) *A Farewell to Arms* likewise spotlights Hemingway's odd fascination with genital wounds. Frederic Henry taunts one of his dowdier nurses, Miss Van Campen, asking if she ever met a soldier "who had tried to disable himself by kicking himself in the scrotum. Because that is the nearest sensation to jaundice and it is a sensation that I believe few women have ever experienced" (144).

Beginning with *Death in the Afternoon*, Hemingway discovered in Hispanic culture a tradition of testicular veneration in which the cojones represent masculine courage (Comley and Scholes 109–10). As a late addition to *Death*, Hemingway added a definition in his glossary: "a valorous bullfighter is said to be plentifully equipped with [cojones]. In a cowardly bullfighter they are said to be absent. Those of the bull are called *criadillas* and prepared in any of the ways sweetbreads are usually cooked when they are a great delicacy. During the killing of the fifth bull the criadillas of the first bull were sometimes served in the royal box. [Bullfighter] Primo de Rivera was so fond of interlarding his discourse with references to manly virtues that he was said to have eaten so many criadillas that they had gone to his brain" (365). As more than one critic has suggested, such possibly ironic passages reveal Hemingway's potential awareness of his own obsession.

Many critics resort to loaded sexual metaphors to debunk the pretensions to virility conveyed by Hemingway's excessive investment in the genitals: "In the work of Hemingway death is less a threat to a man's existence than to his *cojones*," complains Stanley Cooperman in a 1962 analysis that contrasts Frederic Henry's response to his wounding on the Great War's Italian front to the matadors of *Death in the Afternoon*. "For this reason he can speak of 'dying well' or 'dying badly,' while admitting that soldiers, as contrasted to bullfighters and fishermen, 'never do die well' *since they are tossed on their backs to receive rather than give* the final blow" (92; emphasis added). For Cooperman, this image of men rendered effeminate because they are "on their backs," in the traditionally female position of sexual penetration, marks Hemingway's escapism rather than his bravery. Unlike existentialists such as Jean-Paul Sartre, who defined proactively what it meant to "live well" despite knowing one must confront the "obscenity" of death, Hemingway could never transcend his "emasculatory horror" and fell back on empty rituals of action.

Obviously, not all critics agree with this argument. Thomas Strychacz offers a poststructuralist reading of *cojones* by exploring the figural as opposed to literal value of the term: "The very quality that makes *cojones* useful as a sign of manhood is precisely its status as metaphor. One could not otherwise distinguish between a heroic and cowardly bullfighter on the basis of equipment that both possess. . . . It is because there is no natural and necessary relationship between the signifier *cojones* and its signified (testicles) that the term can be liberated to mean the valor, gutsiness, and pride befitting a man. Put simply: a man does not draw valor from his testicles, but his testicles draw meaning when associated with his valor" (153–52). Although Strychacz does not discuss *To Have and Have Not,* his approach offers a device for deconstructing the gendered language of the text. When in chapter 17 Harry will tell himself, "All I've got is my *cojones* to peddle" (146:19–20), he effectively complains that the economic deprivation of the Depression is forcing him to resort to the primal behavior of self-preservation to survive instead of employing more figurative senses of valor, such as devotion to ideals of law and order.

49:6 the hurricane: Harry refers to the 20 October 1926 hurricane that struck into Havana with 145-mile-per-hour winds, killing some six hundred Cubans. The tenth of eleven hurricanes that particular season destroyed many outlying villages and caused nearly $100 million in damage ($1 billion in today's money). A good contemporaneous account of the event is Carlton Bailey Hurst's 1932 memoir of life in the American diplomatic service, *The Arms above the Door* (319–29).

49:12 the delegate: This local representative of the government would be in charge of monitoring the harbor for smugglers. Presumably, Mr. Sing has bought him off. Otherwise foreigners like Harry would be expected to notify him of their presence in the area and present their customs paperwork for their boat. In his memoir of the 1934 marlin season, Arnold Samuelson briefly describes Hemingway's dealings with the Cabañas delegate (117).

49:17 sea grape: Coccoloba uvifera is a flowering plant whose fruit turns purple as it ripens, resembling a grape. In an odd metatextual moment, Hemingway seems to refer to this line in *For Whom the Bell Tolls* as Robert Jordan, prompted by the smell of pine boughs and sap in the Spanish forest where he hides, recalls all the pleasant odors that he has enjoyed in life: "Which would you rather smell? . . . Or the wind from the land as you come in toward Cuba in the dark? That was the *odor of the cactus flowers, mimosa and the sea-grape shrubs*" (260).

49:26–27 **running lights:** Small lights on the sides and sometimes masts of boats mounted for visibility; port-side is red, starboard green.

50:20 **sculling:** To scull is to row with an oar. As Hemingway makes clear, Mr. Sing's small boat here only has one oar, and its paddler is not very adept—he cannot scull backward, which forces Harry to put himself in a position of physical vulnerability as he grips the small boat's gunwale to pull it astern of his cruiser.

51:10 **binnacle light:** A binnacle is a case that stands in front of a ship's wheel to hold navigational instruments. With the implementation of dashboards in motorized ships, the binnacle light referred to a lamplike illumination canister mounted directly atop the steering cabinet so the compass could be read at all times. In many models, the compass was built into the device itself. In seafaring fiction, the binnacle light is often a Gothic device, adding an eerie touch of spectral mystery and suspense. One of Hemingway's heroes, Joseph Conrad (1857–1924), includes a useful example in his short story "The Secret Sharer" (1910) when the nameless captain fishes a mysterious naked swimmer out of the sea:

> "What is it?" I asked in a deadened voice, taking the lighted lamp out of the binnacle, and raising it to his face.
> "An ugly business."
> He had rather regular features; a good mouth; light eyes under somewhat heavy, dark eyebrows; a smooth, square forehead; no growth on his cheeks; a small, brown mustache, and a well-shaped, round chin. His expression was concentrated, meditative, under the inspecting light of the lamp I held up to his face; such as a man thinking hard in solitude might wear. My sleeping suit was just right for his size. A well-knit young fellow of twenty-five at most. He caught his lower lip with the edge of white, even teeth.
> "Yes," I said, replacing the lamp in the binnacle.
> The warm, heavy tropical night closed upon his head again. (88)

53:13–54:3 **by the throat with both hands. . . . Don't think you can't hear it crack, either:** Harry's murder of Mr. Sing is arguably the most shocking moment of violence in all of Hemingway. Other novels and stories contain no shortage of death, of course. But while their protagonists' actions may raise questions about concepts such as bravery, patriotism, and guilt, those texts do not involve outright homicide. The only scene with comparable moral implications occurs in *A Farewell to Arms*, when Frederic Henry shoots a disobedient sergeant in the back during the retreat from Caporetto (204), an incident that has sparked much debate about how readers are to interpret the lieutenant's character. Still, that episode is nowhere near as graphic as Mr. Sing's snapped "talk-box," whose drama is amplified by Hemingway's tone of hardboiled flippancy: "I took him by the throat with both hands, and brother, that Mr. Sing would flop just like a fish" (53:27).

In the "Literature" section of Harold E. Stearns's 1938 update of his *Civilization in the United States* (the first edition [1922] was credited with helping spark the decade's expatriate movement), John Chamberlain objects vigorously to a protagonist committing murder in this fashion:

> It is perfectly true that Harry has often been wronged, and since the law of the jungle is "My life or yours" he has some justification for his own willingness to double-cross the double-crossers, cheat the cheaters, and murder the murderers. But when Harry kills the suave Chinaman, Mr. Sing, after taking a thousand or so dollars from him on condition that he will smuggle twelve Chinese from Cuba to the United States mainland, the scene makes Hemingway's hero a repellent person at the start. And when Harry, with the money in his pants, puts the twelve Chinese ashore in Cuba, even the 'honor among thieves' axiom fades away; Harry is no one to keep a bargain with a dirty Chink. It is perfectly obvious to the reader that Harry is a bum, yet Hemingway would have you believe that he is a great symbol of wronged humanity. (40)

Other critics have not been quite so harsh. For Philip Young, the murder scene questions whether Harry is "tough or simply brutal, which is not at all the same thing. Even Eddy, Harry's rummy companion (whom he was going to kill too until chance made it unnecessary) is shaken by that one, and asks the reader's question for him, 'What did you kill him for?' Harry's answer, 'To keep from killing twelve other chinks,' is not completely convincing" (95).

In a more objective reading of the scene, Jopi Nyman connects Hemingway's emphasis on the "talk-box" to the ABC's threats against *lenguas largas* to explore how the novel defines masculinity as the power to control speaking, whether through one's one own (masculine) silence or violence against others' ability to make (feminine) speech: "In the most significant trait of this passage Harry genders the throat of the man he kills as feminine: it is *she* that cracks, not it. Consequently, the passage illustrates the power of the masculine over the feminine, which in this case is dressed up as an act of violence. By destroying the feminine with its Otherness, the masculine can feel safe, and to be able to govern the world" (158). Nyman's reading connects as well with Lisa Tyler's discussion about how the dental plate Albert Tracy's widow will lose in the Key West yacht basin in the penultimate chapter reflects a silencing of feminine speech in the novel (See 252:13–14; Tyler 58).

54:21 **the old coaling dock at Tortugas:** There are actually two abandoned coaling docks on Garden Key; it is unclear which Hemingway refers to. Today, the northern one is closed to the public, but the southern one, next to the dock where tourists first step onto the island, is a popular snorkeling site, thanks to the remains of its metal pilings.

54:22 **snapper line:** Known in the nineteenth century as a "snood," a snapper line, according to the OED, is "one of a number of short lines each carrying a baited hook, attached at regular distances along the main line."

56:7 **grains pole:** A "grains" is simply a long instrument with one or more barbed prongs for spearing or harpooning fish. A grains pole also makes a significant appearance in "After the Storm," when its unnamed narrator attempts to break open a porthole on a sunken boat with the object: "I could just reach [the window] with the grains pole and I tried to break it with that but I couldn't. The glass was too stout. So I sculled back to the boat and got a wrench and lashed it to the end of the *grains pole* and I couldn't break it" (*CSS* 284).

NOTE

1. The original manuscript for *To Have and Have Not* includes a reference to an "incorruptible essayist" that may be a not-so-veiled swat at Eastman, which suggests just how much ire Hemingway maintained for the writer before their tussle in Maxwell Perkins's office (See MS 32, item 212, folder 6, page 91). In the original chapter 23, Hemingway describes a writer in Key West with many similarities to Richard Gordon: as a leftist, this unnamed author stands on a false sense of principle at the same time he reneges on debts owed to friends who lend him money to support his political causes. A reader is tempted to think this invective is aimed again at John Dos Passos until another interesting detail creeps in: the essayist has white hair. Eastman (1883–1969) was distinguished for his snowy mane. Although not as widely remembered in Key West as Hemingway, Eastman was a habitué of the island, although, for understandable reasons, he visited more often *after* his wrestling rival departed the city for Cuba in 1939.

CHAPTER FIVE

"Now it was all simple except for Eddy," begins the denouement. Having watched Harry kill one man, the reader must now wonder whether our antihero is capable of murdering his rummy mate. Hemingway does not let the mystery linger for long. By the end of the second paragraph, Harry decides to let Eddy live, in part because he knows he would regret murdering someone whose only two crimes were being in the wrong place at the wrong time and being a chatty Cathy when "hot." Sparing the rummy proves Harry's smartest move yet. As he discovers, Eddy added his own name to the boat's exit papers before the boat left Havana. Had Harry Morgan killed him and dumped his body, he would have had to come up with an explanation for his missing mate when he passed through American customs in Key West. The novel's first section then ends with a small coda in which Eddy Marshall shows up the next night to Harry's house uninvited, perhaps to ask for money, perhaps to talk about the murder. When Harry's wife, Marie, says she feels sorry for Eddy because he is a drunk, her husband can only deadpan, "He's a lucky rummy."

61:28–29 **crew list:** To prevent illegal immigration, boats entering and exiting Cuba were required to supply lists of all crew and passengers.

62:11 **Sand Key light:** Once known as Dolphin Island, Sand Key is an extremely small reef formation roughly eight miles southwest of Key West that guards the channel to the island. In 1826 a 110-foot lighthouse was built on its sand surface, creating a memorable landmark. Because the sand's shape often shifts due to hurricanes and storms, sometimes disappearing altogether, the lighthouse can seem to float on the ocean's surface. A wounded Harry will see the light at the beginning of part 2, "straight, thin and brown rising out of the sea right where it ought to be" (67:18), reassuring him he and his wounded mate Wesley are on the right path home after the bloody encounter that will cost him his arm.

63:17–18 **the Eastern and the Western Dry Rocks:** Two other reef formations in the waters approaching Key West.

63:19 **La Concha Hotel:** A seven-story luxury hotel located at 430 Duval Street in Key West, visible on the approach into the harbor. The tallest building in Key West, it was built in 1924 and opened two years later. Hemingway occasionally stayed there, but the association has spawned numerous inaccurate tales. As one travel guide erroneously claims, Hemingway "is known to have written many of his novels in one of the suites there. Having drinks on the rooftop bar or meeting his mistress in secret were among his pastimes at La Concha" (Jenkins 1). The author seems to confuse La Concha with the legend of Hemingway and Jane Mason cavorting at the Ambos Mundos in Havana (which is perpetuated in Hilary Hemingway and Carlene Brennan's *Hemingway in Cuba* [19–20]). One story that can be verified about La Concha: Tennessee Williams wrote *Summer and Smoke* in the mid-1940s while staying at the hotel before he bought his home at 431 Duncan Street.

63:28–29 **"Ah, Harry," he said, "I always knew you were my pal:** In *Cosmopolitan*, "One Trip Across" ended with this line from Eddy, who has no clue how seriously Harry considered murdering him to cover up killing Mr. Sing. Why Hemingway added the subsequent scene at Harry Morgan's house to the novel version is unclear. (The draft is included in MS 31, item 211, folder 23 with tear sheets from "One Trip Across.") Most likely, he decided to give readers a glimpse of Harry's wife, Marie, before introducing her more fully in part 3.

64:3 **Gracie Allen:** The leading comedienne of her day, Grace Ethel Cecile Rosalie Allen (1895–1964) is best remembered as the wife of George Burns (1896–1996), the husband / straight man who survived her to become a mainstay of Neil Simon comedies and television talk shows in the 1970s and 1980s. Allen's charm was to "play dumb" with her guileless persona. At the time this scene in *To Have and Have Not* occurs, Burns and Allen were radio stars—though not quite stars of their own eponymous show. Instead, they appeared on *The Robert Burns Panatella Show* in 1932–33 and *The White Owl Program* in 1933–34, with *The Adventures of Gracie* not debuting until 1934 (and running only until 1935, when the show was renamed for its sponsor: *The Campbell's Tomato Juice Program*). Aside from this reference, Hemingway's closest connection to Allen is through Gertrude Stein, of all people. In January 1935 *Vanity Fair* published a mock interview between the "ditzy" queen of comedy and the Mother Goose of Montparnasse called "Impossible Interview: Gracie Allen vs. Gertrude Stein" (25). Written by humorist Corey Ford (1902–1969), the piece features an oft-republished caricature of its subjects by Miguel Covarrubias (1904–1957), one of the era's best-known illustrators. Although the publication postdates the appearance of "One Trip Across" by more than a year and a half, Hemingway would have appreciated the mocking of his former mentor as a literary counterpart to Allen's daffy persona.

PART TWO

Harry Morgan (Fall)

The novel's second, and shortest, section was published originally as "The Tradesman's Return" in *Esquire* February 1936: 27, 193–96. The magazine version does not include section breaks; Hemingway divided the text into three chapters in the typescript of the original compiled draft of *To Have and Have Not* (MS 31, item 211, folder 23). The section subtitle identifies the season as autumn, but it is important to recognize that the year is not the same as that in which "One Trip Across," or part 1, was set. Internal evidence suggests the year is instead 1934. Specifically, mention of the end of Prohibition, which was not formally repealed until 5 December 1933, means the timeframe has advanced by nearly eighteen months. Scott O. McClintock suggests that the gap is a trick meant to teach readers to pay close attention to the subtle historical references: "Perhaps Hemingway is having a little game with his reader's expectations, dating the three parts of *To Have and Have Not* in such a way that we are tempted to assume the continuity of a single year in the time sequence. . . . Only by alternating between U.S. and Cuban frames of historical reference do we see the length of the gap between parts 1 and 2. We must become 'expatriot' readers [Hemingway's intentional misspelling of *expatriate*], abandoning the perspective of a single national frame of reference in order to accurately read Hemingway's intercultural text" (116).

CHAPTER SIX

As dawn rises across the Gulf Stream, Harry Morgan and his current mate, Wesley, struggle to return from a liquor run to Cuba that has gone horribly awry. Shortly after loading in El Mariel, a post-Prohibition center for booze trafficking, the men were intercepted by Cuban authorities, who fired on them when Harry refused to stop and surrender their illicit cargo. Wesley is wounded in the leg and lies on the cockpit floor, blubbering and cursing his captain; Harry has taken a shot to the right arm, rendering it useless. As the boat takes shelter in the mangroves of Woman Key, Harry wonders if the "blowing" that augurs an impending storm will prevent their rendezvous boat from meeting them before one or both of the bootleggers bleeds to death. He decides to dump his haul and head back to Key West for medical treatment rather than risk the wait. With Wesley insisting he cannot move, Harry must heave the forty-pound sacks overboard by himself—and do it with only one hand, too.

67:15 **American shoals:** Located nineteen miles southeast of Key West near Big Pine Key, the site is home to the American Shoal Lighthouse, the last of the Keys lighthouses, built in 1880, some fifty years after its counterpart on Sand Key (see 62:11).

68:5 **Woman Key:** Located ten miles west of Key West, Woman Key is a small, uninhabited mangrove island that is part of the Mule Keys.

68:6–7 **where the boat was to come out to meet them:** Rumrunners typically rendezvoused with smaller, lighter motorboats, sometimes even rowboats, which would carry the cargo for the final leg of its journey. Although he lies to Wesley about it, Harry is certain that due to the brewing storm the boat scheduled to meet him on this run will not show up (see 72:18–73:4). This is why he must dump the liquor; because of the gravity of their wounds, he and Wesley must lose their cargo so they can return to Key West for immediate medical treatment.

69:3 **Wesley:** Hemingway introduces Harry's newest mate. There are several possible explanations for why he did not revive the character of Eddy Marshall when he wrote "The Tradesman's Return" in late 1935 as a follow-up to "One Trip Across." Given that his working title for the tale was "White Man, Black Man, Alphabet Man," he may have needed a specifically African American foil for Harry to balance the contrast in masculine strength and perseverance he intended to dramatize among those three characters. A more likely explanation, however, is that when he began the story, the inspiration for Eddy Marshall—Joe Lowe—had recently died on Lower Matecumbe Key, in the devastating Labor Day hurricane of 2 September 1935 (see 8:17). Because there was little mystery among Key Westers about Eddy's real identity, Hemingway may have found it unseemly to revive his "rummy" character for this story.

69:15: **The man, whose name was Harry Morgan:** When published autonomously in *Esquire,* this nonrestrictive clause introduced Harry Morgan's name to readers, even though Hemingway continues to refer to him as "the man" until after his encounter with Captain Willie and the alphabet men. In the context of the novel, the clause may seem redundant, given that readers are seventy pages into Harry's story. Yet the construction serves at least two functions. It calls attention to the subtle shift out of the first-person narration in the opening "Spring" section (i.e., "One Trip Across") to the more external and objective third person of "Fall" (or "The Tradesman's Return"), which readers may have not yet noticed. Both the reintroduction and the shift emphasize the discontinuity of the novel's structure, with Hemingway choosing to call attention to the tripartite division of the plot instead of cohering it into a unified whole.

70:16–17 **Why they run liquor now? . . . Prohibition's over:** As a Key Wester, Wesley ought to know the answer to his own question. The repeal of Prohibition, made official with the 5 December 1933 ratification of the Twenty-First Amendment to the U.S. Constitution, did not end rum-running. The trade continued as a means of avoiding alcohol taxes.

72:6–27 **whetstone . . . coaming**: A whetstone is used for sharpening knives. As Harry subsequently notes (75:1), this is hardly the weapon with which Wesley can reap revenge on his captain for inveigling him in their predicament. A coaming is a protective barrier installed around openings on ships such as hatches, shafts, and even decks to prevent water from seeping aboard.

CHAPTER SEVEN

As Harry strains to sink his cargo, another Key West charter boat, the *South Florida,* unexpectedly enters the channel of Woman Key. Aboard are two Washington, DC, bureaucrats, Dr. Frederick Harrison and his obsequious secretary, who immediately peg Harry and Wesley for rumrunners. In a moment of J. Edgar Hoover–styled grandiosity, Harrison decides he will seize Harry's boat and take the wounded captain into custody. The *South Florida*'s owner, Captain Willie Adams, is a friend of Harry's, however, and warns him to get out of the area as quickly as he can. As the preening Harrison and his secretary threaten to make their guide's life miserable if he does not obey their orders, Captain Willie chews them out, letting them know they have no clue how Key West families are suffering during the Depression. The limited options that leave many Conchs with no recourse other than smuggling to survive are a direct fault of the government, which pays an unlivable wage of $6.50 a week for relief work. To give Harry time to get away, Captain Willie heads out to sea until dark with his captive passengers.

76:4–5 **a white boat with a buff painted house:** By "house," Hemingway means the wheelhouse or pilothouse, the enclosed portion of the bridge where the steering wheel is installed.

76:1 **abeam:** As a direction, abeam means directly perpendicular to a boat's center.

76:2 **Captain Willie:** Following Carlos Baker, most scholars associate Willie Adams with Hemingway's first Key West fishing guide, Edward "Bra" Saunders (1876–1949). Born in the Bahamas, Saunders emigrated to the Keys as a child and by 1928, when Hemingway met him, was one of the most experienced guides working the island docks. He was also a founder of the island's fledgling charter-boat industry (Jennings 101). As Baker writes, Saunders introduced Hemingway to "every shoal and key and mangrove swamp from Homestead to the Dry Tortugas" (*A Life* 192). With his brother Berge as mate, Saunders captained the rowdy 1928 and 1929 fishing expeditions that Hemingway arranged for friends whom he collectively dubbed "The Mob," including John Dos Passos, painter Waldo Peirce, Bill Smith, and Henry

"Mike" Strater. During one of these trips Captain Bra told the men a story about a four-hundred-foot steamship called the *Valbenera* that sank during a September 1919 hurricane. Supposedly, Saunders was one of the first wreckers to try to salvage the ship, though whether he "nearly killed himself in successive vain attempts to crack open her portholes to get at the loot inside," as Baker describes it (194), remains a matter of dispute. Regardless, the story became the basis for "After the Storm," Hemingway's first attempt at using his Key West experience in fiction. For many years, biographers accepted Baker's account that Hemingway learned the *Valbenera* anecdote in spring 1928, within weeks of moving to Key West. More recently, Michael Crowley has argued that the storytelling session did not take place until 1929 (192–97). Either way, "After the Storm" remains one of the two or three best entries in the otherwise disappointing 1933 story collection *Winner Take Nothing*. Although Hemingway employed Saunders less frequently in the 1930s, he did choose Captain Bra among all the seasoned Key West fishermen he knew to help him pilot the *Pilar* home from Miami upon its 1934 purchase.

77:7 **the man called Harry:** Unlike the nonrestrictive clause at 69:15, this nominative phrase serves no real narrative purpose. Hemingway may not have called Harry by his first name in nearly ten pages, but Captain Willie does in the preceding sentence ("'What do you say, Harry?' the old man called as he passed"). The resulting repetition suggests just what a thin line separates the dramatic punch of Hemingway's trademark techniques from degenerating into mere stylized tics.

77:17 **a good skate:** A slang phrase meaning "a good fellow," ironic in usage because a "skate" originally described a person worthy of great contempt. The phrase fell out of fashion in the 1960s. Its most famous recent usage is likely the 1980 *Peanuts* television special *She's a Good Skate, Charlie Brown,* featuring Charles M. Schulz's plaintive comic-strip characters. The title is a pun that plays off a plot about a skating competition.

78:3: **On board the charter boat *South Florida*:** This paragraph marks what will become throughout the rest of the novel a recurring tendency on Hemingway's part to shift the narrative focus among various characters. Thus far the storytelling has been "focalized," as narratologists like to say, through Harry. (Many theorists prefer *focalization* to the conventional terminology of *point of view* because the term does not imply a visual perspective and because the various taxonomies into which "focalizing" is divided are considered more specific than "first" and "third person.") In the succeeding sentences (78:6–12), Hemingway will employ interior monologue, allowing us to hear Captain Willie's silent admiration for Harry's cojones: "Damned if I'd cross [from Cuba to Key West] a night like last night," the old salt thinks. "Damned if I'd ever run liquor from Cuba."

78:11 **Mariel:** El Mariel is a small city located twenty-five miles west of Havana, best known today as the site from which some 125,000 Cubans were allowed to emigrate by boat to the United States over a six-month period in 1980 (the "Mariel boatlift"). Captain Willie's line here—"They bring [liquor] from Mariel now"—refers to a brief window of time in spring and summer 1934 when this port and Bahía Honda were the two main pickup points for liquor runs. As Eduardo Sáenz Rovner notes, when "the Cuban authorities launched a campaign to break up the operation . . . they discovered that numerous customs agents were caught up in the illegal activity. The government responded by firing the customs administrator in El Mariel and expelling from the country several Americans involved in the smuggling operations" (28). Cuban distilleries—more than two dozen of them were in operation at the time—protested the crackdown by threatening to stop liquor production. One should note here that Hemingway is not adhering to a strict sense of recent history here; by autumn 1934 when this portion of the novel is set the "open port" at Mariel would have been shut down.

79:7, 11, 19 **Doctor:** Before we learn that the name of Captain Willie's customer is Frederick Harrison, all we know of this ruddy-faced man with the "contemptuous mouth" and white canvas hat is this honorific. Hemingway makes it clear what kind of "doctor" Harrison is *not*:

> "Are you a doctor?' Captain Willie asked.
> "Not of medicine," the gray-eyed man told him. (79:19–20)

In other words, the bureaucrat has a PhD—a degree that Hemingway, always self-conscious about his own lack of college education, as well as his reputation as the "dumb ox" of modernist literature, ridiculed as next to useless.[1]

79:10–11: **Write down the number on the bow:** Harrison refers to Harry's vessel registration number.

79:9 **two-cylinder Palmer:** Brothers Ray and Frank Palmer began building two-cylinder engines in 1884 when the joint owners of the Mianus (Connecticut) Electric Company—a manufacturer of telephones—were unable to find a suitable motor for their pleasure boat. They formally went into the boating business twelve years later. Leicester Hemingway's autobiography notes that Bra Saunders's boat was propelled by "a slow-chugging Palmer" (114), thus strengthening the association between Captain Willie and the real-life fishing guide.

80:8–10 **one of the three most important men in the United States today:** On the typescript of "The Tradesman's Return," Frederick Harrison (whose name isn't specified until 80:12–13) is called *Henry* Harrison, which may have sounded a little too similar to Harry Hopkins for Hemingway. (See MS 31, item 211, folder 23, pages 10–14; we can assume this is the original draft of "Tradesman" because of its prospective title: "Man and Alphabet Man.") Often described as a chief architect of the New Deal, Hopkins (1890–1946) was a key adviser to President Franklin D. Roosevelt, overseeing three crucial agencies: the Federal Emergency Relief Administration (1933–35); the Civil Works Administration (1933–34); and the Works Progress Administration (1935–43, though Hopkins in the buildup to World War II was assigned to serve as an emissary to Great Britain and led the WPA in name only at the organization's end). Hopkins even visited Key West in 1935 to assess rehabilitation efforts and to attend a WPA production of *The Pirates of Penzance.* One frequently reproduced photograph captures him with cast members and Julius F. Stone Jr. (see below). Given Hopkins's prominence in the period—he was indeed one of the three most important men in America in the mid- to late-1930s—most *Esquire* readers would have taken Harrison's depiction as a skewering of the administrator. Either Hemingway or the magazine or both decided to avoid any potential libel issues and replace references to the character's name with dashes. Thus, Harrison's secretary (confusingly named "Harris" in "The Tradesman's Return") introduces his boss: "He's——" (192). In the magazine version, the secretary's line at 80:0–21 ("He's one of the biggest men in the administration") reads, "He's the most intimate friend and closest adviser of——" (192), which readers would have assumed referred to President Roosevelt.

Despite the similar sounding name, Frederick Harrison is generally considered an acidic satire of not Hopkins but Julius F. Stone Jr., the director of the Key West Administration, the municipal corporation formed in July 1934 to save the city after it declared bankruptcy. As the head of the Florida division of the Federal Emergency Relief Administration (FERA), Stone was the driving force behind the KWA's establishment, and he promptly assumed governance of the island with an imperious zeal. (Thus, the secretary's declaration at 80:5 that Harrison will soon become "governor-general of——," presumably referring to Key West, especially given the doctor's boast at 80:16–17 that "every one in this stinking jerk water little town" will soon know his name even if he has to "grub" the city "out by the roots.") In what is by no means a coincidental character trait, Stone, like the doctor, held a PhD, his in organic chemistry. As the son of a leading Ohio industrialist with deep ties to Ohio State University, Stone was no stranger to privilege and entitlement. He had previously served the Roosevelt administration as director of federal projects for the CWA, showing no compunction about cutting employees in need of relief when budgets demanded belt-tightening. To some residents, he was a cigar-store Mussolini; others nicknamed him the "Key West Kingfisher," a local Huey P. Long, the infamous Louisiana governor (Hanna and Hanna 361; McIver, *Dreamers, Schemers, and Scalawags* 130). Among Stone's most highly praised accomplishments was the KWA's Volunteer Works Corps (see 81:15–16), which encouraged residents to pledge volunteer hours to clean up the island, in terms of sanitation, landscaping, and home maintenance. Among his most ridiculed was his recommendation that locals wear shorts to enhance the leisure atmosphere, a suggestion both impractical and offensive to the morally conservative Conch culture.

Hemingway loathed Stone for turning Key West into a tourist trap. In 1934 and 1935, the KWA printed pamphlets highlighting the Hemingway residence at 907 Whitehead Street as a sightseeing stop, an irritation that the author would parody in his August 1935 *Esquire* essay, "The Sights of Whitehead Street" (*BL* 192–97). Although he never denounced Stone by name in print—again, Hemingway was always leery of exposing himself to a libel suit—he did relish condemning KWA and FERA administrators in general. In one 1934 letter, he speaks of Key West as a "F.E.R.A. Jew administered phony of a town" (*SL* 410). Given the preponderance of racial epithets in *To Have and Have Not,* readers may breathe a sigh of relief that anti-Semitic slurs do not seep into the depiction of Dr. Frederick Harrison. Instead, we have a fairly conventional portrait of the ruling class of "haves": Harrison is pompous and pretentious, dictatorial and elitist, but also effete and ineffective when it comes to action. Put in his place by Captain Willie, the most power he can muster is a whimper: "Oh, shut up," he tells the fisherman (80:12).

We never see Harrison after his encounter with Harry's boat, which is unfortunate; he might have made an interesting foil in part 3. Stone exerted his presence in Key West far after his tenure as head of the KWA; surprisingly, he was only in office a short six months when he accepted a promotion within the Roosevelt administration, becoming the chief field officer for FERA with responsibility for all of Florida. Even so, he remained in Key West, eager to make his mark in the tourist industry that he deserved the lion's share of credit for creating. After leaving government service to earn a law degree, he returned to the Keys in the early 1940s and set up permanent office, he and his family living for the better part of two decades in the Southernmost House, at 1400 Duval Street. A series of bad investments caused Stone flee a barrage of lawsuits by relocating to a vacation estate in Cuba. Unfortunately for him, Fidel Castro thereafter seized his property in the Cuban Revolution. Stone in turn expatriated to Australia, where he died in 1967.

81:15–16 working here in Key West for the government for six dollars and a half a week: Shortly after Florida governor Dave Schmidt ceded control to the Key West Administration in July 1934, Julius F. Stone Jr. initiated a series of projects for the island designed to both jumpstart its moribund economy and clean it up to tourist-worthy standards. Although upward of $1 million was slated for the effort, Stone initially declined to pay for labor, asking citizens to donate their time and efforts out of civic pride. As the media would report in 1935, some four thousand locals promptly signed up for the Volunteer Works Corps, each earning a certificate of appreciation for their combined contributions of 2 million hours of effort. The KWA soon instituted a pay scale, however, offering between thirty-two and eighty cents per hour, depending on the worker's skill level. In giving the specific wage of $6.50 per week, Hemingway may have been estimating or citing an informal average. At the time he drafted "The Tradesman's Return," the KWA was paying between $22 and $42 per month for 128 hours of work, or between $5.50 and $10.50 per week (Long, "Workers" 55).

81:9 **marl:** Henry R. Mount's definition in *Hemingway's Tribute to the Soil* (2006) is the most specific for the novel's context: "Marl is defined as white to gray accumulation on lake bottoms caused by the precipitation of calcium carbonate ($CaCO_3$) in hard water lakes. Marl may contain snail and clam shells, which are also calcium carbonate. While it gradually fills in lakes, marl also precipitates phosphorous, resulting in low algae populations and good water clarity" (71). As Mount goes on to note, references to marl also appear in "Big Two-Hearted River" (*CSS* 175) and *Islands in the Stream* (411).

82:18–19 **G men . . . Edgar Hoover:** By the mid-1930s, the director of the Federal Bureau of Investigation (1895–1972) had transformed the image of the federal law-enforcement agent from a crooked, lazy sinecure at the "Department of Easy Virtue" into a daring "G-man" who mercilessly quashed bootlegging, bank robbery, and kidnapping. Central to this transformation was the rise of such "celebrity" criminals as George "Machine Gun" Kelly, John Dillinger, Kate "Ma" Barker, and Lester "Baby Face" Nelson, all of whom were either captured or killed by the Bureau in 1933–34. (Before it was officially christened the "Federal Bureau of Investigation" in 1935, the FBI was known as the "Bureau of Investigation" [1908–32], the "United States Bureau of Investigation" [1932–33], and the "Division of Investigation" [1933–35].) Appalled at how these villains were treated as folk heroes, Hoover launched a highly publicized "War on Crime" campaign. While he wrote editorials and made speeches on the moral tenacity of the "G-man," actual agents such as Melvin Purvis (1903–1960) led the manhunts. Not surprisingly, Hoover and Purvis squabbled over who deserved the credit and the fame for these captures. In his role as bureau director, Hoover had a decided advantage, and he became a controversial symbol of law enforcement, at once winning over fans with blunt talk about "sob-sister judges" and "shyster lawyers" while alienating civil libertarians and other government agencies who resented his showboating.

Hoover appears not to have known or at least not to have cared about Hemingway until the early 1940s. The author's activities in Cuba during World War II, when Hemingway led U-boat surveillances aboard the *Pilar,* both concerned and irked the director. The FBI opened a file on Hemingway on 8 October 1942; it would run until 1974, more than a decade after the author's suicide (and two years after Hoover's). As many critics who have analyzed the file conclude, the interest in the writer was personal more than ideological, despite constant mentions of Hemingway's ties with Communists in the 1930s. Hemingway offended FBI agent Raymond Leddy in Havana in 1942 by referring to the agency as the "American Gestapo." Hoover, in turn, took gibes at the author's character: "His judgment is not of the best," he wrote in a 19 December 1942 memo, "and if his sobriety is the same as it was some years ago, that is certainly questionable" (qtd. in Mort 118). By August 1943 Hoover was more concerned Hemingway would write a book mocking the FBI.

The truly bizarre connections between the agency and the author would not arise until the final months of Hemingway's life, inspired in part by his association with Fidel Castro and other leaders of the 1959 Cuban Revolution. When Hemingway checked into the Mayo Clinic the winter before his suicide, he was convinced the FBI was following him. Thanks to the doctor who notified the bureau, he was correct (Culleton 89–91).

Hoover led the bureau until his death on 2 May 1972 at the age of seventy-eight. Forty years later, he remains a much-loathed symbol of government and law-enforcement overreach, perhaps second only to Richard Nixon.

83:12 **alphabet man:** In 1933, the Roosevelt administration created a bewildering number of federal agencies to save the United States from the economic stagnation of the Great Depression. Many of these were established within the president's first hundred days of office. Most were known by their initials: the Federal Emergency Relief Administration (FERA), the National Recovery Administration (NRA), the Civilian Conservation Corps (CCC), the Civil Works Administration (CWA), and the Public Works Administration (PWA), to name just a few. By late 1933, critics were complaining of the vast expansion of the federal bureaucracy. One such critic was former Roosevelt ally Al Smith (1873–1944), who, with Roosevelt as his vice-presidential candidate, had lost the 1928 Democratic presidential bid to Republican Herbert Hoover. (Smith attempted to win a second Democratic nomination in 1932, but FDR defeated him in the primaries.) In November 1933 Smith gave a speech credited with popularizing the phrase "alphabet soup" to describe the capriciousness with which the Roosevelt brain trust (derided as an oblivious caste of academicians) created new government divisions: "It looks as though one of the absent-minded professors had played anagrams with the alphabet soup. The soup got cold while he was unconsciously inventing a new game for the nation, a game which beats the cross-word puzzle—the game of identifying new departments by their initials" (10). Accordingly, FDR's ever-proliferating departments became known as "alphabet agencies," while the bureaucrats running them were derided as "alphabet men." Thus, the original title of "The Tradesman's Return": "White Man, Black Man, Alphabet Man." As Captain Willie makes clear here, a Roosevelt administrator to a struggling American worker is just a "stool from Washington" (83:2).

83:18 That chap your brother? Not only does Frederick Harrison speak with British affectations ("chap"), he is such an elitist he has to ask whether Captain Willie and Harry are literally brothers. Such a mistake even on the part of an alphabet man seems a bit farfetched and marks the point where Hemingway sacrificed the realism of character for the sake of a satirical point. As previously noted, *brother* was a common proletarian endearment, as in "Brother, Can You Spare a Dime?" (See 17:10).

84:4 Rios: Although the name "Rios" does not appear in the infrequently published Key West directories of the Hemingway era, it does pop up in at least one local memoir. In *Magnolia Dairy: My Memories of Old Key West in the 20s and 30s* (1997), Nilo C. Lopez writes: "The ships that came from Cuba would take back shipments of fish from Rio's Fish Markets. I remember Senor Salvador Napoles who was a bookkeeper for Rio's company. Family members told me that one ship was named the *Mascote*. Other ships I do not remember. They were the *Governor Cobb*, the *Cuba*, and later, the *Florida*. I remember the *Cuba* and the *Florida* when they went from Key West to Tampa and returned here and then back to Cuba" (np).

84:10–11: grits . . . grunts: "Grits and grunts" is a favorite Conch dish that was especially popular during the Depression because it was so cheap. Recalling the era in his 1963 memoir of his older brother, Leicester Hemingway describes the acquired taste: "In town many people were living on grits and grunts, a classic poor man's diet in the keys. Hominy grits were less than ten cents a pound and grunts, members of the snapper family, were small eating fish you could catch in any channel, or from any pier, with a little patience" (148).

NOTE

1. It was Wyndham Lewis who bequeathed Hemingway with this rather unfortunate nickname in his April 1934 review of *Winner Take Nothing*. See Meyers, *Critical Heritage* 186–209.

CHAPTER EIGHT

This two-and-a-half-page chapter follows Harry and Wesley home from Woman Key. Harry is strangely sanguine. He appreciates the risk Willie takes for him with the alphabet men and forgives Wesley for being weak and cowardly. ("Ain't no nigger no good when he's shot," he rather uncharitably says. "You're a all right nigger, Wesley" [87:1–2].) In the context of the novel, Harry's relationship with Wesley parallels his relationship with Eddy Marshall. In both cases he possesses the heroic resolve—the cojones, in other words—that the mates lack. His strength and endurance place him in the tradition of the Hemingway hero. Aside from reinforcing this theme, this chapter is notable mainly for its storytelling experimentation. Hemingway reveals for us Harry's innermost thoughts not only through interior monologue (employed with Captain Willie in the previous chapter) but also through the related (and highly celebrated) technique of stream of consciousness.

85:6 **depression . . . on the bum:** By "depression," of course, Hemingway refers to the Great Depression, which most historians date as beginning with the 29 October 1929 stock market crash known as "Black Tuesday." World War II's industrial production demand for weaponry is typically credited with ending the economic crisis in the early 1940s. According to *The New Partridge Dictionary of Slang and Unconventional English*, "on the bum," meaning to live as a beggar, is a relatively recent coinage, dating only to 1907 (Partridge 1:101).

85:9 **bitt:** A bitt is a vertical device used to tie off mooring line. It may be as small as a metal cleat or as big as a wooden post.

85:11 **Garrison Bight:** Contemporary visitors to Key West will recognize Garrison Bight as the name both of a main waterway channel and a historic marina on the island. The channel runs along the eastern side of Fleming Key from Man of War Harbor to Trumbo Point before turning east into the bay along present-day Northern Roosevelt Boulevard, Eisenhower Drive, and the Palm Avenue Causeway. Because the channel was not dredged until the late 1940s, Hemingway's reference is to the marina, which was home to Charter Boat Row, the site where tourists would have engaged boat captains such as Harry Morgan or Willie Adams. Just because the Garrison Bight Channel antedates *To Have and Have Not* does not mean it has been overlooked in literary history, however. Elizabeth Bishop's poem "The Bight," written on her thirty-seventh birthday, captures the look of the area in 1948 as the Garrison channel was under construction:

> Some of the little white boats are still piled up
> against each other, or lie on their sides, stove in,
> and not yet salvaged, if they ever will be, from the last bad storm,
> like torn-open, unanswered letters.
> The bight is littered with old correspondences.
> Click. Click. Goes the dredge,
> and brings up a dripping jawful of marl.
> All the untidy activity continues,
> awful but cheerful. (61)

85:19 **Boca Grande**: Hemingway is not referring here to the city of Boca Grande, Florida, 100 miles due north of Key West (and some 350 miles by road), even though that round-trip would certainly keep Frederick Harrison and his secretary detoured long enough for Harry to escape. Instead, he means Boca Grande Key, some 14 miles west of Key West, part of the same Mule Keys that also includes the aforementioned Woman Key (see 68:5).

86:4 **That's Cubans for you:** This paragraph expands on the background Captain Willie introduced at 78:11, explaining more specifically why Cuban authorities would open fire on Harry and Wesley. As previously noted, El Mariel became one of two main loading points for Cuban liquor bound for the United States in 1934 because its customs inspectors were easily bribed. Harry is convinced that "somebody didn't pay somebody so we got the shooting." A historical reading of the encounter might suggest he and Wesley have the misfortune of making their run during the period in which the Cuban government, embarrassed by its reputation as a smuggler's haven, set out to shut down Mariel's laxity toward rum-runners.

86:1 **the Trumbo dock:** Trumbo Point is a man-made cape that sits directly above the Garrison Bight bay area in the north-central corner of Key West. It is named after Howard Trumbo (1875–1931), the chief engineer in charge of filling in 174 acres of Key West harbor to house the terminal of the Florida East Coast Railway. The point was a matter of much contention during the prolonged building of the railway because the United States Navy objected to Flagler's beginning the project without proper approval. During Hemingway's time, one of the docks was reserved exclusively for ferries transporting cars to Key West, the ferry a necessity since the overland highway was not completely accessible to vehicles until 1938. Hemingway's first Key West car, purchased by Pauline Pfeiffer's generous uncle Gus (who also financed their Whitehead Street residence), arrived in this manner (McLendon 21).

86:4–27 Wonder who those buzzards were. . . . We did right not to wait: This passage marks Hemingway's first use of stream of consciousness, which will culminate in Marie Morgan's monologue in chapter 26 (257:1–261:7). This technique is distinguished by its use of free association, which allows it to depict the pattern of a character's thought process as random and spontaneous instead of orderly and logical. The differences between interior monologue and stream of consciousness are a matter more of degree than type; in general, the former conveys a sense of structure or purpose in the act of thinking, while the latter suggests that a character experiences ideas instead of creating and constructing them. As narratologist Seymour Chatman writes, "Interior monologue is marked by syntax: it ascribes present tense verbs and first person pronoun-reference to the thinking character (or the implication of these where the syntax is truncated). Stream of consciousness . . . goes beyond syntax: it constrains the arrangement of semantic elements according to the principle of free association" (189). The term "stream of consciousness" comes from William James's *Principles of Psychology* (1890), although its initial use in narratology is credited to May Sinclair, whose essay, "The Novels of Dorothy Richardson," published in April 1918 in the *Egoist*, adapted it from James. Despite the example of Richardson's 1915 novel, *Pointed Roofs* (and the twelve subsequent entries in her *Pilgrimage* sequence), the work that popularized the technique's use was, of course, James Joyce's *Ulysses*. Other modernists associated with stream of consciousness include Virginia Woolf and William Faulkner.

Hemingway's reputation for omission and brevity would seem to preclude his use of a device known for its expansive garrulity. Yet passages of stream of consciousness appear regularly throughout his 1930s work, foreshadowed first by *A Farewell to Arms* but beginning properly with *Death in the Afternoon,* continuing on through *Green Hills of Africa,* and culminating with *For Whom the Bell Tolls*. Mark Cirino points out interesting connections Hemingway drew between stream of consciousness and the Gulf Stream in *Green Hills, The Garden of Eden* manuscripts, and *Islands in the Stream,* noting that the author strove for "prose so fluid that the writing functions like a stream itself" (86–87). Despite this evocative link, most critics agree with Michael S. Reynolds that his greatest use of the technique occurs in "The Snows of Kilimanjaro," in which italicized passages of memories alternate with the central storyline to dramatize Harry Walden's sweeping regrets as he dies from gangrene while on an African safari (*Ernest Hemingway* 146).[1] The contribution of stream of consciousness to *To Have and Have Not* is more suspect. In general, passages such as this one can strike readers as gratuitous since they do not seem thematically significant. Arguably, stream of consciousness works best when it serves as a metafictional expression of a text's effort to reimagine status quo norms of perception, cognition, memory, or the linear construction of time or history—the ways, in other words, that we have been trained to see, experience, and process the world we inhabit. For some critics, Hemingway's more elaborate experiments with the mode in sections involving Marie Morgan and Dorothy Hollis do touch on such themes and help render these characters more human and sympathetic. Shorter bursts of the device, on the other hand, merely wander in and out of moments of free association without apparent purpose. While they may make *To Have and Have Not* a more texturally interesting work than it might have otherwise been, they do not combine to elevate the work to the level of accomplishment achieved in Woolf's *Mrs. Dalloway* (1925) or Faulkner's *The Sound and the Fury* (1929).

NOTE

1. To point out an obvious connection between "The Snows of Kilimanjaro" and *To Have and Have Not,* both protagonists are named Harry. As Carl P. Eby notes, they are by no means alone: "Hemingway's universe is populated by Harrys: *Harry Morgan, Harry Walden,* and Harold Krebs, whose sister calls him 'Hare.' In *The Sun Also Rises,* Jake and Mike fish with the Englishman, Harris. Then there is the Harris in 'Homage to Switzerland'" (*Hemingway's Fetishism* 109–10). As Eby argues, the name is symbolic of Hemingway's hair fetish.

PART THREE

Harry Morgan (Winter)

The final and longest portion of *To Have and Have Not* was only ever published in novel form, despite Hemingway's spring 1937 attempts to sell an excerpt from it to both *Cosmopolitan* and *Esquire*.[1] Composed of seventeen chapters, "Winter" packs a nearly overwhelming panoply of characters into a pair of interwoven plots that dramatize the economic gulf between the haves and the have-nots. Given the overpopulated cast, readers should not be surprised that this third part is also the novel's most complex (some would say inconsistent) in terms of narrative technique. All told, Hemingway will focalize the action through more than a dozen different characters, both major and minor, from Harry Morgan to his wife, Marie; to Richard Gordon; to Freddy, the owner of Harry's preferred bar, as well as several yachtsmen; and, finally, even the townspeople of Key West as they crowd onto a dock to see Harry's dead body returned to the city.

NOTE

1. See my introduction to this study, pages xxxix–xl.

CHAPTER NINE

For the first time in *To Have and Have Not*, readers are given a glimpse of the grittier side of Key West life. Set in what in the 1930s were two of the city's most famous bars, this chapter finds Harry Morgan negotiating the very thing he refused to do in chapter 1: smuggling Cuban terrorists across the Gulf. With the arm wounded in part 2 now amputated, Harry has no means of making a living, especially now that customs officials, in the aftermath of his failed Mariel booze run, have seized his boat. To feed his family, he must accept an offer from shady lawyer Robert "Bee-lips" Simmons, with whom he first trades insults in Freddy's (or Freddie's) Bar before meeting with the terrorists at an unnamed watering hole across town run by a couple named Richards. In between these two meetings, Harry attempts to convince yet another mate, Albert Tracy, to make the run with him. (Albert, in fact, serves as this chapter's narrator.) Indignant at the low wages paid by government work relief, Harry insists he will not allow his family to starve on a subsidy. "You've got two arms and you've got two of something else," he reminds Albert. "And a man's still a man with one arm or with one of those" (97:7–8). The passage is a reminder of the text's persistent preoccupation with testicular fortitude.

91 ***Albert Speaking***: Also for the first time in the book, Hemingway employs a paratextual marker to designate the identity of the narrating "I." Technically speaking, this notation is neither a chapter title nor a subtitle; it is probably incorrect even to call it a "heading," since that term likewise suggests that it *names* the chapter, which is not the case. Rather, the device serves as a cue, signaling information to the reader from what Gerard Genette calls that "interstitial" space between the imagined world of the story and the medium of the printed book through which it is presented (2–3). Hemingway will employ this technique once more in chapter 10 ("Harry") but never again in the novel—another sign of the narratorial inconsistency that makes *To Have and Have Not* intriguingly but perplexingly unique.

Because this is the first chapter narrated *entirely* from an ancillary character's perspective, it marks readers' first extended view of Harry through the eyes of the supporting cast. (The point of view may have switched from Harry to Captain Willie in part 2, but the change is short-term, maintained for only six pages, or roughly half the length of chapter 9.) In commenting on the action, Albert will reflect on Harry's personality with tidbits that imply a complex backstory: "[S]ince he was a boy he never had no pity for nobody. But he never had no pity for himself either" (98:18–20). Yet, as the case will prove in passages narrated by Harry's wife, Marie, this background information is provided in passing and receives almost no elaboration whatsoever. In the end, we will still know relatively little of our hero's biography beyond what the plot dramatizes. Albert's entry into the story also exacerbates a problem that begins with the introduction of Wesley in part 2—namely, the profusion of duplicate characters cluttering the storyline. Between Eddy, Frankie, and Wesley, readers will be forgiven if they must struggle to keep this latest crewmember straight in their minds. That said, Albert is by far the most fully realized of this quartet, and his struggle to feed his family while resisting the lure of black-market work nicely parallels Harry's own temptation into crime.

As with many characters in the book, Albert Tracy is based on a real person. According to James McLendon, he is a composite of two fixtures of Key West's fishing community, Albert "Old Bread" Pinder and Richard Hamilton "Saca Ham" Adams (157). Hemingway met Pinder (1893–1958) in March 1931 when he chartered the fisherman's boat for a Dry Tortugas expedition that also included Scribner's editor Maxwell Perkins and novelist John Herrmann (1900–1959), then husband of Josephine Herbst (1892–1969), who later covered the Spanish Civil War alongside Hemingway while headquartered at Madrid's Hotel Florida (Chamberlin 107). Four years later, Pinder served as pilot and engineer on the *Pilar* during Hemingway's spring-summer 1935 fishing season in Bimini, joined by Adams (1889–1969), who cooked for the party. A period Hemingway letter to Gerald and Sara Murphy's son Patrick describes the pair in Laurel and Hardy terms, with "Old Bread" "fat and a good man" and "Saca Ham" "very tall and thin and . . . a good friend of Bread's" (Miller, *Letters* 126–27). Both men appear in several photographs from the mid-1930s, most notably one reprinted in James McLendon's *Papa: Hemingway in Key West* (1972). Taken on Cat Cay in Bimini, the picture features Hemingway, Henry "Mike" Strater, Pinder, and Adams posing alongside the prize marlin "apple-cored" by sharks after Hemingway peppered the water with Tommy-gun fire (See 6:21). Both "Old Bread" and "Saca" are referenced in passing by nickname in Hemingway's July 1935 *Esquire* column, "The President Vanquishes" (23). They play fuller roles in the previous month's "One Being Shot Again: A Gulf Stream Letter," where they tend to Hemingway after a ricochet from his .22 Colt Woodsman pierces his leg (*BL* 200–02).

91:1 **Freddie's place:** The bar that serves as a central setting throughout much of this third section is based on Sloppy Joe's, then located at 428 Greene Street in Key West (currently the site of Captain Tony's Saloon). Freddy is Hemingway's tribute to Sloppy Joe's owner, Joe "Josie" Russell, owner of the *Anita,* which the author chartered in the summers of 1932 and 1933. This reference is the only one to spell Freddie's with an *-ie*. All future mentions will refer to *Freddy's*. That this inconsistency remains in the novel eighty years after its publication suggests how little editorial concern it has received over the decades. This is one of the many errata testifying to the need for a "corrected" text.

91:2 **Where's Juan?** This reference exemplifies Hemingway's habit of introducing tangential details into the story that receive little to no explanation. Not until 102:21 do we learn from Albert that Juan's last name is Rodriguez. Bee-lips's shady relationship with his client is not clarified in either passage. At 91:5–8 Albert will repeat Harry's charge that the lawyer ratted Juan out to "them"—law enforcement, presumably—so he can defend the man, but the exact nature of Juan's crime is not stated. All we learn of the Cuban is that he is "a poor stinking Gallego," a thief who would "steal from his own mother" and a patsy even to his own lawyer (102:22–23). Given Bee-lips's statement that he has a job for Juan, Hemingway seems to imply the attorney intends to offer his client the smuggling job before deciding to offer it instead to Harry Morgan.

91:9 **Balls to you:** According to *The New Partridge Dictionary of Slang and Unconventional English,* this profane slang expression, which "registers an impatient dismissal of anything specified," is a British colloquialism dating to circa 1923 (Partridge 81). Its UK origins again demonstrate Hemingway's fondness for mother-country idioms and expressions, from "My word yes a most unpleasant business" in "On the Quai at Smyrna" (*CSS* 64) and "potted" in the chapter 3 vignette of *In Our Time* (*CSS* 77) to *The Sun Also Rises*'s "chap" (36) and the great white hunter Robert Wilson's stiff-upper-lipisms in "The Short Happy Life of Francis Macomber" ("damn fine lion," *CSS* 7). "Balls to you" also appears in Hemingway's fictionalized memoir of his 1953–54 African safari, posthumously published in 1999 in condensed form as *True at First Light* (149) and then as 2005's expanded *Under Kilimanjaro* (178). Speaking the phrase in both versions of that fictionalized memoir is a character dubbed "G. C." for "Gin Crazed," a far more comic figure than the noir foil Bee-lips functions as.

91:16–20 **Just then the old man with the long gray hair . . . comes in:** Hemingway did not employ tense shifts in part 2 of *To Have and Have Not*. When the time came to write part 3, however, he returned to the oral storytelling–derived technique he had used in part 1 (See 10:22). Two such tense shifts appear on the first page of part 3. In addition to this paragraph, the opening sentence includes one as the "tall thin lawyer . . . comes" into Freddy's (91:2).

92:1 **What happened to your arm?** This is our first notice that Harry's right arm has been amputated since the timeframe of part 2. As Susan F. Beegel notes, the missing limb is one of the more obvious motifs of "the romantic tradition of piracy" that links *To Have and Have Not* to the popular genre of swashbuckling fiction (109). In fact, the physical disfiguration may be second only to Harry Morgan's name—which affiliates him with the English pirate Sir *Henry* Morgan (ca. 1635–1688; see 37:13)—in associating the rumrunner with buccaneers and corsairs. As Beegel writes, "Amputeeism is a common element in pirate literature, and has a firm basis in grim historical reality" (111). The prosthetic hook Harry will don in chapter 12 (115:19–20) inevitably reminds readers of Peter Pan's nemesis, Captain James Hook, in J. M. Barrie's Lost Boys fantasies. An even earlier amputee pirate is Long John Silver, in Robert Louis Stevenson's *Treasure Island* (1883). Beegel cites a portion of Stevenson's well-known letter to author William Henley (1849–1903), his inspiration for Silver, to suggest what Hemingway may have intended for the deformity to dramatize about Harry's character: "It was the sight of your maimed strength and masterfulness that begot Long John Silver," Stevenson insisted, "the idea of the maimed man, ruling and dreaded by the sound, was entirely taken from you" (113). Although Harry will expose great vulnerability to his wife about being a "maimed man," his conversation with Bee-lips demonstrates how sarcasm and black humor allow him to transform the disability into a mark of tough-guy "masterfulness." When the lawyer asks what happened to his arm, Harry replies, "I didn't like the look of it, so I cut it off" (92:4).

Inevitably, Harry's missing arm serves as a symbol for speculation about the meaning of loss, whether to a body or to a text. (The hasty revision of *To Have and Have Not* invites all manner of comparison to amputation.) It should be noted that had Hemingway not cut much of part 4 of the original text, Harry's arm would not have been the text's only severed limb. Jani Scandura calls attention to a reference in the manuscript's twenty-eighth chapter, "Interlude (in Cuba)," to a dismembered arm found in a shark (presumably from a victim of President Machado's habit of feeding dissidents to the predators): "[The severed arm] becomes a sign of rebellion, a sign of a revolution not wholly squelched, a sign of an encrypted voice rising from the grave. Hemingway collapses the language of tyranny, of capital, into the language of the body." Unfortunately, in excising this passage, Hemingway also capitulated to "the complete tyranny [of capitalism] that the novel anticipates"—that is, he failed to allow this particular missing limb to make "noise in its silence" by revealing "the threat of difference in a repressive, homogenous society, the threat of being anything other than artifice, than a prosthetic illusion" (116–17). Readers perhaps unpersuaded by Scandura's exploration of the metaphorical connections between amputation and repression will nevertheless appreciate the link she makes to Waldo Peirce's Key West scrapbooks, which include a photo of a severed arm found in the belly of a shark during one of the painter's early 1930s fishing trips with Hemingway (119).

93:2–3 **Big Lucie's daughter:** Hemingway hints that Big Lucie is a well-known madam in Key West. Locals would recognize the name as a reference to Big Annie's, a popular brothel located on the corner of Howe Street and Division (now Truman Avenue) in the 1930s. At least one source cites a different location for Annie's, however. Stetson Kennedy includes in his memoir/folklore guide to the city, *Grits and Grunts*, a transcript of an oral history from a local named Hector Barosso, who remembers Big Annie's operating on Stock Island (74), which lies immediately east of Key West across Cow Key Channel and was then the site of a "reasonably sporty little nine-hole golf course" (Jennings 100). Nevertheless, most sources list Annie's and another fondly remembered brothel, the Square Roof, in the same breath as Sloppy Joe's, the Havana-Madrid Club, and other popular dives on the city's western side (see Williams 255).

93:6–9 ain't gonna let no girls out on the streets after six o'clock at night and no girls in any of the places: Whether the Key West Administration or Monroe County issued a curfew to curtail the visibility of prostitution in the city's tourist centers is uncertain. No existing memoir or recollection of Depression-era Key West references such an ordinance; nor is there any mention of such a municipal law in any of the legible copies of the *Key West Citizen* maintained in the Monroe County Public Library's Florida Research Room. (Many of the issues from 1935–36 in the microfilm rolls are marred by splotches and blots that render them illegible.) Given that Hemingway drew from contemporaneous events in Key West, such as the sewer project and the strike Albert will shortly reference (see 94:3), it seems highly unlikely he would invent this detail, especially since it serves no dramatic purpose in the plot.

Regardless of whether the curfew is fact or fiction, the life of a Key West "sporting girl" was hardly glamorous. Only four years after *To Have and Have Not* was published, the city was rocked by the murder of a prostitute at yet another local brothel, this one called Alice's, also known as the Gold Chalice, instead of Annie's (Kennedy *Grits* 65). According to Abraham H. Gibson, "The young woman was strangled with a pair of silk underwear, which were pulled tight around her neck and held fast with a toothbrush" (410). In 1942 a former seaman named Richard Patrick Leroy was tried for the homicide but was acquitted. The United States Navy placed enormous pressure on the city to close the city's brothels, which met with opposition from the citizenry. As Gibson writes:

> many worried that the navy's decision would merely decentralize the industry, driving "the seven known brothels into perhaps fifty unknown." Nor would it do any good to exile prostitutes, one citizen observed, because "others will be here to take their place in a few days, augmenting the present crowd of women that infest all the bars up and down Duval Street." Citizens like J. R. Deland insisted that an island full of frustrated sailors was capable of anything, and thus defended prostitution in the name of family values. "Take away their bawdy houses and

you leave them no place to satisfy their beastial desires except in some dark lane with your innocent daughters," he warned. (413)

93:15 **fine you fifteen dollars:** As per above, it is not clear whether Hemingway invented only the specifics of the fine or the entire law itself. Again, given his tendency to incorporate historical details from the surrounding cultural context into his novels, it seems likely that there was indeed, for however short of a time, a $15 fine levied on the city's sporting girls to keep them out of tourists' sight.

94:3 **Digging the sewer:** Before Julius F. Stone Jr.'s arrival in Key West in July 1934, no municipal sewer system existed. Waste facilities on the island consisted exclusively of outhouses and cesspits, a noxious reality that posed a serious threat to the Key West Administration's efforts to establish the city as a tourist destination. Accordingly, the KWA sought funding from the Works Progress Administration for a joint water/sewer effort budgeted at $1,302,126.93 ($22,536,395.51 in 2016 dollars). Negotiations for the project, which would employ hundreds of laborers to remove paving bricks and existing streetcar tracks along thoroughfares before installing pipeline, took more than a year to finalize. The *Key West Citizen* reported the project's approval on 30 September 1935 ("Key West Sewerage Project") and the comptroller's release of the funds on 24 October ("Sewerage Project Approved"). Work began on 4 November ("Forces Start Work Today"). By 12 December the *Citizen* was reporting that more than 1,894 feet of streetcar "trackage" had been torn out ("Shows Activities Thus Far"). The 21,654 bricks removed by then were hauled to the naval station on the western end of the island, where—in a famous bit of Key West lore—Hemingway would later purchase 19,000 of them for a grand total of $38 for handyman Toby Bruce to build the brick wall that surrounds 907 Whitehead Street. A report on the water/sewer project is included in the U.S. House of Representatives Subcommittee on Appropriations's four-part *Investigation and Study of the Work Progress Administration* (1940).

94:24–27 **Whitehead Street . . . White Street:** Hemingway's directions can be confusing here. Since White Street lies at almost a dozen blocks to the east of Whitehead Street (running parallel), reaching it by taking a left from Whitehead means Harry and Albert drive south on the latter thoroughfare (thus taking them past the Hemingway home at 907 Whitehead), although the description of the trek ("drove up," "head of the street," "head of the town") would seem to suggest they ride north. Turning off Whitehead at its "head" presumably means they take South Street to White Street, whereupon they would dead-end onto the beach just east of the Casa Marina Hotel, driving away from it onto East Roosevelt Boulevard (today *South* Roosevelt).

95:10 **Bee-lips:** This is our first mention of the nickname of the lawyer who wants to hire Harry. (We do not learn his last name, Simmons, until 102:8, nor his first until 250:18.) Since Carlos Baker's 1969 biography, scholars have noted the character is based upon the prominent Key West attorney and politician George Gray Brooks Jr. (1900–1969) (*A Life* 295). According to McLendon, the attorney first met the writer shortly after the latter's arrival in the Keys while Hemingway fished from the ferry docks at No Name Key, with Brooks concerned that this stranger may have been a bootlegger. Supposedly, Hemingway sought out Charles Thompson at Brooks's recommendation (26–27).

Most commentators follow Baker's lead by either insisting or insinuating that "Bee-lips" was "drawn to the life" (*A Life* 295) with little fictional invention. The claim would not necessarily apply to size, for while Simmons is described as "tall" in the opening line of this chapter, Brooks was diminutive. Given what a shady presence the barrister is in the book, the "drawn-to-life" claim hardly bodes well for the character of Brooks, who at various points in his career served as both district attorney and Monroe County state attorney. A pair of *Key West Citizen* articles from summer 1935 suggests how Bee-lips's felonious tendencies may not have been entirely fictional. On 5 July Brooks was arraigned on a charge of embezzling from a client and paid a $200 bail bond ("Brooks Given Hearing Today"). On 12 July, a jury acquitted him after deliberating the case for exactly twenty minutes ("Jury Acquits").

McLendon's biography offers a colorful account of the alcoholic Brooks, based largely on interviews with Joe "Josie" Russell's son-in-law William Cates, who tended bar at Sloppy Joe's in this period. According to Cates, bar patrons dubbed Brooks "Bee-lips" "because of the curious way he wrapped his lips around the Chesterfields he chain-smoked" (152). The lawyer was fond of "rigging," or pranking, Hemingway, sometimes whispering to gay men that the author shared their orientation so they would hit on Papa, other times informing military personnel that he bad-mouthed the armed forces so they would challenge him to a fistfight (152–58). Just how true these stories are is anyone's guess; at least one aspect of the pair's friendship is documentable, however. On 20 February 1937 as Hemingway prepared to depart for the Spanish Civil War, he drew up a pair of warranty deeds transferring ownership of 907 Whitehead Street first to Charles Thompson, who, with a second transfer, would immediately "sell" the property to Pauline for one dollar. This straw-man transaction was likely designed to prevent the Hemingway house from being probated should Ernest die abroad. Brooks's name appears on both deeds as witness; he may have drawn them up. The paperwork was never submitted to the court, however, and its existence was not widely known until it was auctioned to private collectors in 2008 ("Original Ernest Hemingway Signed Deed").

Photographs of Brooks have not been located. Although images of his father, George G. Brooks Sr., are accessible through Ancestry.com, none featuring the younger Brooks are currently online. Something of the lawyer's appearance is discernable in

Erik Smith's 1933 painting of Hemingway and his island friends, in which Brooks appears in profile. There are also circulating privately sketches done by Betty Bruce, wife of Hemingway handyman Toby Bruce, that capture him in his later years. One final bit of Brooks lore circulates in Key West to this day: when he died, the lawyer apparently collapsed on Fleming Street, almost directly in front of the Monroe County Public Library, which holds a copy of the galleys of *To Have and Have Not*.

95:12 **Since the revolution:** The reference places the winter section of the novel squarely in the post-Machado era. Hemingway will not specify an exact timeframe, however, preferring instead to conflate events from early 1934 to mid-1935. The decision may reflect the bewildering instability roiling in the Cuban government in this period: in the five short months between Machado's fall on 12 August 1933 and Carlos Mendieta's Batista-backed installment as "provisional" president on 18 January 1934, no fewer than five separate men led the country: military leader Alberto Herrera y Franchi, who held office for two days, 12–13 August 1933; Carlos Manuel de Céspedes y Quesada of the ABC party (13 August–5 September); Ramón Grau of the Cuban Revolutionary Party (heading a short-termed "executive committee" from 5 to 10 September before taking the reins for a hundred-day government until 15 January); Carlos Hevia, who succeeded Grau for three days (15–18 January); and Manuel Márquez Sterling, named provisional president for a few measly hours on 18 January. Mendieta, representing the National Union party, remained in office until 11 December 1935, at which point he was replaced by a succession of no fewer than three more men before Fulgencio Batista's 1940 election. The leadership instability helps explain why Cuban revolutionaries still run amok in Key West even after Machado's fall.

95:17 **sub-base:** Harry's boat is tied up at Naval Station Key West, located in the current site of Truman Annex on the island's western side. The base dates back to 1823, when a military presence in the Keys was deemed necessary to combat piracy. (The adjacent Fort Zachary Taylor, built between 1845 and 1866, was an army installation until shortly after World War II, when it was transferred to the navy.) The submarine basin is a 2,100-square-yard docking facility constructed in 1917 at a cost of $1.78 million to protect Mexican oil supply lines from German seizure during World War I. Despite the strategic importance of watercraft during the First World War, the navy actually put more emphasis in Key West on air-combat training, establishing a thriving naval air station on Trumbo Point upon leasing that site from the Florida East Coast Railway. After World War I, the sub-basin was all but abandoned. The commanders' quarters at the Navy Station—which in 1946 would become Harry S. Truman's "Little White House"—weren't even occupied between 1932 and 1939. During this time, base personnel consisted solely of seventeen radio operators. The minimal staffing is one reason Hemingway was able obtain permission to moor the *Pilar* in the basin free of charge during these years. The sub base was not only more convenient to Whitehead Street than Garrison Bight and other island docks, its breakwater also provided greater protection against hurricanes.

For better or worse, Hemingway wasn't the only island resident who had designs on the basin. One of the first initiatives of Julius F. Stone Jr. and the KWA in 1934 was to convert the space into a municipal yacht marina. In many ways, chapter 24 of *To Have and Have Not* (227–46) is a protest against this initiative, with Hemingway depicting the yachtsman as haughtily disrespectful of locals gathered to watch the arrival of the Coast Guard cutter with the dying Harry Morgan aboard. Residents with a more vested interest in Key West's economic renewal welcomed the wealthy "haves" into the facility, however. Throughout the mid-1930s, the *Key West Citizen* regularly interviewed yacht owners docking at the sub-basin about its quality, both to promote the site and bolster civic pride. A 14 January 1935 article describes the owner of the *Paula Louise* declaring the city his home port now that it can boast suitable mooring: "Now that the setting [the refurbished basin] pleases, the climate is just right, all other things are in accord with his ideals of comfort and there are perfect facilities for securing all things necessary he has decided to stay where the fish are" ("Owner of Yacht Will Make Key West Port Home").[1] A 29 January 1935 headline makes the point even more succinctly: "Owner of Yacht Says Sub Base Fine Anchorage." The KWA aggressively promoted the basin in yachting periodicals outside of Key West. A December 1935 issue of *Motorboating* reads as if it were copied straight from a press release: "Within the basin proper there are available for docking six piers, each 300 feet long and on both sides of each pier there is an 18 foot depth of water. The piers are eight feet above the low water mark. For the accommodation of boats of low-board, portable ladders are hung from the piers. . . . A nominal fee of one cent per overall foot is charged for a day's docking at the basin" ("Excellent Yacht Basin" 111).

Perhaps the most intriguing document relating to the sub-basin's conversion is a letter to Hemingway from Arnold Samuelson, the aspiring writer who rode the rails to Key West in spring 1934 to learn from Papa after reading "One Trip Across" in *Cosmopolitan*. Samuelson spent that summer and fall serving as Hemingway's mate while fishing in Cuba and as boat caretaker whenever the *Pilar* moored at the basin. The young man abruptly departed the island, however; a year later Samuelson wrote his former employer to confess his hasty exit was the result of trouble with a local girl with whom he had trysted aboard the cabin cruiser:

> It was a cold blooded sexual affair and when she was satisfied she left and I did not ask her to come back or tell her to stay away. One dark night a month later she came again and I let her on board. The rubber was irritating, a heavy brand sold downtown, and she asked me to throw it away, which I did, because she seemed to know her stuff and I had a prophylactic, but I pulled it out before the discharge. She went away to visit in Tampa for a few weeks and when she came back the naval

yard had been turned into a yacht basin with night watchman and I told her she couldn't come on board any more. That wasn't what she wanted. She came to tell me she was pregnant. (qtd. in Hendrickson 178)

For understandable reasons, this story isn't told in Samuelson's posthumously published memoir, *With Hemingway: A Year in Key West and Cuba* (1981). Instead, there the author explains his departure from Key West by claiming that after "the Key West naval yard was changed into the city yacht basin . . . three shifts of WPA watchmen were employed to be responsible for the boats, so it was no longer necessary to have anyone sleep on the *Pilar*" (179–80). The existence of Samuelson's letter wasn't widely known until Paul Hendrickson excerpted it in *Hemingway's Boat* (2011). If mention of the basin's conversion to commercial use seems incongruous in such a personal context, the reference suggests how Samuelson associated its transformation with the loss of innocence the pregnancy represented for him.

The basin's days as a yacht marina ended in 1939, with the approach of World War II. The facility was closed to private craft on 11 September, three days after President Roosevelt declared a national emergency with Germany's invasion of Poland. Over the next six years, the navy would invest more than $30 million in construction on the island, with the basin and adjacent anchorage hosting some fourteen thousand ships by V-J Day in 1945 (Roth 48). The navy yard would remain operational until 1974, when most of the island's military facilities were decommissioned. The drawdown dealt a severe blow to the local economy, triggering the city's worst downturn since the Depression.

96:11 **I went out on strike against those wages:** With this line, Hemingway associates Albert Tracy with a specific walkout staged by Key West laborers on 3 December 1935. Relations between workers and the various alphabet agencies operating on the island had been stormy since the previous May, when the KWA announced a new wage scale for Fall 1935—when the Works Progress Administration (WPA) was set to assume responsibility for relief programs from the Federal Emergency Relief Administration (FERA). On 28 May a small group of workers protested at KWA headquarters, prompting WPA officials to raise the scale by a modest 10 percent. That August and September, despite this victory, workers were frustrated by the WPA's scattershot payroll disbursements, which were often late and cost each recipient a five-cent check-cashing fee because they weren't drawn on local banks. On 15 October 1935, two hundred workers walked out, citing the fee as one of four grievances. Besides a wage increase and a reduction in their 128-hour-per-month contracts, workers also demanded that the WPA make ice water available at project sites, an amenity FERA had provided but that the WPA insisted was beyond its budgetary abilities. The KWA agreed to supply the concession if workers returned to their jobs immediately, which they did, once promised their other demands would be reviewed. An envoy of Key West officials negotiated in person in Washington with WPA chief Harry Hopkins, but in early December, when talks dragged on, the workers struck. Led by a foreman named Luis Alvo, whom the WPA had fired for complaining about inadequate safety for his canal-digging crew, more than thirteen hundred of the fourteen hundred workers on the relief payroll joined the walkout (Long, "Workers" 53–61).

Had Hemingway chosen to delve deeper into the background of the strike, he could have made use of some colorful details. For starters, a racial component of the protest quickly emerged, with pro-WPA forces in the city accusing Alvo, a Cuban, of working against "American" (i.e., "white") interests. As the *Key West Citizen* reported on 6 December, the Ku Klux Klan attempted to threaten strikers back to work by parading along Division Street (now Truman Avenue) in full regalia. The *Citizen* implied the KKK cut an intimidating swath: "The figures in this [mob] were masked and hooded and called to mind days when men clothed in like habiliments was an ordinary sight in Key West" ("Large Number Attend" 1). The *Jacksonville Journal*, by contrast, described the turnout as consisting of "twenty-one men robed in sheets, with pillow cases on their heads . . . [who] carried revolvers in their hands . . . [followed by] a long line of people on bicycles and automobiles" (qtd. in Long, "Workers" 60). Either way, marchers proceeded to Chicha's—a bar mentioned in *To Have and Have Not* at 193:12—and announced on the establishment's blackboard the Klan's commitment to protecting any worker willing to cross the picket line and return to work. The group also proceeded to the corner of the street where Alvo lived but chose not to cross in front of his house when the strike leader was spotted brandishing pistols in his doorway. The very real threat of violence was a major reason Alvo promised city leaders he would call for ending the strike. By 9 December 1935, after the WPA agreed to another 10 percent increase, work had resumed on the city's many ongoing construction projects, including the sewer installation detail to which Albert Tracy was assigned.

Equally germane to *To Have and Have Not*, the walkout briefly brought Communist organizers to the island. After the strike ended, Alvo and sixteen other laborers aligned themselves with the Leftist National Workers Alliance, though their small numbers quickly doomed them to irrelevance. Nevertheless, when Albert accuses Harry of "talk[ing] like a radical" (96:29), it is easy to hear in Harry's angry reply ("I ain't no radical. . . . I'm sore" [97:1]) how accusations of Communist sympathies were used to minimize proletarian disgruntlement, even among workers.

96:23–25 starve you Conchs out of here so they can burn down the shacks and put up apartments and make this a tourist town: During the KWA's control of the island, Conchs were convinced that Julius F. Stone Jr. aimed to drive undesirable locals off the island to accommodate tourists. Since the real-estate boom of the 1990s drove housing prices in Key West up, no line from *To Have and Have Not* is today cited more often in the city.

97:6–7 You've got two arms and you've got two of something else. . . . I got those other two still: Again, far be it from Hemingway to miss the opportunity for a cojones reference.

98:16 Since when ain't you a Conch? Albert's comment is further internal evidence that Harry is a native Key Wester, despite references to his life as a policeman in Miami. Harry's answer ("Since the first good meal I ever ate") ties into stereotypes of Caribbean docility. As Harry implies, because no Conchs have "any guts," they are content to remain poor and exploited.

98:28–29 We turned into the runway and drove around to the back of the place: Harry has driven Albert to the Key West airport, still located today at 3491 South Roosevelt Boulevard, though a far more developed operation than it was in the mid-1930s. The bar where the meeting is held is based on Raul's Club, owned by Raul Vasquez (1890–1957), a legendary bootlegger-cum-entrepreneur who first came to infamy in the city for operating a clandestine speakeasy out of the back of his house at 1117 Duval Street. (The second floor of the house currently operates as the Speakeasy Inn.) Raul's Club opened in the 1930s at the location of the former Club Miramar; Vasquez owned it until the late 1940s, when health considerations forced him to sell. The bar and dance club garnered national press for its backyard marine garden, which included grouper trained to eat out of Vasquez's hand. The 1941 Federal Writers guide to the city describes the spectacle:

> Ripley in "Believe it or not" and Lowell Thomas, radio news commentator, have told the story of the domesticated fish which come when called to the side of the pool in the rear of the club, and take food from the owner's hands. An interesting part of the demonstration is the "side scratching." Without other persuasion than the promise of a morsel, a snapper, grouper, or muttonfish swims obediently to a submerged rock, stretches itself upon it, while the demonstrator strokes its side. The reward is a morsel of food which the demonstrator holds an inch or so above the fish's head. From its reclining position the fish flops into the air to snatch the food from the hand of the demonstrator. (*Guide* 95–96)

In this and preceding guides—including the one that famously irritated Hemingway in 1934 and inspired the article "The Sights of Whitehead Street: A Key West Letter" (*BL* 192–98)—Raul's Club is listed at No. 17 on lists of sites for tourists to visit.

Hemingway does not invest much detail in describing the "place" where Harry and Albert meet the terrorists. We pass through a kitchen into a backroom, without any reference to the popular dance floor and gambling rooms Raul's was known for, much less its marine garden. As such, readers unfamiliar with Raul's Club may assume the bar is little more than a dingy roadhouse. This impression is bolstered by

Albert's comments about Freda Richards, presumably the owner's wife. At 99:8–13, Albert mentions he knew Miss Richards when she worked in the city's tenderloin district as a "sporting" girl, or prostitute: "Two or three of the hardest working married women in town used to be sporting women and this was a hard working woman, I tell you that," Albert notes. McLendon reports a titillating bit of gossip, told to him by a "confidential source" (72), that "Miss Richards" was inspired by a local he dubs "Mavis Lee," a pseudonym for the proprietress of what is presumably Big Annie's (i.e., Big Lucie's in the novel). That the owner of one of the city's famous clubs would marry the owner of one of the city's most famous brothels seems a bit too good to be true, however. Raul Vasquez was divorced from his first wife, Concepcion, in 1936, according to the Florida Divorce Index, although he did not remarry until 1941.

99:9 **jungle town:** A racially derogatory reference to the Afro-Bahamian and Afro-Cuban district of Key West. The section encompasses Whitehead, Thomas, and Emma streets west to east bordered on the north by Southard and Angela streets and Virginia Street to the south. Before it was known as Jungle Town, the area was referred to as La Africa; today it goes by Bahama Village. The site most associated with Hemingway in this area is the Blue Heaven Billiard Parlor located on the corner of Thomas and Petronia. It was here the author refereed and sometimes even participated in boxing matches. Michael Pearson's *Imagined Places: Journeys into Literary America* (1991) includes a detailed, picturesque tour of Bahama Village led by Kermit "Shine" Forbes (1914–2000), whom Hemingway aficionados in Key West in the 1980s and 1990s often sought out due to his local fame as one of Hemingway's last living sparring partners at the Blue Heaven (166–77). Shine even makes a cameo in a 1997 video by rock star John Mellencamp for his Keys-inspired song, "Just Another Day."

99:16–17 **four Cubans:** As Steve Paul writes in his excellent article "Tropical Iceberg: Cuban Turmoil in the 1930s and Hemingway's *To Have and Have Not*," appreciating fully the backdrop of the Cuban revolution requires a reader "to know more than Hemingway delivers in the novel" (129). This need is nowhere truer than in the case of the identity of the Cubans with whom Harry negotiates inside this fictionalized version of Raul's Club. Whether by design or accident, this quartet of revolutionaries is virtually indistinguishable from the trio that approaches Harry Morgan in Havana in the opening pages of part 1. Just as in the scene at the Pearl of San Francisco Café, one terrorist is calm and rational (the first is never named, but the one here identifies himself as Emilio at 163:25), while his foil is dangerously hotheaded, if not sadistic (Pedro in chapter 1, and here Roberto, whose name we learn at 100:11). Had the original radicals not been gunned to death by Machado's *porra* on pages 6–7, a reader could be excused for assuming these are the same men.

Clues to their specific ideological orientation reveal, however, that in historical terms they come from politically dichotomous ends of the spectrum. Most critics agree that the trio in chapter 1 belonged to the ABC Party, which was right-wing and fascistic, although, as previously noted (see 4:24), at least one—Cuban scholar Mary Cruz—links them to the Directorio Estudiantil ("Selection" 92). This latter group is less ideologically obscure. As we discover in chapter 18's conversation between Harry and Emilio, they are extreme leftists—though they are *not* Communists, as Hemingway makes a point of specifying at 166:14.

As Paul notes, the Bradley portions of the novel that Hemingway cut in June 1937 *do* identify the affiliation of this latter group (136–37). In manuscript, Richard Gordon is introduced in chapter 21, reading an account of the bank robbery that costs Bee-lips, Albert, Harry, and all four Cubans their lives. Discussing the audacious crime with his wife, Helen, Gordon notes, "That's the Joven Cuba crowd did that. It's a wonderful story if anybody could write it. They stuck up the City Hall in Havana and they've been kidnapping all this last year to get money for this revolution. . . . They're the extreme left wing of the autenticos" (MS 31, item 204, folder 1, page 132). Gordon refers to the Authentic Cuban Revolutionary Party.

Founded by Antonio Guiteras (1906–1935), Joven Cuba ("Young Cuba") was established in May 1934 to oppose the increasing power of the military after Batista engineered the deposing of President Ramon Grau San Martin, in whose administration Guiteras served as interior minister. So radical was Joven Cuba's agenda that the U.S. State Department branded Guiteras "Cuba's Public Enemy No. 1," leading others to dub him the "John Dillinger of Cuba." The association with the infamous bank robber was not at all inappropriate; Gordon's mention of them in the manuscript refers to a daring 18 October 1934 heist Joven Cuba staged at Havana City Hall that netted the group more than $150,000 to finance its upheaval. While Guiteras was not directly involved in that action, he did participate in at least one kidnapping, on 3 April 1935, when the group successfully ransomed a member of a prominent pro-Machado family, Eutimio Falla Bonet, for $300,000. Guiteras was killed on 9 May 1935, but Joven Cuba carried off at least one more daring abduction, attempting to ransom railroad president Antonio San Miguel for upward of $500,000. This time the family refused to pay, and Miguel was released three days later. The failed plot spelled the end of Joven Cuba, which disintegrated within six months of Guiteras's death (Karol 70–81). Not surprisingly, during the Batista regime, Guiteras was vilified as a vainglorious hoodlum. Castro's followers lionized him, however, and in the aftermath of the 1959 revolution, he became a state-sanctioned hero, a proto-Castro figure, despite the fact that he was avowedly anti-Communist.

100:25 **Cabañas:** This small city sits west of Mariel. Its size made its harbor easier for agents to enter the country undetected than Mariel or Havana. Cabañas is the site from which the inspiration for *The Old Man and the Sea* launched his skiff (not Cojimar, as in the novel itself). See Hemingway's April 1936 *Esquire* column, "On the Blue Water: A Gulf Stream Letter":

> An old man fishing alone in a skiff out of Cabañas hooked a great marlin that, on the heavy sashcord handline, pulled the skiff out to the sea. Two days later the old man was picked up by fisherman sixty miles to the eastward, the head and forward part of the marlin lashed alongside. What was left of the fish, less than half, weighed eight hundred pounds. The old man had stayed with him a day, a night, a day and another night while the fish swam deep and pulled the boat. When he had come up the old man had pulled the boat up on him and harpooned him. Lashed alongside the sharks had hit him and the old man had fought them out alone in the Gulf Stream in a skiff, clubbing them, stabbing at them, lunging at them with an oar until he was exhausted and the sharks had eaten all that they could hold. He was crying in the boat when the fishermen picked him up, half crazy from his loss, and the sharks were still circling the boat. (*BL* 239–40)

102:7 **Where did you see her?** Harry discovers that Bee-lips has already taken the Cubans to the yacht basin to show them his boat. This not only makes him more suspicious of the lawyer's role in the plot but undercuts his own negotiating position. Hemingway hints that his hero had hoped to keep the boat's legal status from the Cubans, presumably because they could refuse to pay the $1,000 guaranty against the boat's seizure since it has already been seized.

102:15 **I never learned it:** As Mr. Sing did in part 1 (36:26), Harry pretends not to understand Spanish so he can make sure the revolutionaries are not conspiring against him. This habit is one of the recurring devices Hemingway employs to dramatize his characters' street smarts. Both Albert and Bee-lips know Harry understands the terrorists' conversations. Albert states it at 101:23–24, while Bee-lips's reaction, which Albert describes at 102:16–18, reveals not only his awareness but his amusement at Harry tricking the men ("He is so crooked himself that he's always pleased if people aren't telling the truth.")

104:2 **county road:** "Old County Road" was the local name for the four-mile stretch today known as Flagler Avenue, after Henry Flagler (1830–1913), the financier behind the Florida East Coast Railway. What inspired Hemingway to locate Albert's home here is unclear. According to 1935 Florida Census records, neither of the character's inspirations—Albert Pinder or Richard Hamilton Adams—resided on Old County Road in this period. Pinder lived at 1501 Seminary Street, five blocks north of County Road, while Adams's home was at 1030 James Street, near Garrison Bight.

104:7–8 **my old woman is giving me hell:** This brief scene between Albert and his (unnamed) wife serves as a contrast to the previous scene between Harry and Marie at the end of the spring section ("One Trip Across") and scenes to come at 125–28 (chapter 14).

NOTE

1. After the 1935 Labor Day Hurricane, yachting enthusiasts would have little choice but to dock at the sub base. Competing facilities in Long Key and Matecumbe were destroyed.

CHAPTER TEN

As with the preceding chapter's paratextual cue (*"Albert Speaking"*), this short, two-and-a-half page rumination identifies the center of consciousness with an italicized marker telling us who "speaks": *"Harry."* Hemingway likely thought this second notation was necessary to ensure that his audience did not assume the "I" here continued Albert's first-person narration from chapter 9. Instead, we are given a glimpse of Harry Morgan's thought process as he rationalizes his decision to run the terrorists to Cabañas ("I didn't ask for any of this and if you've got to do it you've got to do it" [105:3–5]). In terms of narrative mode, some readers might struggle to decide whether the chapter employs interior monologue or stream of consciousness. Harry's introspection is certainly as abrupt and jumpy as the latter can be ("I can't make a mistake. Not a mistake. Not one" [106:29–107:1]). What this one long paragraph lacks, however, is the free association that distinguishes stream of consciousness from other modes. Instead, the tone is deliberative. Harry plots to retrieve his boat from the authorities, then scrambles to remember if the Cubans betrayed any inclination to kill him once at sea and steal his boat. Because he intently weighs options and measures consequences ("I've got to think right all the time" [106:29]), the narration is properly categorized as *monologue intérieur*.

105:8–9 But I can't take no rummy nor no nigger: This is as close as Harry Morgan comes to mentioning Eddy Marshall and Wesley, his mates from parts 1 and 2, respectively.

105:18–19 Do you suppose that Bee-lips is so dumb he won't know that's what they'll do? Hemingway foreshadows Bee-lips's eventual fate, not revealed until 165:25–29.

106:1–2 I heard that word: By pretending not to speak Spanish, Harry has overheard the Cubans at the Richards' bar reveal the reason they need to hire a getaway boat. In keeping with his iceberg theory, Hemingway does not reveal what exactly what "that word" was. Harry simply refers to both the target and the plot itself as "it." ("If they do it they'll have to do it just when it closes" [106:2–3].) For readers, the first hint that a bank robbery is imminent will not come until chapter 16, when Hemingway will mention the First State Trust and Savings Bank (141:16).

106:3–4 **the coast guard plane down from Miami:** Hemingway refers here to the Coast Guard air station located on Dinner Key in Biscane Bay outside Miami, the closest departure point for an aircraft that could locate a boat escaping from Key West to Cuba in the mid-1930s. In chapter 18, the bank robbers will quiz Harry about whether a plane can "get here" from Miami before dark (157:5).

106:21–23 **Did any of them look like sailors? Did any of them seem like they were sailors?** Harry is convinced the Cubans will kill Bee-lips so as not to leave any living conspirators behind. Now he worries they intend to murder him and Albert at sea and steal his boat.

106:16 **Maybe Walton's:** This is the novel's only mention of Walton. Given the feminine pronoun ("I can hire her"), it would be interesting to know whether she was based a historical person. Unfortunately, census records for Key West in the 1930s are incomplete, and no telephone books were printed in the city during the Depression because of the economy. As a result, Walton, whoever she was or was based upon, seems lost to time.

CHAPTER ELEVEN

The opening of this chapter can seem a rehash of chapter 9 inasmuch as we return to Freddy's Bar to discover Harry Morgan trading further insults with Bee-lips as they work out minor details of their plan. About the only new information we learn from their conversation is that the crooked lawyer plans to leave Key West for good with his cut of the Cubans' money. The second half of this four-page interlude is more interesting. To steal his boat back from customs officials, Harry must sneak into the Navy sub-basin and cut the moorings, towing it out in the ebb tide by sculling in a rowboat. Harry and Bee-lips arrange to meet later, after the captain hides his craft on the far side of the island, but Harry is troubled by the degree to which the lawyer has been corrupted. Both men know somebody will die at the Cubans' hands—perhaps an innocent bystander—but only Harry is troubled by the inevitability.

108:3 **out at Richard's:** The singular possessive may lead readers to think Hemingway refers to a character with the first name of Richard—a confusing possibility, since we are yet thirty pages from meeting Richard Gordon. A greater likelihood is that Hemingway really means the plural possessive *Richards'* and simply misplaced the apostrophe. Although we never learn the specific name of the Raul's Club–inspired establishment where Harry, Bee-lips, and Albert meet with the Cuban quartet (98–103), that the former sporting woman greeting them there is named Freda Richards and is identified as the owner's wife makes this reading a logical assumption. The wayward apostrophe demonstrates once again how many textual errors there are to correct in *To Have and Have Not*.

108:5 **he says to Harry:** Another shift from past to present tense.

108:10–11 **Not since that law. Say, how long are they going to have that six o'clock business?** This is the third reference, following 93:6–9 and 93:15, to the municipal ordinance likely passed in the mid-1930s to keep prostitutes from propositioning tourists in the city's bars. Again, no specific substantiation of such a law has been discovered.

109:11–12 **You know they've been financing this revolution with kidnapping and the rest of it:** As previously noted, in 1935 Joven Cuba committed at least two bold kidnappings to finance its anti-Batista agenda, first successfully ransoming Eutimio Falla Bonet for $300,000 that April and then, after leader Antonio Guiteras's death in May, failing to secure the $500,000 demanded for seventy-eight-year-old Antonio San Miguel, president of the Guantanamo & Western Railway. Eight other members of Joven Cuba were violently detained in the ransoming of a young manufacturing heir named Paulino Gorostiza Jr. (see Paul 129–42).

110:25 **the Porter dock:** This wooden dock was formerly located at the northern end of Duval Street. It was owned by prominent Key West businessman William R. Porter (1873–1957), whose Porter Dock Company, a shipping concern, occupied 324 feet of frontage in this area. Porter Dock was open to the public and offered free docking and would thus hardly provide discreet cover for Harry to hide a boat wanted by customs agents.

111:12 **the cable schooner:** At this time, the schooner *John W. Atkins*, working for Western Union's International Ocean Telegraph Company division, operated in Key West repairing telegraph cables to Cuba. The ship was named after the company manager who on 25 December 1900 made the first successful international telephone call by reaching Havana over telephone line connected to existing telegraph wire. (The famous reply to Atkins's call was, "I don't understand you.") The *John W. Atkins* was captained by G. R. Steadman, who in 1939 assumed command of the *Atkins*'s replacement, the *Western Union,* the last large sailing vessel constructed in Key West. The *Western Union* was built by the same Thompson family whose scion Charles was Hemingway's closest friend and whose other son Karl inspired the character of Key West sheriff Roger Johnson in *To Have and Have Not.*

111:23–24 **He put his mouth on his own self all right:** This idiosyncratic expression appears to be Hemingway's invention. In saying Bee-lips "mouth[ed] himself" at 111:25–26 as well, Harry effectively says the lawyer has unknowingly revealed his true amorality. The odd phrase is part of a pattern of motifs throughout the novel related to the mouth and speaking, including the *lengua largas* references beginning at 4:20. The critic who comes closest to exploring this pattern is Jopi Nyman, who, in exploring the significance of Mr. Sing's cracked talk box (see 53:13–54:3), writes, "In [the novel] language provides the speaker with a particular position. For a hard-boiled character this position is both a sign and a site of power, which can be seen in emphasis on the control of language. In the end this control allows one to survive, and survival is connected to individualism, to the privileging of the acting subject" (159). Unlike Harry, Bee-lips lacks this innate control, exposing too much of himself with language, which allows him to be manipulated by the Cubans.

CHAPTER TWELVE

After a chapter that feels as if the narrative wheels are beginning to spin in place, we are given a shocking and wholly unexpected glimpse into Harry Morgan's private life. Indeed, chapter 12 includes one of the most controversial and notorious scenes in all of Hemingway, one at once kinkier *and* more romantic than the sexual perversion William Faulkner exploits in *Sanctuary* (1931). For all his bluster about cojones, Harry has lost confidence in the bedroom and worries that his amputated arm renders him an inadequate lover. His wife, Marie, reassures him of his manliness by demonstrating the erotic gratification she can derive from his stump. Of course, given the censorship strictures of the 1930s, Hemingway cannot explicitly picture the Morgans' lovemaking, and the resulting elusiveness of Marie's mattress talk ("Go ahead. Go ahead now. . . . Hold it there. Hold it. Hold it now. Hold it" [114:5]) raises legitimate questions about how adept the author was at depicting amorous intimacy. Despite the sensationalism of the scene, an interior monologue from Marie demonstrates that the couple's relationship is healthy and positive, certainly more so than any other marriage in the novel. The happiness in the Morgan home, even amid the struggles of the Depression, documents for readers what Harry has to lose by serving as the Cubans' getaway pilot.

112:26 searching for him and then her hand on him: As the subsequent dialogue implies ("Do you want to? . . . Do you remember when we'd do it asleep?" [112:28, 113:1–2]), Harry's wife, Marie, is touching his penis. The awkward scene that follows dramatizes a reality that even the staunchest aficionado must sometimes acknowledge: Hemingway's sex scenes are more often than not embarrassingly bad. In his classic *Love and Death in the American Novel* (1960), Leslie A. Fiedler suggests why via a contrast to F. Scott Fitzgerald, the "laureate" of the petting or necking party:

> For Fitzgerald, "love" was essentially yearning and frustration; and there is consequently little consummated genital love in his novels. . . . Hemingway, on the other hand, is much addicted to describing the sex act. It is the symbolic center of his work: a scene to which he recurs when nostalgically evoking his boyhood as "Up in Michigan"; illustrating the virtues of the sturdy poor as in *To Have and Have Not;*

reflecting on civil strife and heroism as in *For Whom the Bell Tolls;* or projecting the fantasies of a man facing old age as in *Across the River and into the Trees.* There are, however, no women in his books! In his earlier fictions, Hemingway's descriptions of the sexual encounter are brutal, in later ones unintentionally comic; for in no case, can he quite succeed in making his females human, and coitus performed with an animal, a thing, or a wet dream is either horrible or ridiculous. (316)

Subsequent critics have challenged this assumption by noting that Brett Ashley, in *The Sun Also Rises,* Jig in "Hills Like White Elephants," and even Marie Morgan possess emotional complexity, which is the first breath of life that makes a character seem "human" to a reader. Nevertheless, even staunch Hemingway defenders such as Carl P. Eby are hard pressed to deny that when it comes to sexuality "Hemingway's women are always infused with aspects of masculine desire and fantasy" (*Hemingway's Fetishism* 34). One could argue that Marie's worship of Harry's penis is one such aspect. By the time Hemingway has this devoted wife cooing over her husband's endowment ("They don't know what I've got. They won't never know what I've got" [113:12–13])—a line made even ickier by the fact that "they" refers to the Morgans' daughters, whom Harry fears the couple's lovemaking will wake—Marie can seem a rather transparent dream of phallic thrall and subjection. However, she could also be a loving wife acting out this fantasy in order to buck up her maimed husband's masculinity. Ultimately, the problem with Hemingway's sex scenes may not be the debatable reality of his female characters as much as the language of intimacy. What can render his representations of coitus "ridiculous" are the interjections by which Marie and other women voice their responses to sexual stimulation: "Ah, Harry. That's it's. Ah, you honey" (113:13–14). And later: "There. There. There" (113:26–27). These recall the artless murmuring Hemingway requires of Liz Coates in "Up in Michigan," even if Liz is voicing pain instead of pleasure: "Oh, Jim. Jim. Oh" (*CSS* 62). That said, Hemingway has fared no better with critics for trying to poeticize sexuality. None of his lines is more mocked than Robert Jordan's infamous postcoital question to Maria in *For Whom the Bell Tolls,* "Did thee feel the earth move?" (160).

113:8 **a flipper on a loggerhead:** A loggerhead is a turtle distinguished from other members of the Chelonioidea superfamily by its size (it is the largest of the turtle species) and flippers. Loggerheads were abundant in the waters around Key West, although they were never as profitable as the smaller green turtles that made up the bulk of the late nineteenth-century turtling industry. Today they are protected from butchering by the Endangered Species Act. Bryan Christy's nonfiction crime account, *The Lizard King: The True Crimes and Passions of the World's Greatest Reptile Smugglers* (2008), includes an illuminating chapter called "Law of the Jungle" on prosecuting loggerhead poachers, many of whom behave as if they could be Harry Morgan's grandchildren.

113:10 **coot:** As much as it may sound like Conch slang, the verb *coot* meaning *to copulate* is actually an accepted scientific term for turtle mating. Its sanctioned usage dates back to British physician Henry Stubbe's 1667 article, "Observations made on a Voyage from England to the Canbee Islands." Stubbe likely learned the word during his brief tenure as His Majesty's Physician for Jamaica, from 1661 to 1665.

113:21 **nurse shark:** When Marie asks, "[D]id you ever do it with a nigger wench?" (113:17–18), Harry compares the experience to handling this species of shark, known scientifically as *Ginglymostoma cirratum*. Nurse sharks are distinguished by their small mouths and deep throat cavities, which cause them to consume their prey by sucking at their food like suckling infants. Whether Hemingway means to imply that black women are sexually omnivorous or whether he intends a specific fellatio connotation is unclear and, in the end, irrelevant. Either way, the passage is another lamentable lapse into racism. Morrison analyzes this passage, seeing within it a basic antithesis between the "devouring" animal and traditional notions of femininity as "nurturing" and "nursing," effectively alienating black women from language (85).

114:2 **I've had that thing:** Critics generally interpret this line as implying Marie has had a hysterectomy. See both Miriam B. Mandel (467) and Kim Moreland (83). The suggestion nicely reinforces the bond between the couple, with Marie's surgery paralleling Harry's amputation.

114:5 **Put the stump there. Hold it there. Hold it. Hold it now. Hold it:** The text implies that Harry brings Marie to orgasm with the nub of his lost arm.

114:11–12 **a hotel in Miami:** Marie does not acknowledge Harry's law-enforcement stint in Miami, suggesting that the Morgans vacationed on the mainland at some point, though whether "just like we used to" means before or after her husband served on the police force is unclear.

114:24 **I'm lucky, she was thinking:** Hemingway introduces the first of two passages detailing Marie Morgan's inner thoughts. This one paragraph of interior monologue is far less famous than the five pages of stream of consciousness that will end the novel, but it is an important humanizing moment, helping readers envision Marie as a fully dimensional character. Doing so is a necessity, given that in chapter 19 Richard Gordon will glimpse Marie and completely misjudge her (176–77). Through these passages, Hemingway effectively trains his audience not to "misread" the have-nots as the haves do. Of course, an argument can be made that the author fails at this, for the novel's rampant racism reveals how Hemingway lacks the empathy toward African American, Afro-Cuban, and Chinese characters he expects readers to develop for the Morgans.

115:20–21 Harry wore a hook strapped to his right arm: This is our first sight of Harry wearing his hook. As previously noted at 92:1, this is one of the more obvious images linking our hero to the pirate tradition.

116:12–13, 15 Listen, are you letting your hair grow out? . . . You keep it like it is: Harry's preference for short hair firmly integrates him in the tradition of Hemingway heroes who like their women vaguely androgynous. In addition to Marie, the expatriate wives of "Cat in the Rain" (1923) and "The Sea Change" (1931), Brett Ashley in *The Sun Also Rises,* Maria in *For Whom the Bell Tolls,* and, most famously, Catherine Bourne in the posthumously published *The Garden of Eden* (1986) are just a few of the women who are close-cropped if not completely shorn. Additionally, Catherine Barkley in *A Farewell to Arms* expresses a desire for short hair (292–93). The motif has been exhaustively discussed since the late 1980s. Although it functions differently in each text, the overall idea is best expressed by Mark Spilka: "Hair was for Hemingway the public expression of his own private obsession with androgyny; his easy, imaginative access to a women's manipulative, talkative, stylistically inventive powers; his secret envy of her breasts and womb; his confessed desire to rest confident in her supine passivity; and his honest awareness of her oppression by men much like himself" (*Quarrel* 291). Spilka's cleverly named chapter, "Hemingway's Barbershop Quartet," is worth examining for how extensively this fetish operates (279–314). See also Eby's *Hemingway's Fetishism* (72–87). In *To Have and Have Not,* Marie's short hair is less a sign of her androgyny or gender fluidity than of the couple's symbiotic relationship.

CHAPTER THIRTEEN

With yet *another* chapter set in Freddy's Bar centering around yet *another* unpleasant exchange between Harry Morgan and Bee-lips, we begin to appreciate more fully how the repetition of scenes and stylistic devices erodes part 3's dramatic tension. The complicating action should ratchet up the pressure on Harry. After customs agents grill him about his missing boat, he learns from Bee-lips that his bête noire, Frederick Harrison—the "alphabet man" from part 2 and Hemingway's fictional stand-in for Julius F. Stone Jr.—has discovered via an anonymous WPA informant where the vessel is hidden. As the men speak, authorities are on their way to reseize it.

With Harry's trip and the much-needed $200 the Cubans have agreed to pay the struggling charter-boat captain now in jeopardy, we should feel our main protagonist's desperation intensify. Yet Hemingway stages this chapter completely from the exterior, prohibiting us from witnessing any internal aspect of Harry's reaction to this gut-punching news. We only see him lash out at the lawyer with the same insults volleyed in previous scenes ("You're poison. . . . You're like a buzzard" [121:7–8]). As Bee-lips reminds Harry who did him the favor of landing him this work, readers may begin to sympathize with Virginia Woolf's 1927 complaint that Hemingway sometimes suffered from a "tendency to flood the page with unnecessary dialogue," resulting in a "lack of sharp, unmistakable points by which we can take hold of the story": "When fictitious people are allowed to speak it must be because they have something so important to say that it stimulates the reader to do rather more than his share of the work of creation. But, although Mr. Hemingway keeps us under the fire of dialogue constantly, his people, half the time, are saying what the author could say much more economically for them" (qtd. in Meyers, *Critical Heritage* 106).

For readers who feel swept away by the "flood" of dialogue, one "sharp, unmistakable point" we may fail to "take hold of" is the shift in atmosphere that occurs in this chapter. It is an important shift that will culminate in Richard Gordon's bizarre encounter with the veterans from the Matecumbe work camps in chapter 22 (200–19). With a seemingly pointless conversation between Freddy's patron Big Rodger and a Cuban taxi driver called Hayzooz (119–20), Hemingway introduces an aura of absurdity that will make Key West seem increasingly hallucinatory and grotesque—no longer merely hardboiled in its desperation, but surreal and macabre, too. The chapter ends with Harry taking the only available step to make his trip across. Over a Chesterfield cigarette, the captain asks to charter the boat of bar owner Freddy Wallace, putting the men's friendship at severe risk.

118:16 **Don't get plugged:** See 10:17.

119:6 **snotty:** A favorite colorful word of Hemingway's. It will also appear in Marie Morgan's final description of Harry, at 258:1. In Hemingway's other work, *snotty* appears as early as "The Battler" (1924), in which addled boxer Ad Francis confronts Nick Adams: "Who the hell do you think you are? You're a snotty bastard. You come in here where nobody asks you and eat a man's food and when he asks to borrow a knife you get snotty" (CSS 101). It appears fourteen years later, in the Spanish Civil War story "Night Before Battle," in which the term describes the waiters at a restaurant operated by an anarchist syndicate because they are "all over-tipped" (CSS 449). In *The Sun Also Rises* Jake and Bill Gorton use it to characterize a German waiter at the Hotel Montoya during the Pamplona San Fermin, mostly to defer their own lurking awareness that they are behaving as inconsiderate tourists (214). According to Carlos Baker, Hemingway used the word in the same period to acknowledge to Sherwood Anderson that *The Torrents of Spring*, his parody of the author, was a graceless act for an emerging writer who had benefitted from a mentor's help (*Writer as Artist* 42). In fact, at least in this case, the word was actually "snooty" (SL 206). A decade later, he would admit to Maxwell Perkins that his own pugnacity had soured literary critics on his work: "I have been very snotty and [critics] hate you for that too" (SL 471). During World War II, he would claim to have killed a "snotty SS kraut" general who refused to surrender German escape routes (qtd. in Reynolds, *Final Years* 205). Perhaps most tellingly, the word appears in Robert Jordan's interior monologue in *For Whom the Bell Tolls* as a warning against feeling superior to the father he considers a *cobarde*, or coward: "Don't be snotty too soon. And then don't be snotty at all. We'll see what sort of juice you have tomorrow" (339).

119:14–120:12 **Big Rodger, Hayzooz, Sweetwater:** The conversation between Sloppy Joe's patron Rodger and Cuban cab driver Jesus, or "Hayzooz," as Hemingway insists on spelling it, may just be the example par excellence of a gratuitous passage in the novel. The only real narrative purpose to Rodger's attempt to tease Hayzooz about the paternity of his new bride's child is to dramatize what Alfred Kazin called "the noisy, shabby . . . rancor and tumult of all [these] human wrecks" residing on a "great white stretch of beach promising everything and leading nowhere" (Stephens, *Critical Reception* 175). "Leading nowhere" is a fairly accurate description of the men's exchange, for the conversation only hints at the disarming absurdity of the later scene set in Freddy's featuring the discombobulated vets building the

Overseas Highway (200–18). What makes the joke here ineffective is that it needs explaining: Hayzooz negates Rodger's ribbing by insisting his wife's baby is his (as in his possession) regardless of whether it is "his" biologically, because when "you buy the cow" you "get the calf," too. Whether Big Rodger, Hayzooz, or Sweetwater—the friend of Jesus's who is also identified as a local "character"—are based on real Sloppy Joe's patrons has not been documented.

119:29–30 **carta del oro:** Literally, "gold card," but here it is the label phrase used to describe top-shelf Bacardi.

120:19–20 **WPA trucks . . . building the fish camp out at Boca Chica:** WPA refers to the Works Progress Administration (WPA), a central alphabet agency in Roosevelt's New Deal program that employed some 8.5 million different workers over the course of its lifespan (1934–41), including upward of 3 million at its 1938 peak. The organization poured more than $11 billion into the American economy in its seven-year existence, funding a range of initiatives from labor-intensive infrastructure projects that built bridges, highways, and dams to arts programs that funded the creation of creative works and performances. The WPA was designed to replace the Federal Emergency Relief Administration (FERA), whose efforts to alleviate unemployment and lost wages in the first two years of Roosevelt's presidency (1933–35) were ineffective, hobbled as they were by bureaucracy, disorganization, and a lack of centralization. WPA construction projects left an indelible imprint on Key West, funding not only the "relief work" Albert refers to on 93:3–4 but importing artists and photographers to the city whose work shaped the island's tourist aesthetic. (Murals by WPA painters, for example, adorned the walls at Raul's Club.)[1] The "high" trucks to which Bee-lips refers here are most likely trailer trucks.

The construction project from which the anonymous informant telephones the location of Harry's hidden boat to Frederick Harrison is the Boca Chica Fish Camp, located on the southwestern end of Boca Chica Key, about five miles from the Key West lighthouse. The facility was built by local fishing entrepreneur Captain Thomas Luther Pinder (1884–1961), one of three men credited with developing Key West's charter-boat fishing industry. (Bra Saunders is another.) The *Key West Citizen* first reported on plans for the camp on 18 September 1935 ("Fishing Camp at Boca Chica Now Proposed"); on 7 November the paper noted that Pinder had hired the longtime manager of the Long Key Fishing Camp, which had been destroyed in the Labor Day hurricane two months earlier, to run the tourist stop ("George Schutt to Manage New Fishing Camp"). The camp was completed quickly. By 30 November the *Citizen* favorably reviewed the facility, with an article headlined "Fishing Camp at Boca Chica Well-Equipped." Although Pinder seems to have had modest interaction with Hemingway, the two are depicted together in Tom Swicegood's Key West 2012 historical novel, *The Submariner's Son,* which dramatizes the relief efforts for the 1935 Labor Day hurricane (155–57).

120:22 **Customs House:** The Customs House in Key West is located at 281 Front Street. Built in 1891, it currently serves as home to the Key West Art and Historical Society.

120:23 **Herman Frederichs:** The Germanization of Frederick Harrison's name makes Harry's rather blatant point that Roosevelt's "alphabet men" are as dictatorial as Nazis.

123:4–6 **the nickel machine, the two dime machines and the quarter machine and at the picture of Custer's Last Stand:** McLendon writes that slot machines were essential gear for Key West bars in the 1930s as gambling ("the other industry, as it was called") replaced manufacturing and military money on the island (65). The print of Custer's Last Stand that hangs behind Freddy's bar was a real-life Sloppy Joe's fixture as well. Hemingway describes it in his August 1935 *Esquire* column, "He Who Gets Slap Happy: A Key West Letter," about the vets building the Overseas Highway. Published before many of the men died in the Labor Day hurricane, the essay uses the lithograph as a comic device to poke fun at the vets:

> "Can you pick out Custer, Buddy?" asked [one] vet earnestly.
> "There's Custer," said your correspondent, pointing to where the general brandished his sword while the Sioux closed in on him.
> "That's right," said the vet happily. "That's him."
> "Givin' him hell isn't he?" said [a] second veteran, his eyes never leaving the scene where the squaws were already scalping the bodies of the dead of the seventh cavalry.
> "That ain't nothing compared to what he done in France," said the first vet proudly. (19)

123:12 **Chesterfields:** The Liggett & Myers Tobacco Company of Durham, North Carolina, introduced the Chesterfield brand in 1912. The cigarette was known for its strong Turkish aroma. It was also notorious for its 1926 advertising campaign promoting itself to the burgeoning women's market with the slogan "Blow Some My Way."

123:18 **on her ways:** Ways are the V-shaped structures that hold a ship out of the water either for construction or repair.

NOTE

1. As Jani Scandura notes, "WPA grants . . . brought to Key West artists such as Loren MacIver, Richard Jansen, Avery Johnson, W. Townsend Morgan, William Hoffman, [and] Walton Blodget" to spruce up the city's visual flair (76).

CHAPTER FOURTEEN

Harry returns home for a quick lunch before picking up Freddy's boat. While there, he retrieves his Thompson gun, which signals to Marie just how serious the situation is. As with three out of the four previous chapters, this short scene does little to shore up the slackening suspense. Hemingway misses a major opportunity to enlarge Harry Morgan's tragic heroism by depicting him as a loving father. Although the Morgan daughters are introduced in this chapter, none of the girls has a name, and Harry complains unsympathetically that bearing girls is a sure sign of working-class exhaustion ("Those damn girls. That's all the old woman and I could get with what we've got" [127:27–29]). Both Harry and Marie are given interior monologues, but neither deepens their characterization. The passages simply repeat what we already know about the couple: Harry is angry about the corner the economy has painted him into, while Marie is captivated by his animal aggression. The only new element introduced here is the wife's unexpected emotion as her husband departs. Catching a glimpse of Harry's grinning face, Marie bursts into tears. Her crying is an omen, for this is the last time she will see Harry alive.

125:1 **the girls:** This is the first we see of the Morgan daughters. Harry's disregard for them throughout part 3 ("Those girls aren't much, are they?" [126:7]) is a curious departure from what Bernice Kert calls the "protective instinct" Hemingway exhibited toward women, the "paternalism" that by the beginning of the 1930s "came to be expressed in his using the term 'daughter' with his wife and woman friends" (*Hemingway Women* 234). As the father of three sons, the author made no secret of his longing for a daughter. As he complained to painter friend Waldo Peirce when doctors informed him that his third child, Gregory (1931–2001), would indeed be a boy, "I want a girl very much but so far have never had a legitimate or illegit daughter so don't know how to go about it" (*SL* 343). After *To Have and Have Not,* Hemingway would populate his fiction with daughter-lover figures, such as Maria in *For Whom the Bell Tolls* and Renata in *Across the River and into the Trees.* Yet actual daughters, as opposed to surrogate fantasies of youth and dependency, are rare in his work, perhaps because, as Nancy Comley and Robert Scholes write, "Hemingway viewed the family configuration from the position of a son, which allowed only for figures defined as mother, father, brother and sister" (28). Given the theme of economic determinism in *To Have and Have Not*, Harry's attitude is probably less misogyny than his awareness that "girls" have little opportunity or value to trade during the Depression. The only industry open to them is "sporting," or prostitution.

126:5 She cut the meat as for a small boy: The analogy is deliberate: Harry's lost arm leaves him infantilized in many everyday aspects, dependent on Marie for activities as basic as cutting one's food. This dependency may explain the tough-guy tone he takes with his wife, barking orders ("Where's my dinner? What are you waiting for?" [125:16]) and rejecting her affectionate gestures ("Leave me alone. . . . I got to think," Harry grumbles when Marie kisses him on the mouth [127:16]).

126:17–21 Shit." . . . "I don't like to hear shit at my own table: This brief exchange encapsulates the difficulties readers face in deciding how they feel about profanity in Hemingway's fiction. When Marie says "shucks," her husband teasingly replies with "shit," prompting her to insist she dislikes cursing in the house, to which Harry responds, "You talk worse than that in bed sometimes" (126:19). Marie clarifies that she dislikes cursing at the table, inspiring Harry to let out another "Oh, shit" (126:21). For some readers, the passage may exemplify a complaint the *Springfield Republican* voiced in its review of the novel: "The author falls back upon profane and bawdy talk, which exists for no recognizable purpose of delineation" (qtd. in Stephens, *Critical Reception* 176). Others may get past the apparent pointlessness of the salty language by deciding Harry and Marie's repartee dramatizes the playfulness of their marriage. If asked to justify Harry's crudity, Hemingway would probably cite his September 1934 *Esquire* column, "Defense of Dirty Words: A Cuban Letter." Responding to columnist Westbrook Pegler's complaint that he indulged in obscenities, Hemingway responded, "I doubt if a day has passed in my life in which I have not heard what Mr. Pegler calls dirty words used. Therefore how could a writer truly record any entire day and not use dirty words?" (158). Profanity was thus a mark of realism. In many ways, *To Have and Have Not* represents a turning point in the acceptance of such swear words. Scribner's had previously required Hemingway either to cut expletives such as *shit* or replace them with dashes, most notably in *A Farewell to Arms,* where an exceedingly shocking word for the time, *cocksucker,* could not even be printed as "c—s—r," as Hemingway had recommended (*TOTTC* 110; Trogdon, *Lousy Racket* 78). Harry Morgan's story met with little objection, however, with the publisher even allowing *fuck* to appear in print (see 225:18–19). Yet whether the victory over prudery is sufficient reason to include "dirty words" is debatable, especially when, as in this instance, they are gratuitous. (One could cut this passage and the novel would not be weaker for the excision. That's not the case with the *fuck* Harry later lets out. Because it adds rhetorical emphasis to the novel's proletarian credo, it cannot be considered unnecessary.)

What is not debatable is that Hemingway's use of profanity colored his reputation in his lifetime. As one 1950s writer put it, he was the man "who took obscene words off the backhouse wall and put them in print" (qtd. in Reynolds, *Final Years* 292).

127:19–20 the picture of September Morn: Paul Emile Chabas's painting *Matinée de Septembre* sparked scandal in 1913 when a reproduction of its nude female bathing in Savoy's Lake Annecy was exhibited in Chicago. Hardly graphic even by the standards of its day, *September Morn* inspired self-appointed censor Anthony Comstock to declare the image contained "too little morning and too much maid." New York impresario Harry Reichenbach stoked the controversy by feeding disapproving quotes to mocking journalists while simultaneously flooding the postcard, poster, and reproduction markets with prints. In the end, more than 7 million copies of the image appeared, on everything from dolls to umbrellas to tattoos (Ellis 91). By 1935, Chabas's painting was considered as gauche as C. M. Coolidge's Dogs Playing Poker series. Considering Hemingway's sympathy for the proletariat, it seems unlikely he incorporates it into the Morgans' décor to mock their taste in art. Instead, he is showing that despite its economic disadvantage the working class aspires to aesthetics in the home, much as Freddy does in his bar with his lithograph of Custer's Last Stand. Cheap reproductions are simply all that workers can afford.

128:24 mongol cheek bones: From 128:18–29 Marie offers a lengthy description of her husband, characterizing him, among other things, as "tall, wide-shouldered, flat-backed," animalistic, with swift and light gestures and a broken nose on a face that "[e]verytime I see [it] makes me want to cry" (128:28–29). As Debra A. Moddelmog notes, Harry is the "only Hemingway hero whose face and body are developed into a clear image," unlike his heroines, who are almost always "described frequently and specifically." For her the passage is "exceptional because Marie's reverie constitutes one of the few times a narrator in Hemingway's fiction looks at the world through a woman's eyes." This fact suggests that Hemingway resisted "lingering on the male hero's body" because he feared gazing upon a man from a masculine perspective would "not only feminize" his characters but "produce homosexual implications" (126). Of the many characteristics Marie emphasizes, the most salient are the "mongol cheek bones." In the next chapter, the unpleasant tourist Mrs. Laughton will specifically compare Harry to Genghis Khan (136:13).

CHAPTER FIFTEEN

Almost forty pages into part 3, Hemingway finally introduces the "haves" of Key West, with a scene at Freddy's that contrasts tourists to locals. As Harry arrives to pay Freddy a deposit on the boat he borrows, three obnoxious tourists have taken up residence at the bar to pontificate on the character of Key West. One pompous fop, James Laughton, postures as a writer, although Hemingway implies he is far from a *working* writer. His wife, whom we are told has "the face and build of a lady wrestler," openly lusts for Harry, while Professor John MacWalsey marvels at the island's reputation as "the Gibraltar of America," even as he admits he has seen little of the town beyond the interior of Freddy's. Despite the distraction these outsiders pose, Hemingway shifts focus long enough for Harry and Bee-lips to pay Freddy his deposit—minus Bee-lips's 10 percent commission. In terms of drama, the scene shows Harry struggling with his loyalty to his longtime friend as he considers confiding to Freddy his reasons for chartering the vessel. The chapter ends with a return to the Laughtons (now sans MacWalsey), who are joined by Richard Gordon (making his first appearance in the novel) and his wife, Helen (whom Freddy regards as the prettiest and most sympathetic of the city's new winter people). For the first time, we hear of "the famous beautiful Mrs. Bradley." In fact, a spat between the Gordons reveals that Richard Gordon is pursuing an attraction to the woman, deeply upsetting Helen. Yet the closing line also implies Mrs. Gordon has her own extramarital interest: she is disappointed not to find Professor MacWalsey waiting for her in Freddy's.

129:3 in shorts: Among Julius F. Stone Jr.'s many controversial initiatives for making Key West tourist-friendly was his recommendation that locals wear shorts to reinforce the island's new sporty vacation veneer. Socially conservative Conchs were offended by the suggestion, complaining that shorts were tantamount to underwear. Locals weren't the only ones who mocked Stone's habitual Bermudas. Dubbing the administrator "the Rehabilitator in Chief," in a 1934 letter Robert Frost dismissed him as "a rich young man in shorts with hairy legs" (qtd. in Reynolds, *1930s* 187). Jani Scandura's *Down in the Dumps: Place, Modernity, American Depression* (2008) includes an interview with an elderly survivor of the era who remembers Raul Vasquez barring Stone from entering Raul's Club, the inspiration for the Richards' bar in chapter 9, for baring his kneecaps: "I don't mind [if] you come and eat and have a little gambling or whatever," Eveillo Cabot recalls Vasquez telling the island's would-be czar. "But before you come in you've got to put on clothes. You're almost naked" (96). It should be noted that Hemingway was hardly revered for his sartorial formality around town. Most Key West histories point out his fondness for T-shirts, cut-offs, sandals, and a rope for a belt. In *To Have and Have Not,* the tourists' shorts are intended as a sign of how little actual labor "haves" contribute to society.

129:9 **nerts:** This colloquial variation on *nuts* dates back only to the 1920s. H. L. Mencken offers a humorous paragraph on its history in his 1945 supplement to *The American Language* (originally printed in 1921 and updated through 1936):

> When it came in, in 1925, its etymology must have been apparent to everyone old enough to vote, yet it seems to have met with no opposition from guardians of the national morals, and in a little while it rivaled *wham* and *wow* for popularity in the comic strips. My researches indicate it was coined in Hollywood, that great fountain of American neologisms. There arose there, in the early 20's, a fashion for using openly the ancient four-letter words that had maintained an underground life since the Restoration. It was piquant, for a while, to hear them from the lovely lips of movie beauties, but presently the grand dames of Hollywood society prohibited them as a shade too raw, and they were succeeded by euphemistic forms, made by changing the vowel of each to *e* and inserting *r* after it. *Nuts* was not one of these venerable words, but it had connotations [testicular, obviously] that made it seem somewhat too raw, so it was changed to *nerts,* and in that form swept the country. (300)

Hemingway seems to agree with Mencken's etymology lesson when he has Professor MacWalsey subsequently say, "I thought it was an obsolete phrase, something one saw in print in—er—the funny papers but never heard" (128:17–19). But MacWalsey would disagree with Mencken's claim that it arose in the movies: "Isn't it from Brooklyn originally?" he asks (130:1–2). Strangely enough, although Hollywood spared moviegoers the horrors of imagining testicles by substituting *nerts* for *nuts, nerts* was ultimately deemed too evocative of cojones and was banned in 1954.

130:13 **Papa:** Given that this sarcastic sobriquet is addressed to Mr. Laughton, not Harry Morgan, it is safe to assume Hemingway isn't alluding to his own famous nickname.

130:17 **Shut up, you whore:** Harry's brutal dismissal of Mrs. Laughton may lose him sympathy with contemporary readers sensitive to the gender politics of the slur. In a polite bit of understatement, Baker calls the insult "pointed" but argues it isn't undeserved because of the "yahoo-like advances" of this "literary slummer." Harry's viciousness, the critic adds, dramatizes his resistance to the moral corruption of the "haves," who condescend to locals with an air of entitlement. In this way, Harry is unlike Richard Gordon, who cannot resist the vulgar opportunism of Helène Bradley (*Writer as Artist* 213). Beegel effectively agrees, noting it is Mrs. Laughton who treats Harry as a whore, "a 'have not' whose sexual favors can be purchased. He simply reverses the insult upon her, accusing her of soliciting when she is the one who expects to pay" (115).

130:20 **Hello, Big Boy:** Hemingway's hardboiled idiom can strike readers as strained if not artificial, as if he were merely imitating the pulp penchant for condescending nicknames without amalgamating it into his own voice. Yet Robert E. Gajdusek cites this line among several other instances in which Harry is called "boy" despite his age (forty-three) to dramatize the struggle to maintain his masculine dignity (97).

131:13 **crut:** Hemingway retrieved this word from 1924's "The Battler," in which Nick Adams describes the brakeman who throws him from the train at the beginning of the story as a "lousy crut" (*CSS* 97). According to most dictionaries, the word came into use in the early 1920s as an alternative to *crud,* which connoted venereal disease.

132:7 **the money in my box in the bank:** Another foreshadowing of the Cuban revolutionaries' plan to rob the Key West bank. Hemingway has thus far still not specified why they need a getaway charter, so this is a clue readers may only appreciate in retrospect. By promising to store Harry's guaranty in the bank, of course, Freddy has no way of knowing it will be shortly stolen. When Bee-lips smirks, "That's a good place" (132:10), he takes delight in noting the irony of the robbers stealing their own money.

132:17–18 **at the front of the street:** Now that Harry will carry the Cubans in Freddy's borrowed boat instead of his own, he can meet them on Porter Dock at the foot of Duval Street, as per Bee-lips's instructions at 110:25.

132:26–134:14 **the plan:** As Harry and Bee-lips hash out their cover stories to claim they aren't involved in the robbery, the differences in their characters become clear. Harry is loyal to Freddy, believing he owes it to his friend to tell him the truth about what he smuggles out of Key West. Bee-lips, meanwhile, insists not only that he wouldn't trust Freddy but that he doesn't care about protecting others from the overzealous Cubans. His plan may very well endanger the taxi driver who will unknowingly deliver the robbers to Porter Dock. While Harry insists they find a driver without children so they aren't responsible for leaving a local family fatherless, Bee-lips is blithely content to find "one that don't think" so suspicions toward them won't be aroused. When the lawyer aspires to a facetious level of morality ("Well, I never killed anybody")—implying he may know about Harry's murder of Mr. Sing, possibly from the rummy Eddy Marshall—Harry turns his defense back on him as a mark of cowardice: "Nor you never will" (134:8).

The conversation ends with a reference to "crummy" that reminds readers of that word's World War I association with lice, which is the presumed referent for "them" when Harry says, "Can you get them from talking?" (134:11). When Bee-lips replies, "paper your mouth," tying into a pattern of mouth imagery in the novel (see 53:13–54:3, 111:23–24), he simply means "cover your mouth." In manuscript, Hemingway attempted a pun in response by having Harry fire back, "Paper your cuts then." When he tamed this down in the proofing stage to "paper yours," he made an editing error that has yet to be corrected. A reader closely following the dialogue will realize Harry answers his own insult:

> "Just being with you makes me feel crummy." [Harry]
> "Maybe you are crummy." [Bee-lips]
> "Can you get them from talking?" [Harry]
> "If you don't paper your mouth." [Bee-lips]
> "Paper yours then." [Harry]
> "I'm going to get a drink," Harry said.

The confusion occurs because in both manuscript and typescript Bee-lips had a rejoinder between these two final lines: "'Repartee,' Bee-lips said. 'Listen to it.'" That no editorial eye has caught this mistake again suggests how desperately the novel needs a corrected edition.

134:20 **Cuba Libre:** In his cocktail guide to Hemingway (cleverly titled *To Have and Have Another*), Philip Greene tells the legend of how this highball mixing two ounces of rum to four ounces of Coca-Cola was invented shortly after Cuba's liberation from Spain in 1898. As American military and business interests controlled the island for three years after Spain's defeat, they imported the soft-drink sensation, much to the delight of Cubans, who found its sweet flavor mingled well with Bacardi. The name of the drink is a reference to the rallying cry of the liberation campaign, "*Viva Cuba libre!*" which became the toast accompanying its downing, *Por Cuba libre!* Exactly where and by whom the drink was named remains a mystery: "One version of the story concerns a United States Army Signal Corps messenger named Fausto Rodriguez. In 1900, he visited a local bar with an officer, who ordered a Bacardi and Coke. Nearby soldiers took notice, and before you knew it, they were all toasting this great new drink." As Greene notes, only two things cast credibility on the legend: first, it wasn't narrated until a 1966 Bacardi advertising campaign and second, the campaign was the brainchild of none other than Fausto Rodriguez, then Bacardi's chief publicity officer in New York (64).

As Greene rightly recognizes, *To Have and Have Not* isn't endorsing the Cuba Libre. By telling Freddy he will have what Mrs. Laughton is drinking and then promptly changing to "straight whiskey" when he learns this is her preference, Harry dismisses the drink as both feminine and affected—a drink for the "haves," not the common man.

135:17–18 **Professor MacWalsey, Laughton:** Carlos Baker's biography was the first to identify the prototypes on which Hemingway based the tourists in Freddy's Bar. Few have followed his suggestion that economics professor John MacWalsey was partly inspired by *Esquire* editor Arnold Gingrich (1903–1976), perhaps because Gingrich didn't comment on the "rough approximation" Baker attributes between him and the character (*A Life* 295). More attention has been given to University of Washington English professor Harry H. Burns (1905–1979). Upon meeting Hemingway in Key West in July 1936, Burns stayed at Whitehead Street for two weeks before accompanying Ernest and Pauline in their car to New Orleans, where the trio enjoyed a stay at the Hotel Monteleone before the Hemingways headed on to Wyoming for their annual fall stay at the Nordquist L-T Ranch. (This trip to the Big Easy may be why Marie Morgan expresses her desire to vacation there at 114:14.) During their three-week friendship, Hemingway gave Burns the sobriquet MacWalsey, a nonsensical name Ernest and friends had bandied about that summer in Bimini. (In addition to letters to Burns, the name appears in correspondence with Jane Mason describing sister-in-law Jinny Pfeiffer's love interest, Helen Duncombe.) Hemingway informed the professor in October 1936 that he was creating a character in tribute to him; his affection for Burns may be why MacWalsey is one of two "haves" who is a sympathetic (albeit flawed) character. (Helen Gordon is the other.) In his correspondence with Baker, Burns had little reaction to his immortalization other than to say he saw no resemblance between himself and his fictional counterpart, a quote Baker does not cite in *Ernest Hemingway: A Life*.

The best single source on Burns is Bert Bender's article "Harry Burns and Professor MacWalsey in Ernest Hemingway's *To Have and Have Not*" (2008), which discusses not only Burns's friendship with Hemingway but Baker's efforts to pry information from the recalcitrant professor. Burns insisted to the biographer that his letters from Hemingway had been destroyed in a footlocker during World War II. Later, he shared one surviving missive, the October 1936 letter, which he claimed had been tucked in a book and forgotten. Bender had been a student of Burns's in 1964, finding him a congenial if disinterested teacher. Only decades later did Bender discover the connection to Hemingway, and he set out to fill in the slim anecdotes Baker was able to corral in his biography. Through reminiscences from Burns's former department chair at the University of Washington, Bender paints a portrait of a man whose passing association with a great writer compensated for an unspectacular career as a scholar. As Bender is astonished to discover, the October 1936 letter wasn't mislaid in a book. Instead, as Bender's source reveals, for years Burns was in the habit of carrying it in his pocket, strategically showing it off to colleagues as proof that he had contributed to American literature, at least anecdotally if not academically (35–50).

The identity of Mr. and Mrs. Laughton is more problematic. Baker claims the couple is "a thinly disguised portrait of Jack Coles and his wife," paraphrasing a spring 1936 letter to John Dos Passos, whose description of Mrs. Coles's complexion and physique parallels that of the distinctly unfeminine Mrs. Laughton (*A Life* 295). A decade after his authorized biography, Baker included this source, dated 12 April 1936, in the first major collection of Hemingway correspondence, *Ernest Hemingway: Selected Letters, 1917–1961,* where the specific passage reads, "Jack Coles is here [Key West] with his new squaw who looks something like one of these new style wrestlers. The hero. Not the villain. You can tell the hero always because he is pimpled. The villain is bearded. The Coles are ideally happy and read aloud from the new collected works of Havelock Ellis" (*SL* 447). Although the tourists in Freddy's Bar are too busy discussing the etymology of *nerts* to recite Ellis's fashionable sexology theories, the similarity of the physical description does seem undeniable (129:6–7). Accordingly, nearly every subsequent biographer has followed Baker's example, usually describing "Jack Coles" as a mutual friend of Hemingway and Dos Passos but without any attempt at elaborating (see McLendon 157; Meyers, *Biography* 294). M. C. Rintoul's *Dictionary of Real People and Places in Fiction* (originally published in 1993) even includes entries on "Coles, Jack" and "Coles, Mrs. Jack," citing Baker as its authority (312).

There is a good reason additional information on the Coleses has proved elusive: the couple did not exist. Strong circumstantial evidence suggests the 1936 letter refers to John Cheney Cowles (1894–1972) and that, whether by design or accident, Hemingway dropped the *w* when writing to Dos Passos. (Baker did not transpose the letter incorrectly; the name is clearly spelled "Coles" in the original, which is held in the Outgoing Correspondence file for 1936 at the Kennedy Library.) Cowles was the grandson of *Chicago Tribune* coowner Alfred Cowles and had worked in the advertising department of the newspaper's European edition in the early 1920s. He and Hemingway probably met through Donald Ogden Stewart (Bill Gorton in *The Sun Also Rises*). In his 1975 autobiography, *By a Stroke of Luck,* Stewart mentions Cowles as "the wonderfully congenial brother of one of my Yale classmates" (83). When Hemingway traveled to New York in February 1926 to sign his contract with Scribner's to publish *The Sun Also Rises,* he and Cowles carroused together, with Hemingway noting in particular his newfound acquaintance with Cowles's bootlegger (*SL* 193). During his stay, Hemingway presented Cowles with a copy of the Boni & Liveright edition of *In Our Time,* which had been published the previous October. Inside the book he inscribed verses from two of his poems, "The Age Demanded" and "The Earnest Liberal's Lament," dedicating them to Cowles with the line "To Jack Cowles on Valentine's Day (this has no sexual significance) Ernest Hemingway." The inscription was in return for Cowles presenting him with a copy of the original 1924 Three Mountains Press edition of *in our time,* which was already a rare collector's item. Cowles apparently kept his copy of Hemingway's earlier limited edition volume, *Three Stories and Ten Poems,* for when it appeared on the auction market in 1993 his inscription to a friend named Harry was dated 1938. An unexplained reference to Cowles shows up in 1930, when Hemingway notes that his dog was poisoned (*SL* 322), suggesting Cowles was frequenting Key West by this point.

Two specific clues link Cowles to Laughton. First, in the manuscript and typescript of *To Have and Have Not,* Laughton is named "Bowes" (MS 30, item 204, folder 14, page 58 and MS 32, item 212, folder 4, pages 31–32). In the second version of the typescript, the name is rendered "Bowles" (MS 33, item 215, folder 2, page 56). Not until the setting copy (MS 32, item 213, folders 10–16) is the name changed. In Richard Gordon's initial appearance in chapter 19, the beginning of the "haves" section, he and Helen discuss the bank robbery and Bee-lips's murder, with Gordon identifying Joven Cuba as the culprits, before referencing their social circle and dismissing "that awful Bowles and his wife." Later in the same chapter, as Gordon quizzes Freddy's Bar owner Freddy Wallace about Harry Morgan, Freddy mentions Bowles as another writer wintering in Key West, and Gordon promptly dismisses him as "a twerp" (MS 31, item 204, folder 7, page 132). That Hemingway might harbor ill will toward a man with whom he had socialized only a decade earlier isn't surprising, given his long history of broken friendships. The cause of that ill will is harder to specify, but the second clue linking Cowles and Laughton—a pair of letters from Cowles, from September and October 1936—hints that a falling out occurred between the pair over "The Snows of Kilimanjaro," which had just appeared in the August 1936 issue of *Esquire.*

The first letter, dated 20 September, suggests that Hemingway challenged Cowles to a fight after Cowles had the audacity to criticize the story:

Dear Earnest [sic]:

Ever since you came into my ken, I have admired both you and your work. Also, as every man of prominence is subject to criticism and you came in for your share, I have said to many people that your poses should be discounted, since the important consideration was what you really were, not what you were pretending to be. However, suddenly your fatuous story in July [sic] Esquire filled me with rage and indignation and I linked your desire to pick a fight with me as part of your exhibitionism.

As surely as you are convinced now, and were at the time, that you can whip me, as surely as you wanted to fight only because you knew you could whip me, I admit one reason I didn't want to fight was because I expected a licking. But also,

I had not wronged you and I saw no reason for taking punishment just because you wanted the publicity of another knockdown.

However, if you insist upon carrying out your intention the next time we meet, I hope I have the courage and the grace to take a beating I don't deserve. You owe me an apology, but only to wipe out an ungenerous act, and permit us to be friends again. I value your friendship, but as is I don't trust it.

Very sincerely yours,
John Cowles
PS. This has been lying around for a month to see if it was what I wanted to say. *It is.*

Hemingway responded with a letter that has not been located. From Cowles's 30 October reply, it's apparent the writer responded aggressively, taking a potshot at Cowles's wealthy family by claiming Cowles associated Helen, the middle-aged wife in his story, with his "aunt." (Whether Hemingway meant Cowles's literal aunt or his female companion—Cowles did not marry his second wife, Elizabeth Hudson, until November 1937—is unclear.) The letter's middle portion finds Cowles criticizing Hemingway's dependence on personal experience, his tendency to recycle biographical legend, and his lack of grace in citing F. Scott Fitzgerald as an example of a writer corrupted by glamorizing the rich. (As is well known, when Hemingway republished "Snows" in subsequent story collections, he changed the specific reference to Fitzgerald as "ruined" in *Esquire* to a fictional "Julian.") "I am delighted you weighed 198 lbs. stripped that morning, had just killed two grizzlies and remembered having beat up three strapping buck niggers in Bimini," Cowles writes, apparently summarizing Hemingway's description of his own state of mind as he wrote the letter. "Such thoughts must put a man into cracking good shape to whang out words on a typewriter." Cowles then reveals more tantalizing details about the apparent confrontation between the pair over the story:

> However, what was really on my mind that day, was thinking of a writer of your power and impact, devoting approximately three thousand words of a ten thousand word story to asides which contained but a rehash of episodes already described in previous works. Also one dirty crack at an erstwhile friend whose present mental moral and physical condition cannot be in too good shape to receive said jibe. It's a small matter, Earnest, but a dirty one. For you to patronize "poor Scott Fitzgerald" is not pretty. To return to the burden of your alleged story and why I was indignant and outraged. These sentiments did not arise in me because, as you so pertly observed, the middle-aged resembled my aunt, but because you have a guy all fucked out, who wants a lust for his woman, but cant get a heart on[.] Granted this is a sad

case, but we all come to it in our given span. Then what? (This a rhetorical Question) Out of the strength of your imagination and the depths of your genius, you fetch up death. Good old standbye death. Not content with this divertissement, you add the wow cap of sending him to heavan in an airplane.

Whether Hemingway responded to this letter is not known, but if he did, Cowles did not reply, for his file in the Kennedy Library contains only the 30 September and 30 October items. Cowles seems to have unburdened himself of his Hemingway connections after the spat. If the inscription on the front end of his copy of *Three Stories and Ten Poems* is any indication, he gave the book to a friend the summer after *To Have and Have Not* was published: "For Harry Because I Like the way he Talks about Earnest [sic] Hemingway, June 18, 1938, Sheridan [Wyoming], G.H., John Cowles." Unlike many of the minor characters who passed through Hemingway's life, Cowles was not interviewed for Baker's biography. Instead, he lived a quiet life in Meriden, New Hampshire; Key West; and, from the 1950s on, in Naples, Florida. A 1959 *Popular Mechanics* article on the unique octagonal home the Cowleses built in Naples features a photograph of the then sixty-five-year-old, who described his profession as "writer" (Hunn 88). (Cowles likely lived off family money.) It was at this home that on 16 April 1972 Cowles shot himself in the head, despondent over the death of his wife a year earlier. His suicide is yet another tantalizing connection to Hemingway.

135:26–27 the Gibraltar of America: Gibraltar is a British territory located on the southern tip of the Iberian Peninsula. No larger than two-and-a-half square miles, it is home to the fabled Rock of Gibraltar, best remembered in North America as the logo of the Prudential Insurance Company. This 1,389-foot promontory has long symbolized stability and invincibility. Gibraltar itself has specific imperial associations with the British Empire, which jointly captured it with the Dutch in 1704 during the War of Spanish Succession. (Spain officially ceded the territory nine years later.) By describing Key West as "the Gibraltar of America," Professor MacWalsey cites a nickname that dates back to the nineteenth century and the island's strategic position as the southernmost outpost of the American empire. MacWalsey, however, is talking less about military importance than cultural peculiarity. Calling Key West "a strange place," he emphasizes the island's distance from the mainland, suggesting its culture has little connection to the rest of the United States. In noting that Key West sits farther south latitudinally than Cairo, Egypt, he reminds us that for seven centuries (711–1462), Gibraltar was under Islamic control after the Umayyad Caliphate seized the territory from the Visigoths. The reference to Egypt adds an additional layer of exoticism to the setting that complements Mrs. Laughton's comparison of Harry Morgan to Genghis Khan (see 136:1 entry). The phrase "the Gibraltar of America" is by no means tied to Key West alone, however. In the nineteenth century, this was the nickname of Quebec, Canada, because of its reputation as a fortressed defense.

136:13 Ghengis Khan: The fabled Mongolian Emperor (1162–1227) who conquered Eurasia in the early thirteenth century. Hemingway misspells the name, which should be rendered "Genghis." By having Mrs. Laughton compare Harry Morgan to Khan, Hemingway establishes a thematic link back to Marie Morgan's description of her husband's "broken mongol cheek bones" (128:24).

136:18 Tamerlane: Sarcastically playing off his wife's attraction to Harry, Mr. Laughton suggests another historical dictator with Eastern ties might next enter Freddy's bar: the Persian leader of the Timurid dynasty, Timur, or "Tamerlane" (1336–1405). Hemingway's spelling of the name suggests a familiarity with Edgar Allan Poe's 1827 poem. Other variations include *Tamburlaine,* as in Christopher Marlowe's 1587–88 tragedy.

136:24 He seemed to like me for what I really am. Mrs. Laughton expresses the central theme of the novel's female "haves," their marital dissatisfaction and, more specifically, anger at husbands who have lost sexual interest in them. Unlike Professor MacWalsey, Mr. Laughton dislikes hearing his wife say "nerts" and finds her vulgarity unattractive.

137:13 a face like a ham with a broken nose: Few foodstuffs are more appropriate to hardboiled fiction than ham. The word seems a veritable cognomen of the genre: Dashiell *Ham*met, Mike *Ham*mer. The dish is pluripresent in the genre, undoubtedly because it evokes the working-class life. "A face like a ham" is a common trope in 1920s and 1930s noir.

137:17–21, 137:27 All this time the writer sat there . . . worrying: Here the narration focalizes through Freddy, culminating in his dismissive view of the prowess of male "haves" like Mr. Laughton: "Any one would have to be a writer or a F.E.R.A. man to have a wife look like that" (137:19–21).

138:1–2 His legs ached all the time: Joe "Josie" Russell often complained of the back strain that came from manning the bar at Sloppy Joe's, which he found more wearing than charter-boat fishing or bootlegging. This passage recalls Hemingway's 9 April 1936 letter to Maxwell Perkins: "Mr. Josie is laying off the operation of his highly successful joint because he is getting bartender's foot from standing up all day and all night and the day after the farewell ball of the Fireman's Convention he is going over to Cuba with me and we plan to put in two weeks of intensive recuperation from our arduous winter" (*SL* 443).

138:11 **A tanned face, sandy-haired, well-built man . . . came in:** The entire passage from this point to the chapter end's at 141:12 does not appear in the original manuscript or typescript. The scene, which introduces Richard and Helen Gordon, is Hemingway's most extensive addition to the novel during his hasty June 1937 revision and was necessitated by paring the Bradley narrative to a sliver of its former heft. In draft, Gordon enters the novel with a twenty-nine-page chapter 19, which follows him from a conversation with Helen in his rented cottage off Rocky Road to Freddy's Bar, where he discusses the bank robbery with the owner and his patrons. Intriguingly, Harry Morgan isn't the only subject of their conversation. The deleted scene at Freddy's also includes a strange metafictional dissection of Hemingway's own literary productivity, with the author allowing his characters to criticize him *by name* for failing his own celebrated work ethic. As Gordon informs Freddy's clientele, "Hemingway" is considered a "big slob" who has no investment in politics. What impresses the patrons, however, is the writer's earning capacity, not his ideology: "'Hemingway makes money,' somebody said. 'That big bastard is shot in the ass with luck,' someone else said. 'I've never seen him working yet'" (MS 31, item 204, folder 1, page 143).

138:15 **Richard Gordon:** Literary legend says that Hemingway created Harry Morgan's unsympathetic counterpart, the novel's chief "have," to skewer fellow author and friend John Dos Passos (1896–1970). As Kenneth Lynn puts it, "Gordon is a vicious caricature of Dos Passos, and the question is what had the novelist done to incite it" (457), for Dos Passos had been a loyal supporter and colleague for more than a decade. While each man would claim they met in Schio, Italy, in May 1918 (Dos Passos had actually departed by the time Hemingway arrived), their friendship didn't truly begin until 1924 in Paris, during the heyday of expatriate modernism. By that point, Dos Passos had already authored a celebrated World War I novel, *Three Soldiers* (1920), and he plied his influence to help launch Hemingway's career, both urging Horace Liveright to publish *In Our Time* in 1925 and encouraging Hemingway not to hold back on his parodic drubbing of Sherwood Anderson in *The Torrents of Spring*. (Dos Passos makes a cameo in the satire.) Dos Passos was also the friend who first recommended Key West to Hemingway, describing the city as he had visited it in 1924 during a hiking expedition as "a vacation paradise, like no other place in Florida" (qtd. in Carr 231). As Ernest and Pauline made the island their home, Dos Passos was a frequent guest and founding member of the Mob, the band of fishing buddies Hemingway summoned to the Keys for excursions to Cuba and the Dry Tortugas. Dos Passos even met his wife, Katherine "Katy" Smith—one inspiration for Helen Gordon (see 138:28–29)—while visiting the Hemingways' first Key West apartment, at 314 Simonton Street, in late April 1928.

By 1936 as Hemingway drafted *To Have and Have Not*, Dos Passos was at the peak of his career. His eleventh book, *The Big Money*, was the culminating installment of a triptych, called *U.S.A.*, which also included *The 42nd Parallel* (1930) and *1919* (1932). Published on 6 August 1936, *The Big Money* proved a major critical success, landing its author on the cover of that week's *Time Magazine*, while racking up solid if unspectacular sales. Considering the sorry state of Hemingway's career in the mid-1930s, it's not hard to understand why biographers claim the seeds of Richard Gordon lay in simple jealousy. In manuscript, Hemingway fired away with both barrels at every Dos Passos quality that had irritated him over the years, including his perceived sycophancy with wealthy friends such as Gerald and Sara Murphy, his habit of borrowing money, and his lack of athletic zest. As Donald Pizer notes, Gordon's most readily identifiable similarity to Dos Passos is his career as a writer of radical fiction (117). Dos Passos was tireless in his leftist advocacy, not only producing proletarian novels but working to exonerate convicted anarchists Sacco and Vanzetti in the 1920s and covering labor strikes for the *New Masses* during the Depression. Had Hemingway published his original manuscript, the connection between Gordon's and Dos Passos's politics would have been irrefutable, for in the deleted Bradley party scene Hemingway mocks *U.S.A.* by attributing faux titles to Gordon that are clearly takes on Dos Passos's major achievement, including *The Ruling Classes, Brief Mastery,* and *The Cult of Violence* (MS 31, item 202, folder 3, pages 179–80). More privately, the Gordons' marriage also resembles select aspects of the Dos Passoses', especially John and Katy's "peripatetic existence," their tendency to travel year-round, despite their lack of regular income, with long stays at Cap d'Antibes with the Murphys. (Helen Gordon mentions Cap d'Antibes at 183:16.) In what may be the bitterest insult, Hemingway mocks the couple's inability to have children.

Not all critics believe readers should associate Gordon with Dos Passos, however. Robert E. Fleming catalogues the differences between the character and the writer, noting the physical dissimilarities: "Gordon is described as a handsome man; part of the irony of his character is that his handsome exterior conceals moral and artistic corruption. Dos Passos, prematurely balding, skinny, and adorned with thick glasses, was hardly good-looking" ("Libel" 601). Nor does any evidence suggest that the Dos Passos marriage fell prey to infidelity as the Gordons' has. By all accounts, Dos Passos's shy temperament made him the antithesis of a ladies' man, as unlikely to make advances on other women as other women were unlikely to "collect" him the way Helène Bradley does Gordon. For Pizer, the Gordon/Bradley seduction scene suggests that the real target of satiric excoriation is Ernest Hemingway himself—it was Hemingway, after all, who cultivated his attraction to Jane Mason, the inspiration for Mrs. Bradley, striking a friendship whose flirtatious intimacy has led many to assume their relationship was adulterous, despite a lack of concrete evidence (see 138:28–29). Accordingly, Pizer argues that Dos Passos was merely a "scapegoat" for Hemingway's own self-recrimination, a "sacrificial offering who was to bring relief" for Ernest's failure to live up to his ideals of integrity (120–21). Yet Fleming cautions against associating Gordon with *any* specific individual. He argues Gordon is designed "to attack a *type* of writer who flourished during the political turmoil of the 1930s," one who represents "a composite figure" of novelists who turned radical because the critical tide had turned toward politicized fiction.

It should be noted that Hemingway's portrait of Gordon was completed before his friendship with Dos Passos ended for good in spring 1937, over the Spanish Civil War. Hemingway revised the novel after the pair quarreled that May over the execution of Dos Passos's friend and translator José Robles, leading one to wonder whether he cut the more gratuitous aspersions against the Gordons, fearing that Dos Passos would be more inclined to sue for libel now that they were estranged. Hemingway would continue to disparage Dos Passos for the rest of his life, most notably in *A Moveable Feast,* where the former friend is described as a "pilot fish" who ruined Hemingway's marriage to Hadley Richardson by introducing him to the wealthy expatriate class that turned him into a "bird dog who wants to go out with any man with a gun, or a trained pig in a circus who has finally found someone who loves and appreciates him for himself alone" (209). For his part, Dos Passos never specifically addressed the Gordon character. He did parody Hemingway as the belligerent blowhard George Elbert Warner in his 1951 novel *Chosen Country* and its posthumously published sequel, *Century's Ebb* (1975). Yet his own memoir, *The Best Times,* speaks nostalgically of Hemingway and Key West in the 1930s.

138:28–29 **the prettiest stranger in Key West:** Richard Gordon is a wholly unsympathetic character, but the same cannot be said of his wife, Helen. In chapter 23, she delivers one of the most justifiably angry protests against masculine power and privilege in all of Hemingway. Along with Professor MacWalsey, Helen is the rare "have" with any depth to her depiction, a point underscored in admittedly chauvinistic terms by Freddy's comment here that she is the most attractive tourist in Key West—more beautiful even than her nemesis, Helène Bradley, whom Freddy gratuitously notes "is getting a little big" (139:1–2). As Kim Moreland argues, Helen is a compelling character because she displays "a psychological complexity that is articulated rather than merely asserted" (89). In other words, her predicament as a woman who has attempted to serve as a "good wife" only to discover neither her husband nor the institution of marriage respects her sacrifice is dramatized as opposed to merely discussed in other characters' dialogue, as is the case with Mrs. Bradley's predatory femininity.

Because Richard Gordon is inexorably associated with John Dos Passos, readers have been tempted to equate Helen Gordon with Dos Passos's wife, Katherine Foster "Katy" Smith (1891–1947). Hemingway had known the Smith family when he was a teenager, during his summers on Walloon Lake outside Horton Bay, Michigan. He and Katy were especially close during the summers of 1919 and 1920 during his recuperation from his World War I wounding and his jilting by Red Cross nurse Agnes von Kurowsky. As with so many women in Hemingway's circle, the degree to which their relationship was romantic remains a matter of speculation. Kenneth

Lynn claims that Katy "once confided to Edmund Wilson's daughter Rosalind that she and Hemingway had been romantically involved for a time" (128). Most biographers, however, portray the friendship as platonic, with the pair enjoying a strong but unconsummated sexual attraction (Kert, *Hemingway's Women* 45–46). What is safe to say is that in Ernest's post-adolescent years Katy embodied the allure of the post-Victorian woman, outgoing, frank, and uninhibited by notions of propriety. His attraction to her is best captured in the short story "Summer People," written in 1926 but not published until 1972, because of an explicit scene in which Nick Adams and "Kate" make love in a hemlock forest. The specific position Hemingway describes (*coitus more ferarum*, to be polite) is intended to demonstrate both Nick's romantic mastery and Kate's liberated sophistication (*CSS* 502).

Hemingway met his first wife, Hadley Richardson, through Katy Smith during the fall of 1920. Although Hadley considered Katy a close friend, she was attuned to Hemingway's attraction to her and for a time regarded her as a romantic rival. As Donald Pizer suggests, Katy's friendship with Hadley would prove a lingering reminder of the guilt Ernest felt after leaving Hadley in 1927 to marry Pauline Pfeiffer. If one assumes "Summer People" is pure fiction, Katy came to represent both Hemingway's "failure to possess her outside of fantasy" as well as "his increasingly powerful and nagging realization of the failure in his life represented by his break with Hadley" (113). Rivalry and competitiveness no doubt shaded those feelings of failure further after Katy married Dos Passos, a man Hemingway was hardly prone to consider a serious adversary when it came to attracting feminine attention.

On a very basic level, if one associates Richard Gordon with Dos Passos, the Gordons' unhappy marriage can be read as Hemingway's effort to deny Katy Smith in fiction the happiness and contentment that, by all accounts, she and Dos Passos shared during their twenty years together. That denial is brutally realized in one particular detail Hemingway twists into fiction. The Dos Passoses wanted to have children, but Katy suffered miscarriages that were the couple's single major disappointment. At 183:12–13, Richard Gordon will chide Helen for failing to produce "anything to cackle about." She insists that Gordon refused to have children because of their money problems. Later, at 185:27–29, she refers to the "ergoapiol pills" he forced her to take "to make me come around because you were afraid to have a baby." Hemingway thus conflates the Dos Passoses' money and fertility problems to insist that Richard Gordon forced his wife to have an abortion. As if this act of invention were not nasty enough, Hemingway leveled another insult aimed specifically at Katy that he would cut for fear of libel. In his original chapter 23—in a scene set at the Key West yacht basin—reference is made to an "incorruptible writer" who, although not Richard Gordon, is based partly on Dos Passos. (Physically, the writer resembles another Hemingway rival, Max Eastman, with whom Hemingway would tussle in Maxwell Perkins's office in August 1937.) This writer's wife is described as the source of honesty problems, for she "likes to steal as much as a monkey does" (MS 31, item

204, folder 5, page 231). Biographers have not located any instance in which Katy was arrested for shoplifting, yet Hemingway, according to Jeffrey Meyers, would angrily refer to Katy as a "thief" during a tension-filled evening at Gerald and Sara Murphy's apartment in 1937, the last ever meeting between Hemingway and Dos Passos (308). The implication is that Hemingway availed himself of some private knowledge, perhaps dating back to his and Katy's Michigan youth, to imply that the Dos Passos's marital contentment was a hypocritical sham.

Yet, as is the case with Richard Gordon and John Dos Passos, as many dissimilarities distinguish Helen Gordon from Katy Dos Passos as connect her. For starters, Helen is repeatedly described as young and referred to as a "girl," while Katy was in her mid-forties by the time *To Have and Have Not* was drafted. Additionally, as Lynn points out, Katy was agnostic, while Helen is embittered by Gordon's unwillingness to respect her Catholic upbringing by refusing to marry her in a church and forcing birth control on her (461–62). Because of Helen's religious convictions, critics have suggested a more obvious model for Helen is Pauline Hemingway, the wife for whom Hemingway converted to Catholicism in 1927. Strengthening the association is that "Helen" is also the name of the dying writer's wife in "The Snows of Kilimanjaro" who also resembles Pauline. But perhaps the most persuasive evidence that Hemingway based Helen on his own wife is that the extraordinary rebuke Mrs. Gordon delivers to her husband again reflects Hemingway's awareness of his failings as a spouse. In giving Helen voice to vent against a man prone to "rages and jealousies . . . and meanness," Hemingway castigated himself for the vanity and delusions of virtue that the literary life encourages. Indeed, for all the insults Helen levels at Richard Gordon, the most piercing is the one on which Gordon's whole sense of identity is based: "You writer" (186:13–14).

More than any other characters in the novel, Richard and Helen Gordon represent the limitations of reading Hemingway as roman à clef. Over the course of his career, he certainly based characters on friends and foils, but his dramatis personae almost always assume their own sets of conflicts and contradictions, their own psychologies. The Gordons' marriage will inevitably raise questions in readers' minds about Hemingway's mixed feelings for John and Katy Dos Passos, as well as the complex reasons for his resentments.

139:1 **Mrs. Bradley:** This is our first mention of the novel's femme fatale, whose role in the drama is restricted to her appearance in a chapter 21 flashback to an odd sex scene with Richard Gordon (188:28–29). As the most villainous "have," she is often interpreted as Hemingway's quintessential "bitch-goddess" (Moreland 83), the most unrepentant of "a group of women [characters] defined by a special combination of sex and money" who appear in his 1930s fiction (Comley and Scholes 41). One of the great misperceptions of *To Have and Have Not* is that Hemingway cut Helène's role in the novel to a sliver of what Arnold Gingrich called the "generic female study" she originally represented (Unpublished letter). In fact, Mrs. Bradley only ever appeared in the manuscript's extended party scene spread across chapters 22 and 23, and only then in vignettes as the narrative lens swings among various attendees at her and her husband's soiree. From her conception, Helène was always more a subject of other characters' conversation than an actual presence, her purpose more symbolic than dramatic. Nevertheless, when she does appear in the manuscript, she makes for a marvelously malignant antagonist, far more interesting in her ruthless carnality than the insults other "haves" level against her behind her back can even begin to suggest. Certainly Helène is a cartoonish character, with none of the psychological complexity of Hemingway's other "rich-bitch" wives, whether Margaret in "The Short Happy Life of Francis Macomber" or Helen in "The Snows of Kilimanjaro." Yet her one-dimensional malevolence also infuses a great pulp or noir electricity in the novel that is far more invigorating than the static cackling of Mrs. Laughton. I may be the one critic ever to suggest *To Have and Have Not* could benefit from more rather than less Helène Bradley, but had Hemingway made her a centerpiece of part 4's aborted dynamite run to Cuba—a betrayer of the revolution, perhaps—he could have created as unremorseful a hardboiled heroine as Velma Valento in Raymond Chandler's *Farewell, My Lovely* (1941) or Phyllis Nirdlinger in James M. Cain's *Double Indemnity* (1943).

As it stands, however, Helène Bradley is yet another character deemed more interesting for whom she is based on rather than what she does. Late in life, Hemingway obliquely referred to Jane Mason (1909–1981) as "the worst bitch I knew (then)" ("Art of the Short Story" 6), and while the matter at hand was the inspiration behind Margaret Macomber, the bile bespeaks the anger vented on Helène Bradley throughout *To Have and Have Not*. Hemingway first met the attractive, athletic socialite in September 1931 on the *Ile de France* as he and Pauline returned to Key West via Havana from a summer in Europe. Hemingway was immediately smitten and involved both her and her laconic husband, Grant, in his social circle. Grant's duties as Pan Am vice president meant Jane more often than not saw Ernest by herself, leading to either an intensely platonic flirtation or a full-blown affair, depending on the source. Jane Mason was a frequent guest aboard Joe "Josie" Russell's *Anita* during the Cuban fishing holidays of 1932 and 1933; the boat's logbook includes an intriguing entry from May 1932, noting "Ernest loves Jane" (Baker, *A Life* 228). Hemingway's affection cooled the following year, however, after Mason broke her back either falling or leaping from a balcony at her hacienda in the Havana suburbs of Jaimanitas. The injury occurred on the heels of a potentially dangerous automobile accident involving her and Hemingway's oldest sons, making Ernest leery of her emotional instability. As James Mellow writes, "There was a wild, awesome streak in her nature that Hemingway would come to understand [as manic]. . . . She was subject, as Hemingway was, to mood swings, shifting from enthusiasm to a black despondency, and had apparently made one or two ineffectual attempts at suicide" (*Life without Consequences* 413). Hemingway would later claim to have written the Nick Adams story "A Way You'll Never Be" to comfort "a nice girl going crazy from day to day" (Baker, *A Life* 228), although the title can't help but read as a passive-aggressive denial of the validity of her woes.

During her convalescence, Mason confided details about Hemingway to her psychotherapist, Lawrence Kubie. Two years later, when Kubie sent Hemingway an analysis of his fiction, which the *Saturday Review of Literature* had commissioned, Hemingway was livid enough to threaten a lawsuit. Although both Mason and Kubie denied the article drew from their sessions, Ernest was convinced Jane was unreliable and indiscreet and distanced himself from her. He was also annoyed by her flagrant affair with big-game hunter Richard Cooper and began channeling his resentment toward both in the story of a cowardly husband (based on Grant Mason) mysteriously shot dead by his philandering wife during an African safari. If the interviews in Denis Brian's *The True Gen* (1986) are to be trusted, Mason was far from offended by her depiction as the "rich bitch" Margaret Macomber. Brian quotes an anonymous "Friend" on why: "I know it's strange that Jane should be proud to be the model for the Macomber woman, but, you see, all her life she came close to being famous without being famous. . . . She'd been in international society since she was a teenager, but she never got the acclaim she wanted. President Calvin Coolidge said she was 'the likeliest young lady that ever crossed over the threshold in the White House.' That's about the biggest compliment she ever got" (84). Hemingway's sister Madelaine, or "Sunny" (1904–1995), is even more piquant in Denis's book: "People are pleased to have a place in history and 'a prize bitch' is better than an absolute nobody" (84). That Mason knew of her depiction in "Macomber" before the story appeared in *Cosmopolitan* in September 1936 was confirmed in the late 1990s when her granddaughter, Alane Salierno Mason, discovered its earliest handwritten draft in a family steamer trunk. (The manuscript was auctioned at Christie's in 2000, fetching $248,000.)[1] Jane Mason also knew as early as February 1937, from Arnold Gingrich, that Hemingway had created a character with at least "six recognizable characteristics" of hers. As noted on pages xxxviii–xxxix, Gingrich informed Mason he had encouraged Ernest to remove the offending passages. There is no evidence that Jane was privy to the manuscript before its publication, however. Although she and Ernest had spent time swimming and fishing in Cuba as late as December 1936, their friendship was effectively over. By the time of Gingrich's letter, Hemingway was already in the thick of his next extramarital obsession, with Martha Gellhorn.

Hemingway never displayed much gallantry toward Mason in the years that followed. In fact, mentions of her are invariably accompanied by the epithet "bitch." Mason herself went on to a chaotic life, divorcing Grant Mason and then marrying three more times, her final husband none other than Arnold Gingrich. A 1964 stroke left her incapacitated; as a result, most of Baker's portrait of the Hemingway-Mason relationship drew from correspondence with Gingrich, Grant Mason, and

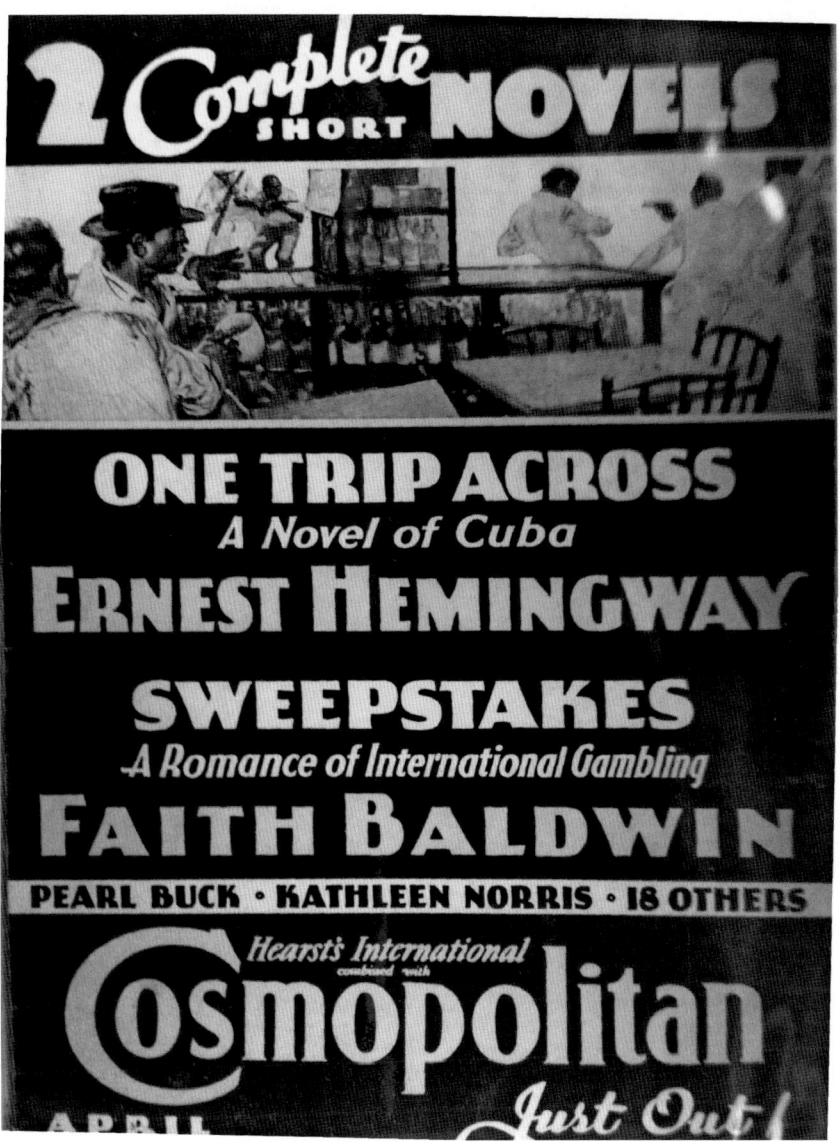

This promotional window card for "One Trip Across," designed for in-store display, suggests how *Cosmopolitan* promoted Hemingway's first Harry Morgan story as a violent shoot-'em-up in April 1934. (Courtesy Park Bucker)

Hemingway with John Dos Passos (*left*), Captain Edward "Bra" Saunders, and an unidentified Key West fishing guide, taken, according to painter Waldo Pierce's notation, at Dry Tortugas. (Courtesy Colby College Special Collections, Waterville, Maine, and the Waldo Peirce Collection/Karen Peirce)

One of the atrocity photos Cuban journalists slipped Walker Evans to smuggle out of Havana as he photographed its streets for Carlton Beals's *The Crime of Cuba* (1933). The graphic image suggests how the terrorist group ABC warned potential informants against collaborating with the government of President Gerardo Machado. In chapter 2, anti-Machado radicals will show Harry Moran a similar photograph. (The Metropolitan Museum of Art)

Hemingway (*left*) a few months after "One Trip Across" appeared in *Cosmopolitan* during his first Cuban fishing expedition aboard his cabin cruiser, the *Pilar*. To his left are his Cuban "choferservicial," or chauffeur, Ignacio, nicknamed "El Gallego"; his pilot, Carlos Gutierrez; and Arnold Samuelson, the aspiring Minnesota writer who rode the rails to Key West after reading the story and ended up as the *Pilar*'s night guard. (Ernest Hemingway Collection. John F. Kennedy Presidential Library and Museum, Boston)

Hemingway's Key West bête noire, Julius F. Stone Jr., the New Deal bureaucrat or "alphabet man" who engineered the island's transformation from an economic Depression casualty into a tourist mecca. Part 2 of *To Have and Have Not*—originally published in *Esquire* as "The Tradesman's Return"—mocks Stone as the Roosevelt toady Dr. Frederick Harrison. (Courtesy Monroe County [Florida] Public Library)

John and Katy Dos Passos aboard Sloppy Joe's owner Joe "Josie" Russell's boat, the *Anita,* in 1932. Although Hemingway had introduced his literary compatriot to his childhood friend from Michigan in the late 1920s, by the time of *To Have and Have Not* he viciously ridiculed the couple's happy marriage by depicting them as the adulterous, childless Richard and Helen Gordon. (Courtesy Ernest Hemingway Collection. John F. Kennedy Presidential Library and Museum, Boston)

A rare picture of the Hemingway home at 907 Whitehead Street, taken from the nearby Key West lighthouse, before handyman Otto "Toby" Bruce built a brick wall around it to keep away tourists. (Courtesy Monroe County [Florida] Public Library.)

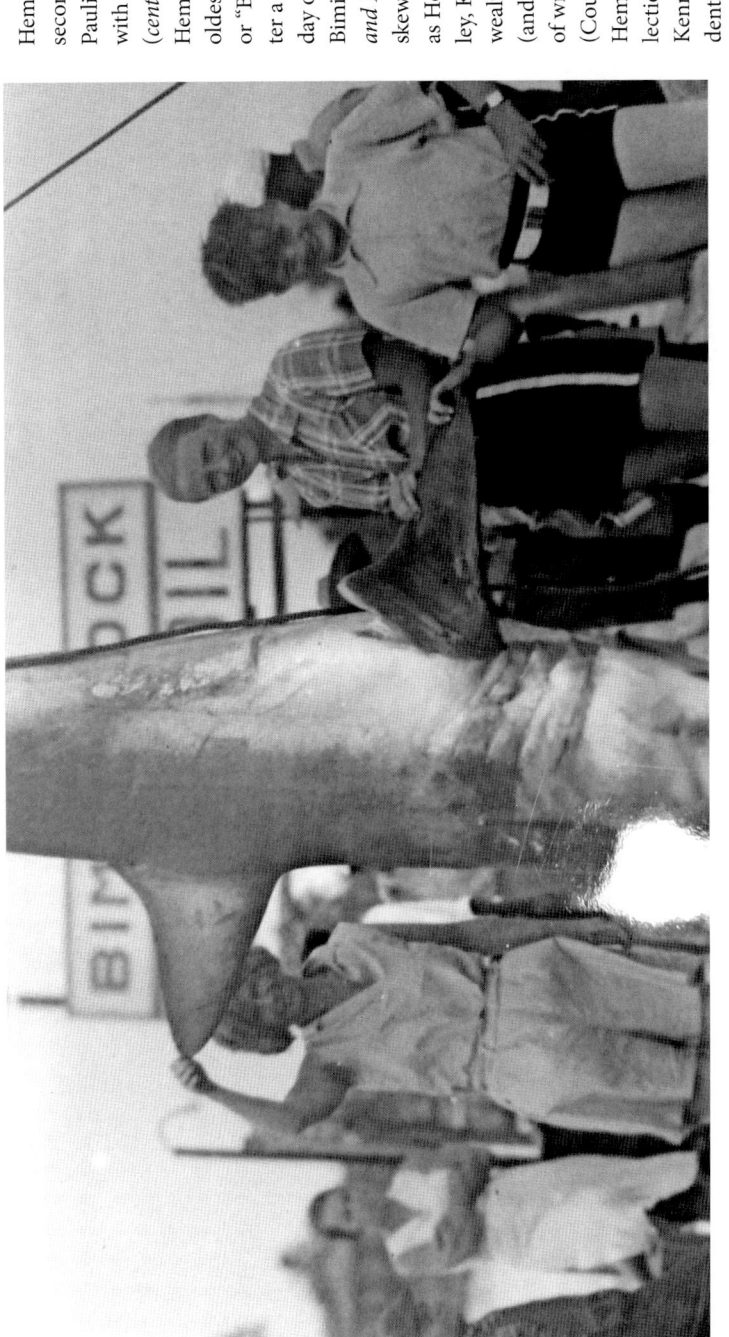

Hemingway's second wife, Pauline Pfeiffer, with Jane Mason (*center*) and Hemingway's oldest son, Jack, or "Bumby," after a successful day of fishing in Bimini. *To Have and Have Not* skewers Mason as Helène Bradley, Key West's wealthy collector (and seducer) of writers. (Courtesy Ernest Hemingway Collection. John F. Kennedy Presidential Library and Museum, Boston)

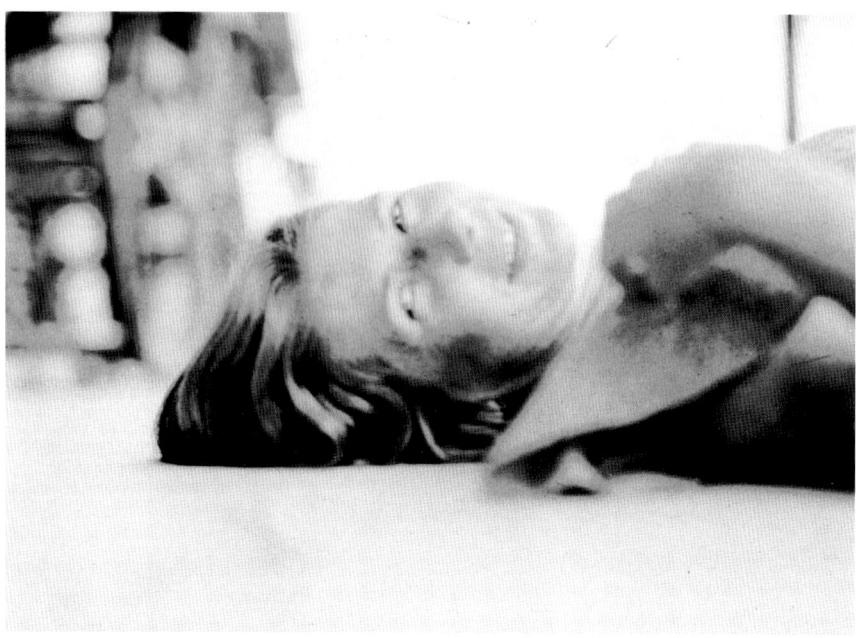

Aware of her husband's attraction to the younger, more glamorous Jane Mason, Pauline dyed her hair blonde and struck a fashion-model pose in hopes of maintaining his affection. Helen Gordon's virulent critique of her husband's literary self-absorption in chapter 21 reflects Hemingway's guilt over his growing indifference toward Pauline. (Courtesy Ernest Hemingway Collection. John F. Kennedy Presidential Library and Museum, Boston)

Artwork by painters and illustrators from the Works Progress Administration (WPA) captures the duality of life in Key West during the tourist boom Julius F. Stone Jr. orchestrated: on the one hand, picturesque, postcard waterscapes of the submarine basin–turned–yacht club, where Hemingway takes readers on a tour of the decadence of the wealthy in *To Have and Have Not*'s chapter 24 (*above*), and on the other, the grimy resilience of native fishermen and boat captains like Harry Morgan (*below*). (Top photo courtesy Florida Memory, State Archives of Florida [Tallahassee]; bottom photo by the author)

The Square Roof, one of the notorious brothels of Jungle Town, the Afro-Bahamian and Afro-Cuban neighborhood on the island's west side, not far from the sub-basin where Hemingway moored the *Pilar*. Richard Gordon wanders past the bordello during his drunken tour of Key West bars. In real life, the poet Elizabeth Bishop once had her picture taken on the establishment's steps during a visit. (Courtesy Florida Memory, State Archives of Florida [Tallahassee])

A period photo of the First National Bank on Duval and Front streets, called First State Trust and Savings in *To Have and Have Not*. Built in 1891, the building remains a Key West landmark, although today it houses T-shirt and trinket shops. (Courtesy Florida Memory, State Archives of Florida [Tallahassee])

A scene from Sloppy Joe's Bar: Hemingway's close friend and sometime fishing guide Joe "Josie" Russell (*above*), the inspiration for Freddy Wallace, owner of the fictional Freddy's Bar where Harry Morgan has an unpleasant encounter with the tourist class. (Courtesy of Benjamin Bruce. From the Toby and Betty Bruce archives)

Painter Waldo Peirce, a founding member of the self-proclaimed "Mob" that fished and caroused with Hemingway in Key West, captured the boozy bonhomie of Sloppy Joe's in this 1936 painting, featuring bartender Al Skinner pouring Hemingway a beer while Peirce and his then wife, Alzira, look on. (Courtesy Karen Peirce)

```
                                    15

        In the Old Days--Carlos killing the other boy
                       The executions at Cabano.
           One Trip Across                              First Juxtaposition/
        In between--The Massacre in the Park            1st theme Key West
           Tradesman's Return                           Decline of Harry.
        The hunting and death of J̶u̶a̶n̶ the agitator     the individual   gradual
                                    friend of Juan      Destruction of Key West
              The Robbery--                             Rise of Harry--
        Death of Juan's child--                         The Hurricane--
              Rummy's End--                             The Vets    Death of Eddy
                                                                    ie Joe Lowe

          Story of the Dynamite trip and its capture--
          -------------------
           The betrayal--consequences--nothing to blow up
           the b̶r̶i̶d̶g̶e̶--K̶e̶e̶p̶-̶t̶h̶e̶ troops from coming in from Camp Columbia--
               Atares
        A night at San Sauci
                   the
                Paco--Langosta and his boat--
           Departure of Juan for Spain--                2nd Theme
        Fall of Machado                                 The J̶u̶x̶t̶a̶p̶e̶s̶ contrast
        Hotel Nacional                                  between the two islands
        Atares                                          How a load of dynamite
        Burial of Mella (End of Communism)              50 lbs to the case changes
                                                        enroute--what goes on in one
                                                        and other at same time--
                                                        Mrs. Miller-Big Annie-Mary Trev
                                                        Bra's Annie-Rosalind Grooms-

        Suppḻa̱mentary themes                            3rd theme
        Lopez Mendez--Jose Antonio                      Decline of the Spaniard Dream
        Gattorno and Lilliane--                         Survival of San Sauci
        Mrs. Mason vs. Mrs. Miller                      Death of the Revolution
                                                        Rise of the Army
                                                        Decline of Key West
                                                           Rise of the beaurocracy
                                                             (temporary)
```

Fig. 1. Page of ink notes in Hemingway's hand (Item 211) outlining ideas for <u>To Have and Have Not</u>.

A transcription of Hemingway's original plan for *To Have and Have Not*, revealing three tiers of themes, friends he intended to include in the plot, and specific historical events he planned to dramatize—almost none of which made it into the final text. (Courtesy Sarah Finch Brown)

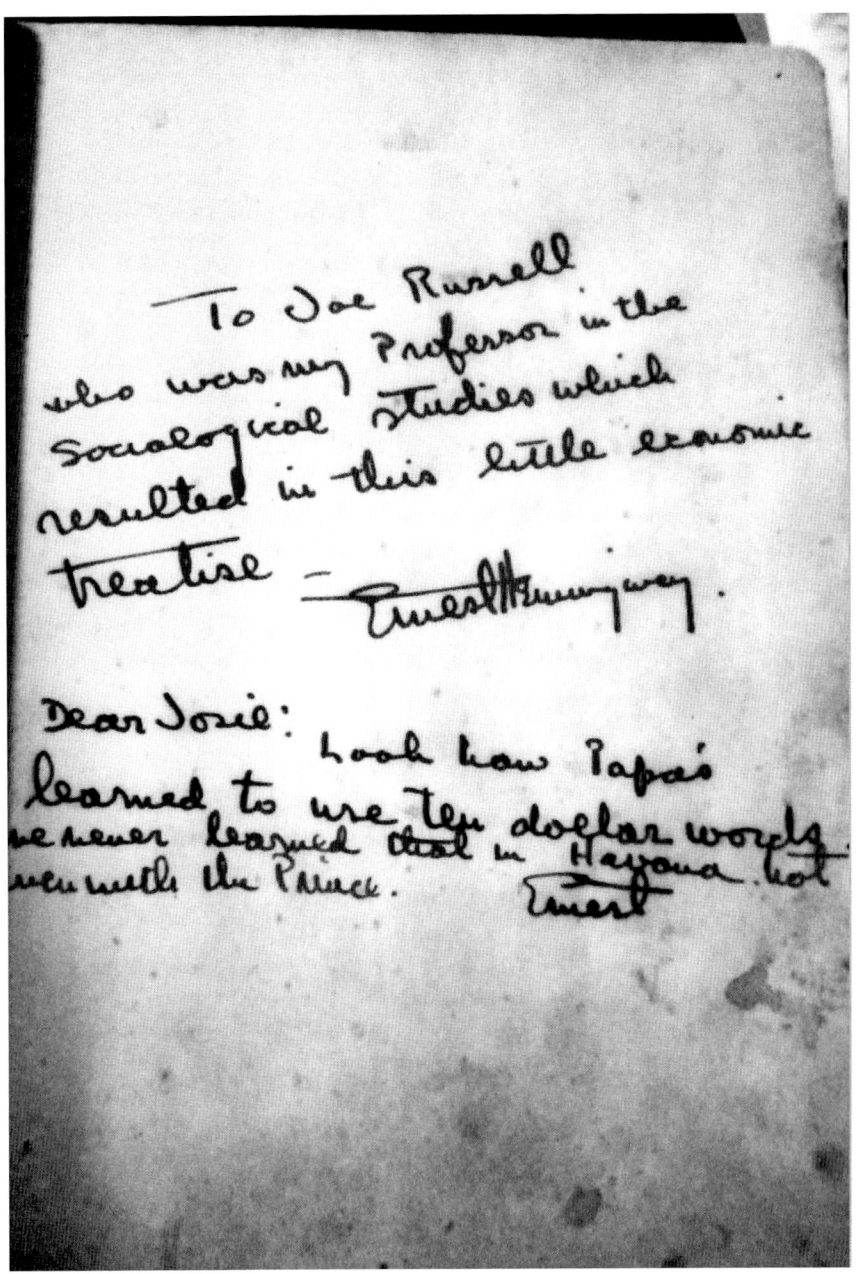

The dedication Hemingway wrote for Joe "Josie" Russell in the captain's presentation copy of *To Have and Have Not* suggests the debt the author owed his friend for inspiring Harry Morgan. (Courtesy of Benjamin Bruce. From the Toby and Betty Bruce archives)

The pulp paperback cover of *To Have and Have Not* conveys not only the sexual longing Marie Morgan feels for her husband, Harry but also the most indelible detail Hemingway created for his doomed boat captain—not his cojones, but his missing limb. (Author's collection)

others. Dennis Brian includes stray quotes from Mason in *The True Gen,* including a claim regarding Margaret Macomber: "Ernest never told me he was writing a character based on me" (85), which was either evasive or a symptom of her memory loss. A rounded portrait of her would not emerge until Bernice Kert's *The Hemingway Women* (1983). Thanks to interviews with the elusive, frail figure conducted shortly before her 1981 death, Kert was able to fill in Mason's background and character and redeem her from her unfortunate and frankly unfair "rich-bitch" reputation. Mason's aforementioned granddaughter, Alane Salierno Mason, also produced a pair of valuable essays on her for *Vanity Fair* and the *Boston Review* that draw on newly discovered correspondence.

For all that is now known about Jane Mason, one specific aspect of her relationship with Hemingway remains unverifiable. As a result, biographers and critics are forced into unenviable speculation about whether or not they were sexually intimate. Hemingway, not surprisingly, boasted that they were, even describing to his oldest son, Jack, how Mason would climb along the outside window ledge of his room at the Ambos Mundos Hotel to reach their trysts—a move that, as James Mellow wryly notes, "almost certainly must have been far more noticeable than sneaking in by way of the door" (*Life without Consequences* 424). Mason, however, denied the pair were lovers, citing her loyalty to Pauline. (Mason often visited Pauline in Key West after the Hemingways' divorce.) And yet Gingrich insisted otherwise to Brian, weirdly asserting, "It's not embarrassing when you know all [her] husbands and all the non-husbands for, God, forty years. . . . It was all very incestuous" (88). In the end, perhaps the best summation of the mystery comes from Kert: "So how does one describe the relationship of Ernest Hemingway and Jane Mason? Ambiguous to say the least" ("Jane Mason" 116).

140:7 **She interests me both as a woman and as a social phenomenon:** Gordon's windy assertion typifies what Hemingway regarded as the pretentiousness of "phony" proletarian writers. Helen Gordon offers two sarcastic replies to this comment—"Do people go to bed with a social phenomenon?" and "is [sex with a rich woman] part of the homework of a writer?" that put Gordon in his place. Helen's sarcasm is unsuccessful, however, for Gordon insists that marital fidelity interferes with the writer's ability to investigative sociology: "A writer has to know about everything. . . . He can't restrict his experience to conform to bourgeois standards" (140:12–14). For Hemingway, the term *bourgeois standards* would ring of parody.

141:11–12 **She hadn't found John MacWalsey either:** Hemingway implies that Helen Gordon is romantically attached to the economics professor. In chapter 23 we will learn their affair is in its earliest stages; the two have only kissed. Still, Helen Gordon is convinced that MacWalsey will love and respect her as Richard Gordon has failed to.

NOTE

1. See Alane Salierno Mason's "Comedy with Animals" 23–26.

CHAPTER SIXTEEN

Set at Porter Dock, this scene finds Harry Morgan making sure Freddy's boat is seaworthy. Harry also hides his Thompson gun with the engines below the cockpit floor for easy access. When Albert Tracy unexpectedly appears asking to be hired as a mate, Harry relents. Government work has been cut to three days a week in Key West, giving Albert little choice but to turn for help to the man who attempted to hire him in chapter 9. Only now Harry lies and tells Albert they have been hired to take a party tarpon fishing, not to run the Cubans to Cabañas—a sign that the captain is attempting to protect his mate. After sending Albert on an errand to buy spark plugs and gas, Harry stares at a red-brick building barely a block away at the corner of Front and Duval streets. For the first time, we learn the name of the Cubans' target: the First State Trust and Savings Bank. As Harry walks to Freddy's for one final drink, he makes sure to take a circuitous path to avoid the scene of the impending crime.

143:3 receiver just behind the bolt: *Receiver* is the term used to describe the frame or body of a firearm. It generally houses the bolt, trigger, and magazine assemblies.

143:19 a grunt fishing boat . . . on the way around to the fish market: Grunts, first noted in the "grits and grunts" line (84:10–11), are a family of fish with the scientific name Haemulidae. There are 150 different species and 19 different genera among them. In 1930s tourist guides to Key West, the fish market and wharf are marked as stops Nos. 7 and 8 at the end of Elizabeth Street. The market and wharf were a public attraction because catches were not hung at a counter or displayed on ice but purchased live from fish cars or smack wells, making for an entertaining spectacle as fisherman scooped them live onto the dock for customers.

143:24–26 sandy island . . . the shark camp: Harry here looks out to Wisteria Island, colloquially known as Christmas Tree Island, which lies some two thousand feet off Mallory Square. The small land mass was created at the turn of the twentieth century through Navy dredging; the name *Wisteria* was officially given to it in 1925 after a steamer that sank and burned while moored there. In the 1930s the island was purchased by a colorful and legendarily influential state representative named Bernie C. Papy (1902–1964), known colloquially as the "King of the Keys." The island's shark camp was operated by Captain Ray Knopp, the "King of Shark Fisherman." As recently as 2011–12, Wisteria Island was at the center of controversy. For many years the island has been Key West's last remaining bastion of undeveloped bohemia, a site where boaters and squatters alike could find shelter from the relentless tourist economy. When the previous owners (who had also developed nearby Sunset Key) announced a development plan, locals researching the island's history discovered documents raising questions about the legitimacy of its deeding. After investigating, the U.S. Department of the Interior declared the federal government still owned the land, despite the developers having paid property taxes on it for forty-plus years.

144:7–8 three days a week on the relief now: Hemingway conflates historical events here to give Albert a dramatic reason for needing work from Harry.

144:17 Why don't you smack her? Harry is not being ironic here; Hemingway is insisting that his hero would never tolerate Marie "giv[ing] him hell" as Albert does from his woman. The awkward exchange is meant to demonstrate how much manlier Harry is than other male characters. As Mark Spilka notes, in his final two marriages (both occurring after *To Have and Have Not*) Hemingway "qualifies as a male batterer": "In one of two known incidents of direct abuse, he slapped his third wife, Martha Gellhorn, with the back of his hand when she insisted on driving home one night from a Havana party because he had been drinking." Later, during World War II, when he was courting her, Hemingway slapped Mary Welsh after she complained about the drunkenness of a group of battalion-commander friends while staying at the Ritz Hotel (*Eight Lessons,* 207). As Spilka goes on to note, Hemingway was also verbally and emotionally abusive. On 30 September 1951, following a volatile telephone argument with Hemingway over their troubled son Gregory, Pauline, his second ex-wife, died from shock on an operating table after an adrenal tumor heightened and then dropped her blood pressure due to stress (*Eight Lessons,* 210; see also Hawkins 270–71).

144:20 Marine Hardware: Although various marine hardware shops operated in Key West in the 1930s, Hemingway likely intended this as a reference to his friend Charles Thompson's store, part of the varied Thompson family enterprises that dominated the eastern end of Caroline Street around the present site of Land's End Marina. In addition to selling boating supplies, the Thompson family operated a 125-boat fishing fleet, an ice house, the turtle kraals, a cigar-box manufacturing plant, and a pineapple canning company, among other ventures. Thompson and his wife, Lorine, were Ernest and Pauline's closest friends in Key West; the couples met during the Hemingways' first spring on the island. As Michael S. Reynolds writes, "Had Hemingway not connected with Thompson, he might never have returned to Key West [after 1928]; had Pauline not found Lorine, she might never have agreed to the return" (*American Homecoming* 172). Charles accompanied Hemingway on his 1933–34 safari and appears as "Karl" in *Green Hills of Africa*. Karl Thompson was actually an older brother of Charles's and happened to serve as Monroe County sheriff in the 1930s, inspiring the character of Sheriff Roger Johnson in *To Have and Have Not*.

144:28 **flywheel:** A flywheel is a disk attached to the crankshaft of an engine that allows for the constant distribution of power. When a piston is applied to the flywheel to create torque, the flywheel stores the energy generated by the rotation. The energy is subsequently released through the mechanical system when the piston is removed.

145:2–3 **tarponing:** *Megalops atlanticus,* as the species of tarpon native to the Atlantic is scientifically known, is a game fish notable for its upturned mouth and the distinctive blue-green glint to its silver back scales. Tarpon are a basic mainstay of the charter-fishing industry because they are found in abundance in shallows, flats, bays, and other coastal proximities, making them easily accessible. More importantly, they are known for the acrobatic agility and the fight they put up when hooked, often making for a spectacular show for anglers. Hemingway's most extensive comments on tarpon occur in his debut *Esquire* column, "Marlin Off the Morro: A Cuban Letter" (1934), in which he notes tarpons' fondness for congregating around smacks and fish cars (*BL* 120), and "The Great Blue River" (1949), in which he describes fishing for them in the Havana harbor (*BL* 356–57).

145:7 **jacks:** A reference to jack crevalle, or *caranx hippos,* a voracious, predatory fish mentioned in Hemingway's March 1935 *Esquire* essay "Sailfish Off Mombasa: A Key West Letter" (197). In *To Have and Have Not,* Albert suggests that because the jacks will devour Harry's bait mullet they should stock up on more of the latter fish. His very specific questions here imply that he suspects the tarponing story is a cover, especially since tarpon are out of season. Albert specifically asks Harry about ferrying the Cubans they met with at the Richards' club (145:14–15), and while Hemingway doesn't describe his reaction to Harry's claim that he never heard back from the men, the dialogue suggests he knows full well they are not preparing for an ordinary charter.

146:1 **The First State Trust and Savings Bank:** This is our first concrete hint that the Cubans are plotting a bank robbery; previous clues are simple foreshadowing. "First State Trust and Savings" was not the actual name of the financial institution operating on Front Street in the 1930s. The bank, founded in 1891, was actually called the First National Bank. Hemingway bore more than a smidgen of resentment toward it. A half-decade earlier, amid the windfall of *A Farewell to Arms,* he had attempted to cash a thousand-dollar royalty check there, only to be refused by President William Y. Porter (of Porter Dock fame). According to lore, Hemingway whisked into a nearby Front Street bar whose owner was only too happy to accommodate him. That bar happened to be the original Sloppy Joe's, then called The Blind Pig, before Joe "Josie" Russell relocated it to Greene Street (McLendon 38; McIver, *Hemingway's Key West* 47–48). It should be noted that this story, while a mainstay of anecdotal biographies, has not been corroborated.

CHAPTER SEVENTEEN

Winding in and out of interior monologue, this chapter is largely given over to matters of conscience as Harry Morgan wrestles with his complicity in the coming crime. Initially, his concern is for Freddy, with whom he again feels compelled to be honest out of loyalty. Only Harry knows Freddy would never stand for allowing an institution as central as Key West's leading bank to be robbed. Harry briefly considers hiding out in Freddy's Bar to avoid the Cubans. "I could just let it all slide and do nothing," he thinks, but inaction would do nothing to solve the issues of his poverty and poor prospects (147:22–23). Considering the predicament of Conchs in general, Harry realizes how economic oppression instills apathy into the working class, lulling the average wage earner into starving instead of fighting for his right to a living. Harry decides he will not allow himself to be further emasculated; his cojones are all he has left to sell. Accordingly, he plants an alibi with Freddy and returns to the dock to await the Cubans. On his way out, he reencounters the Laughtons and once again brushes off the obnoxious wife's come-ons. The chapter ends with the omniscient narrator informing us of the Gordons' whereabouts. As Richard Gordon heads to the Bradleys for what he hopes will be a tryst, Helen saunters a nearby beach, pining for Professor MacWalsey.

147:1 **he wanted to tell him about it:** In manuscript this chapter begins with Harry confiding the plot to Freddy in the bar's back room. After six lines of dialogue, Hemingway changed his mind and decided the boat owner must remain unaware of the robbery. That Freddy would allow the heist to happen without informing law enforcement is implausible. As the barkeep notes in this deleted passage, the bank employees are honest working people like Harry, and putting them at risk is "awful" (MS 30, item 204, folder 7, page 70). The change also had the additional benefit of reinforcing the novel's theme. As Harry broods over his obligations to Freddy and other citizens of Key West, he begins to realize how conspiring with the revolutionaries has isolated him from his fellow man: "I have to do it alone," he insists (148:19–20).

147:5–14 **In the old days, maybe. . . . I got it [the Tommy gun] in Cuba on a trip the time when I peddled those others:** A serious flaw of *To Have and Have Not* is that Hemingway introduces tantalizing bits of information about Harry Morgan's background without ever telling the whole story. We learn that Harry was once a Miami policeman but not why he left the force (44:14–17). Similarly, Hemingway here refers back to the conversation on 133:9–13, when Harry says to Bee-lips that he and Freddy have twice partnered up since the war, implying that the pair bootlegged together during Prohibition: "You know how much stuff I've handled for him." Even more intriguing is the suggestion that Harry ran guns as well as rum. As noted at 6:21, Tommy guns were prevalent among both pro- and anti-Machado forces. Since Harry reports that he picked up his machine gun while "peddl[ling] the others" in Cuba, one assumes he supplied weapons to the revolution, although "the time" suggests he did it only once. The disinclination to elaborate on these anecdotes probably reflects Hemingway's sense of genre. In hardboiled fiction at this time heroes such as Hammett's Continental Op and Sam Spade were not haunted by their pasts, as gumshoes and noir protagonists would increasingly become, from the late 1940s on. In *For Whom the Bell Tolls*, Hemingway would shift 180 degrees when it came to protagonists' backstories. To determine his personal standard of heroism outside of political ideology, Robert Jordan obsesses over the past, specifically, his grandfather's Civil War service and his father's suicide.

147:19–20 All I've got is my *cojones* to peddle: The verb *to peddle* appears only four times in the novel, as well as once as a noun in 237:14, when a grain broker in the Key West yacht basin refuses to acknowledge how common people whom capitalism has allowed him economic advantage over have been reduced to selling novelties door-to-door ("we don't want no peddlers, get out of here, the door slammed in [their] face"). Despite the relative scarcity of references to it, peddling serves as a central motif of the novel's proletarian theme. Harry has only his manhood from which to make his living, while Marie's lone saleable commodities, her hips, are devalued goods because of her age (175:3). The importance of peddling may be best understood in regard to the difference between the producer and service economies. In an essay on James M. Cain's *Mildred Pierce* (1941) and its depiction of the rise of the service sector in the American marketplace, Donna M. Campbell argues that Cain's characters resist the economic redefinition of the self from producer to server: "For Cain's characters, the quest for self-definition results less from a shift in class than a shift in self-perception: in key scenes in several of his novels, down-but-not-really-out characters confront, recognize, and thereafter reject what Cain calls a 'varlet' mentality, which they implicitly define as the willingness to work for wages and tips instead of holding out for the big payoff from their carefully planned but improbable schemes" (2). Forced by economic circumstance to become a waitress, Mildred Pierce must cross "the psychological Rubicon between production and service, autonomy and dependence, that results from wearing a uniform and taking tips" (4–5). Of course, Mildred *recrosses* that boundary by rising from the wait staff to the owner of her own restaurants by virtue of her culinary skills, all the while profoundly anxious about her past as a "varlet." Yet her relationship with her shrewish daughter, Veda, ultimately confirms that status, for Mildred abandons her business to shepherd Veda's career as an opera singer, only to lose both her daughter and her second husband, Monty, when the two run off together. In the end, Mildred ends up remarried to her first husband and is back to baking the pies that originally supported her family during the Depression. Like Marie Morgan, she is overweight and worn down by labor, and any sense of self-possession is neutralized by what she has lost over the course of her ups and downs in the economy: "She has escaped the service industry," Campbell notes, "but only at the cost of destroying all that she has worked for and of losing her two daughters in the process" (13).

If the tragedy of *Mildred Pierce* is "the cultural anomie that results when service substitutes for the production of commodities" (15), one might argue that the tragedy of *To Have and Have Not* is the inability to imagine any alternative economic identity to service. As a charter-boat captain, after all, Harry occupies a liminal position between the producer and service economies: on the one hand, he owns his own business, but on the other, he is selling a service to a wealthier class, upon whom he is dependent. (As the episode in part 1 with the deadbeat tourist Johnson demonstrates, the wealthier class has no qualms ripping him off for this service.) When Harry insists he has only his cojones to peddle, he is admitting that there is no escape from the service economy; even his bravery and masculine strength are services he must now sell to the Cuban revolutionaries to get by. In this regard, it seems significant that as Harry lies mortally wounded on the *Queen Conch* in chapter 18, the only dream of escape he can muster is an "honest" position in the service sector: "I should have got a job in a service station or something" (174:21–22). Because Marie is a woman, her position is even more tenuous, for aging devalues the sexuality that is her only possible commodity to peddle, prostitution being merely one more insidious example of a service relationship in the economy. As a motif, peddling is the counterpart of the novel's theme of "taking it": both represent the limits of agency and the passive entrapment of stoic endurance in an economy without outlets for autonomy, not even in crime.

148:6–7 One bunch of Cuban government bastards cost me my arm shooting at me with a load when they had no need to: Harry alludes back to 86:1–6 in part 2, Hemingway's most explicit description of the political confusion in post-Machado Cuba that enabled Mariel to serve briefly as an "open port." As Harry insists, even if the Cuban government did decide to shut down the trade in undeclared rum, there was no need for the violence that cost him his arm.

148:21–26 There were Conchs that would starve to death before they would steal all right. . . . They started starving when they were born; some of them: Reviewing

To Have and Have Not for the *Saturday Review of Literature,* Bernard DeVoto complained that the "dice which Mr. Hemingway is rolling are so openly and flagrantly loaded" that it was impossible to think of Key West's laboring class as victimized by the economy—not when Harry Morgan's major characteristic is the "gonadotropic" strength he exerts in the face of flaccid male "haves" such as Laughton and Gordon (qtd. in Meyers, *Critical Heritage* 224). Such a reading overlooks the ethnocentrism that creeps into the novel in lines like this passage, in which Harry critiques "some" of his fellow Key Westers for their passivity. Having imbibed the Protestant work ethic through his midwestern upbringing, Hemingway was not necessarily sensitive to the more laidback tropical attitude, often interpreting the pace of island life as laziness.

150:6. **the Bradleys' big winter home:** Grant and Jane Mason did not own a home in Key West. Their estate was located west of Havana in Jaimanitas. In the manuscript, when Hemingway describes the Bradley home in detail he essentially transplants the estate across the Gulf of Mexico.

150:7-8 **Mrs. Bradley collected writers as well as their books:** This entire final paragraph was added to the setting copy in pencil, a late addition reflecting the hasty need to stitch in threads of the Gordon/Bradley subplot after cutting the original chapters 22 and 23, in which it was developed (MS 32, item 213, folder 14, page 113). In this section of the manuscript, Hemingway had explored the theme of literary patronage, more specifically the power of the rich to corrupt writers with money and favors. This was a concern Hemingway felt intently by 1936 as he fished in Bimini with wealthy sportsmen such as Michael Lerner, Richard Cooper, Tommy Shevlin, Winston "Wolfie" Guest, and Baron Bror von Blixen-Finecke—not to mention Jane Mason, only occasionally accompanied by her husband, Grant. As Scott Donaldson writes, Hemingway cultivated the lifelong belief that "an inverse relationship existed between money and morals" (*By Force of Will* 53–54), an axiom that enabled him to romanticize the (relative) poverty of his early apprentice years in Paris but that also aroused deep feelings of hypocrisy during the Depression as his sporting interests affiliated him with the yachting class. His anxiety about the effect of this circle on his art is spelled out explicitly in "The Snows of Kilimanjaro": "You said that you would write about these people; about the very rich; that you were really not of them but a spy in their country; that you would leave it and write of it. . . . But he would never do it, because each day of not writing, of comfort, of being that which he despised, dulled his ability and softened his will to work so that, finally, he did no work at all. The people he knew now were all much more comfortable when he did not work" (*CSS* 44).

What makes "Snows" compelling fiction is precisely the element that the Helène Bradley / Richard Gordon subplot lacks: self-excoriation, Harry Walden's brutal estimation that he has betrayed his work ethic by growing too comfortable availing himself of the luxuries proffered by the rich. Whether in manuscript or the final version of the novel, Gordon never admits to his hypocrisies, even after other characters enumerate them for him. Instead, *To Have and Have Not* levels a more simplistic, transparent value judgment against the affluent likewise vented in "Snows": "The rich were dull and they drank too much. . . . They were dull and they were repetitious" (*CSS* 53). Hemingway also voiced this complaint a tad more expansively in his *Esquire* essay "Out in the Stream: A Cuban Letter" (1934), in which he complains that the rich are dull because they only care about "how to get more wealth, or horses, or what is wrong with themselves, with psychoanalysis, or horses, or how not to lose what they have, or horses" (*BL* 177).

Arguably, the word *collected* in this passage reveals one anxiety Hemingway felt about befriending "haves." Fishing and hunting may have been the passion he shared with the rich, but his entry into their world was his status as a famous writer. While most of his moneyed friends were awed by his literary talent and treated him as an equal, Hemingway's perpetual defensiveness convinced him he was just another acquisition. In this view, the rich traded on his capital, trafficking in his reputation and renown as they would any other commodity. In years to come, for example, he would claim "The Snows of Kilimanjaro" was inspired by a wealthy female admirer who, upon his return from Africa in April 1934, offered to fund a second safari if she could tag along (Baker, *A Life* 289). Whether that story is true is a matter of conjecture, but in "Snows" Hemingway deployed a choice word to dramatize the writer's sense of feeling procured by the rich: "The steps by which [Helen] had acquired him . . . were all part of a regular progression in which she had built herself a new life and he had traded away what remained of his old life" (*CSS* 46).

Despite its use of the term *rich bitch*, "Snows" is sympathetic toward Helen Walden, the wife coping with her dying husband's abusive anger. Helène Bradley, however, is by design a one-dimensional villain. In the manuscript she escorts Richard Gordon to her bedroom to show off the collection of signed first editions she displays in a glass case. Both the location of the display and the transparent flattery of inviting Gordon to autograph his books as a record of his having been invited into her temple literalize the seductions of wealthy admirers to an almost comical degree. (The detail of the autographed books may trace to a September 1934 letter from Mason to Hemingway in which she notes that she ordered first editions of his books, hoping Ernest will "take plume in hand and sign them.")

Thanks to the prurient emphasis on Mrs. Bradley's unquenchable sex drive, critics are often misled into regarding her as a simple "nymphomaniac" (Mellow, *Life without Consequences* 487; McIver, *Hemingway's Key West* 71). Yet the manuscript of *To Have and Have Not* includes a telling exchange between Helène and Tommy Bradley that humanizes this femme fatale and provides dramatic justification for her predatory approach to writers. When she confronts Tommy for walking in on her lovemaking with Richard Gordon, her cuckolded husband shrugs, wondering how he was supposed to know she had company. When Helène says she should have locked the door, Tommy says, "I cured you of that," leading her to remember an "awful time" involving broken doors and trousers thrown out of windows. Helène insists she wanted to kill her husband then but continues to love him and her sexual escapades are meaningless (MS 32, item 212, folder 6, pages 100–01). As the conversation reveals, Tommy cheated on Helène first. More than mere revenge, her sexual aggression represents a seizing of male sexual privilege that protects her from the romantic vulnerability typically stereotyped as feminine. The added character dimension makes her a fascinating foil to Marie Morgan, who is equally willful but draws her strength from her perfect partnership with Harry. Again, it is unfortunate that Hemingway deleted this detail from the published novel; it had the potential to redeem Mrs. Bradley from the conventional wisdom that she is a cartoonish stereotype.

CHAPTER EIGHTEEN

The longest single chapter in the novel also happens to be the most action-packed section of part 3. Harry and Albert have barely finished preparing Freddy Wallace's boat for their crossing when shots ring out at the First State Trust and Savings Bank on the corner of Front and Duval streets. The Cubans from Richards' bar stream from the building, guns still blazing, appearing a second later on Porter Dock with an abducted cab driver. When Albert tells Harry not to start the engines, the most sadistic of the terrorists, Roberto, blasts him with a Tommy gun. With Albert crumpled at the boat's stern, Harry has little choice but to take to sea. He and the four bank robbers race away, initially trailed by boats that cannot match their speed.

Once at a comfortable distance from Key West, Harry begins plotting to seize back control of the boat. He allows the youngest of the revolutionaries, Emilio, to defend their violence and explain their intent to save their homeland from military rule. Harry pretends to sympathize, but as the chapter flows in and out of interior monologue, we hear the captain's inner objections to overthrowing oppression with bloodshed, especially when it victimizes honest workingmen such as Albert. Amid Harry's ruminating, Hemingway delivers a controversial line that some interpret as his pre–Spanish Civil War resistance to political calls-to-arms: "What the hell do I care about his revolution. F——his revolution" (168:4–5).

Pretending to check the engines, Harry slips below deck and retrieves his own submachine gun. He manages to shoot all four men, but one survives at least long enough to plant what will prove a fatal bullet in his belly. "I got a chance still," Harry tells himself. "I got a kind of chance" (173:5–6). He cuts the engine and hopes the Coast Guard will find him in time. As he lies on the cockpit floor, his thoughts turn to Marie and how she will survive without him. His nausea makes him susceptible to the roll of the sea, but he suffers the choppy water stoically: "[H]e lay quietly and took it" (175:18). A similar line will appear in a different context in chapter 22, spoken at Freddy's bar by one of the crazed World War I veterans living on Matecumbe laboring on the Overseas Highway. The repetition will establish contradictory meanings for the motif that Hemingway declines to resolve: is the ability to "take it" a litmus of heroic endurance or a passive submission to the sadism of surrounding forces that render humanity grotesque?

151:19, 22–23 **Thompson machine gun . . . the bop-bop-bop-bop:** This refers back to the Tommy gun the *porra* fired on the ABC revolutionaries in the novel's opening scene (6:21).

153:5–6. **The bullets whocked like three slaps:** From the beginning of part 3 readers likely predict Albert's death. Harry's efforts first to hire him and then to protect him by turning him away from the run suggests that the mate is not only doomed but that Harry will bear responsibility for his demise by involving him in the plot. Nevertheless, Albert's murder before the getaway boat even leaves Porter Dock comes as a shock, for it happens so quickly on top of the bank heist as to catch us off-guard.

The OED does not contain an entry on the onomatopoeic verb *to whock*, but the word appears in books as early as the 1830s, so it is clearly not Hemingway's invention. Nevertheless, it seems to have been a conversational staple of his when describing bullets hitting their target. Fourth wife Mary Hemingway employs it in a diary entry describing Papa's attempt to land the first lion of his 1954 safari: "We heard the whock, but [the lion] didn't fall and he didn't roar" (Baker, *A Life* 516).

154:4 **Crawfish bar:** Also known as Kingfish Shoals, this sandbar lies just shy of five miles west of Key West on roughly the same latitude as Fort Zachary Taylor. As revealed by the description of Harry's navigating that follows on 154:11–15, the boat channel out of Key West carries the men southwest past the Navy sub-base/yachting basin and the fort.

154:28–29 **One, Ray's, is running the mail from Matecumbe:** This reference to speed boats employed as mail carriers demonstrates how Hemingway did not feel bound to a strict historical timeline in his writing. Before the 1935 Labor Day hurricane, a mail train from New York arrived in Key West each business day at 11:50 A.M. and departed at 5:40 P.M. With the Florida East Coast Railway destroyed by the disaster, however, the postal service was forced to truck mail to the island, considerably slowing delivery. Moreover, with the Overseas Highway as yet incomplete, speedboats had to service the forty-mile leg between Upper Matecumbe and No Name keys. Since part 3 takes place before the hurricane, when the train was still in service, Hemingway's mention of "running the mail" is an anachronism.

155:1 **on Ed. Taylor's ways:** Neither census records, telephone books, nor business guides to Key West in the 1930s (which are not plentiful by any means) list any "Ed. Taylor" in the boat building/repair business. As with the earlier reference to Walton (106:6), Hemingway appears to have invented names for fictional characters mentioned only in passing.

155:7–12 **old Postoffice . . . the yellow hotel building . . . lighthouse . . . the big winter hotel:** In this paragraph Hemingway identifies several major Key West landmarks. The yellow building dominating the skyline is the La Concha Hotel, first described at 63:19 and 86:19–20 as Harry returns to Key West from his two disastrous trips to Havana in both part 1 and part 2. A careful reader will notice the hotel is described as white, not yellow, on the earlier approach into Key West. The post office refers to the Customs House referenced at 120:21; upon its completion in 1891, the building originally housed both customs and mail offices (along with federal court and lighthouse personnel). The Key West Lighthouse is located on Whitehead Street, directly across from the Hemingway House, while the "big winter hotel" refers to the Casa Marina Hotel on Reynolds Street, built in 1920 and, due to the Depression, shuttered from 1932 to 1934, when the KWA reopened it as a centerpiece of its tourism rehabilitation program.

156:22–23 **Sand Key . . . the stake on little Sand Key shoals:** The "widening spire" Harry Morgan sees is the Sand Key Lighthouse, first noted at 62:11 as Harry and Eddy return to Key West after murdering Mr. Sing at the end of part 1 and subsequently at 67:14 at the beginning of part 2 as the wounded Harry and Wesley attempt to find the island after Cuban authorities ambush their liquor run. Hemingway was fond of trawling the flats of nearby Little Sand Key shoals, which were home to kingfish.

157:1 **We cut the telephone wire:** Notifying the Coast Guard to a pursue a Cuba-bound boat of bank robbers via seaplane would have required Key West authorities to telephone Miami, where an air station had been established in 1932 on Dinner Key in Biscane Bay. The Miami station played a vital role in protecting the Keys. As the 1935 Labor Day hurricane approached the Florida straits, Lieutenant William Clemmer dropped warnings to Keys residents from his aircraft. After the storm, Clemmer set a record, evacuating sixteen injured people at once in his FLB, or flying airboat, as Coast Guard pilots called their seaplanes. Cutting the telephone line to the mainland, the terrorists fail to appreciate how Prohibition duties had challenged the Coast Guard to upgrade radio capacities with shore radio stations, including one in Ft. Lauderdale, Florida. As Harry knows, a radio operator at the Key West Naval Air Station could notify superiors through the wireless immediately of the boat's general direction, with a plane tracking them at least until dark, when it would be recalled. Thus, even if the slow Coast Guard vessel assigned to Key West could not interdict Harry's boat (as Harry notes, it only moves at twelve knots per hour [156:17]), the plane could easily foil the getaway by notifying either outlying vessels or Cuban authorities of its coordinates.

157:7 **Cappy:** As yet another sign of how corrupted the text of *To Have and Have Not* is, the condescending name Roberto gives Harry is spelled here with a *-y* instead of an *-ie* as throughout the rest of the chapter.

158:1–2 He is a good revolutionary but a bad man: Revolutionaries appear throughout Hemingway's fiction, reflecting his fascination not simply with war and political upheaval but with the moral contradictions of violence. In characterological terms, insurrectionists tend to fall into two camps: the sincere but naïve true believer Emilio will shortly reveal himself to be and the brutal thug for whom ideological conviction is an excuse for sadism. Roberto clearly falls in this latter category. As such, he not only resembles the ABC terrorist Pancho in Havana (4:20) but also Andre Marty, the homicidal Stalinist commander of Robert Jordan's brigade in *For Whom the Bell Tolls*. Pablo, the cowardly guerilla in *Bells*, offers a more reformed variation on this character type: after forcing nationalists off the cliff in Ronda, Pablo is broken by his sadism and must through Jordan's leadership reconnect with his ideals of valor and heroism. A predecessor to Emilio is the naïve hero of the short story "The Revolutionist" (1925), a Hungarian communist who travels Italy enjoying art galleries on his way to Switzerland, seemingly disillusioned by politics and escaping into aesthetic ideas (*CSS* 119–20). To symbolize Emilio's naïveté, Hemingway makes the young man a poor sailor. As Harry notes at 159:27, Emilio fails to recognize that his navigation "is about twenty-five degrees off and that the compass dial [is] swinging."

161:8–9 Harry kicked the machine gun over the edge . . . while Albert turned over twice in the white, churned, bubbling back-suction of the propellor wash before sinking, the gun went straight down: The tough-guy banter Harry exchanges with Roberto over the dead body of Albert may seem excessively callous until this masterful moment when Hemingway reveals his hero's wisecracks are a distraction designed to lull the terrorist into a false sense of security. When Harry suggests they dump the mate's body overboard, Roberto is amused and asks if the one-armed man understands how much a dead body weighs. "You ever lift a dead man before, Cappie?" the terrorist wonders, to which Harry replies, "No. . . . You ever lift a big dead woman?" (160:23–25). Seconds later, Roberto chides, "Listen, I'm sorry I killed him. . . . When I kill you I feel worse," and Harry essentially rolls his eyes (161:2–3). To hoist the corpse to the stern, Roberto must set down the Tommy gun, allowing Harry to kick it into the ocean while the terrorist is occupied. The moment is a cleverly contrived sequence that again demonstrates Hemingway's skill at building suspense through action.

161:15. *ametralladora*: Spanish for *machine gun*.

162:13 You're drunk. Every time you're drunk you want to kill somebody: In Hemingway's world, a man who cannot handle his liquor lacks self-discipline and thus always proves himself unworthy of others' respect. Here that trope is deployed ironically. As events subsequently demonstrate, Roberto is actually wise to warn that the bank robbers "make a mistake if [they] don't kill [Harry] now" (162:11–12). Yet his fellow terrorists have so little regard for him, both because he drinks at a time like this and because his violence heightens when he is intoxicated, that they dismiss his concern—a fatal mistake.

163:7 **grease cups . . . stuffing boxes:** Also known as a "gland seal," a stuffing box is the chamber around a propeller shaft where it exits a hull. The box prevents water from leaking back into a vessel. In some models, lubricant is pumped into the chamber to facilitate propulsion. Other models employ a grease cup, a reservoir that releases the lubricant at an adjustable rate.

163:9–14 **Not yet, he thought. . . . I better wait:** For many readers, this passage is indicative of how perfunctory interior monologue can seem. We enter Harry's thoughts but for no real purpose other than to hear him caution himself against acting hastily in ambushing the terrorists. Chapter 18 includes at least three such moments, but instead of tightening the suspense they slacken it with repetition and pointless self-interrogation.

163:25 **Emilio:** This is the first mention of the most sympathetic terrorist's name.

164:7–23 **It would be a pretty night to cross, he thought:** Yet another instance of gratuitous interior monologue. This time Harry realizes he must somehow skew east to avoid sighting the glare of Havana, which will appear on the horizon in as shortly as an hour. The long passage includes at least one extremely awkward transition that proves almost comical in attempting to capture the flux of Harry's thinking: "That was lucky getting rid of that gun. Damn that was lucky. Wonder what Marie's having for supper" (164:12–14). Strikingly, interior monologue was a stylistic indulgence of Sherwood Anderson's that a decade earlier Hemingway had relentlessly mocked in *The Torrents of Spring*. Anderson's *Dark Laughter* (1925) is full of risible rhetorical questions that characters pose to themselves that mark the author's infelicitous effort to invest them with depth. That Hemingway would repeat the same narratological sin suggests how far he could drift from his belief in unornamented prose.

165:16 **Simmons:** This is only our second mention of the lawyer Bee-lips's surname since 102:8. Coming after so many scenes featuring the shady lawyer, it cannot help but feel an afterthought. As Emilio implies, Roberto murdered Bee-lips so not to leave any witnesses behind in Key West.

166:7–14 **We are the only true revolutionary party. . . . But we are not Communists:** When Hemingway cut the manuscript passage in which Richard Gordon explicitly names Joven Cuba as the culprits behind the bank robbery (see 99:16–17), this passage of dialogue from Emilio became the only real clue identifying the specific political party to which the terrorists belong. The ideals the young revolutionary espouses do, in general, correspond to the program Joven Cuba promoted in its short lifespan: an end to imperialism and to the "old politicians" embedded in the Cuban establishment and a push for land reform to abolish the sugar oligarchies. Yet Antonio Guiteras and his followers were not Communists. As K. S. Karol notes, from its founding in 1925 the Communist Party was but one revolutionary faction in Cuba, and one frequently overshadowed in the anti-Machado movement by more visible opposition forces such as the ABC Party, whom Harry Morgan meets with in the opening scene, and the Directorio Estudiantil Universitario or Student Dictatorship (of which Guiteras was a founding member) (78). To their detriment, Communists had engaged in last-minute negotiations with Machado in August 1933, while the dictator's regime was on its last legs, making them suspect among other revolutionary wings. By the time he founded Joven Cuba in 1934, Guiteras had little use for them. Not only did he "condemn the Party's political opportunism in general and its dealings with Machado in particular," but the Communist insistence on competing for power against the first legitimate post-Machado government coalition, in office from September 1933 to January 1934, in which Guiteras had served as interior minister, made them veritable enemies. (Fulgéncio Batista cemented his alliance with the United States by crushing Communist pockets in this period.) Karol blames the party's inflexible Stalinism for its miscalculations, which rendered it "isolated and in the minority" in the 1930s, "quite incapable of grasping the real nature of Cuba's crises or of affecting its development" (81). After Guiteras's assassination in May 1935, remaining members of Joven Cuba slowly aligned themselves with the Authentic Cuban Revolutionary Party, which is why in the deleted discussion of the robbery Gordon calls Joven Cuba "the extreme left wing of the *auténticos.*"

Historical accuracy was probably not Hemingway's main motivation for having Emilio distinguish his band of bank robbers from Communists. As Sara Finch Brown notes, the clarification "But we are not Communists" was added to the setting copy of the novel during June 1937 revisions. This was at a time when Hemingway was actively working alongside international Communist Party members such as Joris Ivens on behalf of the Spanish Republic. The addition may reflect his need to distinguish the robbers' revolutionary program from that of his fellow partisans, who no doubt would have been offended to discover Communists portrayed as either naïve or sadistic, trigger-happy criminals—just as party stalwarts were indeed offended in 1940 when *For Whom the Bell Tolls* dared criticize the Communist presence in Spain. As Brown suggests, Emilio's line seems an understated effort to suggest that "*these* revolutionaries (members of Joven Cuba) deserve to be damned; but they are not Communists, who do *not* deserve the same condemnation" (52).

166:12–13 *guajiros . . .* **sugar estates:** In general terms, *guajiro* describes the rural Cuban peasantry. The name derives from the Guiajiro Indians of Venezuela, who were enslaved and brought to Cuba in the seventeenth and eighteenth centuries—although, oddly enough, the Cuban *guajiro* is assumed to be white, even though its population does include a small percentage of blacks and mulattos. More specifically, the *guajiro* is also a folk character. He is the subject of many 1930s watercolors by Antonio Gattorno, whose first U.S. exhibition Hemingway and John Dos Passos helped sponsor in January 1935. Writing in the exhibition catalogue, Dos Passos commended Gattorno for capturing "always a look of poverty, a malarial refinement and sadness and isolation of a transplanted race" (qtd. in Carr 337).

166:20–22 **The end is worth the means. They had to do the same thing in Russia:** Emilio attempts to justify the violence of revolution. The passage is best appreciated in relation to the manuscript's deleted chapter 28, "Interlude (In Cuba)" (see my introduction, xxxiv–xxxv).

166:27–29 **I was out on strike plenty of times in the old days when we had the cigar factories in Key West:** Another reference to Harry Morgan's backstory that remains frustratingly fleeting. Cigar-making became Key West's dominant industry in the latter half of the nineteenth century, thanks in part to tariffs that hiked the price of Cuban-made tobacco products to exorbitant levels. As Maureen Ogle notes, "By the early 1880s, close to one hundred factories employed over two thousand workers and produced 42 million cigars annually. By the 1890s, about a third of Key West's eighteen thousand people were Cuban," many having migrated specifically to work in the industry (82). Labor conflict was constant, however, with walkouts wracking production. In 1893 alone seven different strikes disrupted output. Tensions exacerbated as owners imported workers of Spanish descent to replace unruly Cubans, many of whom either campaigned outright or plotted in secret for Cuba's liberation before independence was won in 1898. The result was a legal battle over alien labor laws that went all the way to the U.S. Supreme Court. In frustration, many factory owners relocated to Tampa, which promised lower taxes and closer proximity to major transportation. By the 1910s the industry was all but obliterated on the island. Given that Harry's age (forty-three) means he would have been born in the early to mid-1890s, the reference to "old days" can seem somewhat anachronistic. Although Tampa factories suffered through a nine-month strike in 1910, the heyday of Key West strikes would have occurred when Harry was a toddler.

167:8–25 **You do not know how bad things are in Cuba. . . . Now we are ruled by rifles, pistols, machine guns, and bayonets:** Emilio's description of post-Machado Cuba reflects the left's anti-Batista, antimilitary sentiment. From the moment he emerged from the September 1933 Sergeants' Revolt to become the Army's designated strongman, Fulgéncio Batista insisted that civil order was possible only through military policing. A 14 October 1934 interview with the *New York Times Magazine* articulates this position:

> The army has no desire to enter politics, but we have been forced to take a hand in the affairs of the nation. The entire social structure is abnormal at present. Political factions disagree violently and frequently shake the confidence of the public in government. Small groups, without consideration of the rights of others, attempt to impose their will on the government or individuals by force. . . . When this happens, what can the army do? Our sole function is to maintain peace and order. In doing so we have come into direct conflict with many classes and have gained the enmity of people. We are accused of usurping civil authority. The army is always subordinate to civil power, but when the latter proves itself too weak to cope with the situation, then military authority must step in. (Phillips, "Batista" 4–5)

Despite the facetious selflessness expressed here, Batista's forces could prove every bit as brutal as the *machadistas*. On 2 October 1933, they quashed deposed army officers ensconced at Havana's Hotel Nacional. On 9 November, the troops mowed down surrendering rebels who had taken refuge at a former Spanish fortress overlooking Havana Bay called Atarés. Throughout 1934, the army broke strikes among tobacco, sugar, and transportation and utility workers. In March 1935 a teacher-led, labor union–supported general strike brought Cuba to a veritable standstill. Batista's puppet president, Carlos Mendieta, declared martial law, giving the army the right to initiate a repressive reign of terror that culminated in May 1935 in Antonio Guiteras's murder. As a result of the strike, military personnel replaced local elected officials in municipal management offices, civilian servants were purged from public administration ranks, and the military became the most influential source of patronage and employment. Even if Emilio's dialogue does not mention Batista, the mulatto colonel—who as recently as five years earlier had been a stenographer in Machado's military courts—is the figure the passage indicts.

168:4–5 What the hell do I care about his revolution? F——his revolution. Harry's dismissal of Emilio's justification for revolutionary violence is arguably the second most-cited passage of *To Have and Have Not*. The only line quoted more often is the captain's dying "one man alone" declaration, which is still seventy-five pages away and is the ideological antithesis of this paragraph. In truth, the two passages should be quoted in tandem, for the space between them marks the conversion proletarian heroes typically undergo, from rugged individualism to collective action (Foley 284). That this conversion comes too late for Harry Morgan can sometimes confuse readers who are perhaps further distracted by the profanity and the question of why this *fuck* is censored when its second appearance is not.

170:5 **Where's your balls now?** This is the most explicit testicular reference in the novel.

170:25–172:14 **The gun made a big flame in the dark. . . . Harry sat down in a backward lurch.** This shootout scene is every bit as intense as the opening ambush at the Pearl of San Francisco Café in part 1. It again demonstrates how masterfully Hemingway wrote action sequences. Through the hatch of the engine pit, Harry carefully sights Emilio, shooting him in the back of the head before dispatching the two nameless Cubans, who are close enough he can smell the bullets burn through one of the men's coats. His final victim—or so he assumes—is Roberto, who has ducked from his chair while the boat, now unpiloted, spins in a circle. When Harry spots the "big-faced murdering bastard" crawling along the floor in the dark, he takes him out with satisfaction. His mistake is not firing additional bursts into the unnamed pair sprawled on the bench above the engines. One of the men manages to sit up and shoot Harry in the gut. What makes the scene gripping is the straightforward prose. Unlike a great deal of hardboiled writing at the time, Hemingway eschews the descriptive flourishes that often turned gunplay into overheated cartoons. For example, when in *Red Harvest* Dashiell Hammett describes firing a handgun as "throwing lead" (*Novels* 74), there is a sense of the language calling attention to its own metaphorical novelty and ingenuity instead of depicting the immediate danger of being shot. Only once does this shooting scene veer into comparable hyperbole when Hemingway refers to the "flame-stabbing gun" (170:29).

172:29–173:1 **like hitting a pumpkin with a club:** This simile may be the most disturbing description of violence in the scene, substituting, as it does, the sound of a pumpkin being smashed for a bullet entering a head.

174:1 **Some mess:** For the only time in part 3, Hemingway returns to the "some—" refrain employed throughout part 1 or "One Trip Across" ("some nigger," "some Mr. Sing," see 8:5, 19:7–8, and 28:13). *To Have and Have Not* might have proved more cohesive had the "Winter" section evoked it more than once.

175:3 **She's too old to peddle her hips now:** See 147:19–20 on the use of *to peddle* in the novel.

CHAPTER NINETEEN

Barely a page and a half in length, the scene that follows Harry's shooting finds Richard Gordon catching a glimpse of Marie Morgan as he rides his bicycle home from Freddy's Bar. No critic commenting on Gordon and the theme of writers' mores in *To Have and Have Not* will fail to cite this chapter, for it represents Hemingway's core critique of proletarian fiction. Knowing neither Marie's name nor her identity, Gordon has no idea of her struggles or resolve. Instead, he can only judge her physically and assumes that because of her "big ox" girth her husband must resent her. When Gordon arrives home he rudely orders his own wife to leave him alone so he can work. He decides he will include a portrait of Marie in his novel-in-progress about a textile strike. Specifically, he plans to compare her to the beautiful and buxom Jewess that is his fantasy protagonist. As the writer congratulates himself for a scene that is both "terrific" and "true," Hemingway intends for us to see Gordon as self-deluded.

176:15–16 the front door the termites had tunneled and riddled: A seemingly throwaway tidbit of description that actually demonstrates Hemingway's eye for realistic detail. As Carol Hemingway notes, "A termite called woodworm thrives in the Key West culture, where little by little it destroys woodwork and furniture." The original furnishings Pauline Hemingway purchased for 907 Whitehead Street in the 1930s eventually fell victim to this local scourge; by the time the home passed from the Hemingway family in the early 1960s, "many pieces of furniture were brittle shells" (32).

177:3–4 her husband when he came home at night hated her: For most critics in here, Hemingway's depiction of Gordon's thought process is excruciatingly heavy-handed. As Philip Young writes, he is "underlining with a crayon what at his best he would feel no need to remark at all" (74).

CHAPTER TWENTY

In a mostly descriptive interlude, Hemingway details the damage from the shootout to Freddy Wallace's boat. No action advances the plot; the chapter's biggest revelation is the name of the borrowed vessel, the *Queen Conch,* which is finally specified. Nevertheless, the short scene heightens the suspense by drawing a parallel between the Gulf Stream's deceptive placidity and the eerie silence aboard the vessel. For every bullet hole and spilled stream of gasoline sloshing in the bilge that Hemingway details, he also notes the Sargasso weed drifting in the current and the fish that swirl in the shadows of the boat's bottom. Most naturalistically, he focuses on a pair of ugly ocean predators too primitive to understand why the "ropy, carmine clots and threads" of draining blood have evaporated from the splintered holes where they congregate while smaller competitors feast on dribbles from the hand of a dead terrorist that hangs overboard.

In the cockpit, Harry Morgan lies on his side mistaking the sloshing sounds around him for his own insides. Turning cold and numb, he struggles to find a position that will stop his hemorrhaging before he bleeds to death. At least eighteen hours have passed since the shootout, and except for a distant tanker on the horizon, Harry has few immediate prospects for salvation. Extending the motif of the individual's stoic suffering, Hemingway writes, "There was nothing to do about the cold but take it." The question is how long Harry can take it before death takes him.

178:4 **Frolic green:** The color is referenced as early as Michael Drayton's 1593 poem "The Ballad of Downsabel": "She wore a frock of *frolic green* / Might well become a maiden queen." Yachting magazines of the 1930s and 1940s typically advertise frolic green as a paint option, alongside Nile green and orange buff.

179:2 **Sargasso weed:** Also known as *gulfweed* and *sargassum,* Sargasso weed is a type of brown algae that floats in dense masses in regions of the Atlantic Ocean. The name comes from the Portuguese word *sargaço,* which sailors borrowed from a native rock rose that vaguely resembles the weed. For most literary readers, this mention of sargassum will bring to mind Jean Rhys's *The Wide Sargasso Sea* (1966), the brilliant revision of Charlotte Brontë's *Jane Eyre* (1847) that gives voice to Edward

Rochester's first wife, Bertha, nineteenth-century British literature's prototypical madwoman in the attic. The Sargasso Sea is a two-thousand-mile-long, seven-hundred-mile-wide stretch of the Atlantic just west of Bermuda, so named because of the density of sargassum; both it and the weed itself served as symbols of oceanic mystery long before either Hemingway or Rhys, from Jules Verne's *Twenty Thousand Leagues under the Sea* (1870) to Dylan Thomas's 1934 poem "When Once the Twilight Locks No Longer." Coincidentally, before her unlikely comeback with *The Wide Sargasso Sea*, Rhys (1890–1979) was a forgotten footnote among Lost Generation writers. She was in expatriate Paris in the same era as Hemingway, publishing both *The Left Bank and Other Stories* (1927) and *Quartet* (1929), a roman à clef of her affair with Ford Madox Ford, as well as other compelling novels in the 1930s.

180:2–4 They were reluctant now to leave a place where they had fed so well and unexpectedly: With his piscatorial knowledge, Hemingway gives us two images of opportunistic fish feeding off the bloodshed on the *Queen Conch*. The first, smaller, school of striped fish eagerly "mills" every drop falling from the unnamed terrorist sprawled over the starboard gunwale, a clever verb that demonstrates Hemingway's skill at le mot juste: in pushing and stirring the blood drops until they froth into dispersing, the fish exhibit a carnivorous frenzy that suggests the innate vampirism of the novel's naturalistic universe. Two nearby suckerfish offer an image of a dumber malevolence. Having devoured the blood draining from the boat's lower splinter holes, the fish nevertheless hover underneath, incapable of understanding that their feeding ground has run dry.

180:8 scupper: A scupper is a drain built into the edge of a deck to remove standing rain or seawater.

180:11 bilge: A bilge is the drainage hold of a boat where excess water collects—or, as in Harry's case, leaking gas from the gunfight's stray bullets. Pumps are typically built into the bilge to keep it empty and prevent the water's weight from sinking the craft.

181:12–13 you could not pull yourself up over yourself and there was nothing to do about the cold but take it: Harry lies on the cockpit floor with his knees raised. His hope is to use his body as a blanket to rid himself of the cold of his shock, an urge satisfied only momentarily as the position causes him to hemorrhage and further drain away his life. By describing the cold as something else Harry must "take" or suffer, Hemingway links this central to motif to the question of the workingman's stoic capacity to endure.

181:21–22 Portuguese men-of-war: Despite its resemblance to a jellyfish, this member of the physalia genus is actually a conglomerate organism composed of distinct, physiologically integrated entities. The man o' war is recognizable by its surface polyp, known as the sail, a translucent, gas-filled bladder that allows it to float on the ocean's surface above the long string of filaments that are its reproductive, alimentary, and defensive systems. The name comes from the creature's resemblance to pirate-era frigates at full sail. In *The Old Man and the Sea,* Santiago calls the man o' war "the falsest thing in the sea" for its deceptively benign appearance. He despises the animal for the venom it often leaves on his fishing lines, which raises welts and sores like poison oak up and down the old man's arms. Santiago describes how much he enjoys watching sea turtles devour the creature, as well as how much he enjoys the sound of them popping when he steps on ones that have washed up on his home beach (9).

181:24 **Tampico:** A port city in the Mexican state of Tamaulipas on the country's Gulf Coast, Tampico remains a major site of oil exporting today, as it was in the 1930s. In terms of literature, its closest association with Hemingway may be Joseph Hergesheimer's 1920 novel *Tampico,* an expatriate tale that modestly anticipates the themes of Lost Generation literature. Unlike many of the Cuban cities named in *To Have and Have Not,* Hemingway had no real association with Tampico, other than recognizing it as the departure point of northbound tankers in the sea lanes outside of Key West.

CHAPTER TWENTY-ONE

For sheer unpleasantness alone, this is the novel's most gruelingly tedious chapter. Exploring the breakup of Richard and Helen Gordon's marriage, it is meant to document how the privileges enjoyed by "haves"—freedom from work and want, in particular—erode marital bonds by sapping individual moral resolve. Both Gordons, we learn, have allowed themselves to be seduced. Helen has let Professor MacWalsey kiss her while sitting on the Gordons' own couch, and Richard has succumbed to Helène Bradley's predatory lust (as witnessed by the lipstick covering him, which he makes no effort to hide). Amid the dialogue-delivered recriminations, we discover that Gordon refused to marry his wife in the church and that Helen believes her husband a fake of the first order. Indeed, the chapter is the novel's most explicit critique of authorial hypocrisies, with the irate wife voicing a line that critics interpret as Hemingway's critique of John Dos Passos: "I've seen you bitter, jealous, changing your politics to suit the fashion, sucking up to people's faces and talking about them behind their backs" (186:21). Helen even extends her attack by comparing her husband unfavorably to her father, who may have been a drinker but possessed a moral compass she associates with authentic manhood. (Adding insult to injury, she tells Richard that MacWalsey reminds her of her father.) Although Gordon slaps Helen's face, the exchange is emasculating and ends with him creeping back into the Key West night in hopes of finding his pride in one of the city's many bars.

As dismally astringent as the dialogue is, the chapter's structural defects are an even greater reason for its dramatic failure. In manuscript, Hemingway had limned the couple's infidelity firsthand. As previously noted, a long scene set at the Bradleys' house party depicts Helène Bradley seducing the spineless Gordon with the resolve of a praying mantis. Afterward, he returns to his rented home only to flip on the lights to discover MacWalsey and Helen necking on his living-room sofa. Cutting the party scene forced him to compromise this material. In a major miscalculation on Hemingway's part, Helen's petting is discussed but not dramatized, robbing part 3 of one of its more unexpected twists. Equally unfortunate, Richard's bedroom scene with Helène Bradley is condensed into a brief flashback. Although Hemingway retains the scene's kinkiest revelation—Gordon is not man enough to complete the sex act after discovering Helène's husband, Tommy, has no objection to his wife's adultery—the italicized-memory device blunts the tawdry shock of the Bradleys' open marriage. Had Hemingway had more time and attention to replot this section of the narrative, he likely could have done the infidelity motif better justice. As it stands, chapter 21 is unbearably bitter in tone and unbearably botched in execution.

183:6 **No," she said. "I'm not a bitch:** Philip Young describes Helen's rhetorical evisceration of her husband as "the most spectacularly abusive speech in American literature" (48).

183:14–19 **Whose fault was that? Didn't I want children? But we could never afford them. But we could afford to go to the Cap d'Antibes to swim and to Switzerland to ski. We can afford to come down here to Key West:** As previously noted, this passage takes a veiled swat at John and Katy Dos Passos for their inability to produce children. Hemingway turns the couple's fertility woes into a charge of irresponsibility by insinuating they chose expatriate vagabonding over a settled family existence. Cap d'Antibes is the peninsula of France's Cote d'Azur resort town Antibes, located between Nice and Cannes. In the 1920s and early 1930s, it was home to Gerald and Sara Murphy's fourteen-room Villa America, where the Dos Passoses often stayed while in Europe (as did Hemingway, F. Scott Fitzgerald, Cole Porter, Pablo Picasso, and many other luminaries). Hemingway and Dos Passos also skied together in Montana-Vermala, Switzerland, in late 1929 while visiting the Murphys, who stayed at the Palace Hotel with Dorothy Parker in tow. Since this trip occurred shortly after Dos Passos's marriage to Katy, it is likely this is the holiday Hemingway was thinking of when he wrote the passage. Switzerland is not the most vilified skiing spot associated with Dos Passos, however. That honor belongs to Schruns, Austria, where during the winter of 1926 Hemingway's first marriage began to unravel as he courted the attention of Pauline Pfeiffer. The final chapter of *A Moveable Feast* is set in Schruns and blames the Murphys and Dos Passos (though not by name) for tempting Hemingway from the artisanal values he associated with his first wife, Hadley (197–211).

183:19 **twirp:** The reference here is to Professor John MacWalsey, the lone character in the novel than whom Richard Gordon can feel manlier.

184:5 **And what's his last name? Thomas?** "John Thomas" is the notorious nickname Oliver Mellors gives his penis in D. H. Lawrence's *Lady Chatterley's Lover* (1928). By the same token, Constance "Connie" Chatterley calls her vagina "Lady Jane." A 1927 version of the novel was actually entitled *John Thomas and Lady Jane*. Not surprisingly, given the novel's notoriety in the 1930s, ribald "John Thomas" references abounded in the popular culture, with far more people knowing the reference than had ever read the book. When it comes to phallic euphemisms, Hemingway had no reason to feel superior to Lawrence; in love letters to Martha Gellhorn, he would soon nickname his own penis "Mr. Scroobie."

185:28 **ergoapiol pills:** Ergoapiol was the brand name of a menstrual relief medication manufactured by the Martin H. Smith Company of New York. Ingredients included apiol (an organic chemical compound found in parsley), ertoin, oil of savin, and aloin. Advertised as curing amenorrhea, or the absence of menstruation, the capsules were widely known as an abortion cure-all for women in the early stages of pregnancy.

186:1 **quinine and quinine and quinine:** Although best known as a malaria treatment, quinine, an extract from the South American cinchona tree, was another widely recognized abortifacient in the 1930s.

186:2–6 **dirty aborting horror . . . half catheters and half whirling douches . . . Lysol:** In addition to pills and tablets, to dramatize how Richard Gordon's aversion to children has spoiled the couple's marriage Helen reels off an unpleasant list of other era abortion options. The embittered wife implies that on one occasion her husband took her to an actual abortionist, who "messed up" her insides. Whether she has resorted to the other remedies is unclear; Helen may merely cite them to illustrate how the invasive reality of reproductive management debunks notions of romantic love. When employed mainly by midwives as a birth-control device, catheters were inserted into the cervix to irritate the uterus and induce menstruation. "Whirling douches" refers to devices such as the Marvel "Whirling Spray" Syringe, which advertised itself as a more effective vaginal cleansing tool than traditional douches by emitting spinning water rather than a straight stream when its bellow was squeezed.

Lysol was associated with birth control mainly because its manufacturer, Lehn & Fink, marketed it as a feminine hygiene product from the late 1920s through the 1960s, despite its inflammatory and sometimes even toxic results. In *Devices and Desires: A History of Contraceptives in America* (2002), Andrea Tone provides some appalling statistics: "By 1911, doctors had recorded 193 Lysol poisonings, including 21 suicides, 1 homicide, and 5 deaths from uterine irrigation. In 1915, a Chicago man killed his wife, who had just given birth to their child, when, confusing the toxic substance with her regular medicine, he gave her the toxic substance to drink. As Lysol became more commercially available, injury and death rates grew. Coroners in New York City reported 40 suicidal and 4 accidental Lysol deaths in 1925 alone" (171). These figures become all the more upsetting when one recognizes Lysol was never a reliable or particularly effective contraceptive. As Tone notes, "The Lysol douche did not prevent pregnancy; a 1933 study undertaken at Newark's Maternal Health Center . . . found that 250 of 507 women who used Lysol for birth control became pregnant" (170).

186:15 **mick:** A common North American epithet for a person of Irish descent. The name comes from the common prefix *Mc* or *Mac,* meaning *son of.*

186:21 **I've seen you bitter, jealous, changing your politics to suit the fashion, sucking up to people's faces and talking about them behind their backs:** This line is typically interpreted as Hemingway's most pungent insult to John Dos Passos's proletarian commitment. It tends to be cited alongside a passage from *A Moveable Feast* in which Dos Passos is described as moving "one dollar's width to the right" on the political spectrum "with every dollar that he made" (208). Yet because Helen's accusation of fickleness and hypocrisy appears in the initial draft of *To Have and Have Not* (completed in January 1937), it predates by at least four months Dos Passos's disenchantment with the Russian Stalinists managing Spain's Republican government during the Spanish Civil War, which marked the beginning of his conservative turn. As such, it is probably not fair to read the line as a commentary on Dos Passos at all but more on proletarian writers in general.

188:20–21 **slapped her hard and suddenly across the face:** For Hemingway's tendency to condone physical abuse toward women, see 144:17.

189:1 **white ceiling with its cake-frosting modeling:** This line echoes a similar image in *The Great Gatsby* in which Nick Carraway, visiting his cousin Daisy Buchanan's East Egg mansion for the first time, observes the "frosted wedding cake of the ceiling" (8).

189:6 **"Don't stop," Helène had said:** The voyeurism of this sex scene, in which Tommy Bradley interrupts Gordon and Helène Bradley's lovemaking, has a curious legacy in Key West fiction. Variations on it appear in Thomas McGuane's *Ninety-Two in the Shade* (1972) and Thomas Sanchez's *Mile Zero* (1989).

189:20 **That's only Tommy:** Tommy Bradley is based on Jane Mason's first husband, George Grant Mason Jr. (1904–1970), a founder of Pan American Airways. In 1907 Mason's father, George Sr., and his uncle, Henry, had inherited the bulk of the $50 million estate of their uncle, a stockbroker known as "The Silent Man of Wall Street" for his self-effacing presence in finance circles. Following his graduation from Yale, the younger Mason worked in banking before pursuing his aviation interests by backing pilot Juan Trippe in the airline industry. Hemingway biographies usually depict Mason as "tall, good-looking . . . but unassertive" (Meyers, *Biography* 243) or passive to the point of "unintrusive" (Mason, "To Love and Love Not" 108). Much of this impression channels Hemingway's own mixed feelings for Mason, whom he classified as belonging to a species of "Husbandus Americanus Yalemaniensus Twirpi Ciego" (Donaldson, *MacLeish* 249) for his "blind" detachment toward his wife. Inherent in Richard Gordon's seduction scene then is a fascination/revulsion with not only aggressive female sexuality but the masculine inability to dominate it. Hemingway's intrigue with cowed husbands peaks with "The Short Happy Life of Francis Macomber," in which the titular hero resembles Grant Mason. Behind his back, members of Hemingway's clique—including Jane herself—chided Mason as "Old Stoneface."

CHAPTER TWENTY-TWO

If chapter 22 is the single biggest victim of Hemingway's rushed revision of *To Have and Have Not,* its successor offers the single best-executed episode in the novel's "haves" portion. After leaving his wife, Richard Gordon bicycles to Key West's bar district to drown his woes in *ojen* (Spanish absinthe), beer, and whiskey. Unfortunately, he finds little sanctuary from the grotesqueries of Key West. At the Lilac Time, he encounters an out-of-towner named Herbert Spellman, whose obsequious flattery may be inebriated prattle, a homosexual advance, or outright lunacy. Gordon cannot decide which; he only knows he does not deserve the young Brooklynite's fawning compliments, which celebrate Gordon's novels for all the wrong reasons. The proletarian writer then runs into the sheriff, who informs him that a tanker near Matecumbe Key (presumably the same tanker mentioned at the end of chapter 20) has come upon Harry Morgan and the drifting *Queen Conch.* Gordon is eager to see the Coast Guard tow the getaway boat into the Navy Yard and decides to wait out its arrival at Freddy's Bar.

The wait proves anything but relaxing. Freddy's is packed with WPA laborers on leave from the backbreaking task of completing the Overseas Highway between Lower Matecumbe and No Name keys, which was then dependent on ferry service. Most of these laborers, as Hemingway documents, are World War I veterans sent to Florida after the Bonus Marches of 1932 and 1933, when tens of thousands of former soldiers streamed into Washington, DC, demanding cash payment for bonds issued to them in the 1920s in appreciation for their military service. Contemporary readers would have recognized these men as future victims of the 1935 Labor Day hurricane that killed 259 members of the WPA crew, a tragedy Hemingway had already angrily addressed in his essay "Who Murdered the Vets?" Although *To Have and Have Not* cannot be said to allude to the disaster in any discernable way, the palpable sense of victimization the men exude makes it clear they have been brutalized by forces beyond their control. Their only freedom is to beat each other up in a gruesome effort to show who can take the most pain—a scenario that grows more macabrely slapstick the longer it goes on.

Among the vets, Gordon finally meets one sane spokesman for their condition, Nelson Jacks. "We are the desperate ones," he explains, insisting that the government keeps the vets in the Keys to quarantine the threat of revolution they represent: "The ones with nothing to lose. We are the completely brutalized ones" (206:11–12). When Jacks finds out he is talking to Richard Gordon the novelist, however, he turns surly and silent. Pressed for his opinion of Gordon's books, the Communist organizer bluntly dismisses them as "shit" and leaves.

Gordon's night does not improve. Without warning, Professor MacWalsey appears at Freddy's. Although his wife's paramour expresses a strange empathy for Gordon's cuckolding, the writer is in no mood to forgive him. Gordon challenges MacWalsey to a fight, only to get knocked out by Freddy's no-nonsense bouncer. The bouncer and the professor pour the unconscious man into a cab, but Gordon awakens and stumbles off before MacWalsey can return him home. The chapter ends with the point of view shifting to an ornate interior monologue from MacWalsey, who attempts to diagnose the compulsive self-destruction of Gordon, himself, and the other "haves." Stymied by his sense of moral powerlessness, MacWalsey acts upon the one bit of initiative he can muster:

He returns to Freddy's.

193:6 If "Jungle Town" was the racist name for the black section of Key West, "Conch Town" referred to the neighborhoods historically home to families of white Bahamian immigrants. Conch Town's geographical borders were fluid, but the core of the district clustered in the blocks concentrically centered upon the Key West Cemetery.

193:7 **grits and boiled grunts:** Captain Willie first mentions this Key West staple in chapter 7 (84:10–11).

193:10 **Cuban bolito houses:** *Bolita* is the name for a Cuban lottery extremely popular in South Florida in this period. According to legend, a Cuban émigré named Francisco Gonzales, or "Pancho Macaro," first brought the diversion to Key West circa 1885. The game was ostensibly illegal in Florida, but authorities turned a blind eye to bookie establishments such as the ones Richard Gordon passes along this stretch of Division Street (aka the future Truman Avenue). As with most lotteries, gamblers bet on which numbers were randomly selected from a bag of little balls, which is the literal translation of the word *bolita*. Numbers were drawn in Cuba on Wednesday and Saturday then broadcast to the island over the radio.

As McLendon notes, bolita was so popular in Key West that in addition to over-the-counter operations salesmen or brokers walked assigned territories in the city soliciting bets for bookies known as "bankers": "All the transactions from route salesman to banker were made in cash, and it was not uncommon for a major banker to have $100,000, even $200,000, in cash in his house. In the tradition of accredited banks, bolita banks and bankers were scrupulously honest. Winning numbers were posted in street corner booths and strategically placed all over town for all to see" (65).

193:11–194:11 The Red House, Chicha's, the pressed stone church . . . the convent . . . the embowered entrance of the Lilac Time: The general route Richard Gordon follows in this expansive passage takes him west from the old residential section of Key West into the heart of its bar/tourist district. In 1934 John and Katy Dos Passos rented a house at 1401 Pine Street, which seems a likely starting point for the trek. (More recently, the couple had stayed at 803 Waddell Avenue in the southern district near the Casa Marina, which doesn't correspond to any of the sites mentioned in this passage.) At some point, Gordon cuts south to Rocky Road, the older, colloquial name for Division Street. In quick succession he passes the two real-life gambling dens cited here—The Red House and Chica's—before reaching St. Mary Star of the Sea, Key West's major Catholic Church at the time, on the corner of Windsor Lane. The convent next to it is the Convent of Mary Immaculate. Tourists visiting present-day Truman Avenue will spot nothing of the "black-domed bulk" mentioned here. The original 1886 building was demolished in 1966 after residents lost a fiercely contested preservation campaign with the bishop of Miami. According to Joy Williams, "the convent is probably the most-mourned lost building in Key West. . . . Many fragments of the convent—fanlights, gingerbread trim, shutters—can be found in various homes in Key West today, and over the convent grounds, next to the St. Mary Star of the Sea church, the afterimage of the lovely structure seems to hover in the air" (143).

The rest of Gordon's walk is not so clearly mapped. The "brightly lit main street" with fourteen different types of businesses itemized in quick succession would be Duval, of course, and the "one good restaurant" standing out among the "five bad ones" is most likely Delmonico's, a favorite of Hemingway's. Whether Gordon turns onto Duval or whether he continues on Division Street is unclear, however. Hemingway's use of the adverb "past" implies the writer hustles straight through the intersection, continuing west. Yet, by the time the paragraph wends through the list of Duval's drugstores, pool rooms, and "Jew stores" to reach "a hotel on the corner with taxis opposite" (194:2–3), one is tempted to assume he has traveled five blocks north to La Concha Hotel. After all, this Key West landmark has already been mentioned three times in the novel (63:19, 86:19–20, 155:9–10), and it, along with the Casa Marina, would be the only two hotels in Key West with which general readers of the day were likely to have any familiarity. If Gordon does indeed take a northern jag, he would appear to turn left onto Fleming Street to cut "behind the hotel" to reach "the street that led to jungle town"—presumably, Thomas Street. From there, however, the trajectory makes less sense. "[T]he big unpainted frame house with lights and girls in the doorway" (194:4–5) seems a reference to Key West's most exotic brothel, the Square Roof; Hemingway's image matches descriptions of the establishment by friends of Elizabeth Bishop, who a few years later went there for tea with Tennessee Williams and New Directions Publishing founder James Laughlin, whose recollection of the adventure, excerpted in Gary Fountain's *Remembering Elizabeth Bishop: An Oral Biography* (1996), offers an extensive glimpse inside the establishment (82–83). The only problem is that the Square Roof sat on the corner of Emma and Petronia, three blocks southwest of Fleming Street, which makes for a circuitous loop to say the least. Perhaps regardless of geographical fact Hemingway felt compelled to reference the other major cat house of Key West's red-light district after alluding to Big Annie's all the way back in chapter 9 (93:2–3) with the description of Big Lucie's daughter. A detour may be implied by the reference to Gordon moving "then on back," meaning, perhaps, he turns back up Thomas Street. Or "back" may merely indicate that he moves deeper into the red-light district via Fleming. That seems the more plausible explanation, given that Gordon is described as passing the backside of the Monroe County Courthouse on the corner of Thomas and Fleming, with the county jail next to it, before arriving at his bar of choice, the Lilac Time, presumably at the intersection of Thomas and Southard streets.

194:12 The Lilac Time: In chapter 9, Hemingway took us inside the Richards' club behind the Meacham Field airport on the island's southeastern side, our first glimpse of a Key West bar that wasn't Freddy's, the characters' usual hangout. For our second foray outside of the thinly veiled Sloppy Joe's, we visit a fancier establishment with a distinctly Cuban atmosphere. The setting is based on Pena's Garden of Roses, often described as a beer garden but which also featured a dance floor and a gambling area. The bar—No. 15 on the Key West Administration's 1934 map of recommended tourist stops—was located at 508 Thomas Street. Among the island sites mentioned in *To Have and Have Not,* it enjoyed a relatively short vogue: it was torn down in 1942 during the Naval Base expansion precipitated by World War II. The local legend surrounding the bar involved the elusive hiding spot where the Spanish proprietor—usually referred to in island histories by his nickname "Pena," though his full name was Albino Morales (1888–1976)—stored his liquor. According to lore, during Prohibition only Morales and one trusted black bartender knew where he kept his cache, meaning when certain spirits ran low he or his right-hand man would have to disappear into the Key West night to restock. Patrons spent the resulting time waiting for their drinks speculating about Pena's hideaway—a cave being the most popular guess. (Morales's name shows up at least twice in the *Key West Citizen* during the dry era for violating liquor laws.) In manuscript, Hemingway had toyed with calling Pena's the Bower of Flowers and the Bower of Roses before settling on the slightly more fictional Lilac Time.

194:27 **ojen:** As Philip Greene explains, *ojen* is a Spanish anisette manufactured until the 1980s by the Manuel Fernandez Company of Jerez. It bears some similarities to Anis del Mondo, which Hemingway famously redubbed "Anis del Toro" in "Hills Like White Elephants" (*CSS* 211). An ojen special, Greene speculates, would have included Peychaud's bitters, sugar or syrup, and seltzer. The drink is a powerful one: the Spanish legend *una copita de ojen* suggested "perhaps it's best to have only one cup of Ojen"—advice Richard Gordon doesn't take (Greene 180–82).

195:24 **Herbert Spellman:** Given that virtually every character in *To Have and Have Not* has been identified with a real-life Hemingway friend, enemy, or mere acquaintance, it is curious that this cameo appearance by a Lilac Time habitué has generated absolutely no speculation about his inspiration. Herbert Spellman shares initials with novelist and short-story writer Harry Sylvester (1908–1993), who met Hemingway in 1936 while honeymooning in Key West. Sylvester was just beginning his career at the time; in the following decade, he would produce three acclaimed Catholic novels—*Dearly Beloved* (1942), *Dayspring* (1945), and *Moon Gaffney* (1947)—before fading into obscurity. Interviewed by Dennis Brian for *The True Gen*, Sylvester would recall bonding with Hemingway over boxing and Knute Rockne stories from his days as a Notre Dame undergraduate (104). Together the pair trained light-heavyweight boxer Emory Blackwell for a 19 March 1936 bout with Baby Ray Atwell held at Key West's Navy Field Arena (Reynolds, *1930s* 224). In October 1936 Sylvester capitalized on the friendship by publishing "Hemingway: A Note" in *Commonweal* (9–10). Much to Hemingway's embarrassment, the article made a case for reading its subject as a Catholic writer. Even worse, it repeated dubious legends about the famous author's adventures in World War I Italy that Hemingway himself likely narrated during garrulous drinking marathons with Sylvester.

When the Spanish Civil War broke out, the pair supposedly debated the conflict along with military historian and future general S. L. A. Marshall, who would recall the exchange for Carlos Baker. Although Sylvester is not mentioned in Baker's biography, subsequent scholars have availed themselves of the Marshall correspondence, housed with Baker's papers at Princeton University, to untangle Hemingway's complex feelings about the conflict. In Marshall's recollection, Hemingway was initially "disinterested," claiming to have friends on both sides, while Sylvester was "hot for the Rebel cause" (qtd. in Vernon 11–12). Accordingly, most Hemingway biographies have labeled Sylvester pro-Franco—as many devout Catholics were outraged by the Republican government's abuses against the Church. Sylvester protested this depiction of himself and insisted he had remained neutral throughout the war (Brian 103–04). Regardless, Hemingway considered Sylvester sympathetic enough to the Nationalist side that, on 5 February 1937, as he prepared to depart for Spain he felt the need to justify his support for the Loyalists to his young friend in a letter: "The Spanish war is a bad war, Harry, and nobody is right. All I care about is human being and alleviateing their suffering which is why I back ambulances and hospitals. The rebels have plenty of good Italian ambulances. . . . I know [the Loyalists have] shot priests and bishops but why was the church in politics on the side of the oppressors instead of for the people[?]" (*SL* 456). Critics seeking evidence of Hemingway's burgeoning partisanship in the war inevitably cite this note, along with a comparable 9 February 1937 letter of conscience to his very Catholic Pfeiffer in-laws in which he likewise defends siding with the Loyalists.

Considering how little tolerance Hemingway held for conflicting opinions, it is tempting to suggest the Spellman character allowed him to vent his impatience with Sylvester in the same way Hélène Bradley skewers Jane Mason and Richard Gordon Dos Passos. After all, in praising Gordon's novels, Spellman brags of his indifference to social oppression, much as pro-Nationalists excused the Catholic Church's collusion with repressive forces: "What do I care what Douglas Aircraft does? What do I care what A.T. and T. does? They can't touch me" (197:26). The Spellman-Sylvester connection gains further valence when we recognize the encounter between Gordon and Sylvester was added to the novel during the slapdash revisions of June 1937, a point by which Hemingway had dropped any pretense that "nobody" in the war was "right." Yet, in the end, the facts bear out no real evidence of a feud. Jeffrey Meyers claims Hemingway and Sylvester nearly came to blows over the war (*Biography* 602), but in his interview in Brian's *The True Gen*, Sylvester dismisses the accuracy of the depiction of his politics (103–04). Hemingway would express irritation to his mother-in-law two years later, after Sylvester claimed Guernica was a Communist propaganda plot hatched to discredit Franco (*SL* 476). Despite this, the pair seems to have remained on friendly terms up through the decade's end. Sylvester's papers at Georgetown University include a cashed $100 check written to Hemingway dated 31 May 1939. The younger writer was even present when Hemingway moved out of Key West the following December, upon officially leaving Pauline for Martha Gellhorn. According to a story he told Meyers, Sylvester watched over the Hemingway sons as their father boarded the ferry to Havana for the final time (*Biography* 344–45).

If Sylvester's relationship to Spellman is tenuous at best, the more formalist question is what thematic purpose this encounter with Richard Gordon serves. Robert E. Fleming suggests the fawning admirer embodies the type of reader a true writer avoids, one who, like Don Quixote, "has been addled by reading books—in this case books of criticism rather than romances but, like Don Quixote's romances, far removed from reality" (*Face* 68). In this regard, Spellman is a counterpart of Hélène Bradley. If she collects writers, Spellman is the reader more than happy to be "collected" by a writer, the fan whose unquestioning appreciation leads him to mistake clichés for truth. And in this way Spellman may again be a veiled commentary on Harry Sylvester, whose Commonweal essay contorted Hemingway to reinforce his own religious beliefs. Much as Spellman enjoys all the wrong elements of Gordon's novels (their formulae and stock characters), Sylvester misread his friend to suit his own desires.

196:13–14 **Margaret Van Brunt:** Hemingway apparently invented this character by borrowing the middle name of Coles Van Brunt Seeley Jr. (b. 1895–1924), the fellow Red Cross volunteer ambulance driver wounded alongside him in July 1918. The reference to the fire at 196:16 appears to be fiction as well.

197:8 **Sylvia Sidney:** The former Sophia Kosnow (1910–1999) was a successful Hollywood actress in the mid-1930s. While not a major box-office draw, she was a respected character actress who in 1936–37 appeared in popular films such as Henry Hathaway's *The Trail of the Lonesome Pine*, Alfred Hitchcock's *Sabotage*, Fritz Lang's *Fury* and *You Only Live Once*, and William Wyler's *Dead End*. Equally important, she was politically active in the Hollywood Anti-Nazi League (HANL) alongside Hemingway's friend Donald Ogden Stewart (Bill Gorton in *The Sun Also Rises*), among many other moviemaking elite. Hemingway probably cited Sidney not simply because she fit Spellman's ideal of a "beautiful Jewish agitator"; she supposedly donated a $1000 bill during a fundraising dinner for *The Spanish Earth*, Hemingway and Joris Ivers's propaganda film promoting the Loyalist cause (Koch 229).

199:7 **The sheriff:** As another sign of how dilatory Hemingway's attention to detail was while writing *To Have and Have Not*, we should note his habit of not providing full names until well after a character is introduced. We do not learn that Bee-lips's full name is Robert Simmons, for example, until 250:18, nearly 160 pages after the shady lawyer is introduced, at which point the detail seems gratuitous. (The Simmons surname is mentioned twice, at 102:8 and 165:16, however.) Similarly, we are not told that Freddy, Harry Morgan's favorite bartender, has the last name of Wallace until 178:8, some eighty pages after he first appears in chapter 9. The sheriff is another example. Hemingway simply refers to him by his title until 251:20–21, at which point—very late in the narrative—we are told his name is Roger Johnson. Interestingly, at this time in Monroe County, the sheriff was Karl Thompson (1887–1972), older brother to Hemingway's closest Key West friend, Charles Thompson. Hemingway had previously borrowed Karl's first name to lightly fictionalize Charles in *Green Hills of Africa*. Karl Thompson served eight years in office, from 1933 to 1941.

200:6 **those Vets from up on the Keys:** The veterans doomed to perish in the 1935 Labor Day hurricane arrived in the Keys between November 1934 and January 1935 as employees of the Federal Emergency Relief Administration (FERA). As previously noted, many were members of the Bonus Army. This ragtag coalition of World War I vets had poured into Washington, DC, in 1932 to demand immediate payment of a $500–$625 reward for their service promised to them in 1924 as part of the World War Adjusted Compensation Act. Unfortunately, that law stated the bonuses were not redeemable until 1945, a compromise Congress had reached to enable the bill's passage. (Three previous attempts to reward veterans had been voted down, with President Calvin Coolidge on record as promising to veto any legislation that did not defer the compensation.) Eight years later, in 1932, veterans argued that the Depression necessitated immediate payment, since soldiers who had served in the Great War were among the country's highest unemployed and homeless demographics. Their protests were credited with costing Herbert Hoover his 1932 reelection bid (see the entry on Anacostia Flats below), and Franklin Delano Roosevelt was intent on avoiding Hoover's mishandling of their demands. It was FDR's right-hand man, Harry Hopkins (see 80:8–10), who suggested housing the men in Civilian Conservation Corps–styled camps to work on public construction projects. The camps would have the additional benefit of isolating the men and keeping them out of the public eye.

All told, FERA constructed twenty-five camps (officially known as Veterans Rehabilitation Camps) in Florida and South Carolina. Three such camps were located in the Keys: Camp One on Upper Matecumbe or Windley Key and Camp Five and Camp Three at the northern and southern tips respectively of Lower Matecumbe Key. The peak population numbered seven hundred men, most of them assigned to rickety barracks. Conditions at the camps were less than ideal; not only were the vets woefully unprepared for the backbreaking labor of highway construction, but the lack of sanitation led to tensions that frequently exploded into violence. Nor did it help that bootleggers and prostitutes set up shop in the men's proximity, eager to siphon off FERA paychecks. FERA administrators attempted to alleviate strikes by organizing softball leagues and creating lending libraries for the former soldiers, but many of the men preferred to spend their off time carousing in Key West. For those opposing the New Deal, the Bonus Army program was a handy target for deriding Roosevelt's public-works projects as "shovel-leaning" boondoggles. The same week that the hurricane decimated Matecumbe and killed hundreds of the vets, *Time* ridiculed the camps as "playgrounds for derelicts" (qtd. in Dickson and Allen 233).

200:26–27 the loud-speaking nickel-in-the-slot phonograph was playing "Isle of Capri": Often described as the prototype of the modern jukebox, a nickel-in-the-slot phonograph allowed patrons to enjoy recorded music publically for a mere five cents per play. Early versions contained predecessor earphones that allowed four separate listeners to hear the sound at the same time. Later models, such as this one at Freddy's, included the famous gramophone bell for community listening. Although the term "jukebox" did not come into vogue until 1940, automated players known as "audiophones" were on the market as early as 1928. These differed from nickel-in-the-slot machines by offering a selection of different 78 rpms, whereas the older machines played only one.

Unlike the technology at Freddy's, the song playing is quite contemporary. Written by composer Hugh Williams (real name Wilhelm Grosz) and lyricist Jimmy Kennedy, "Isle of Capri" dates only to 1934. The version stocked in the nickel player is probably by Ray Noble and His Orchestra, with a vocal by Al Bowlly; their rendition topped the U.S. pop charts for seven weeks in 1935.

201:1–5 They fell and rolled on the sidewalk: *To Have and Have Not* was not the first work in which Hemingway had written about the bizarre violence to which the veterans in the Matecumbe camps were prone. Barely a month before the hurricane hit the Keys, he devoted a portion of his August 1935 *Esquire* column to the men's unruly presence in Key West, titling the essay "He Who Gets Slap Happy: A Key West Letter." "The finest lot of Slap Happies your correspondent has ever been privileged to hoist a beer with hang out around Mr. Josie Grunt's bar in Key West when the veterans from the C.C.C. camp at Matecumbe come in on payday," Hemingway boasted. He then went on to describe one vet with a broken leg who would summon strangers to his side, only to bash them in the head with his crutch, just for the pleasure of knocking them out cold (19). In the essay, Hemingway equates the vets' violence with the complaints of readers who "write letters to [*Esquire*] complaining about . . . lousy letters such as this one." Much as the vets are "slap happy," throwing wild punches out of bitterness and contempt, his critics' grousing is wasted energy on the part of discontented "four-letter" effetes who are "mean" but unthreatening. "It has been a long time since your correspondent cannot take it and he is still able to hand a little back," Hemingway insists. "The only way [a writer] can judge the impact of anything he writes in a periodical is by the type and quantity of four letter folk that protest. If you hit them they write" (19). As this passage suggests, "He Who Gets Slap Happy" is the source of the motif of "taking it" in the novel.

202:14 Camp Five: As noted in the 200:6 entry, Camp Five was located at the northern tip of Lower Matecumbe Key. Hemingway probably cites it here instead of Camp One or Three because of his memories of surveying the hurricane devastation at this particular site. As he wrote Maxwell Perkins on 7 September 1935, he, Bra Saunders, and J. B. "Sully" Sullivan were "the first in to Camp Five of the veterans who were working on the Highway construction. Out of 187 only 8 survived. Saw more dead than I'd seen in one place since the lower Piave in June of 1918" (*SL* 421).

202:23–24 nigger bartender: It is unfortunate that Hemingway chose to describe Sloppy Joe's African American bartender this way, for Alfred L. Skinner (1894–1949) was not only a fearsome fixture at the bar but a beloved Key West legend as well. A well-known 1930s painting of Sloppy Joe's regulars by WPA artist Erik Smith features the three-hundred-pound World War I veteran alongside Hemingway, George G. Brooks Jr., Julius F. Stone Jr., and Joe "Josie" Russell, among others. "Big Al" also appears in a 1936 canvas by Hemingway friend Waldo Peirce, who depicted the bartender pouring Ernest a beer under the watchful eye of Peirce and his wife, Alzira. Although actual photographs of Skinner remain undiscovered, the

Monroe County Library does possess at least one image from his funeral, published in Sharon Wells's *Sloppy Joe's Bar: The First Fifty Years* (1983). Skinner also makes a cameo in John Hersey's "To End the American Dream," included in his *Key West Tales* (1993), which tells the story of Hemingway attempting to write *To Have and Have Not* while challenged to a boxing match by a visitor to Sloppy Joe's (199).

203:8 **Sometimes it feels good:** At Sloppy Joe's, Richard Gordon agrees to buy beers for a pair of vets caught up in what can only be described as a strangely sadomasochistic relationship. One vet, a freckle-faced redhead identified as Joey, enjoys being beaten, while his unnamed pal finds gratification in meting out the brutality. "I had [Joey] down and I was hitting him on the head with a bottle," the second man excitedly recounts of their tussle at Camp Five. "Just like playing a drum" (202:13–15), Joey insists on revealing a secret to Gordon: not only do the beatings not hurt, they are actually pleasurable. The question that haunts this exchange is whether Hemingway implies a sexual relationship between the men. James H. Meredith makes this suggestion in his essay "Hemingway's Key West Band of Brothers: The World War I Veterans in 'Who Murdered the Vets?' and *To Have and Have Not*" (2009). The argument is only partially based on a literal interpretation of Joey's claims that he "can take it" and that "it don't hurt." First, Meredith notes how frequently when depicting isolated groups of both soldiers and men "on the bum" Hemingway evoked the threat of homosexual assault. The fear of male rape is implied in *A Farewell to Arms* and the 1927 short story "A Simple Enquiry" (*CSS* 250–52), but its most explicit evocation is in *A Moveable Feast*, when Hemingway describes predatory tramps or "wolves" on lake boats whose mantra was "Oh gash may be fine but one eye for mine" (18–19). As Hemingway boasts to Gertrude Stein, as a young man he carried a knife in the presence of such company "in order not to be interfered with."[1] Meredith also notes that in the broader culture of the 1930s "hobosexuality" was commonly ascribed to homeless men to vilify the transient lifestyle. Considering both the intertextual and contextual evidence, readers who wonder whether Joey's "secret" involves carnality should not dismiss the suspicion. Hemingway seems to stage Joey's confession to provoke the question (Meredith 256–57).

204:3 **the Tortugas:** Hemingway previously mentioned the Dry Tortugas in part 1 when Mr. Sing facetiously suggests Harry could drop his cargo of Chinese illegals there (see 32:17–22). The reference here is important because it reveals the little-known role that Fort Jefferson on Garden Key played in managing the veterans during their consignment to the Upper Keys. While Joey and his friend play their game of Punch and Judy, Gordon begins a conversation with a tall man with the scar running the length of his face who will shortly introduce himself as Nelson Jacks. As he reveals, Jacks and a handful of other vets have just returned to Key West from the Tortugas because they "raised enough hell" that the authorities "couldn't keep us there." As early as December 1934, FERA relocated vets accused of "drunkenness, insubordination and theft" to Fort Jefferson, which served as an unofficial penal colony (Dickson and Allen 222). Hemingway implies suspected Communists such as Jacks were also sent there to quarantine their "radical" influence over the men.

204:6 **He's a red:** Nelson Jacks is an honest to goodness Communist organizer, but the question of how many actual "reds" operated in the FERA camps remains a matter of speculation. Camp One was beleaguered by two strikes in February 1935; when protestors agitated for improved conditions for a third time with an ominous "or else" capping their demands, FERA ordered in the National Guard to police the vets. To quell any bad publicity, Julius F. Stone Jr. denounced organizers as "Reds" and "anti-government agitators" to the United Press ("Soldiers Rushed to Vets Camp" 1). In an interview with the Associated Press, one of the four men elected to lead the strike committee, Herschel McMorris of San Pedro, California, denied the presence of either "Communists" or "Radicals." B. M. Duncan, identified as the chief engineer of the Matecumbe project, attributed the strike to "a chronic band of kickers who have been making trouble at the camp" ("Ex-Service Men" 2).

204:21 **Cool the son-of-a-bitch:** *Cool* as slang for *beat up* came into use in the 1920s. Hemingway would employ it again in *Islands in the Stream,* in a scene that fictionalizes his famous 1936 Bimini dockside brawl with Joseph Fairchild Knapp (1892–1952). In the novel, Thomas Hudson's buddy Frank encourages Roger Davis to "cool the son of a bitch" when a drunk taunts the men (40).

205:3 **postal savings:** Before Roosevelt created the Federal Deposit Insurance Corporation, which went into business on 1 January 1934, the U.S. Postal Savings System was the only federal guaranteed deposit program in the country. Established in 1911 (and shut down in 1967), postal savings paid 2 percent annually on investments up to $2,500 in the 1930s. The minimum deposit was $1, although customers could purchase ten-cent stamps and fill a postal-savings card that could then be redeemed for either cash or a higher-denomination certificate. The FDIC was not the only Depression-era competition that spelled doom for the system. Beginning in mid-1935, U.S. savings bonds began to be issued that paid a slightly higher return rate of 2.5 percent. Previously, customers could only invest in the postal savings system and then trade the certificates for savings bonds. In this passage, two of the camp residents are pummeling a "white faced" third for stealing their drinks off Freddy's bar. The vets are furious with the victim because they know he invests all his FERA pay in postal savings and then tries to drink for free.

205:13 **slappy:** Hemingway's word choice marks the scene's most overt connection to his August 1935 *Esquire* column featuring the vets, "He Who Gets Slap Happy: A Key

West Letter" (see 123:4–6). The term *slap happy* was a recent coinage. According to *Cassell's Dictionary of Slang,* its usage began in the 1930s, arising in boxing circles to describe punch-drunk fighters (Green 1300).

205:16 **the old rale:** Although *rale* or *râle* is a medical term describing abnormal respiratory sounds—usually a crackling or bubbling of breath—Hemingway used *old rale* to mean syphilis. The phrase shows up several times in his correspondence and at least one other time in his fiction in *True at First Light* (274; see also *UK* 375). In a 1951 letter to Charles Scribner denouncing novelist James Jones of *From Here to Eternity* fame, Hemingway claimed the term "goes back to nearly Chaucer's time" (*SL* 724). Perhaps its most surprising appearance is in a quote from Malcolm Cowley's 10 January 1949 *Life Magazine* profile, "A Portrait of Mister Papa." The piece ends with a typically stoic Hemingway statement about the strength and endurance of character that writing demands: "Any writer worth a damn is just a writer," he insists. "Go out and do your stuff. You can't do it? Then don't take refuge in the fact that you are a local boy or a rummy, or pant to crawl back into somebody's womb, or have the con or the old râle. You can do it or you can't do it in that league I am speaking of" (101).

205:23–24 **War is a purifying and ennobling force:** Nelson Jacks is being sarcastic when he tells Richard Gordon this. The veterans' violence and masochism is proof of the exact opposite. The inability to reconcile the men's grotesque behavior and the notion of war as heroic may inspire readers to recall Frederic Henry's famous dismissal of the rhetoric of glory in *A Farewell to Arms*: "Abstract words such as glory, honor, courage, or hallow were obscene beside the concrete names of villages, the numbers of roads, the names or rivers, the numbers of regiments and dates" (185). In "Who Murdered the Vets?," his post-hurricane dissection of the Matecumbe tragedy, Hemingway described the men in the FERA camps as "what you get after a war"—namely, a cross-section of damaged men, "many of them husky, hard-working and simply out of luck, but many of them close to the border of pathological cases" (qtd. in Trogdon, *Literary Reference* 170, 169). As Jacks goes on to inquire of Gordon, the real question is whether war transforms men into ghoulish caricatures of brutality or whether society simply relies on men already predisposed to such behavior to serve as soldiers. Jacks seems to insist on the latter; as he cynically brags to Gordon, "not three men in this room were drafted": "These are the elite. The very top cream of the scum" (205:27–29).

206:1 **Wellington, Waterloo:** Arthur Wellesley (1769–1852) is the first and best-known Duke of Wellington in England, a title bestowed on him in 1814. To date there have been seven subsequent heirs, all descendants of the original soldier/statesman. Often referred to as "Wellington" or "The Wellington," Field Marshal Wellesley led the Anglo-Allied Army that, alongside a Prussian contingent, defeated French emperor Napoleon Bonaparte (1769–1821) at the Battle of Waterloo on 18 June 1815. In 1814, after abdicating the throne he had held since the turn of the century, Napoleon was exiled to Elba, where he plotted a return to power that came to be known as The Hundred Days. His resumption of the emperorship was virulently opposed by the Great Powers of Europe (Great Britain, Austria, Russia, and Prussia), who collectively declared him an outlaw. Intent on striking before the Great Powers could organize their forces, Napoleon entered Belgium, first defeating Prussian troops at Ligny and then British forces at Quatre Bras. Forced to retreat toward Brussels, Wellington decided to square off against the French army just south of the village of Waterloo. In a famous military misjudgment, Napoleon delayed his attack until midday to give the wet ground time to dry so his heavy artillery would not be mired in mud. The wait allowed the Prussians time to join Wellesley's troops by mid-afternoon and defeat the French by evening. Napoleon's reign was effectively over; he abdicated the throne a month later and spent his final years on the island of Saint Helena, off the African coast. The location was not of his choosing; to avoid revolutionary reprisals, he petitioned for British protection in July 1815. Fearing a second escape from Elba, the British sent to him as remote an outpost as it could identify. Napoleon died on Saint Helena six years later, at the age of fifty-one.

206:1–2 **Mr. Hoover, Anticosti Flats:** Hemingway mistakes Anticosti (an island in Quebec) for the *Anacostia* Flats, a swampy area along the Anacostia River that flows from Maryland into the nation's capital. Scribner's has yet to correct this error.

In 1932 more than twenty thousand World War I veterans poured into Washington, DC, to join the Bonus Expeditionary Force demanding immediate payment of the military service dividend awarded by the 1924 World War Adjusted Compensation Act. Washington, DC, police chief Pelham Glassford selected a park on the eastern side of the Anacostia River to house the influx. The site served both logistical and political purposes: not only was it spacious enough to accommodate the large numbers of unemployed men and their families; it was also remote enough to sequester the protest and minimize the visibility of Communists, who constituted a minor but vocal segment of the Bonus Army. Housing was improvised from materials from a local dump, while area residents donated food and shoes. Although Glassford designed the layout of the camp with quadrants and streets, his "vision of an army-style camp" quickly gave way to "to the reality of a junkyard city, one of many 'Hoovervilles' like it throughout the nation" (Dickson and Allen 110).

The camp's first residents arrived on 6 June, one day before a twilight march on the Capitol that saw nearly a hundred thousand locals turn out to watch the Bonus Army parade. Life in the shantytown was relatively peaceful; as many journalists were startled to note, Anacostia was integrated, with residents disregarding Jim Crow laws as whites and blacks coexisted. The Salvation Army set up a lending library, and a makeshift post office operated on the grounds. The few incidents of violence centered mostly upon efforts to expel suspected Communists, some of whom were hazed or beaten, and two of whom may have actually been murdered and dumped in the river. By and large, however, "Camp Marks" (as it was unofficially known, after an accommodating local policeman) was considered an orderly protest—at least initially. Locals felt safe enough to freely roam the flats, both to witness the spectacle and to contribute to relief efforts.

Although the House of Representatives passed the Wright Patman Bonus Bill authorizing immediate payment on 15 June, the Senate tabled debate, meaning it would not vote on the measure during the ongoing legislative session. Despite expectations that the Bonus Army would disperse, the Anacostia camp and other impromptu housing sites throughout Washington, DC, lost few residents. Under the enigmatic Walter W. Waters (1898–1959)—sometimes called "Mussolini Waters" for his domineering leadership style—the veterans dug in and continued regular marches through the capital's federal corridor. By late July, with Congress out of session, officials in charge of public safety declared the protest over and issued eviction orders. On 28 July federal troops under the command of General Douglas MacArthur (1880–1964) dispersed protestors along Pennsylvania Avenue before marching into the Anacostia camp and burning hovels as residents fled. The resulting news coverage was a public relations disaster for Herbert Hoover (1874–1964), whose inability to remedy the downturn of the Great Depression had made him vulnerable in his 1932 reelection bid. Although MacArthur violated Hoover's explicit, twice-issued orders not to enter Camp Marks, the president declined to reprimand the general publically and instead vilified the marchers, insisting that a majority were not veterans at all but derelicts, criminals, and—no surprise—Communists. The image of the U.S. military unleashed upon its own veterans haunted Hoover throughout his entire campaign. On 8 November 1932, he lost to Franklin Delano Roosevelt by a margin of 7 million votes, with commentators citing the disaster at Anacostia Flats as a major reason for the defeat.

206:14 Spartacus: The story of the legendary gladiator/slave rebel known in Greek as Σπάρτακος or Spártakos (109–71 B.C.E.) appears in as few as three, often contradictory, sources: Plutarch's *Life of Crassus* (written 75 C.E.), Appian of Alexandria's *Civil Wars* (books 13 through 17 of his *The Roman History*, written in the second century), and Florus's *Epitome of Roman History* (also second century). About the only point this trio agrees on is that Spartacus was a general in the Third Servile War, waged against the Roman Empire from 73 to 71 B.C.E. Born in Thrace, he may have been enslaved and sold to a school for gladiators in Capua, where he would have been trained for combat in the infamous arenas. Or Spartacus may have been a mercenary conscripted into the Roman army whose punishment for deserting was fighting as a gladiator. Eventually escaping from Capua with seventy-eight other men, the warrior hid in the environs of Mt. Vesuvius until his legions were joined by upward of seventy thousand other rebels. The contingent battled its way across Italy to Cispaline Gaul, supposedly, according to Plutarch's *Crassus,* in hopes that the men could return to their individual homelands. For reasons that remain unclear, however, the warriors turned south. Confronted by the Roman general Crassus, they were defeated in the Battle of the Siler River. Crassus ordered six thousand rebels to be crucified, but, contrary to popular iconography, Spartacus was not one of them. Again according to Plutarch, he was killed attempting to fight his way to dispatch his Roman nemesis with his own sword, his body not recovered.

Contemporary readers are most familiar with the Spartacus story from the eponymous 1960 Stanley Kubrick movie starring Kirk Douglas. (From 2010 to 2013, STARZ-TV produced a soft-core, blood-and-guts adventure series based on the legend, but it was at best a cult hit.) Based on a 1951 novel by Howard Fast, Kubrick's blockbuster transformed the warrior into a martyr for freedom and free speech as opposed to the militaristic plunderer he most likely was, elevating him into a symbol of the 1950s fight against McCarthyism and the Hollywood blacklisting. In direct contradiction of classical sources, the final scene even depicts Spartacus nailed to a cross on the Appian Way—a powerful symbol, to be sure, but hardly a subtle statement about the persecution of supposed anti-American behavior during the Cold War. The movie's most iconic moment is also an allegorical indictment of the hearings held by Senator Joseph McCarthy and the House of Representatives counterpart, the House Un-American Activities Committee (HUAC), both of whom between 1947 and 1959 recklessly smeared Americans accused of Communist leanings by demanding public accountings of their political beliefs and affiliations. (Both Fast and screenwriter Dalton Trumbo, among others, were victims of these witch hunts.) When Crassus captures the slave rebels after their final defeat and demands that they identify their leader from among their throng, as a gesture of solidarity, man after man stands up and shouts "I'm Spartacus!"

Of course, *To Have and Have Not* predates this depiction of Spartacus by more than twenty years. In Hemingway's time, the most influential image of the rebel warrior was a Marxist revolutionary group known as the Spartacus, which had existed in Germany during the Great War. A precursor to the Communist Party of Germany, the Spartakusbund was most famous for its 1918 manifesto, also named after the gladiator. Their identification with the rebel general was undoubtedly inspired by Karl Marx's 1861 reference to Spartacus as a "real representative of the ancient proletariat" in a letter to Friedrich Engels (qtd. in Kodat 488). The Spartacus League was indirectly responsible for a January 1919 uprising known as the "Spartacist uprising," or Spartakusaufstand, in which workers in Berlin, disillusioned with the Weimar Republic economy staged a spontaneous strike. Paramilitary groups of alienated, defeated World War I veterans known as the Freikorps fired upon strikers, killing roughly a hundred, before murdering two of the Spartacus League's founders, Karl Liebknecht and Rosa Luxemburg.

In his original draft of *To Have and Have Not,* Hemingway has Nelson Jacks specifically compare the vets in Freddy's bar to the German Spartacists. When Richard Gordon points out that the Spartacists were routed in 1919, Jacks replies, "Yes. . . . I was there" (MS 31, item 204, folder 8, page 304). When Gordon asks how he managed to witness this short debacle of an attempted revolution, the Communist admits to going AWOL from "Cobbentz," Hemingway's mangling of the German town of Koblenz, which the American army occupied in December 1918, before turning the Rhine region over to the French (who referred to the city as "Coblence"). Why this story was removed from the setting copy so it does not appear in the published novel is unclear; Hemingway may have thought that too few readers would remember the German Spartacists, or the 1919 "January uprising" (Januaraufstand). He did, however, allow this more general reference to the vets as "worse than the stuff the original Spartacus worked with" to depict the men's degradation.

207:2–3 up under Riverside Drive there's old guys with long beards . . . you can piss in their beards for a dollar: Riverside Drive is one of New York's City toniest addresses, home at various points to everyone from William Randolph Hearst to George Gershwin to Saul Bellow. The Westside thoroughfare runs from 72nd Street to 181st and passes several notable memorials, including the Soldiers and Sailors Monument, honoring Civil War veterans, at 89th Street and Grant's Tomb, the final resting place of Ulysses S. Grant, in Riverside Park. "Up under Riverside Drive" refers to the mudflats between the bluff where the drive sits and the Hudson River. Despite its name, before 1937 Riverside Park was nothing but a six-mile stretch of mucky land that was home to the New York Central railway. According to Robert A. Caro in his magisterial biography of New York City parks commissioner Robert Moses (1888–1981), *The Power Broker and the Fall of New York* (1975), the park was notorious for housing "derelicts who had built tar-paper shanty towns considered so dangerous that the police stayed away from them" (66). Hemingway would have glimpsed something of this scene when he boasted to his family on 7 May 1918 that he had "been all up and down Riverside Drive" during a New York City stop on his way to his Red Cross posting in Italy (*SL* 7). During the Depression, Riverside Drive was home to at least two large Hoovervilles. A 1933 *New Yorker* article, "Riverside Residents," tours the more northern of these squatter camps, although it makes no mention of the sexual deviancy to which Hemingway refers. Another Hooverville, located at 77nd Street, called Camp Thomas Paine, was populated, according to press reports, by many Great War vets who had participated in the Bonus Army marches of 1932. In April 1934 Moses ordered the camp's demolishment to create the Henry Hudson Parkway and develop Riverside Park into an attractive green space, a $100 million initiative known as the West Side Improvement Project. Coincidentally, the parkway was completed on 12 October 1937, exactly three days before the publication of *To Have and Have Not.*

207:27 **saltcellar:** Before the popularity of shakers, salt was served from dishes that might be glass, pewter, or silver, ranging in size from tiny bowls to large "standing" salts not intended to be passed around a table. Whatever size the saltcellars at Freddy's bar, they would undoubtedly make for formidable weapons when wrapped in a towel and whapped upside a drunk's head.

208:7 **Wallace:** Another instance of the odd name repetition that can create confusion among characters in *To Have and Have Not*. We learn at the beginning of chapter 20 that Freddy's last name is Wallace (178:1), but he also has an employee whose *first* name is Wallace, "a heavyset young fellow" who pulls "the saltcellar man" out of the bar. In chapter 24, we will meet a third Wallace, Wallace Johnston, one of the yacht owners at the Key West sub-basin (228:18).

209:5 **boogie:** Joey uses a derogatory reference for African Americans to describe the bartender Hemingway based on Sloppy Joe's Al Skinner. According to the *Oxford English Dictionary*, this racial epithet dates to the 1920s. While the *OED* suggests it is a derivation of *bogey*, Mary Cruz posits a likelier connection to the term *boogie-woogie*, which, of course, also entered the popular lexicon in the Jazz Age (*Cuba and Hemingway* 142). Use of the term to describe this style of music derives from *boogie* as slang for a Harlem rent party, as in *pitch a boogie*. Hemingway would later employ the epithet in a 2 April 1945 letter to Colonel Charles T. "Buck" Lanham, lamenting his return to Cuba from World War II: "When Mary comes down here [Cuba] we can let her kill a Boogie instead of a Kraut" (*SL* 580).

To Have and Have Not should have had *two* uses of this racial epithet. In the *Esquire* version of part 2, published as the short story "The Tradesman's Return," Harry refers to his mate Wesley as a "boogie" (196). Why Hemingway cut this reference from the novel is unclear. Because the *Esquire* version of "Tradesman" appears in *The Complete Short Stories of Ernest Hemingway*, the word appears there as well (419).

209:27 **Gastonia:** A reference to the Loray Mill Strike that began 1 April 1929 and continued for upward of five months, which became a symbol of Depression-era labor struggles and the influence of unions in labor management in general. The outbursts of violence associated with the strike—including the deaths of Police Chief O. F. Adderholt and organizer Ella May Wiggins in different skirmishes—would inspire no fewer than a half-dozen novels by the mid-1930s. Gastonia is the city in southwestern North Carolina's Gaston County where the events took place.

In spring 1929, organizers for the National Textile Workers Union, a Communist labor union, arrived in Gastonia to protest worker exploitation at the state's largest mill (which was owned by a northern company, coincidentally). When the walk-off began in April, workers demanded a minimum wage ($20 a week) and a reduction of the number of tasks expected of each employee. Unfortunately, the union's ideological indoctrination agenda proved off-putting to many laborers who soon returned to work out of economic necessity. On 7 June an armed confrontation occurred at the tent city the Union constructed to house workers whom mill owners had expelled from their homes. Chief Adderholt died of a gunshot wound after the melee, resulting in the prosecution of union chieftain Fred Beal and a dozen other strike leaders. When a mistrial was declared on 9 September, Gastonia residents reacted violently by abusing mill workers. The union, in turn, called for a rally the following week; Wiggins was shot in the chest when her car was ambushed en route to the event. While a jury found Wiggins's murderers not guilty, at their retrial Beal and seven colleagues were convicted and promptly fled to Russia. The union abandoned the strike effort in the wake of the violence.

Richard Gordon's invocation of Gastonia is one of the clearest links between him and John Dos Passos, even though the writer did not travel to North Carolina during the strike. Dos Passos did ask the *New Republic* to send him to report on the violence, but according to Edmund Wilson's essay "The Literary Consequences of the Crash," the magazine considered him too partisan (496). Dos Passos did, however, write about Gastonia for *Labor Defender* in August 1929. He was also a close friend and supporter of Fred Beal's and felt profoundly guilty that he was unable to report on the strike directly. In 1931 Dos Passos compensated for missing Gastonia by observing a similarly well-publicized coal-mining strike in Harlan County, Kentucky, joining Theodore Dreiser and other luminaries in a fact-finding mission into labor conditions. For Hemingway, Gastonia was the ultimate example of a literary bandwagon. Not only had Sherwood Anderson fictionalized events in *Beyond Desire* (1932), but the strike was the subject of several other proletarian novels, including Mary Heaton Vorse's *Strike!* (1930), Olive Tilford Dargan's *Call Home the Heart* (1932), Grace Lumpkin's *To Make My Bread* (1932), Myra Page's *Gathering Storm* (1932), and William Rollins Jr.'s *The Shadow Before* (1934).

210:13 **I thought they were shit:** Hemingway reserves his most pungent insult for proletarian writing for Jacks's assessment of Gordon's novels.

210:24 **Western Stories, War Aces:** Hemingway is probably referring here to *Western Story Magazine,* published by Street & Smith from 1919 to 1949, the most popular of the Western pulps that proliferated between the 1920s and the 1950s. Although several such publications were subtitled "Western Stories"—and despite the example of *Spicy Western Stories,* which debuted in November 1936—there was no major pulp with this title. *War Aces* belonged to the "aviation pulp" or "flying pulp" genre, which also included *Flying Aces, Battle Birds, Wings,* and more than forty others. Produced by Dell Publishing, the magazine debuted in 1930, but most sources say its run ended a mere two years later, after only twenty-eight issues. Hemingway also refers to *War Aces* in a contemporaneous Spanish Civil War story, "Night Before Battle," published in *Esquire* in January 1939 (*CSS* 456). Why he cited this title of the many aviation pulps that, unlike *War Aces,* were still publishing in the late 1930s is unclear. *War Aces* did have a bit of notoriety that competing pulps did not. It is referenced in a 1933 *Vanity Fair* assessment of pulp fiction that critics frequently cite as evidence of the highbrow/lowbrow divide in era reading tastes. Written by Marcus Duffield, "The Pulps: Day Dreams for the Masses," takes a snide potshot at the periodical by describing it as escapist drivel: "Chicago soda-jerkers living in tenements with their mothers and three sniveling little sisters are transformed into dare-devils of the sky reading *War Aces.* Cheap girls in Pennsylvania hosiery mills and Kansas City ten-cent stores find their handsome lovers in *True Confessions.* The pulps manufacture daydreams on a wholesale scale" (26).

212:2 **Ginger Rogers:** Born Virginia Katherine McMath in 1911, Fred Astaire's dance partner was at the peak of her popularity in the mid-1930s as Hemingway wrote *To Have and Have Not.* Since her 1930 breakthrough in *Young Man of Manhattan* (featuring her famous catchphrase, "Cigarette me, big boy"), Rogers had appeared in nearly three dozen films, including the classics *42nd Street* and *Gold Diggers of 1933,* the latter of which includes her performance of the Al Dubin/Harry Warren hit popularly known as "We're in the Money." In *Flying Down to Rio* (1933), RKO Pictures teamed Rogers with Astaire for the first of nine musicals that elevated the art of dance in cinema to unprecedented heights. Although best remembered for this partnership, Rogers would actually hit her career peak with her 1940 Best Actress Academy Award for *Kitty Foyle,* which proved popular enough to inspire a fashion trend in the early years of World War II. In the 1950s, Hemingway and Rogers would share a Hollywood agent, Leland Hayward, who helped bring *The Old Man and the Sea* to the screen. Rogers died in 1995 at the age of eighty-three.

213:21 **scab:** Gordon's newfound friend, Joey, and his vet buddies offer to "cool" Professor MacWalsey, who has unexpectedly reappeared in Freddy's. Describing him as a "scab," Joey uses a term that dates back to the early eighteenth century—although until the 1930s it was often used more as a verb than a noun (Green 1232).

214:12 **He defaulted and ruined the bank:** Amid the vets' drunken wordplay, Hemingway references what may be the most cataclysmic symptom of the Depression, the tidal wave of bank failures that destabilized the American financial system until the Roosevelt administration took extreme measures to ensure its security. Between 1929 and 1933, nearly 40 percent of the twenty-five thousand banks operating in the United States failed, wiping out some $7 billion in deposits. Upon entering the White House, Roosevelt instituted a bank holiday from 6 to 13 March 1933, during which time Congress passed the Emergency Banking Act that allowed for the assessing of banks' financial viability, empowering the government to assist those with insufficient deposits and closing those unlikely ever to recover. "I can assure you that it is safer to keep your money in a reopened bank than under the mattress," FDR insisted in his 12 March address to the nation, the first of his famous fireside chats (Roosevelt 106). The intervention worked; when banks reopened, depositors returned to institutions in droves to reinvest cash in the monetary system. Three months later, in June 1933, Roosevelt shepherded into law the Glass-Steagall Banking Reform Act, which created the Federal Deposit Insurance Corporation to insure member deposits up to $2,500. The FDIC helped stem the shuttering of institutions; in 1934, only sixty-one banks folded.

Mention of a bank failure leads to the novel's second reference to the postal savings system (214:19). As previously noted, the FDIC's deposit guarantee would, by the late 1960s, render post-office certificates redundant, for with the federal government ensuring accounts, consumers had little motive for investing their money in other institutions. Among the veterans in the Keys, casual evocation of the post office leads to suspicion that one of the carousers is saving his paycheck instead of spending it all on alcohol. The accusation leads to another seriocomic round of fisticuffs, with the two buddies accosting Gordon pushed out the door, "holding and punching, kneeing and butting" (214:25).

215:8 **puss:** In this passage, another vet claims that Red caught "the old rale," or syphilis, from fighting a boxer named Benny Sampson with a habit of rubbing his open sores across competitors' faces while in the ring. Hemingway's use of "puss" for mouth is yet another invocation of the hardboiled idiom. Although the Irish slang dates to the nineteenth century, it was enjoying a resurgence of popularity, thanks to detective and gangster novels and movies. Despite Hemingway's fondness for citing the names of real-life fighters, Benny Sampson is a fictional character.

The passage is also notable for reeling off the vets' colorful nicknames for each other: in addition to "Red" or Joey, we learn of "Poochy" and "Suds."

215:27 **Brest:** This city in northwestern France was the disembarkation point for nearly eight hundred thousand of the 2 million American soldiers arriving in Europe during the Great War. The large number of Allied military passing through the city made it a major hub for the influenza plague of 1918–19, with transport ships unknowingly carrying the virus back across the Atlantic Ocean.

216:17–18 **Nobody seemed to know but all enjoyed the atmosphere of serious philological discussion:** The discussion of the "old rale" perks the academic interest of Professor MacWalsey, who wonders aloud "what the derivation is," a question that the vets, not surprisingly, are not prepared to answer. "I've always heard it called the old rale since my first enlistment," one vet tells the professor. "Some call it ral. But usually they call it the old rale" (216:9–11). MacWalsey hypothesizes that it is an old English term, which impresses the vets. By describing the conversation as a "serious philological discussion," Hemingway is clearly mocking both the pedantry of academia and the vets' dipsomania.

217:21–22 **the influenza epidemic in 1918:** Across the globe, an estimated 100 million people died as a result of the Spanish flu outbreak that lasted from January 1918 until December 1920. Notable victims of the pandemic include Gertrude Stein and Alice B. Toklas's close friend Guillaume Apollinaire (1880–1918), intellectual Randolph Bourne (1886–1918), William Randolph Hearst's mother, Phoebe Apperson Hearst (1841–1919), and German economist Max Weber (1864–1920). As noted in the entry for 215:2, troop transportation is thought to have played a major role in spreading the virus. The first reported American cases occurred in Haskell County, Kansas, with more than five hundred diagnosed instances in a single week in March 1918.

219:13 **the old Model T taxi:** Between 1903 and 1908, Henry Ford and the Ford Motor Company manufactured a sequence of ever-improving prototype automobiles, from the earliest Model A to the Models R and S. Yet not until the Model T entered the marketplace in late 1908 did the horseless carriage truly became a mass-market sales success. This was due not only to design and mechanical innovations that allowed the machine to run more reliably in adverse conditions but to the implementation of the assembly line in 1913, which reduced the price from $850 to an affordable $300 a decade later. That cost savings was balanced by a lack of consumer choice, however. After 1913 the Model T was available only in a single color, black. The car's famous nickname, "Tin Lizzie," stuck late in its production history. In 1922 during a race near Pikes Peak, Colorado, one contestant promoted his car as "Old Liz," for its lack of hood and paint. Noting Old Liz's resemblance to a tin can, observers redubbed the car "Tin Lizzie." Rather than an insult, when Lizzie won the race the name became a testament to the Model T's durability. Mass production on the Model T ended in 1927, when Ford introduced a newly revamped Model A. Although Hemingway does not specify what year the taxi is, the car would be close to a decade old by the time of the story's action, effectively qualifying as "old."

219:28–220:1 **Past the park. Down the street from the place where they sell mullets." . . . Rocky Road:** As previously noted, before the late 1940s Rocky Road was the name for present-day Truman Avenue. In a 17 January 1931 letter to Waldo Peirce, Hemingway refers to the newly rented Whitehead Street house as sitting "out near the mullet seller" (qtd. in Reynolds, *1930s* 60).

221:15–16 **Is he your brother?** The taxi driver's innocent question to Professor MacWalsey ironically emphasizes the theme of proletarian solidarity by demonstrating how little unity exists among upper-class "haves." As noted at 17:10, "brother" was

PART THREE · 181

a leftist term during the Depression, signifying comradeship and the investment in collective survival. When MacWalsey weakly answers, "In a way," he admits how his class has failed to nurture fellowship and the collective bond, stranding each other in self-interest.

221:29–222:1 If I had been a better man I would have let him beat me up: The professor's awareness of his failings leads to this oddly formal interior monologue in which he assesses his failures and admits he is too weak to break his dependency on the "anaesthetic" of alcohol. Although MacWalsey rakes himself over the coals for the "grave and deadly sin" of stealing another man's wife, his fears of feeling the pain his actions have caused will not allow him to minister further to Gordon. While the main point is to document thematically the weakness of character among the "haves," the monologue's real purpose seems more stylistic: it allows Hemingway to indulge in the stuffy tone and stilted syntax ("[Alcohol] is probably a vice for which I only invent excuses" [222:9–10]) he was apt to employ when satirizing his dramatis personae.

NOTE

1. In his interview in Brian's *The True Gen,* Henry "Mike" Strater claims Hemingway carried a pocketknife to protect himself from rape by homosexual bums (97).

CHAPTER TWENTY-THREE

A late addition to the novel, this chapter is the book's political cri de coeur. Aboard the Coast Guard cutter towing the *Queen Conch* back to Key West lies Harry Morgan, clinging to life, barely able to speak. As the cutter's captain and mate grill him about whether he killed the four Cuban revolutionaries by himself, Harry struggles to articulate the lesson of his death: "No matter how a man alone ain't got no bloody fucking chance" (225:18–19). The meaning is lost on the Coast Guard crew, who speculate about whether Harry will survive until they dock.

223:2 **the hawk channel:** This major waterway lies between the keys of the Florida straits and the Atlantic reefs to their east, running all the way from Biscayne National Park to Key West. With its three- to five-mile width and a depth of thirty feet, the channel provides the safest navigable route from the mainland to the islands.

223:7 **Robby:** It is not clear whether this is a fictional character or whether Hemingway refers to a boatbuilder in the Keys known as "Robby." As Miriam B. Mandel notes, no 1930s records indicate anyone with the family name "Robby" operated in the period, but it may be a first name or a nickname (498). It is possible that "Robby" refers to a Conch family that in the 1960s and 1970s would produce wooden skiffs popular among tarpon fishing guides in the Keys. A recent interview with novelist Thomas McGuane testifies to the importance of Willy Roberts boats in the era McGuane wrote *The Bushwacked Piano*, *Ninety-Two in the Shade*, and *Panama*: "The first of the real dedicated skiff builders was Willy Roberts. I had a Willy Roberts skiff and he built wooden boats on Tavernier Key. He was a conch and a wonderful craftsman whose peculiarity was that he hated painting boats. You could get a substantial discount on one of his boats if he didn't have to paint it. His family origins were in the Abacos. They had been loyalists during the American Revolution and fled the Carolinas. He came from a long line of boat builders. Most of the guides in the '60s had Willy Roberts boats" (Pero). During Hemingway's time, the patriarch of the Roberts family was Samuel Winreal Roberts (circa 1893–1951), whose obituary identifies him as "a retired boat builder" (Parker-Brady-Zimmerman Ancestor Tree).

224:9 gimbal: As used in this example, a gimbal or gimbal ring is a device that keeps an object (in this case, a water bottle) level by suspending it within a pivoting or rotating structure. On ships gimbals are used to correct for the pitching and rolling of waves. They are used to stabilize everything from gyroscopes and compasses to stoves.

225:18–19 No matter how a man alone ain't got no bloody fucking chance: The most frequently cited line in *To Have and Have Not* is also, not surprisingly, the novel's most debated sentence. From the earliest reviews on, reviewers and critics have argued the significance of Harry's assertion, no matter how self-explanatory its meaning might seem. At the heart of the disagreement is the question of whether Harry's conversion to a collectivist stance is dramatically efficacious, coming so few pages after dismissing Emilio and his fellow conspirators' fight against tyranny with "F—his revolution" (168:5). By "dramatically efficacious," we do not mean the question of whether Harry's dying declaration is realistic coming from such a rugged individualist or whether it is a plot contrivance devised to give the text a climactic epiphany (which its late addition to the text would suggest). We mean, rather, how effectively the novel's "message" affects the reader. Unlike nonpolitical fiction, proletarian novels are, in general, designed with a pragmatic aim in mind—their goal is to ignite the audience's outrage and recruit them to the cause of the class struggle. The issue for critics is whether Harry's newfound stance is sufficient to energize readers' political sensibilities to accomplish this intent. For Michael Szalay, the answer is no: "*To Have and Have Not* does not really depart from [Hemingway's usual position of libertarian individuality], for though Morgan's parting lines would seem to suggest some form of activism, some mode of protective affiliation, nothing in the novel is adequate to this demand" (106–07). As Szalay complains, the text provides no demonstration of collectivism's positive accomplishments: Hemingway's disdainful, dismissive portraits of radical writers, New Deal bureaucrats, and governmental relief brand *every* attempt at social change as hypocritical and compromised by self-serving motives, thereby precluding the text from providing any model for actualizing the collectivism Harry suddenly espouses.

Surprisingly, perhaps, many devoted Hemingway scholars agree. As Arthur Waldhorn argues, Harry Morgan is depicted simply as a victim of forces outside of his control and is not even afforded the consolation (or "largesse") of the "separate peace" enjoyed by other Hemingway heroes, from Nick Adams to Robert Jordon. As a result, Harry's final words bespeak the entire muddled message of the novel: "To which of many possible queries did Hemingway intend [Harry's "one man alone" speech] as an answer: Has modern society wiped out any chance for a 'separate peace'? Should a man who fails to achieve a 'separate peace' declare a private war? If a man alone has no chance, should he join with others to crush his oppressors? Regrettably, no straightforward response may be offered, for among other crippling faults, *To Have and Have Not* is hobbled also by lame thinking" (153).

Only a small minority of critics have regarded Harry's conversion as an effectively plotted moment of protest. Foremost among these is Malcolm Cowley, who in his original review of the novel, declares the death scene "beautifully done": "This might be the message that Hemingway carried back from Spain, his own free translation of Marx and Engels: 'Workers of the world unite, you have nothing to lose.'" Even so, Cowley recognizes that this message is not effectively integrated into the novel, and he surmises (correctly) that Harry's declaration was inserted late in the composition process, for "it doesn't grow out of what has gone before" (qtd. in Meyers, *Critical Heritage* 235).

Despite the general consensus that the passage does not jell with the rest of the novel, Harry's "one man alone" speech has inspired any number of political writers who either cite it or allude to it in their own work. New Zealand author John Mulgan (1911–1945) titled his 1939 novel *Man Alone,* and Richard Wright has his character Cross Damon effectively paraphrase Harry's speech in *The Outsider* (1953): "The search can't be done alone. . . . Never alone. . . . Alone a man is nothing" (585). Crime writer James Lee Burke even has his recurring character Dave Robicheaux discuss the meaning of Harry's line in the twentieth installment of his Robicheaux series, *Light of the World,* published as recently as 2014 (251).

226:3 **Sombrero:** This reference is confusing for most readers unfamiliar with the colorfully named keys along the waterway to Key West. Sometimes known as Dry Banks, Sombrero Key is a reef that lies eight miles southwest of Marathon, north of American shoal (see 67:15). The lighthouse to which Hemingway refers went into operation in 1858. At 142 feet, it is the tallest of the navigational markers in the Hawk Channel.

CHAPTER TWENTY-FOUR

With Harry Morgan having made his dying declaration, the Coast Guard arrives at the Key West yacht basin to a crowd eager to learn the specifics of the bank robbery. As the marina's Cuban watchman struggles to keep locals on the far side of the gate, he is confronted by two "haves" who demand access to their luxurious vessel. The men turn out to be Wallace Johnston and Henry Carpenter, two Ivy League graduates in their late thirties whom readers quickly realize are Hemingway's stereotype of embittered homosexuals (or bisexual, in Carpenter's case: "You don't know what you are even," Johnston snaps at him [229:22]). After the men bicker in an unpleasant exchange that recalls Richard and Helen Gordon's ugly dialogue in chapter 21(see 186:21), Hemingway switches to omniscient mode to provide stylistically experimental synopses of the men's lives and circumstances. Johnston is "interdit de sejour," or banned, in Paris, presumably for sexual proclivities that Carpenter now provides so his patron can avoid paying blackmail to "bus boys and sailors." Carpenter finds himself in this subservient position thanks to the Depression's banking crisis, which has bled his trust fund down to a monthly pittance—albeit one that, as Hemingway didactically notes, is still six times as much as Albert Tracy earned working for the WPA.

Still in omniscient mode, the narration then tours other yachts in the basin, cataloguing the sins and despairs of the rich. In the reception history of *To Have and Have Not,* this fifteen-page excursus is second only to Mr. Sing's murder in terms of controversy, with critics evenly divided over whether Hemingway's mordacious yet rhythmical inventory of venality succeeds or bungles. After learning of Carpenter's "inevitable suicide," we are introduced to an alcoholic grain merchant who, because his doctor has barred him from booze, cannot drink away news of an Internal Revenue Service investigation; a dully contented family whose daughter is about to marry a member of Yale's Skull and Bones fraternity, not being sophisticated enough to understand that a "man who is tapped for Bones is rarely also tapped for bed"; two Estonian sailing enthusiasts awaiting payment for hackneyed seafaring articles published in a columns called Sagas of Our Intrepid Voyagers; and "a professional son-in-law of the very rich and his mistress," among others.

Hemingway devotes the bulk of the chapter to the mistress, Dorothy Hollis, who also happens to be married to a famous Hollywood director. Unable to sleep, Dorothy contemplates women's woeful prospects for happiness. Because men are by nature not "built for" monogamy, she surmises, women have few options as they age other than to enter "bitch-hood," their sole means of steeling themselves against their husbands' infidelity, alcoholism, and abuse. "The bitches have the most fun," she notes, "but you have to be awfully stupid really to be a good one" (244:27, 245:8–9)—at least if Hélène Bradley is any evidence. Depending on one's perspective, Hemingway's attempt at imagining feminine woes is either "surpassingly awkward" (Mellow, *Hemingway* 487) or a "remarkably fair" presentation of "what is tender and affectionate" in a character whose "clear-cut preference for monogamy" is doomed to disappointment (Hovey 163). As Dorothy takes a dose of luminol to cure her insomnia, her ruminations turn into the novel's second most famous takeoff on Molly Bloom's closing soliloquy in Joyce's *Ulysses,* considered by most far less affecting than Marie Morgan's imminent stream of consciousness memorial to Harry in chapter 26. The specific reason the passage can strike a reader as infelicitous has to do with how Dorothy ultimately soothes the anxieties of "Bitch-hood": she masturbates herself to sleep.

227:2–3 the old submarine base now transformed into a yacht basin: See 95:17. As previously noted, the all-but-abandoned sub-basin where Hemingway docked the *Pilar* in Key West was converted into a yacht marina from 1934 until the advent of World War II. The "finger piers" Hemingway describes at 227:8 are the basin's most distinctive feature.

228:18 Wallace Johnston: Hemingway introduces the novel's third character with the name of Wallace, alongside Freddy Wallace and the bouncer at Freddy's. This is also the second character with the last name of Johnson/Johnston, after the tourist who stiffs Harry in Havana in part 1. At 250:20–21, we will learn that the sheriff's last name is Roger Johnson.

229:5 stick her: Short of saying "fuck her," Hemingway could not have been more graphic in conveying the repulsion Johnston feels for Hélène Bradley. As the conversation implies, Johnston's companion here, Henry Carpenter, has slept with Mrs. Bradley, declaring her "marvellous" (229:4). Johnston is unswayable in his judgment against the Bradleys' moral corruption, insisting that Hélène represents everything he loathes in a woman and her husband, Tommy, everything he despises in a man.

229:22 You don't even know what you are: Johnston's insult suggests that Carpenter is bisexual, as opposed to Johnston himself, who is homosexual. As Carpenter tells him, the sexual favors he grants Johnston spare the yachtsman the temptation of cruising busboys and sailors who might afterward blackmail him. When Johnston declares he never pays extortionists, Carpenter offers a clever riposte: "You're too tight to"—meaning too cheap, not too drunk (230:5).

230:25 I lost three hundred: Johnston and Carpenter have been to the casino, where the latter has lost heavily. Although Hemingway gives no clue as to which establishment they have been gambling at, the proximity of the yacht basin to The Lilac Time (i.e., Pena's Garden of Roses) suggests they are returning from the same club where Richard Gordon began his drinking binge. The alternative would be the Roberts' bar (Raul's Club), where Harry and Albert meet with the bank robbers. Freddy's bar (Sloppy Joe's) would probably be too blue collar an establishment for Johnston and Carpenter.

232:2 *interdit de sejour*: Meaning "forbidden to reside," this French legal term designates a person who has been banned from a specific area, "a somewhat archaic penality" in this era "usually reserved for drug addicts, white slavers, and thugs" (Ahamed 55). In Johnston's case, the ban is probably the result of his fondness for busboys and sailors.

232:14–15 he would land safely with his knees under some rich man's table: One can read this two ways. Henry Carpenter has a talent for landing *at* a rich man's table, with his knees tucked as he sits in a chair, or he lands *on* his knees under the table. This latter possibility conjures an image of oral sex, with Carpenter willing to crawl under the table to fellate any rich man who will in return support him. Either way, the name "Henry Carpenter" has two potential sources. Henry Carpenter is a minor character in Sherwood Anderson's *Winesburg, Ohio* (1919), the masochistic banker-father of Belle Carpenter, who is featured in the story cycle's eighteenth entry, "An Awakening." Hemingway may have also borrowed the name from a real-life Wall Street broker, Henry Carpen*d*er, implicated in 1926 of a gruesome double murder committed with his cousin, the "half-wit" Willie Stevens four years earlier. Both men were related to Mrs. Frances Stevens Hall, whose husband, Rev. Edward Hall, was the murder victim, as was his mistress, Eleanor Mills. Although Carpender was not a defendant in the murder trial that eventually found Mrs. Hall and Stevens innocent, his name was certainly bandied about in the press as a co-conspirator. The Hall-Mills murder case fascinated F. Scott Fitzgerald, who in 1926 was in the beginning stages of *Tender Is the Night,* which was originally to have concerned a sensationalized matricide. The murder of the adulterous couple has also been discussed as a potential source for *The Great Gatsby,* mainly because it was a major tabloid scandal in 1922, even though the trials of Mrs. Hall and Stevens did not take place until a year after *Gatsby*'s publication. Henry C. Phelps's 2001 essay "Literary History / Unsolved Mystery: *The Great Gatsby* and the Hall-Mills Murder

Case" makes a basic case for the murders' relevance to the novel. More recently, Sarah Churchwell in her eminently readable *Careless People: Mayhem, Murder, and the Invention of The Great Gatsby* (2014) goes over both details of the case and Fitzgerald's potential familiarity with it.

In *To Have and Have Not,* the association between Hemingway's Henry Carpenter and Fitzgerald is strengthened by a potential allusion to the triptych of 1936 essays Fitzgerald published in *Esquire* known collectively as *The Crack-Up,* in which Fitzgerald confesses to a breakdown. As Hemingway says of Carpenter, "[H]is friends had felt for some time that he was cracking up. If he had not been felt to be cracking up, with that instinct for feeling something wrong with a member of the pack and a healthy desire to turn him out, if it is impossible to destroy him, which characterizes the rich, he would not have been reduced to accepting the hospitality of Wallace Johnston" (232:18–25). Hemingway reveals that Carpenter's arrangement with Johnston postpones "his inevitable suicide" for "weeks if not months" (233:4–6).

233:14–15 **barkentine rigged three-master:** A barkentine or barquentine is a three-mast sailing vessel. The lead sail, the foremast, is square-rigged, meaning it is strung between horizontal spars. The second mast is fore-and-aft rigged, meaning it runs parallel, as opposed to perpendicular, to the keel.

233:18 **Internal Revenue Bureau:** Before July 1953, the official name of the revenue-collecting agency of the U.S. government was Bureau of Internal Revenue. President Dwight D. Eisenhower—working from a proposal from his predecessor, Harry S. Truman—changed the name to *Service* to mark the agency's reorganization from a patronage employment system into a civil service organization.

234:7 **Galapagos:** The Galápagos Islands are a series of islands clustered around the equator some five hundred miles west of Ecuador. They are most famous as the site studied by Charles Darwin, who formulated the theory of natural selection and evolution in *The Origin of the Species* (1859) during an 1835 expedition to the islands aboard the HMS *Beagle.*

In one of the best assessments of class in the novel, Randall A. Meeks uses this reference to analyze the conflict between the haves and have-nots through the lens of Social Darwinism, the "economic and social theory" that arose in the latter half of the nineteenth century "as the result of the misapplication of Darwin's theories to the spheres of human social and economic behavior" (82). As Meeks argues, *To Have and Have Not* is "about a world of predators and prey. It is, essentially, a story about some people a little lower on the food chain, caught up in the context of a social-Darwin world that, in this context, demands that there be winners and losers" (89). The philosophy is offered as a way of redeeming Harry Morgan's character from accusations that he lacks the moral character of a Nick Adams or Jake Barnes: "The novel places Harry Morgan in a world marked by a ruthless adherence to Social Darwinism. Hemingway did not set out to write about St. Francis of Assisi in Key West" (87).

237:4–5 **Lake Shore drive, Austin:** One of Chicago's most famous landmarks, Lake Shore Drive is the throughway that parallels Lake Michigan along the city's eastern coast. A 1920 letter from Hadley cites a line supposedly from Ernest in which the roadway is described as "white piping on gray ruffles, indistinguishable from sky" (qtd. in Griffin 147). In the 1920s and 1930s, Lake Shore Drive was also famous as a tony address for business elites. Austin was decidedly not tony. A west-side neighborhood, it was a working-class setting.

237:11–12 **on the L to work, Berwyn:** The L in Chicago is the city's mass-transit train system. Berwyn is the small city directly south of Hemingway's birthplace, Oak Park.

237:16–20 **the leaning drop his father made from forty-two floors up:** The enduring image of stockbrokers and bankers plunging to their deaths by leaping out of skyscrapers at the onset of the Great Depression is an urban legend. According to John Kenneth Galbraith,

> in the week or so following Black Thursday, the London penny press told delightedly of the scenes in downtown New York. Speculators were hurling themselves from windows; pedestrians picked their ways delicately between the bodies of fallen financiers.
>
> In the United States, the suicide wave that followed the stock market crash is part of the legend of 1929. In fact there was none. For several years before 1929 the suicide rate had been gradually rising. It continued to increase in that year, with a further and much sharper increase in 1930, 1931 and 1932—years when there were many things besides the stock market to cause people to conclude that life was no longer worth living (128).

According to a 2008 *Slate Magazine* article, only two "leaning drop" deaths took place on Wall Street during the financial collapse, one involving clerk Hulda Borowski, who fell forty flights on 5 November 1929, and the second, a produce-industry magnate, G. E. Cutler, who jumped from his lawyer's window eleven days later, on 16 November (Rastogi). Even before these deaths, however, popular lore was insisting that the stock-market crash had led to a wave of such suicides. One source of the story was gallows humor, such as a *Punch Magazine* cartoon showing financiers hurtling toward the ground, or comedian Eddie Cantor's oft-told joke that New York hoteliers ask guests if they wished to rent rooms for sleeping or leaping (Galbraith 129–30). Equally influential was a story told by British prime minister Winston Churchill, who claimed in a 1929 *Daily Telegraph* article that under his own hotel window while visiting New York "a gentleman cast himself down fifteen storeys and was dashed to pieces" (Rastogi).

237:18, 237:27 the Aurora-Elgin train, the Aurora-Elgin tracks: From 1902 to 1957, the Chicago Aurora & Elgin Railway (CA&E) offered commuter service from Chicago to Wheaton, Illinois, and then either south to Aurora or north to Elgin (begun in 1903), on electrified tracks. Fifty-two trains served the line, running fifteen minutes apart, with the final destinations alternating between Aurora and Elgin. The commute ran roughly sixty-five minutes (forty-seven of them between Chicago and Wheaton) and cost twenty-five cents one way and forty-five cents round-trip. After the line was abandoned in the 1950s as customers turned to private vehicles for commuting, the right of way lay dormant until 1966, when a "rail-to-trail" conversion led to the creation of the Illinois Prairie Path. Hemingway uses the railway here as a symbol of suburban despair.

238:3–12 the Colt or Smith and Wesson; those well-constructed implements that end insomnia . . . , their only drawback the mess they leave for relatives to clean up: As Hemingway structures this textbook exercise in periodic-sentence construction, he includes an obvious autobiographical reference. When Hemingway's father, Clarence, committed suicide on 6 December 1928, he fired a .32 Smith and Wesson behind his right ear. The handgun had belonged to Clarence's own father, Ernest's beloved grandfather, Anson Hemingway. This entire passage, from 237:29 to 238:15, was a manuscript insert.

239:18 only suckers worry: Another key word in the hardboiled lexicon, *sucker* as a synonym for *dupe* or *fool* dates back to the mid-nineteenth century, as early as 1831, according to some sources, as late as 1857 to others. Its most famous formulation, "There's a sucker born every minute," is credited to P. T. Barnum (1810–1891), although the circus magnate / publicity innovator never actually uttered that phrase. The term gained maximum currency in the 1920s and 1930s thanks to its association with the gangster idiom, but along with *sap* its usage also quickly suffered from stylization. In *Listening to America: An Illustrated History of Words and Phrases from Our Lively and Splendid Past* (1982), Stuart Berg Flexner traces the etymology of the term to the word "suckling" and to the notion of childlike naïveté, as in "one as innocent as a suckling" (320).

239:2 blow: A common slang term for *storm, blow* appears often in Hemingway's fiction, most notably as the title for the 1924 short story "The Three-Day Blow" (*CSS* 83–94).

239:21 Skull and Bones: Founded in 1832, Yale University's secret society has gained a notorious reputation as a training ground for aspiring powerbrokers, thanks to its history of influential members, which to date includes three U.S. presidents (William Howard Taft, George H. W. Bush, and George W. Bush), as well as dozens of congressmen, federal judges, bankers, and academics. Influential members of Hemingway's generation included his friends Archibald MacLeish and Donald Ogden Stewart (the inspiration for Bill Gorton in *The Sun Also Rises*), Henry Luce (founder of *Time Magazine*), and literary critic F. O. Mathiessen. In keeping with Hemingway's defensive dismissals of Ivy League masculinity, the reference here is far from admiring or complimentary. As the author shortly insists, "The type of man who is tapped for Bones is rarely tapped for bed" (239:26–27).

240:4–7 selling something everybody uses by the millions of bottles . . . fifty cents in the medium, a quarter in the small: Biographers agree that this elusively described product is a reference to Sloan's Liniment, a multipurpose patent medicine manufactured by Pauline Hemingway's uncles through the St. Louis–based Richard Hudnut Company (Kert, *Hemingway Women* 294). Hemingway momentarily slips into pseudo-testimonial advertising mode, noting that the product "does just what it says it will. Grateful users from all over the world keep writing in discovering new uses" (240:11–13). Given Hemingway's financial dependency on the Pfeiffers in the 1930s—in particular, the largesse he enjoyed from Pauline's uncle Gus—the parody is both hypocritical and ungrateful, reflecting the resentment he felt toward his second wife as the end of their marriage neared. Sloan's Liniment is explicitly named in *True at First Light* (258) and *Under Kilimanjaro* (146) without the mockery, however.

240:15 Stanley Baldwin . . . Harrow: Stanley Baldwin (1867–1947) served as prime minister of England during the period Hemingway wrote *To Have and Have Not*. Harrow is the exclusive boys' school located in North London's Harrow borough that competes only with Eton College in minting British royalty and statesmen.

240:17 *Alzira III*: During the period Hemingway wrote the novel, the *Key West Citizen* reported the comings and goings of yachts in both the submarine-basin-turned-public-marina and boat berths on the city's north side as part of the tourist initiative. Although no particular vessel was dubbed *Alzira*, the name did have relevance to Hemingway: he borrowed it from the wife of painter Waldo Peirce, his frequent guest in Key West. A painter in her own right, Alzira created two notable WPA murals in 1938–39: *Ellsworth, Lumber Port* in Ellsworth, Maine, and *Shipwreck at Night* in Portland, Maine. She and Waldo Peirce divorced after World War II, after nearly fifteen years of marriage. She then became an organizer for the United Mine Workers. She died in 2010 at the age of 102.

240:20 **yawl-rigged:** To be "yawl-rigged" means a ship has a smaller aft mast and sail at the very back of a vessel. Post–World War II, the specific definition of the term would come to mean the back mast and sail were located behind the rudderpost, with a "ketch" distinguished by them located in front of the post.

240:21–22 **Esthonians:** The Republic of Estonia is a Northern European country located on the Baltic Sea, north of Latvia and south of Finland (and separated from it by the Gulf of Finland). Hemingway slips a gratuitous "h" into the name for its people. Despite the misspelling, a paraphrase of the line, "No well-run yacht basin in Southern waters is complete without at least two sunburnt, salt-bleached Esthonians who are waiting for a check for their last article" has been amended in Estonia to "In every port in the world, at least two *Estonians* can be found" and adapted into a national slogan celebrating Estonian worldliness—this despite the fact that Hemingway's original sentence is meant as a dig.

Exactly what inspired Hemingway to include Estonians in his list of yachtsmen is unclear. None of the legible issues of the *Key West Citizen* available at the Monroe County Library in Key West mention any such visit from foreign, seafaring journalists. (Many of the microfilmed issues from 1935–36 in the library's Florida Research Room are illegible, however.) Nor do national newspaper databases make any mention of Estonian sailors writing yarns for home papers. A *Citizen* article headlined "Tiny Boat Which Crossed Atlantic Starts on Cruise" does appear in the 8 January 1931 issue, detailing the travels of a twenty-nine-foot sailboat called the *Ahto,* which sailed from Estonia to the Florida Keys in 133 days. No mention is made of brothers Kou and Ahto Walter selling their adventures for a dollar a column. Hemingway was in Key West at this time, though, having begun moving into his new Whitehead Street home only five days earlier (Chamberlin 107). It is possible that he made the acquaintance of Kou and Ahto somewhere on the island, although it would have happened at least three years before he purchased the *Pilar* and spent significant time at the Key West sub-basin. Ahto Walter remains the most famous Estonian sailor, having moved to the United States after his oceanic trek and published *Racing the Seas* (1935).

Hemingway does have another, albeit tangential, connection to Estonia that is of interest. Future wife Martha Gellhorn (whom he had not yet met when he wrote the yacht-club scene) was a friend of H. G. Wells, who in the 1930s was involved in an affair with one of the most colorful figures in twentieth-century Eastern European history, Baroness Maura Budberg (1892–1974), a self-professed British spy and aspiring Lenin assassin. Born in Ukraine as Maria Ignatievna Zakrevskaya, Budberg became Wells's mistress in 1920 at the same time that she was the common-law wife of Maxim Gorky. In the 1930s, she lived in intermittently in Estonia, where she owned an estate called Yendel (today known as the Jäneda Manor and Museum). Wells visited her there in 1934, confronting her for lying to him repeatedly over secret visits to Gorky. A year later, the famed writer, then sixty-nine years old, met Gellhorn, twenty-six, supposedly over dinner at the White House with the Roosevelts. Later that year, during a second trip to America, Wells stayed with Gellhorn for several weeks in a cramped house in Connecticut, where he facilitated a deal with G. P. Putnam's for her second book, a quartet of novellas called *The Trouble I've Seen,* for which Wells wrote a preface. In May 1936 Gellhorn stayed with Wells in England. Late in life, she vigorously rejected Wells's insinuations that their relationship had been more than platonic and even threatened to sue his estate when, in the early 1980s, it planned to publish posthumously Wells's memoir of his love life, *H. G. Wells in Love: Postscript to an Experiment in Autobiography* (1984). (Mentions of Gellhorn were replaced with asterisks.) Six months after her London stay, Gellhorn met Hemingway, although she would not introduce him to Wells until 1940 (Kert, *Hemingway Women* 348). What, if anything, Hemingway knew of Wells's relationship with Budberg is unclear. Even if the references to the Estonian sailors predate his own introduction to Gellhorn in December 1936, the Budberg-Wells-Gellhorn connection remains, aside from this passage, Hemingway's only connection to the country. It is also a relatively unexplored story in Hemingway studies, although Andrea Lynn's claim in *Shadow Lovers: The Last Affairs of H. G. Wells* (2001) that "Martha's intriguing association with HG is absent from the Hemingway biographies" (347) is not quite accurate. Bernice Kert's *The Hemingway Women* certainly covers Wells's fondness for Gellhorn, and others mention him in passing. Interestingly, Maura and Martha, thanks to Wells introducing them in London in the 1930s, remained friendly after his death in in 1946; Budberg served as a witness to Gellhorn's post-Hemingway marriage to journalist T. S. Matthews in 1954 (Moorehead 309).

241:10 Dorothy Hollis: Although she only appears in *To Have and Have Not* for five pages, Dorothy Hollis is generally regarded as the novel's third most prominent female character behind Marie Morgan and Helène Bradley. She certainly elicits more critical commentary than Helen Gordon or chapter 15's Mrs. Laughton. The reason for the attention is twofold: beginning at 242:2 Hemingway launches into an extended treatment of Dorothy's private thoughts that weaves between interior monologue and stream of consciousness, in apparent homage to James Joyce's closing chapter in *Ulysses,* popularly known as "Penelope," which dramatizes Molly Bloom's sensuality and erotic embrace of life in contrast to the withheld sexual affections of her husband, Leopold, who avoids coitus with his wife (although not other forms of sexual gratification) out of grief over the loss of their son. While *Ulysses* ends with the implicit promise that Bloom will soon make complete love to Molly, no such optimism surrounds Dorothy. At any rate, only Marie Morgan's forthcoming monologue in chapter 26 will out-Molly this interlude of Dorothy's. The second reason for the attention has to do with Dorothy's actions as she ruminates over her unhappy life: Hemingway depicts her, albeit indirectly, as masturbating herself to sleep. If most critics are sympathetic toward Dorothy as a character, they are generally unimpressed by Hemingway's technique. As Arthur Waldhorn wittily writes, "Although Dorothy Hollis's long inward discourse reveals Hemingway's awareness of Joyce, it does little to direct our sense of the novel's purpose (unless, of course, Dorothy's masturbating illustrates once more that one cannot—or, perhaps, can—manage alone)" (157).

Dorothy is a sympathetic character because of the female dilemma she represents. Married to one incapacitated alcoholic (the Hollywood director John Hollis), she has become the mistress of another drunk, a "professional son-in-law of the very rich" named Eddie, who brings her to Key West on his yacht, the *Irydia IV*. As Dorothy laments, men and women share no real emotional intimacy in relationships. Alcohol may be one contributing factor to their alienation, rendering men either impotent or somnambulant, but the real culprit is the male sexual appetite: men only desire what they have yet to possess, and their relentless inability to maintain fidelity dooms women to "bitch-hood": "The better you treat a man and the more you show him you love him the quicker he gets tired of you," Dorothy realizes (245:1–2). To many critics, the line could have come from the lips of Pauline Hemingway, the wife whom the author was in the process of abandoning for Martha Gellhorn as the novel was published. (The subsequent line, "the good [men] are made to have lots of wives," can strike critics as a little too self-justifying on Hemingway's part.) Dorothy's interior monologue critiques the illusory power a woman derives from being a "bitch": "The bitches have the most fun but you have to be awfully stupid really to be a good one," she decides (245:7–9). In the absence of any sustaining affection for women, Dorothy can only pine for the escape of sleep, which leaves her craving luminol almost as much as she craves love.

As Carl P. Eby notes, the name "Hollis" was added to the manuscript shortly after Hemingway finished his first draft in January 1937. Originally Dorothy's surname was "Knowlton," and she was intermittently referred to as "Dodie McKenzie" as well. Inspiring the change to "Hollis" was a friend and former colleague of Pauline's, named Marjorie Hillis, with whom the second Mrs. Hemingway had worked in the Paris offices of *Vogue* in the mid-1920s, shortly before the affair with Ernest that would lead to their marriage. Shortly after completing the early 1937 draft, Hemingway received a letter from his oldest sister, Marcelline, mentioning she had met Hillis, who was then garnering fame as the author of a popular etiquette guide for single women, *Live Alone and Like It: A Guide for the Extra Woman*. Not unlike a modern-day Nora Ephron collection, this advice book humorously counseled Hillis's female audience on how to find contentment without relying on men—something Dorothy Hollis decidedly doesn't know how to do. As Eby writes, Hemingway's allusion may be a secret, self-recriminating confession to Pauline that he knew deep down he was at fault for their failing marriage. The reference may even be a sly, if not glib, way of signaling that Pauline was better off without him. For the reader, however, the Hollis-Hillis connection functions as a "bitterly ironic" rejoinder to the emphasis placed on individualism by the male characters: "The book's interest in the inadequacies of the individual," writes Eby, "is most convincing and poignant in the arena of human emotional relationships, particularly as seen from a woman's point of view. . . . Emotionally and erotically alienated by the impotence, infidelity, or deaths of their husbands, Dorothy Hollis, Hélène Bradley, Helen Gordon, Mrs. Tracy, and Marie Morgan must all in their various ways struggle with the loneliness and pain of 'living alone'—and they don't like it" ("Wake Up Alone" 101–02). In this way, the allusion to Hillis's book reminds us of the "intensity of Hemingway's sympathy with many of the female characters in the novel," complicating its reputation as among the most misogynistic of his works.

241:20 breakwater: A breakwater is an offshore structure, usually a wall, constructed to diminish the power of waves as they strike the shore. The structures may be man-made or natural; in Key West both are present, with the coral reef surrounding the island an example of the natural type.

242:4 luminol: Contemporary readers honed on police procedurals (whether in novels or on television) are often thrown by this reference, conditioned as they are to think of luminol as the chemical that crime-scene technicians use to test for blood traces. When mixed with a small amount of an oxidant (usually hydrogen peroxide), luminol reacts to the iron in blood to give off a blue glow. German chemist H. O. Albrecht first discovered the chemical's luminescent properties in 1928; as Hemingway wrote this scene in 1937, they were still being refined for crime-scene usage by Walter Specht. Before this usage became commonplace, Luminol was the brand name for a sleeping pill Bayer introduced into the sedative market in 1912. F. Scott Fitzgerald mentions the drug in an essay on insomnia, titled "Sleeping and Waking" (1934): "A typical night (and I wish I could say such nights were all in the past) comes after a particularly sedentary work-and-cigarette day. It ends, say without any relaxing interval, at the time for going to bed. All is prepared, the books, the glass of water, the extra pajamas lest I awake in rivulets of sweat, the luminol pills in the little round tube, the note book and pencil in case of a night thought worth recording. (Few have been—they generally seem thin in the morning, which does not diminish their force and urgency at night.)" (*Crack-up* 65). "Sleeping and Waking" begins with a tribute to Hemingway's "Now I Lay Me," another story about insomnia (*CSS* 276–82).

243:5–6 There's two of nearly everything except stomach and heart: Dorothy's line echoes Harry's reference to testicles to Albert in chapter 9: "You've got two arms and you've got two of something else" (97:5–7).

244:25–26 **Mr. Winchell:** A reference to newspaper and radio personality Walter Winchell (1897–1972), who in 1929 became the first syndicated gossip columnist, when the *New York Daily Mirror* began running his column "On Broadway." At the peak of his fame, Winchell appeared in more than two thousand American newspapers and was heard by upward of 20 million a week thanks to his Sunday evening radio show. Hemingway made frequent appearances in Winchell columns from the late 1930s on.

244:27 **canined:** Hemingway turns "canine" into a verb as an awkward attempt at a synonym for "bitch."

CHAPTER TWENTY-FIVE

Largely perfunctory, the novel's penultimate chapter follows the sheriff as he tours the *Queen Conch* with the Coast Guard skipper. The main point of the conversation seems to be the men's total miscomprehension of the scene. As the skipper surmises, a fight must have broken out among the Cubans, the quartet killing each other over how to split the money. Neither man suggests Harry Morgan might have killed the revolutionaries; the skipper does not even tell the sheriff about Harry's "one man alone" statement. Despite the scene's lack of discernable purpose, the chapter includes a bizarre moment that reintroduces in miniature the extended grotesquery of Richard Gordon's encounter with the vets at Freddy's Bar. As the sheriff and the skipper wrap up their inquiry, Albert Tracy's wife rushes onto the dock demanding to know where her husband's body is. Neither man is aware that Harry and the Cubans dumped it overboard once clear of the Key West channel (161:8). Eager for a glimpse of the dead bodies, the crowd behind the widow surges forward and inadvertently knocks her into the water. Rather gratuitously, Hemingway has Mrs. Tracy scream for divers to find her lost dental plate.

The spectacle of the woman's grief contrasts with Marie Morgan's more dignified bearing at the Marine Hospital, to which Harry has been rushed. When the doctors inform her he cannot be saved, Marie takes her children home. On the way they cross paths on Rocky Road with "some poor goddamned rummy" with a bloody face. In a reversal of chapter 19, it is Richard Gordon.

249:3 **coaming:** A raised seal around any opening on a boat, such as a hatch, that prevents water from seeping into the hull.

250:17 **Robert Simmons:** This is our first mention of the deceased Bee-lips's full name.

251:20–21 **Roger Johnson:** Although the sheriff has appeared in several chapters already, this is Hemingway's first mention of his name.

251:25 **chords:** Another typo that Scribner's failed to correct in proofreading. A chord with an "h" typically refers to a group of musical notes played simultaneously, although it can also refer in geometry to a line connecting points on a plane. In this context, the spelling Hemingway means would not include the "h," as in a vocal *cord*. Although British spelling deems "vocal chords" an acceptable alternative, American usage does not.

252:2–3 **Hay cuatro muertos. Todos son muertos:** Cubans in the crowd are saying, "Four dead. All dead."

252:13–14 **Mrs. Tracy . . . fell into the green water:** As with so much of *To Have and Have Not*, critics are divided over this bizarre moment when Albert Tracy's grieving wife is knocked into the water of the yacht basin and loses her false teeth. As P. G. Rama Rao says, "The tragi-comic scene of Mrs. Tracey's grief, which precedes the scenes of Marie's dignified conduct at the hospital and her grief, looks to be an artificial device deliberately planted there as a foil [to Marie's anguish], and this [contrived contrast] takes away much of its effect" (9–10). For Lisa Tyler, the scene is indicative of the overall way the narrative demeans women's speech so they go unheard: "Women's voices are rarely heard in this novel, and when they are, they are sometimes hard to understand," as when Mrs. Tracy screams, "Losht my plate" at 253:1–2. "Because she is unable to enunciate it clearly, [Mrs. Tracy's] grief—and surely some of her emotion is genuine—is trivialized and made ridiculous" (58).

253:20–21 **since the Isleño had been lynched:** Meaning "The Islander," the Isleño is a reference to World War I veteran Manolo Cabeza, a Key West resident in the early 1920s so nicknamed because he was born in the Canary Islands. The owner of a small bar known as the Red Rooster, the immigrant committed the cardinal Jim Crow sin of living openly with a half-black, half-Cuban woman, purportedly named Angela. Members of the Ku Klux Klan mercilessly beat Cabeza on 23 December 1921, first attacking him in his apartment and then dragging him to Petronia Street, where he was tarred and feathered. On Christmas Day, in retaliation, the Spaniard murdered local cigar-factory worker George Decker, whom he had recognized during the beating despite Decker having worn a traditional Klan hood. Cabeza escaped from the crime scene on upper Duval Street by taxi and retreated to the cupola of the Sandola Building at the intersection of Whitehead and Petronia, where Marines were called in to assist in his arrest. Eventually, Cabeza allowed himself to be taken into custody with promises of protection by then Sheriff Roland Curry. That night, however, Klansmen entered the jail, which had conveniently been left unguarded, and attacked him even more ferociously. Whether Cabeza was still alive by the time his body was dragged to East Martello Tower is unclear. What is known is that his corpse was hung from a tree and riddled with bullets. Cabeza's grave remains a tourist attraction in the paupers' section of the Key West cemetery, marked by a hand-lettered sign.

255:22–23 It was Richard Gordon on his way home: The appearance of Gordon neatly mirrors chapter 19, in which the writer catches sight of Marie and misinterprets her entirely (see 176:4–6). It is significant that Marie expresses pity for this drunken "have" ("Some poor rummy . . . some poor goddamned rummy" [255:18–19]); Marie embodies the compassion that Gordon and his ilk lack when the radical writer dismisses her as fat and unloved by her husband.

CHAPTER TWENTY-SIX

The novel's closing scene follows Marie Morgan's thoughts after Harry's funeral—which, most readers are surprised to discover, she has skipped (257:20–21, 261:3). The other surprising revelation is Marie's animosity toward her children. "I don't care about those girls," she admits to herself. "I've got to do something about them though" (257:6–7). Whether Hemingway intends for us to view Marie as too hardened from the working-class struggle to love her daughters or whether he simply assumes it is not unnatural for a mother to feel this way is not clear. Perhaps he even aims for us to interpret her callousness as an expression of grief voiced in the heat of confusion. Regardless, Marie's statements are likely an impediment to contemporary readers empathizing with her.

Where audiences will feel for the woman, however, is in the memories of her love for Harry. Marie recalls a vacation in Havana nearly twenty years earlier when she dyed her hair blond and was nervous about her husband's reaction: "I was so excited I was choked with it," she remembers (259:16–17). With barely a word, Harry insisted they return to the hotel right then and there. For Marie, the story is proof of their love and commitment.

With Harry now gone, Marie has nothing but emptiness inside. She insists that life is a matter of going dead by degrees. Returning to the theme of "taking it" as a measure of heroic endurance, Hemingway depicts her as snuffing any aspiration or ambition except simple survival: "Nothing is any good to wish," she declares (261:1–2).

Given the darkness of Marie's thoughts, Hemingway was wise to end the novel on a more objective note. The narrative perspective pulls away from Marie to focus on a yacht entering the harbor. Miles farther out, a tanker not unlike the one that found Harry Morgan adrift in the *Queen Conch* hugs a reef so not to waste fuel by riding headlong into the Gulf Stream. The ambiguous juxtaposition between the yacht and the tanker provides one final contrast between the haves and have nots—between the luxurious wastage of the wealthy and the common man's struggle to survive.

257:1–261:27 **I don't know, Marie Morgan was thinking:** The bulk of this final chapter weaves between interior monologue and stream of consciousness. Marie's reflections on Harry and his passing represent the novel's most famous attempt to emulate Joyce's Molly Bloom soliloquy in *Ulysses*. As critics often note, Hemingway's copy of Joyce's 1922 magnum opus reveals he was not familiar with the entirety of the novel; in the copy that Shakespeare and Company bookstore owner Sylvia Beach presented him in his early Paris years, only the pages of the book's opening half and Molly's concluding chapter are cut open (Lynn, *Hemingway* 161). (At the time, books were usually sold with untrimmed page edges, requiring readers to slice the folds with a letter opener or knife.)

Critics generally regard Marie's monologue as a more successful experiment than Dorothy Hollis's in chapter 24 (241:10), although still too clearly derivative of Joyce to qualify as an achievement.

258:1 **snotty:** One of five uses of this word in the novel (see 119:6), this is the only time the attribute is depicted as a virtue. For Marie, Harry's snottiness was apiece with his strength and survival instinct, all of which make him "like some kind of expensive animal."

258:15 **my hair blonde:** Marie's dyed hair was most likely inspired by Pauline Hemingway's efforts to maintain her husband's sexual interest in their marriage by lightening her hair on at least two occasions. The first occurred in July 1929; only a few short years later, she did it again, this time in response to the presence of strawberry-blond Jane Mason, whose attention to her husband made Pauline feel insecure and competitive. As Pauline's biographer, Ruth Hawkins, explains, "throughout their marriage, Pauline's hair held erotic qualities for Ernest, particularly because of its cut and feel. Pauline decided to take things a step further by going blonde, like Jane. In mid-September [1934] Pauline told Ernest that her hair had reached a deep gold shade, with no pink, and she intended to 'just jockey it along' and not do too much else besides keeping the roots light." She even delayed a trip from Key West to rendezvous with her husband in Havana until she could tint her hair "a little golder" (170–71).

During his fourth marriage, to Mary Welsh, Hemingway would experiment with lightening his own hair. Not surprisingly, the motif of dyed blonde hair is pervasive throughout his novels and stories (Eby, *Hemingway's Fetishism* 36–40). One work written during his marriage to Pauline, "The Light of the World," collected in 1933's *Winner Take Nothing*, even features a prostitute nicknamed Peroxide (*CSS* 292–97). Dyed blonde hair is also crucial to the erotic but ultimately destructive gender play in the posthumously published *The Garden of Eden* (1986). Here Catherine and David Bourne take turns cutting and bleaching their hair to achieve an androgynous mutuality that ultimately leads to madness and destroys their union.

258:16 **Prado:** The name refers to the Paseo del Prado, a boulevard that separates Old and New Havana. The roadway runs roughly a mile from the Malecón to just past the Capitol building. Dating back to 1772, the thoroughfare had undergone a redesign by the French architect Jean-Claude Nicolas Forestier in the same year Hemingway first passed through Havana (1928).

260:17–20 **And he was so goddamned good to me:** Hemingway penciled this four-line paragraph into the setting copy.

261:10 **take it every day the way it comes:** Marie here invokes the rhetoric of resilience Hemingway employs throughout the novel, effectively summing up the theme of stoic acceptance and endurance.

261:22–27 **I've got a good start if that's what you have to do:** Hemingway's setting copy originally ended with this line. He then penciled an additional half-dozen short sentences in which Marie reiterates the claim that she is going dead inside, ending with her insistence that when it comes to that enervation, "I'm way ahead of everybody now."

261:28–262:11 **Outside it was a lovely, cool, sub-tropical day:** As noted in my overview of the novel's composition process (see pages xlv–xlvi), Hemingway struggled to find an ending for the final version of the novel after he deleted the Tommy Bradley–Richard Gordon dynamite run to Cuba, which ends with Tommy's boat sunken in the Key West sub base. This late addition reads like an authorial attempt to find a more objective image upon which to conclude than Marie's monologue would have provided. The best way to appreciate these final three short paragraphs is by imagining them as a camera shot in a film: the "eye" of the "you" the text names zooms forward through a window, noting various details, including palm branches sawing in the winter, bicycling winter people, and a squawking peacock. The focus leaves the land to focus on the ocean, where a yacht enters the harbor and, farther out, a tanker runs west along a reef to glide in the current.

The question here is the relationship between these main elements, and in particular the relationship between the yacht and the tanker. If the former is obviously a mark of the luxury and privilege enjoyed by the "haves," the latter seems a more ambiguous symbol. On the one hand, it may represent the economic exploitation of the working class inasmuch as the tanker is employed in hauling the natural resources necessary for the wealthy to sustain their lifestyle. On the other, the concluding detail about the conservation of fuel that the tanker achieves by hugging the reef seems a commentary on the endurance of the poor, another expression of the labor class's ability to "take it." These interpretations may not seem mutually exclusive, but they do create a textual space of ambiguity within which critics disagree about the ultimate meaning of the image. For Jani Scandura, the novel's final paragraphs narrate "the inevitable burial of Key West's working classes, the

Conchs, by rich 'winter people,' FERA, and military ships"—and, by extension, by Hemingway and his readers, who belong to the same "burgeoning tourist colony" as the rich, whether they acknowledge it or not (120). P. G. Rama Rao, by contrast, calls attention to the similarities between the tanker passage and *Green Hills of Africa*'s meditation on the Gulf Stream, suggesting an escape into the eternal (10). As Hemingway writes there, "the Gulf Stream and the other great ocean currents are the last wild country there is left. Once you are out of sight of land and of other boats you are more alone than you can ever be hunting and the sea is the same as it has been since before men ever went on it in boats" (31). Bert Bender likewise cites this passage in relation to *To Have and Have Not* in *Sea-Brothers: The Tradition of American Fiction from* Moby-Dick *to the Present* (1988). When read alongside *Green Hills,* the final passage of *To Have and Have Not* becomes a metafictional window on the text itself, offering a frame for viewing the eternality of the sea in contrast to the emptiness of human life (181).

The most original reading of the novel's ending may come from Robert W. Lewis. In *Hemingway on Love* (1965), Lewis hails the closing passage as "magnificent" in its use of "sexual imagery" and in its "ironic suggestiveness in contrast to the bloody mess and loneliness of the town of Key West that night." In the critic's reading, the peacock in the yard stands as a "beautiful symbol of sex and vanity, the two irreconcilables" while the "everlastingness" of the Gulf Stream stands as a contrast to its "squawk ... an ugly sound from an ugly, beautiful bird" with a simple message: "Meanwhile, endure" (140).

Despite its faults (or perhaps because of them), *To Have and Have Not* endures in the meanwhile of popular culture far longer than its literary reputation suggests it should. Hemingway's 1937 novel will never be hailed as a classic, but it does offer an entertaining vision of the clash between the natural world and human systems such as politics, economics, and the law. Part of the adventure of reading any Hemingway work is the biographical valences that engender so much fascination with the writer's personality. In this regard, *To Have and Have Not* sparks the typical scholarly pursuit of real-life friends and acquaintances who inspired its cast of characters. Yet more so than any other Hemingway text, Harry Morgan's story is a potboiler rich with action and violence. A reader expecting genius will be sorely disappointed, but one hoping for B-grade pleasures is in for a wild ride.

APPENDIX A

Manuscripts

The manuscripts, typescripts, and setting copy of *To Have and Have Not,* including original drafts of "One Trip Across" and "The Tradesman's Return," are housed in boxes 30–33 of the Ernest Hemingway Collection at the John F. Kennedy Presidential Library and Museum in Boston, Massachusetts. The material is divided among fourteen items, the contents of which are outlined below. Materials held at the Harry Ransom Center at the University of Texas in Austin and the Monroe County Library in Key West are listed afterward.

I am indebted to Sarah Finch Brown, who gave me permission to expand on the inventory of *To Have and Have Not* manuscripts at the Kennedy Library she includes in her 1985 master's thesis at Trinity University, written under the direction of Paul Smith.

HEMINGWAY COLLECTION

Item 204: Divides the pencil manuscript of the original draft among twenty-six folders, up to Marie Morgan's final lament for Harry, totaling 451 pages. Includes a typescript of "One Trip Across."

Item 205: A pencil manuscript fifty-five pages in length erroneously entitled "Chapter 40." (The draft in item 204 ends with chapter 29, not 39.) What should be labelled chapter 30 here is the original draft of Tommy Bradley and Richard Gordon's aborted dynamite run to Cuba.

Item 206: A fifteen-page manuscript fragment labeled "A big breeze was blowing. . . . ," which is Hemingway's first attempt at what would evolve into the story "The Tradesman's Return" and eventually be incorporated into *To Have and Have Not* as part 2. The draft is completed but not dramatically successful. Despite featuring Harry Morgan's mate Wesley, it does not resemble the plot of "Tradesman." Set in Cuban waters instead of on the journey back to Key West, the story ends with military police arresting Harry and quarantining Wesley in Havana. There is no Captain Willie or Dr. Frederick Harrison in the story. For a description, see my pages xxvi–xxvii.

Item 207: Two pages of manuscript discards.

Item 208: An eight-page pencil manuscript of the published novel's chapter 23, headed by the phrase "After vets—before yachts," to instruct his typist where to insert the scene.

Item 209: A discarded fragment, written in pencil, describing Harry Morgan's death, which comes to him "easy" because he is "completely tired." Hemingway insists that working-class characters like the charter-boat captain are exhausted by responsibilities and have outlived their resources. This item also includes a false start on the party at Hélène Bradley's house, with several crossed-out sentences suggesting Hemingway's frustration with beginning the scene.

Item 210: Undoubtedly the most baffling fragment filed among the *To Have and Have Not* materials, this short scene set along the Malecón in Havana can lead a researcher to think Hemingway contemplated giving Harry Morgan's death a supernatural element, for it describes a Negro fingering a set of voodoo beads. Once a reader realizes the woman in the scene is named Maria and not Marie, however, s/he recognizes that this manuscript scrap is not related to Harry Morgan's story at all. Rather, it belongs to the little-read story "Nobody Ever Dies" (*CSS* 470–81), which first appeared in *Cosmopolitan* in March 1939, a year and a half after *To Have and Have Not* was published.

Item 211: This item includes tear sheets of "One Trip Across" as it appeared in *Cosmopolitan* in April 1934. It is here that Hemingway penciled in chapter breaks for part 1 of *To Have and Have Not* for his typist. A typescript of "The Tradesman's Return" is also included here, with the original name of the Roosevelt bureaucrat, Henry Harrison, crossed out and replaced with Frederick Harrison. This item also includes the one-page sheet in which Hemingway diagrammed his ambitious plan for the novel (see pages xxx–xxxi).

Item 212: This item is a carbon of the typescript Hemingway's typist prepared of the original draft of *To Have and Have Not*, presumably meant to be used as the setting copy from which typeset galleys would be prepared. The typescript runs 260 pages.

Item 213: This item is the setting copy of the cut or final version of *To Have and Have Not*, featuring many pencil corrections and insertions. The novel now runs 199 pages.

Items 214–18a: Various cuts, insertions, and corrections in the final setting copy. Most of these items run only two or three pages.

HARRY H. RANSOM CENTER

The Ransom Center at the University of Texas in Austin includes two *To Have and Have Not* related items: a copy of the typescript of "One Trip Across" (box 2, folder 8) and a galley copy of the story (Galley folder 5).

MONROE COUNTY PUBLIC LIBRARY

Located at 700 Fleming Street in Key West, the public library's Florida Research Room holds a set of the galleys of the final version of *To Have and Have Not*. The corrections and changes Hemingway made to these are not substantive.

APPENDIX B

A Comparison of the Original Draft of *To Have and Have Not* and the Published Version

For this appendix, I am indebted to Sarah Finch Brown, who gave me permission to expand on her comparison of the original *To Have and Have Not* draft and the published novel included in her 1985 master's thesis at Trinity University, written under the direction of Paul Smith.

Outline of Chapters in Original Manuscript	Outline of Chapters in Published Novel
Part I (Harry Morgan [Spring])	**Part I (Harry Morgan [Spring])**
Chapter 1: Harry Morgan survives *porrista* attack at the Pearl of San Francisco Café and takes the tourist Mr. Johnson fishing; Johnson loses Harry's tackle and skips out on his bill.	Chapter 1: Same as manuscript.
Chapter 2: Harry meets the nefarious Mr. Sing and agrees to smuggle Chinese immigrants from Cuba to Key West.	Chapter 2: Same as manuscript.
Chapter 3: Setting out to sea from Havana, Harry discovers his drunken mate Eddy Marshall has stowed aboard his boat.	Chapter 3: Same as manuscript.
Chapter 4: Harry rendezvouses with Mr. Sing and kills him after loading his human cargo, then returns the Chinese to wade back ashore rather than abandon them at sea.	Chapter 4: Same as manuscript.
Chapter 5: Harry and Eddy return to Key West; while Harry relaxes at home with Marie, his mate, drunk, appears unexpectedly, stopping just short of demanding money to	Chapter 5: Same as manuscript.

Outline of Chapters in Original Manuscript	Outline of Chapters in Published Novel
fuel his bender. This final scene was added to the novel manuscript; it did not appear in the *Cosmopolitan* text of "One Trip Across."	
Part Two (Harry Morgan [Fall])	**Part Two (Harry Morgan [Fall])**
Chapter 6: Harry and new mate Wesley sail into Woman Key wounded after a rum-running expedition runs awry.	Chapter 6: Same as manuscript.
Chapter 7: Captain Willie and Frederick Harrison spot Harry's boat; Harrison demands the captain facilitate a citizen's arrest.	Chapter 7: Same as manuscript.
Chapter 8: After dumping the rum overboard, Harry and Wesley sail for Key West, Harry worried that his wounded arm will be amputated.	Chapter 8: Same as manuscript.
Part Three (Harry Morgan [Winter])	**Part Three (Harry Morgan [Winter])**
Chapter 9: Albert Tracy narrates the story of the crooked lawyer Bee-lips offering Harry a job running Cuban revolutionaries back to their homeland.	Chapter 9: Same as manuscript.
Chapter 10: In an interior monologue Harry explains that he has no choice but to agree to the job; the Depression has left him with few other choices.	Chapter 10: Same as manuscript.
Chapter 11: Albert accompanies Harry to the Richards' bar to negotiate with the Cubans. In item 204, this chapter is headed "Freddy," although Freddy Wallace, the bartender, does not yet narrate.	Chapter 11: Same as manuscript, except that Harry also steals his boat back from customs officials.
Chapter 12: Harry makes love to Marie, who soothes his anxieties over whether his amputation has cost him his masculinity.	Chapter 12: Same as manuscript.

Outline of Chapters in Original Manuscript	Outline of Chapters in Published Novel
Chapter 13: Harry negotiates to borrow Freddy's boat after Bee-lips informs him customs officials have just impounded his.	Chapter 13: Same as manuscript.
Chapter 14: Harry returns home and visits daughters.	Chapter 14: Same as manuscript.
Chapter 15: Harry encounters the Laughtons and MacWalsey in Freddy's as he tries to finalize the run to Cuba. Chapter ends on *THHN* 138.	Chapter 15: Same as manuscript, except that Hemingway introduces Richard and Helen Gordon into the bar. Pages 138–41 are added to sketch out marital tensions between the Gordons—more fully explored in the manuscript's chapter 19.
Chapter 16: Harry agrees to hire Albert for the Cuba run, despite not trusting the revolutionaries. Albert is suspicious about what crime the Cubans intend to commit.	Chapter 16: Same as manuscript.
Chapter 17: In item 204, Harry first admits to Freddy that he borrows the boat to run revolutionaries back to Cuba, but Hemingway crossed out this scene. Instead, the chapter explores Harry's guilt at lying to his friend, knowing he puts the bartender's boat at risk. Does not include the concluding paragraph in which Richard Gordon walks to Helène Bradley's house for an assignation.	Chapter 17: Same as manuscript except for the Richard Gordon paragraph, which also includes a description of Helen Gordon walking along the beach looking for Professor MacWalsey.
Chapter 18: The revolutionaries rob the bank, killing Albert as they load onto Harry's boat. Held hostage, Harry sets off for Cuba, eventually killing his captors, although he is shot in the process.	Chapter 18: Same as manuscript

Part 4: In item 204, Hemingway begins this section with a list of several potential headings: "A Winter Haven for Writers," "The Literary Life," and "Workers in The Art." In item 212, he headed the section "Waiting in Town."

Outline of Chapters in Original Manuscript	Outline of Chapters in Published Novel
Chapter 19: In item 212, Hemingway titled this chapter "The Enquiring Observer." Richard Gordon is introduced for the first time, talking with Helen about the bank robbery; the chapter specifically identifies the revolutionaries as members of Joven Cuba, a post-Machado sect. Gordon bicycles to Freddy's, where locals talk about the "big slob" Hemingway who has failed his talent; on his way home he sees Marie and misjudges her completely.	Chapter 19: This entire chapter is whittled down to two pages in which Richard Gordon observes Marie. Hemingway writes a new introductory sentence to the scene ("The next morning . . .") to plaster over the excisions.
Chapter 20: Freddy's boat, the *Queen Conch*, drifts through the Gulf Stream as Harry lies wounded and suffering from chills.	Chapter 20: Same as manuscript.
Chapter 21: Richard Gordon visits another bar, the Lilac Time, where he and Key West sheriff Roger Johnson discuss the bank robbery with a pair of Marine flyers, who heckle the law enforcement.	Chapter 21: Hemingway essentially condenses the entire Helène Bradley subplot into this scene. As Richard and Helen Gordon hurl marital recriminations at each other, a flashback featuring material from the manuscript's chapter 23 shows Mrs. Bradley seducing the writer. The chapter ends with Gordon leaving home to get drunk.
Chapter 22: Richard Gordon attends a party hosted by Tommy and Helène Bradley. With a masterful use of omniscient narration akin to a cinematic tracking shot, Hemingway leads us through the minds of several partygoers, including Helène's ex-lovers. Eventually, Tommy Bradley and Roddy Simpson discuss Cuba.	Chapter 22: Richard Gordon wanders through two Key West bars, the Lilac Time and Freddy's. In the former he meets Herbert Spellman, who confesses to having once set fire to the Brooklyn domicile of Margaret Van Brunt while the men attended a party there. At Freddy's, Gordon encounters the addled Great War veterans completing the Overseas Highway in the upper keys, along with the Communist Nelson Jacks.
Chapter 23: Descriptions of the Bradleys' party culminate with Mrs. Bradley seducing Richard Gordon and Tommy walking	Chapter 23: In one of the last scenes written for the published book, Harry Morgan delivers his dying "one man alone" speech

APPENDIX B · 211

Outline of Chapters in Original Manuscript	Outline of Chapters in Published Novel
in on them. Except for the seduction scene, which is condensed into the flashback refitted into the published novel's chapter 21, this material was cut; chapter ends with Gordon walking in on Helen kissing MacWalsey on the Gordons' couch, precipitating their marital dissolution.	to the Coast Guard captain and mate who have rescued Harry from the drifting boat.
Chapter 24: The published novel's chapter 22 occurs at this point in the manuscript. The chapter ends with the crowd in the Key West yacht basin waiting for the Coast Guard's arrival before shifting to Hemingway's famous tour of the hidden secrets of various yacht-club members, including Dorothy Hollis.	Chapter 24: Crowd waiting at Navy Yard for Freddy's boat to be towed in; description of the people on the yachts.
Chapter 25: Morgan is taken off boat; Albert's wife is on the dock; Marie goes to the hospital and passes Gordon on her way home; Morgan dies.	Chapter 25: Same as manuscript.
Chapter Twenty-six: As in novel, except that Marie is not told that Morgan is dead. Does not include the yacht and tanker paragraph. From here on out, the manuscript focuses on what Hemingway called "the Bradley part," in which Tommy Bradley replaces Harry Morgan as the novel's chief protagonist.	Chapter 26: Marie's final interior monologue on Harry; the concluding three paragraphs on the yacht and tanker in the horizon.
Chapter 27: Tommy Bradley and Roddy Simpson talk the following morning about the comic view of life and about the human soul; Bradley tells Simpson that he is going to leave Key West until Saturday. From here on out, the revolutionary sympathies Hemingway will emphasize in the published novel are ridiculed as naïve and overly earnest.	

Outline of Chapters in Original Manuscript	Outline of Chapters in Published Novel
Chapter 28: Entitled "Interlude (In Cuba)," this brilliant monologue from a Cuban revolutionary argues for the moral necessity of terrorism.	
Chapter 29: In item 204, Hemingway headed this section "Part-Five." After an exchange of cables between Bradley and Simpson, Tommy returns to Key West and agrees to run the dynamite.	
Chapter 40 (wrongly numbered by Hemingway, who meant chapter 30): In item 205, this section is called "Chapter Forty Thomas Bradley." Richard Gordon accompanies Tommy to Cuba for the dynamite run, with Gordon demonstrating once again his complete ineptitude as a man by having no clue about how to sail. After several derisive comments from Tommy on politics, the run is thwarted by a severe storm. Tommy sails back to Key West, barely surviving. The next day, much to his amusement, he finds that his boat sank overnight in the yacht basin, a final sign of the comic absurdity of humanity's powerlessness to affect political change or to conquer nature.	

APPENDIX C

Focalization and Technique: The Narratology of *To Have and Have Not*

Hemingway's Key West novel is often described as his most experimental thanks to his use of multiple points of view and literary strategies associated with modernism, most famously the stream of consciousness popularized by James Joyce. In actuality, most of this experimentation is confined to Part Three. Part One employs the conventional first person for which Hemingway was known thanks to *The Sun Also Rises* and *A Farewell to Arms,* while Part Two uses third person omniscience (although not *limited* omniscience—that is, the narration is not so focalized through the characters' perspective that a narrating presence external to the story cannot be felt).

The chart below summarizes the focalized foci and techniques throughout the novel.

Part 1 Chapters 1 through 5		
Originally published as "One Trip Across," in *Cosmopolitan*, April 1934.	Pages 1–64	First person, narrated in the voice of Harry Morgan.
Part 2 Chapters 6 through 9		
Originally published as "the Tradesman's Return" in *Esquire* in February 1936		
Chapter Six	Pages 68–75	Third-person omniscience. The narration here cannot be described as limited because although Hemingway hews closely to Harry's perspective, occasional cues reveal the presence of an extradiegetic (or out of the plot) narrator: "The man, whose name

			was Harry Morgan" (69:15) is not a thought of Harry's transcribed into third person, as limited omniscience would be. Instead, it is Hemingway's narrating voice.
Chapter 7		Pages 76–84	After a second (and superfluous) narrative description of the protagonist as "the man called Harry" (77:7), the focalization shifts from Harry Morgan to Captain Willie Adams on an entirely different boat at 78:3.

Several passages of interior monologue provide direct access to Captain Willie's thoughts: "Damned if I'd ever run liquor from Cuba" (78:10). |
Chapter 8		Pages 85–87	The narration returns to Harry as the focalized consciousness, largely written in limited omniscience (without narratorial interjections this time) and some interior monologue (86:1–6). At 86:24–27, interior monologue briefly (and arguably) transforms into the novel's first use of stream of consciousness, although the differences between the two styles, while theoretically easy to define, are in practice harder to determine.
Part 3			
Chapter 9		Pages 91–104	Subtitled "Albert Speaking," this chapter is written in first person in the voice of mate Albert Tracy. There are no extradiegetic intrusions on Hemingway's part.
Chapter 10		Pages 105–07	Subtitled "Harry," this chapter is the first of part 3's many chapters written mainly in interior monologue. Because the thoughts flow in an orderly rather than random fashion, the narration never slips into stream of consciousness.
Chapter 11		Pages 108–11	This chapter opens with a passage from an omniscient observer at Freddy's bar ("You could see they had given [Bee-lips] plenty out at Richard's" 108:2–3).

At 109:17 the narration shifts to limited omniscience, with Harry as the focal consciousness.

At 111:18 the narration shifts to interior monologue for the chapter's duration. |

Chapter 12	Pages 112–17	This bedroom scene between Harry and his wife, Marie, begins in limited omniscience, with Harry as the focalized agent, before shifting at 114:24 into an interior monologue by Marie. At 115:17 the narration shifts to an externalized perspective that views Harry and Marie's dialogue descriptively, without reference to either's interior thoughts.
Chapter 13	Pages 118–24	As does chapter 11, this one begins with omniscient commentary, presumably from an observer at Freddy's bar. At 121:5 Harry and Bee-lips are described as moving to the bar's backroom, but the narration does not shift to limited omniscience focalized through Harry. (There are no descriptions of Harry's thoughts; in other words, the exchange consists entirely of dialogue.)
Chapter 14	Pages 125–28	This short scene between Harry, Marie, and their daughters consists almost entirely of dialogue, with only two passages accessing the characters' thoughts: From 127:23 to 127:30 a bit of interior monologue reveals Harry's worries about losing his home and family. From 128:18 until the chapter ends, the narration shifts into limited omniscience, with Marie as the focalized consciousness.
Chapter 15	Pages 129–41	The omniscient narration continues as we return to Freddy's for an unpleasant encounter with the tourist trade flooding Key West. Although dialogue largely drives the chapter, signs of narratorial judgment reveal the lens onto the action is not objective: Mrs. Laughton has "the face and build of a lady wrestler" (128:7). At 137:19 the narration focalizes through Freddy Wallace with a passage of limited omniscience that runs to 138:9. At 137:28 we enter another passage of free indirect discourse in which Freddy expresses compassion for Helen Gordon. Yet another brief passage begins at 140:29, with Freddy hoping Helen doesn't cry in his bar.

		The chapter ends with one final slip into free indirect discourse, unexpectedly focalizing through Helen to deliver a bombshell: she has come to Freddy's bar looking for the object of her romantic interest, Professor MacWalsey.
Chapter 16	Pages 142–46	As Harry prepares Freddy's boat for the Cuba run, Hemingway employs free indirect discourse to explore his ambivalence as he breaks down and agrees to hire Albert to accompany him. At 146:6 we slide into first person for a brief concluding interior monologue.
Chapter 17	Pages 147–50	A mixture of free indirect discourse and interior monologue, again focalized through Harry, except for the final paragraph, which switches to Richard Gordon, but for only two brief sentences at 150:6–7 as he scurries to Hélène Bradley's house, hoping to find her alone. The rest of the chapter is told from an omniscient perspective, noting information Gordon is not privy to: Mrs. Bradley will seduce him, and his wife, Helen, is simultaneously searching the beach for MacWalsey.
Chapter 18	Pages 151–75	The novel's longest chapter, paradoxically, employs the fewest perspective changes. Harry's focalized consciousness, rendered in free indirect discourse with occasional passages of interior monologue: 154:29–155:2, 155:24–25, 163:9–14, 164:8–165:2, 165:19–23, 168:4–15 (the "F— his revolution" passage), 170:5–6, 170:14–18, 173:4–9, 173:28–29, 174:2–3, 174:7–175:7, 175:10–13.
Chapter 19	176–77	Richard Gordon's famous glimpse of Marie, in which he misjudges her capacity for love because of her appearance, demonstrates perhaps more than any other section of the novel the irony that free indirect discourse allows. The reader is expected to recognize that the narration does not endorse Gordon's view of the Morgans. The chapter includes one brief excursion into interior monologue, at 176:7–13.
Chapter 20	Pages 178–81	This description of the gray sucker fish feeding off the blood draining from the bullet holes on the *Queen Conch* is written in an omniscient voice until 180:17, when it transitions into free

		indirect discourse, focalized through Harry. This section is a rare instance in which Hemingway does not alternate between free indirect discourse and interior monologue.
Chapter 21	Pages 182–92	The vast bulk of this blistering confrontation between Richard and Helen Gordon is staged through dialogue. From 188:28 to 190:7 Hemingway switches to the italicized flashback scene depicting Helène Bradley's seduction of Gordon, which is staged in free indirect discourse focalized through the leftist writer. Hemingway maintains that perspective for an addition four lines, before switching back to dialogue. The final paragraph of the chapter (192:6–15) focalizes again through Gordon as he leaves Helen to cry over the dissolution of their marriage.
Chapter 22	Pages 193–222	Most of this chapter is staged in free indirect discourse focalized through Richard Gordon. At 219:10 the focalization shifts to Professor MacWalsey as he helps an inebriated Gordon find his way home. At 221:22 the narration switches to interior monologue, which remains until the chapter ends.
Chapter 23	Pages 223–26	This chapter begins from an exterior focalization but at 225:6 switches to Harry, as rendered in free indirect discourse, before shifting back to the exterior stance at 226:2 to describe the Coast Guard officers' certainty that Harry will die.
Chapter 24	Pgs. 227–46	The novel's most narratologically complex chapter begins with the watchman of the Key West yacht basin as the point of focus before quickly shifting at 227:6 to Wallace Johnston and his kept man, Henry Carpenter. The omniscient narrator inhabits the thoughts of Carpenter from 231:27 to 233:6, although *not* through limited omniscience. At 233:15, however, Hemingway does employ that device as he shifts into the head of a grain merchant anxious about a tax audit. At 237:29 he shifts back to an omniscient focus, but only for a paragraph on various suicides. At 237:28 we leave the merchant for good and shift to an omniscient description of a pharmaceutical family and a pair of Estonian sailors than runs to 238:8. At that point begins the

		Dorothy Hollis section, which by 238:20 employs free indirect discourse to describe her thoughts. At 242:4 we switch into Dorothy's interior monologue, which itself evolves into stream of consciousness by 242:11. From there until the end of the chapter, Hemingway will interrupt her stream of consciousness monologue with external descriptions of her. At 246:12 we switch back for good to externalized omniscience.
Chapter 25	Pages 247–56	Hemingway employs his external focus until 253:20, when he focalizes through the community perspective of the Key Westers gathered on the yacht club dock as they remember the story of the local lynching of "the Isleño." At 254:3 Marie Morgan becomes the focalized consciousness, remaining so up to 255:22, when we learn Richard Gordon is the "rummy" Marie sees staggering home. At 256:3 until the rest of the chapter, the doctor who pronounces Harry dead is the focalized conscious.
Chapter 26	Pages 257–62	The bulk of the chapter, beginning with an opening attribution ("Marie Morgan was thinking") is written in a combination of interior monologue and stream of consciousness. At 261:28 Hemingway concludes the novel from his externalized, omniscient perspective.

APPENDIX D

Tense Shifts

One of the more curious narrative techniques Hemingway employs in *To Have and Have Not* is the seemingly random shifts from past to present tense. As noted at 10:22 and 91:16–20, such shifts are considered a standard characteristic of oral storytelling, where they vivify action, giving it immediacy that helps interlocutors visualize events. Tense shifts are rarer in written narration, however, for an obvious reason: their inconsistency is at odds with the authorial control and attentiveness we expect of printed stories. Teachers of writing emphasize consistent use of tense for this very reason: high school and undergraduate students often switch from past to present tense and vice versa without a thought, in part because they tend to write as they speak instead of focusing on the formalities of the written word.

The list below is a guide to Hemingway's shifts, which occur only in part 1 and part 3, not in part 2.

Two types of shifts are noted here:

1) Shifts from the timeframe of the plot to the "now" of the narration, which reminds readers that a narrative consciousness is commenting directly to readers. For example, at 49:1, when Harry Morgan describes the rendezvous spot with Mr. Sing ("Bacuranao is a cove where there used to be a big dock for loading sand"), the present tense marks the moment at some time after he and Eddy meet the smuggler that he narrates events. The timeframe referred to here is a perpetual now in which Harry (and Hemingway, at a broader remove) establishes a temporal continuum between the story and its telling. Readers are essentially assured that in between the action and its narration little has changed: Bacuranao remains as it was the night of Mr. Sing's murder, and the living quarters of the government representative described at 48:11–13 ("There is one other house where the delegate lives but it is back from the beach") stands as it did then as well.

2) More interesting and more unusual are tense shifts that occur within the plane of the plot—in other words, transitions that do *not* mark a shift out of the "now" of the story's events to the time of their telling but remain within the former. These are shifts that, like the one at 17:15, often code a narrative happening as dramatically significant, as worthy of intensified concentration on the reader's behalf. When Harry describes the motion that marks the moment a marlin snaps the line

his tourist Johnson has poorly managed, for example, the present tense functions as a kind of temporal italics: "I had the wheel and I kept yelling to Johnson to keep his drag light and reel fast. All of a sudden I see his rod jerk and the line go slack" (17:14–16). Not all of these shifts are marked by "all of a sudden" or "then," but they usually do occur around either action verbs, such as the opening line of part 3 ("We were all in there at Freddie's place and this tall thin lawyer comes in" [91:1–2]) *or* around attribution markers ("'Well, big shot,' [Bee-lips] says to Harry. 'Don't big shot me,' Harry told him" [108:5–6]).

One use of the present tense *not* noted here is its appearance in passages of interior monologue. This is because interior monologue usually occurs in the temporal plane of the past, even though it is written in the present tense. That is, a character's thoughts and feelings occur at a moment in the story marked elsewhere by the past tense, often by a marker of attribution. When chapter 26 begins, "I don't know, Marie Morgan was thinking, sitting at the dining-room table" (257:1–2) the "was thinking" marks the past timeframe in which Marie's thoughts occurred to her in the present tense. The relationship between temporal planes is not unlike that of dialogue: characters may speak in the present tense, but an attribution such as "Harry said" marks that speech act as happening in the past. For this reason tense shifts associated with interior monologue are not included here.

10:22	this nigger . . . comes down the dock
11:4	He's a real black nigger, smart and gloomy
12:7	These big flying fish are
12:28	One out of fifty parties you get know
17:15	All of a sudden I see his rod jerk
18:28	he isn't any good now
19:19	About four o'clock when we're coming back
20:10	where it makes deep so close
21:16	Just then Eddy slaps him on the back. "Mr. Johnson," he says, "you're just unlucky."
23:10	"What's this for?" the nigger asks me
23:16	The nigger gets his ball of twine
22:24	finally he hooks into a fish
28:6	The town is flooded with it
28:16	He hangs around the water
28:24	He seems dumb
29:4	You can get a good meal
39:21	He pointed out a Spanish boy that works around the docks
44:7	I keep them in those full-length, clipped sheep's wool cases
49:1	Bacuranao is a cove
49:11	There is one other house

56:3	There is plenty of water
57:9	he begins to chatter
57:13	Now I tell you it would take a hell of a mean man
60:11	Now I tell you
60:13	Because he's a rummy
60:15	he's as well off dead
60:20	there's no sense
61:7	I tell you
91:2	this tall thin lawyer comes in
91:16	Just then the old man with the long gray hair . . . comes in
92:2	Harry has the sleeve pinned
93:8	Freddy says
93:11	Freddy says
93:15	says Big Lucie's daughter
97:9	Then after a minute he says
102:16	he is so crooked himself
104:6	He drops me in front of where we live
108:3	when he drinks it makes him cocky
108:5	he says to Harry
108:13	Bee-lips says
108:14	Freddy tells him
120:9	He goes out with this stranger
120:13	Just then in comes Bee-lips
238:26	So he rings for one

Hemingway's longest excursion into present tense begins with this particular shift out of past tense as the grain broker calls for a drink to cure his fear of death. The present tense is then maintained as Hemingway shifts focus to the dull, upright pharmaceutical manufacturing family. From there he describes the two Estonians visiting Key West to write about their sailing adventures for their home newspaper. The present tense shifts into Dorothy Hollis's interior monologue at 242:4–5, whose attribution subtly marks a transition back to the past ("Dorothy thought"). Readers can easily overlook this transition, since Dorothy's monologue, as most monologues are, is staged in present tense. But by 242:23 it is clear we are definitively back in the preterit ("She went below"). Except for Marie Morgan's interior monologue in chapter 26, the novel does not shift from past to present tense again after 242:23.

APPENDIX E

Adaptations of *To Have and Have Not*

There is a certain irony in the fact that Hollywood has thrice adapted a Hemingway novel generally considered one of the two weakest efforts of his career. His classic works, of course have a long, albeit mixed history with movies and television: *The Sun Also Rises* has been filmed twice, first as a movie in 1957 and then as a TV miniseries in 1984; *A Farewell to Arms* has been adapted four separates times, most famously as a 1932 movie, followed by a 1957 remake, but also in a lesser-known 1955 TV installment in the American anthology series *Climax!* (with a script by Gore Vidal) and as a 1966 BBC miniseries. Both *For Whom the Bell Tolls* and *The Old Man and the Sea* enjoyed successful adaptions that remain well regarded. That *To Have and Have Not* has attracted producers, writers, and directors despite its critical reputation suggests the appeal of its action-adventure plot rather than its thematic value. Indeed, all three of these versions of the novel jettison its proletarian politics and focus on the smuggling and gunrunning. Below is a basic introduction to the three adaptations. Further information can be found at the Internet Movie Database (www.imdb.com).

> 1. To Have and Have Not (1945), starring Humphrey Bogart as Harry Morgan, Lauren Bacall as Marie "Slim" Browning, and Walter Brennan as Eddie, Harry's alcoholic mate. Directed by Howard Hawks from a script famously coauthored by William Faulkner and Jules Furthman. A Warner Bros. production.

The first and most famous adaptation of the novel, in a further irony, bears the least resemblance to its source material. As noted in my introduction, film historian Bruce F. Kawin writes in his introduction to the published screenplay that director Hawks told him the film came about when he bet Hemingway he could turn the writer's worst work into a profitable movie. When Hemingway demanded to know what his worst work was, Hawks replied, "That god damned bunch of junk called *To Have and To Have Not* [sic]" (16). The adaptation has been studied by several critics, most notably by Gene D. Philips in his work on both Hemingway and Faulkner's associations with Hollywood (*Hemingway and Hollywood* [1980] and *Fiction, Film, and Faulkner: The Art of Adaptation* [2001]). Working from a draft by

Furthman, Faulkner switched the setting from Key West and Cuba to World War II–era Europe, where instead of Chinese immigrants and Cuban terrorists Harry would aid the French resistance. The revised plot bears more than a passing resemblance to *Casablanca* (1942), especially given Bogart's presence, and draws from Faulkner's work on a proposed movie celebrating Charles De Gaulle and the Free French movement, which for political reasons was never filmed. Perhaps the most significant detail retained from the novel is Harry's amputated arm. For readers of the novel, as opposed to Faulkner scholars or Hawks/Bogart aficionados, the most useful critical essay on the adaptation is Mimi Reisel Gladstein's "Hemingway, Faulkner, and Hawks: The Nexus of Creativity that Generated the Film *To Have and Have Not*" (172–86). Gladstein makes the counterintuitive argument that the film is faithful to the novel, despite the "superficial" differences in setting and timeframe (172). Her essay is particularly useful in noting how centrally Hemingway's name was used to promote the movie, especially in the trailer with its pitch line, "Ernest Hemingway takes you to the danger zone of the mid-Atlantic," despite that Hemingway was not involved with the adaptation (173).

> 2. *The Breaking Point* (1950), starring John Garfield as Harry Morgan, Patricia Neal as Leona Charles. Directed by Michael Curtiz (who had also directed *Casablanca*) with a screenplay by Ranald MacDougall (an Academy Award nominee for his 1945 adaptation of James M. Cain's *Mildred Pierce*). Also a Warner Bros. production.

The second adaptation of *To Have and Have Not* centers upon part 3's bank robbery plot and Harry's forced run to Cuba with the terrorists. Here, however, the crime is a racetrack heist, the anti-Batista members of Joven Cuba are hardboiled gangsters, and Bee-lips is renamed Duncan. Instead of Albert Tracy, the mate murdered here is Wesley, from the novel's second part, and the run takes place in California instead of the Florida Keys. The most extraneous addition to the plot is Neal's character, who basically serves as the Hélène Bradley femme fatale, minus the wealth and with her sights set on Harry Morgan instead of Richard Gordon. The film was designed to be a commercial crowd-pleaser, but promotion and publicity plans were derailed by the appearance of Garfield's name in a pamphlet listing members of the Hollywood community with supposed ties to the Communist Party. As film noir historian Alan K. Rode told the *Los Angeles Times* during a 2012 revival, "All the movie moguls were scared, and none were more scared . . . of the hysterical atmosphere of anticommunism than Jack L. Warner. He completely pulled the plug on the movie and put almost no money into promotion. The picture was released, got good reviews and it was absolutely buried. Garfield's contract for another picture was canceled by Jack Warner" (qtd. in King). Garfield died the following year of a heart attack, not yet forty. As a result, *The Breaking Point* became something of a "lost" Hollywood classic, its reputation enhanced by its scuttled history. It is generally considered the strongest of the three adaptations, at least in the genre of film noir.

> 3. *The Gun Runners* (1958), starring Audie Murphy as Sam Martin (the Harry Morgan role), Eddie Albert as Hanagan (the closest thing to a Bee-lips), and Patricia Owens as Lucy Martin (Marie Morgan). Directed by Don Siegel, from a script by Daniel Mainwaring and Paul Monash, with uncredited contributions by Ben Hecht. A Seven Arts/United Artists Production.

Finally, a version of *To Have and Have Not* set in the Gulf of Mexico. The movie also takes place during the Cuban Revolution, albeit the Castro Revolution of 1953–1959 (which was not yet victorious) instead of the anti-Machado / anti-Batista campaigns of the 1930s. This adaptation is best known for being an entry in the oeuvre of director Siegel, who in 1964 helmed the second film noir version of Hemingway's "The Killers" (starring Lee Marvin and Angie Dickinson and featuring a cameo by Ronald Reagan) and would be noted for his long association with Clint Eastwood, including the original *Dirty Harry* (1971). *The Gun Runners* is serviceable B-movie fare, distinguished mostly for the taut performance from Eddie Albert, whose Bee-lips–like role as the American conspiring in the Cuban Revolution is expanded from a mere middleman to that of a financier/power broker. (Audie Murphy, however, is predictably wooden, as the former World War II battle hero was in most of his starring roles.) Fans of 1960s television who only remember Albert as Zsa Zsa Gabor's befuddled husband, Oliver Wendell Thomas, on the corny series *Green Acres* (1965–71) will be astonished at the character actor's menacing presence, a startling counterpoint to his more genial comedic persona in the two movies for which he was nominated for an Academy Award, *Roman Holiday* (1953) and *The Heartbreak Kid* (1972). Fans of Burt Reynolds's classic prison yarn, *The Longest Yard* (1974), will see the continuity between Hanagan and that film's evil warden, Rudolph Hazen. Other than Albert's performance, perhaps the most memorable aspect of *The Gun Runners* is its promotional tagline, which coined the phrase HEMINGWAY-HOT ADVENTURE.

In addition to Phillips's fine work on Hemingway in film, readers are encouraged to examine Candace Ursula Grissom's commentary on the three *To Have and Have Not* adaptations in her sterling study, *Fitzgerald and Hemingway on Film: A Critical Study of the Adaptations, 1924–2013* (2014).

APPENDIX F

Correspondence Regarding the 1938 "Banning" of *To Have and Have Not* in Detroit, Michigan

The history of Hemingway novels being censored or suppressed for obscenity and sexual explicitness is by no means as colorful or as significant as the legendary cases surrounding James Joyce's *Ulysses* in 1933 or D. H. Lawrence's *Lady Chatterley's Lover* in the United Kingdom in 1960. *The Sun Also Rises* met with objection in Boston; more famously, the second installment of the serialized version of *A Farewell to Arms* published in *Scribner's Magazine* was banned there as well after the supervisor of police took issue with the "salacious" language (see Donaldson, *Fitzgerald and Hemingway* 355–62). By far the most interesting case of censorship, however, centers on *To Have and Have Not*, the first Hemingway book to feature an unexpurgated use of *fuck*. When a patron at the Detroit Public Library complained about the obscenity, Wayne County prosecutor Duncan C. McCrea ordered the book removed from the shelves and enjoined local bookstores from selling it. What makes the case particularly intriguing is the source of the original complaint. According to a 13 May 1938 article in the Little Rock–based *Arkansas Catholic*, the chairman of the board of directors of the Detroit Council of Catholic Organizations, Arthur D. Maguire, wrote librarian Adam Strohm objecting to "a book of this character being offered for circulation by an institution supported by the taxpayers of Detroit." Deeming the novel "'utterly filthy from beginning to end,'" Maguire contacted Judge Thomas M. Carter of the Recorder's Court, who passed the complaint to McCrea. According to the article, the prosecutor immediately "called in Librarian Strohm, and told him that if the book was not removed from the shelves of the Detroit Public Library he would prosecute both the Librarian and the Library Commission" ("Novel Is Barred" 2).

It is significant that a Catholic organization lodged the complaint. By spring 1938, Hemingway was arguably the most famous literary supporter of the Loyalist cause in the Spanish Civil War, his newspaper dispatches and essays for *Esquire* and its sister publication *Ken* making the case that fascism in Spain had to be defeated lest Europe erupt into a second world war. The Catholic Church, meanwhile, supported the Franco-led Nationalists, or rightists. There seems little doubt that the ban was as much an effort to stopper Hemingway's very public advocacy for the cause of Republican Spain as much as to protect the youth of America (as Maguire described his intent). When a local coalition of booksellers, led by Alvin

C. Hamer, sought an injunction against McCrea's ban, the prosecutor indulged in some profound literary criticism, dubbing *To Have and Have Not* "a cesspool of printed sewage devoted to obscene, immoral, lewd, lascivious and descriptive matter tending to nauseate the common sense, decency, and modesty of every adult of normal mentality" ("E. Hemingway's Book Branded as Sewage" 9). Judge James E. Chenot denied Hamer's request for a temporary injunction (Stephens, *Critical Reception* 187–88), but it was not until 1939 that the case went to court, at which point the protest against the ban had lost steam, possibly because the Catholic ire at Hemingway was rendered moot by the 1 April 1939 victory of the Nationalists. Regardless, Hamer's legal team seized on the unique strategy of arguing that *"To Have and Have Not* . . . was much less offensive than many books on the market, and because of its poor quality would have been headed for oblivion anyway" (Boys 329). *Hamer v. Duncan McCrea,* Wayne County Circuit Court Chancery Calendar 278506 was docketed on 20 December 1939. After a brief, three-to-four-day trial, Chief Judge Ira Jayne dismissed Hamer's suit, declaring that a permanent injunction was not possible before a jury trial occurred to decide the matter of whether *To Have and Have Not* was obscene. According to U.S. District Court Judge Avern Cohn, who has researched the case, such a decision was not technically accurate but was indicative of the politics of the time (interview). It allowed Judge Jayne to avoid challenging McCrea's authority or that of the police to suppress provocative material without legally declaring the novel obscene. According to Cohn, *To Have and Have Not* was technically never not on sale in Detroit; typically, the authorities suppressed materials by threatening distributors rather than booksellers, making it difficult for material to reach shops. Once the case was dismissed, McCrea and the police could have pressed the issue by raiding bookstores daring enough to sell the novel, but apparently authorities had moved on to more pressing concerns.

The following correspondence concerns the controversy over the Detroit Public Library's handling of *To Have and Have Not.* It supplements the narrative recently published by John Cohassey in *Banned in Detroit: The Suppression of Hemingway's* To Have and Have Not. If nothing else, the letters demonstrate how librarian Adam Strohm was caught in the middle. Pressured on the one hand by the Maguires and McCreas of the world, who demanded taxpayer money not purchase "filth" like Hemingway's novel, Strohm also had to contend with the American Civil Liberties Union's denunciation of the library for supposedly removing the book from its shelves. As Strohm's tart letter notes, *To Have and Have Not* was not technically removed from circulation; it was placed among several other volumes by "writers of standing" whose works could only be checked out by asking the librarian for a copy. A compromise at best, the plan nevertheless ensured that at least a few discerning adults could read the novel.

No record exists of whether patrons who did so thought *To Have and Have Not* was worth the hassle.

AMERICAN CIVIL LIBERTIES UNION
METROPOLIS BUILDING, 31 UNION SQUARE WEST
NEW YORK CITY

May 6, 1938

Board of Trustees,
Detroit Public Library,
Detroit, Mich.

Dear Sirs:

We condemn your action in withdrawing from the shelves of your library Ernest Hemingway's novel TO HAVE AND TO HAVE NOT. As reported in the press.

Mr. Hemingway is generally recognized as one of the most distinguished writers in America. The book you attack has received high praise from leading critics and literary authorities. It seems a reflection of your board rather than of the book that your library finds it necessary to ban it.

We are opposed to all forms of censorship believing that freedom of expression in the arts is essential to the preservation of democracy and the development of culture.

In deploring this act of censorship, may we earnestly urge that you make the book available to the adult reading public.

Sincerely yours,

Hatcher Hughes, Chairman
Barrett H. Clark, Vice-Chairman
Roger N. Baldwin
Stephen Vincent Benet
[et al.]

THE PUBLIC LIBRARY
DETROIT, MICH.

May 14, 1938.

Mr. Hatcher Hughes, Chairman,
National Council on Freedom from Censorship
31 Union Square W.,
New York City, N.Y.

My dear Mr. Hughes:

This is in acknowledgement of your communication under date of May 6th. You and your associates seem disturbed about the fate that has overtaken Hemingway's "To Have and To Have Not" in this city. It is easy to join you in your general efforts for intellectual freedom and freedom from censorship. It is well within facts that this institution has quite definitely and publicly declared against what you term censorship and what sometimes amounts to attempted dictatorship from special groups. We are quite well acquainted with these interests in our institutional service. We have had some tussles with them and will probably have a few more rounds. Their claims of being representatives of American standards are not easily accepted as they very often dwell in the atmosphere characteristic of mediaeval spiritual cramps and are unduly preoccupied with the fact that the human being happens to have a physical body.

Having made that clear you should perhaps also consider the structure and problems with which an institution like the public library has to deal in giving book service. Insofar as I can identify your roster I am afraid that you cannot lay claim to practical experience and responsibility in this sort of public service.

Insofar as the ideal of freedom is concerned we are probably in harmony. When it comes to making that ideal a practical possibility, experience must govern abstract ideas. The very informality of public library service has its limitations and pitfalls. We have no way of measuring the capacity and critical ability of our readers beyond that of individual age, which is very deceptive as a measuring stick. We have no way of following up the effects of reading and, unfortunately, but rare occasions to confer and advise.

It would seem impossible to have it both ways. Could we set ourselves up as an academic institution or as a hospital we would, of course, have some control of our patients, make our diagnosis, and give prescriptions based on fairly reliable tests that would prevent many regrettable failures in the fundamental efforts of a librarian to bring "The right book to the right reader."

I have attended several meetings of librarians where this problem has been discussed without any very satisfactory conclusions, often ending with platitudes and perplexities.

Our attempt to guide in a liberal yet responsible spirit the profitable use of books of real content has not always been successful—perhaps least successful with the adults where inherited inhibitions and puritanical hangovers still seem to paralyse the emancipated attitude worthy of free people. Should we persist in fighting for "right" we would run the risk of creating conditions that would be neither fair to the writers nor profitable to liberalism. The better way would be to trust to educational advances, beginning, of course, with the schools and perhaps invading even the self-appointed guardians of our spiritual and moral welfare. For a public institution to enter militantly and on a campaign of challenges would, of course, arouse antagonism and lay us open to a charge of partisanship. An institution like ours must beware of functioning as a sponsor. After all, this is a citizen's club library and you have to weigh carefully the sensibilities and misgivings of a good many worthy people.

In the case of Hemingway's last book we probably did not watch the road ahead carefully enough. Furthermore we found that a good many followers and friends of Hemingway felt that he had let them down with this book. There were those who opined that he had taken a plunge, made quite a splash and little more. All of them realize that he had observed some facts against which human instincts and feelings properly revolt. In short, while he can be understood by the inquiring mind he can easily be misunderstood by the gluttonous in spirit, as well as draw fire from the smug and closed minded. Doesn't a protest that overshoots its mark, that wallows, draw a blank, whereas another kind of protest indicative of great reserve power makes an indelible mark?

Presumably you know little or nothing about this institution but I can assure you that it is not a reactionary set-up where timid respectability is rated high. The members of the governing board are men of professional rank and high minded business men, some of extraordinarily liberal views, who have not hesitated to declare their independence against self seeking individuals or interests. The staff has had the benefit of liberal college training (without which an appointment is never considered) and professional training as well. They are liberal enough and quite independent in their ideas and practices. If anything, a certain percentage is possibly a little too quickly attracted when the battle cries of the vigilantes for freedom are sounded. This, of course, does not mean that they have the temper of Carrie Nations.

Do I need to say that the books of Hemingway are available here? The particular title under discussion is available now only to adults upon identification and a pledge of good faith.

Some of us here have been dealing with authors and books for a quarter of a century or more. You and your associates may perhaps conclude that we know something about modern writers, not only in America but in other countries, whether English speaking or not.

This, my reply, will, I think, disclose the attitude and policy of this institution and the situation up to date.

Very truly yours,
[Signed] Adam Strohm,
Librarian

NATIONAL COUNCIL on FREEDOM from CENSORSHIP
(Organized by the American Civil Liberties Union)

May 19th, 1938

Mr. Alexander Lindey,
285 Madison Avenue,
New York City.

Dear Alex:

Here is the letter from the Librarian in Detroit in answer to our protest. It's really a very cagey letter. I'm sorry I couldn't get it off yesterday, as promised, but the girls were too busy here to get it copied. If you can give me an angle on how to reply, I'll be grateful. . . .

Sincerely yours,

Hazel L. Rice,
Secretary.

WORKS CITED

Abbott, Megan. *The Street Was Mine: White Masculinity and Urban Space in Hardboiled Fiction and Film Noir*. New York: Palgrave Macmillan, 2002.
Ahamed, Liaquat. *Lords of Finance: The Bankers Who Broke the World*. New York: Penguin, 2009.
Anderson, Sherwood. *Dark Laughter*. New York: Boni & Liveright, 1925.
Baker, Carlos. *Hemingway: A Life*. New York: Scribner, 1969.
———. *Hemingway: The Writer as Artist*. 4th ed. Princeton, NJ: Princeton UP, 1973.
Beals, Carleton. *The Crime of Cuba*. Philadelphia: Lippincott, 1933.
Beegel, Susan F. "Harry and the Pirates: The Romance and Reality of Piracy in Hemingway's *To Have and Have Not*." Curnutt and Sinclair 107–28.
Beidler, Philip D. *The Island Called Paradise: Cuba in History, Literature, and the Arts*. Tuscaloosa: U of Alabama P, 2014.
Bender, Bert. "Harry Burns and Professor MacWalsey in Ernest Hemingway's *To Have and Have Not*." *Hemingway Review* 28.1 (2008): 35–50.
———. *Sea-Brothers: The Tradition of American Fiction from* Moby-Dick *to the Present*. College Station: U of Pennsylvania P, 1988.
Berg, A. Scott. *Maxwell Perkins: Editor of Genius*. New York: E. P. Dutton / Thomas Congdon Books, 1978.
Berman, Ronald. *Fitzgerald, Hemingway, and the Twenties*. Tuscaloosa: U of Alabama P, 2002.
Biesen, Sheri Chinen. *Blackout: World War II and the Origins of Film Noir*. Baltimore: Johns Hopkins UP, 2005.
Bishop, Elizabeth. "The Bight." *The Complete Poems, 1927–1979*. New York: Farrar, Straus & Giroux, 1983. 61.
Bland, John Otway Percy. *Recent Events and Present Policies in China*. Philadelphia: Lippincott, 1912.
Boulard, Garry. "State of Emergency: Key West in the Great Depression." *Florida Historical Quarterly* 67.2 (1988): 166–83.
Braudy, Leo. *The Frenzy of Renown: Fame and Its History*. 1986. New York: Vintage, 1997.
Brian, Denis. *The True Gen: An Intimate Portrait of Hemingway by Those Who Knew Him*. New York: Grove, 1988.
Brooks, Cleanth, and Robert Penn Warren. *Understanding Fiction*. New York: Appleton-Century-Crofts, 1943.
"Brooks Given Hearing Today." *Key West Citizen* 5 July 1935: 1.
Brown, Sarah Finch. "The Composition of Ernest Hemingway's *To Have and Have Not*." MA thesis. Trinity College, Boston, 1985.

Bruccoli, Matthew J. Ed. *Sons of Maxwell Perkins: Letters of F. Scott Fitzgerald, Ernest Hemingway, Thomas Wolfe, and Their Editor.* Columbia: U of South Carolina P, 2004.

Boys, Richard C. "Literary Censorship and the Public Morals." *Michigan Alumnus Quarterly* 53.24 (1947): 323–30.

Burke, James Lee. *Light of the World.* New York: Simon & Schuster, 2014.

Burton, Harry. Unpublished letter to Ernest Hemingway. 1935. Incoming Correspondence. Ernest Hemingway Collection. John F. Kennedy Presidential Library and Museum. Boston.

Calabi, Silvio, Steve Helsley, and Roger Sanger. *Hemingway's Guns: The Sporting Arms of Ernest Hemingway.* New York: Shooting Sportsman, 2010.

Calvino, Italo. *If on a winter's night a traveler.* Trans. William Weaver. New York: Houghton Mifflin Harcourt, 1982.

Caro, Robert A. *The Power Broker and the Fall of New York.* New York: Knopf, 1975.

Carlson, Coralie. "Cuban Crossroads: When Hemingway Met Evans." Associated Press. 29 April 2004.

Campbell, Donna M. "Taking Tips and Losing Class: Challenging the Service Economy in James M. Cain's *Mildred Pierce*." *The Novel and the American Left: Critical Essays on Depression-Era Fiction.* Ed. Janet Galligani Casey. Iowa City: U of Iowa P, 2004. 1–15.

Carr, Virginia Spencer. *Dos Passos: A Life.* New York: Doubleday, 1984.

Chamberlain, John. "Literature." *Civilization in the United States.* 2nd ed. Ed. Harold E. Stearns. New York: Scribner, 1938. 36–47.

Chamberlin, Brewster. *The Hemingway Log: A Chronology of His Life and Times.* Lawrence: UP of Kansas, 2015.

Chatman, Seymour. *Story and Discourse: Narrative Structure in Fiction and Film.* 2nd ed. Ithaca, NY: Cornell UP, 1980.

Christy, Bryan. *The Lizard King: The True Crimes and Passions of the World's Greatest Reptile Smugglers.* New York: Hachette, 2008.

Churchwell, Sarah. *Careless People: Murder, Mayhem, and the Invention of The Great Gatsby.* New York: Penguin, 2013.

Cirino, Mark. *Ernest Hemingway: Thought in Action.* Madison: U of Wisconsin P, 2012.

Cobbs, John L. "Hemingway's 'To Have and Have Not': A Casualty of Didactic Revision." *South Atlantic Bulletin* 44.4 (1979): 1–10.

Cohassey, John F. *Banned in Detroit: The Suppression of Hemingway's* To Have and Have Not. Detroit: Salt & Cedar Letterpress, 2015.

Cohn, Avern. Telephone interview with the author. 5 October 2015.

Comley, Nancy R., and Robert Scholes. *Hemingway's Genders: Rereading the Hemingway Text.* New Haven: Yale UP, 1994.

Conrad, Barnaby. *101 Best Scenes Ever Written: A Romp through Literature for Writers and Readers.* Fresno, CA: Quill Driver, 2006.

Conrad, Joseph. "The Secret Sharer." *The Secret Sharer and Other Stories.* New York: Dover, 1993. 83–113.

Cooperman, Stanley. "Death and Cojones: Hemingway's *A Farewell to Arms.*" *South Atlantic Quarterly* 63 (Winter 1964): 85–92.

Cowles, John Cheney. Unpublished letters to Ernest Hemingway. September–October 1936. Incoming Correspondence, 1936. Ernest Hemingway Collection. John F. Kennedy Presidential Library and Museum. Boston.

Cowley, Malcolm. *Exile's Return: A Literary Odyssey of the 1920s.* 1934. New York: Penguin, 1994.

———. "A Portrait of Mr. Papa." *Life* 10 January 1949: 86–101.
Crowley, Michael. "Reexamining the Origins of 'After the Storm.'" Curnutt and Sinclair 189–205.
Cruz, Mary. *Cuba and Hemingway on the Great Blue River*. Trans. Harold Spencer. Havana: José Martí, 1994.
———. "Selection from 'It Is Hard for You to Tell,' Chapter Three of *Cuba y Hemingway en el gran río azul* (*Cuba and Hemingway on the Great Blue River*)." Grimes and Sylvester. 84–101.
Culleton, Claire A. *Joyce and the G-Men: J. Edgar Hoover's Manipulation of Modernism*. New York: Palgrave Macmillan, 2004.
Curnutt, Kirk. *Dixie Noir*. Waterville, ME: Five Star, 2009.
Curnutt, Kirk, and Gail D. Sinclair, eds. *Key West Hemingway: A Reassessment*. Gainesville: UP of Florida, 2009.
Daly, Carroll John. "Knights of the Open Palm." *Black Mask* 6.5 (1923): 22–47.
———. *The Snarl of the Beast*. 1927. New York: HarperPerennial, 1992.
De La Torre, Miguel A. "Beyond Machismo: A Cuban Case Study." *Sexuality and the Sacred: Sources for Theological Reflection*. 2nd ed. Ed. Marvin M. Ellison and Kelly Brown Douglas. Louisville, KY: Westminster John Knox P, 2010. 221–40.
Dickson, Paul, and Thomas B. Allen. *The Bonus Army: An American Epic*. New York: Walker, 2004.
Donaldson, Scott. *Archibald MacLeish: An American Life*. New York: Houghton Mifflin, 1992.
———. *By Force of Will: The Life and Art of Ernest Hemingway*. New York: Viking, 1977.
———. *Fitzgerald and Hemingway: Works and Days*. New York: Columbia UP, 2009.
Donne, John. *Devotions upon Emergent Occasions: Together with Death's Duel*. New York: Cambridge UP, 1965.
Doran, Sabine. *The Culture of Yellow; or, The Visual Politics of Late Modernity*. New York: Bloomsbury, 2013.
Dos Passos, John. *The Best Times: An Informal Memoir*. New York: HarperCollins, 1968.
Drayton, Michael. "The Ballad of Dowsabel." *The Book of Elizabethan Verse*. Ed. William Stanley Braithwaite. Boston: Turner, 1904. 275–79.
Duffield, Marcus. "The Pulps: Day Dreams for the Masses." *Vanity Fair* June 1933: 26–27.
Eby, Carl P. *Hemingway's Fetishism: Psychoanalysis and the Mirror of Manhood*. Albany: SUNY P, 1998.
———. "Wake Up Alone and Like It! Dorothy Hollis, Marjorie Hillis, and *To Have and Have Not*." *Hemingway Review* 26.1 (2006): 96–105.
"E. Hemingway's Book Branded as Sewage." *Vidette-Messenger* (Valparaso, IN) 16 May 1938: 9.
Ellis, Edward Robb. *Echoes of Distant Thunder: Life in the United States, 1914–1918*. New York: Kodansha, 1975.
Estrada, Alfredo José. *Havana: Autobiography of a City*. New York: Macmillan, 2008.
———. *Welcome to Havana, Señor Hemingway*. Miami, FL: Vista, 2003.
Evans, Walker. *Walker Evans: Cuba*. Ed. Andrei Codrescu. Los Angeles: Getty, 2001.
"Excellent Yacht Basin at Southernmost Port." *Motorboating* July 1935: 11.
"Ex-Service Men on Road Work in Keys Strike." *Palm Beach Post* 1 March 1935: 1–2.
Farrington, S. Kip. *Fishing with Hemingway and Glassell*. New York: David McKay, 1971.
Fiedler, Leslie A. *Love and Death in the American Novel*. New York: Dell, 1960.
"Fishing Camp at Boca Chica Now Proposed." *Key West Citizen* 8 September 1935: 1.

"Fishing Camp at Boca Chica Well-Equipped." *Key West Citizen* 30 November 1935: 1.
Fitzgerald, F. Scott. *The Crack-Up*. Ed. Edmund Wilson. New York: New Directions, 1945.
———. *Dear Scott / Dear Max: The Fitzgerald-Perkins Correspondence*. Ed. John Kuehl and Jackson R. Bryer. New York: Scribner, 1971.
———. *F. Scott Fitzgerald: A Life in Letters*. Ed. Matthew J. Bruccoli. New York: Scribner, 1994.
———. *The Great Gatsby*. 1925. New York: Scribner, 2012.
———. *The Notebooks of F. Scott Fitzgerald*. Ed. Matthew J. Bruccoli. New York: Harcourt Brace Jovanovich / Bruccoli Clark, 1978.
Fleming, Robert E. *The Face in the Mirror: Hemingway's Writers*. Tuscaloosa: U of Alabama P 1996.
———. "The Libel of Dos Passos in *To Have And Have Not*." *Journal of Modern Literature* 15.4 (1989): 597–601.
Flexner, Stuart Berg. *Listening to America: An Illustrated History of Words and Phrases from Our Lively and Splendid Past*. New York: Simon & Schuster, 1982.
Foley, Barbara. *Radical Representations: Politics and Form in U.S. Proletarian Fiction, 1929–1941*. Durham, NC: Duke UP, 1993.
"Forces Start Work Today on Key West Sewer Project; Total of 900 Persons Employed in WPA Project." *Key West Citizen* 4 November 1935: 1.
Ford, Corey. "Impossible Interview: Gracie Allen vs. Gertrude Stein." *Vanity Fair* January 1935: 25.
Fountain, Gary. *Remembering Elizabeth Bishop: An Oral Biography*. Amherst: U of Massachusetts P, 1996.
Fuentes, Norberto. *Hemingway in Cuba*. Trans. Consuelo E. Corwin. Secaucus, NJ: Lyle Stuart, 1984.
Gajdusek, Robert E. "'Some Nigger . . . Some Mr. Johnson': Getting the Reels and the Lines Together." Knott 187–97.
Galbraith, Kenneth. *The Great Crash 1929*. 1954. Boston: Houghton Mifflin, 2009.
Genette, Gerard. *Paratexts: Thresholds of Interpretation*. Trans. Jane E. Lewin. Cambridge: Cambridge UP, 1997.
"George Schutt to Manage New Fishing Camp." *Key West Citizen* 7 November, 1935, 1.
Gibson, Abraham H. "American Gibraltar: Key West during World War II." *Florida Historical Quarterly* 90.4 (2012): 393–425.
Gingrich, Arnold. "Scott, Ernest, and Whoever." *Esquire* December 1966: 186–89, 322–25.
———. Unpublished letters to Jane Mason. February 1937. Ernest Hemingway Collection. John F. Kennedy Presidential Library and Museum. Boston.
———. Unpublished telegram to Ernest Hemingway. 19 May 1937. Ernest Hemingway Collection. John F. Kennedy Presidential Library and Museum. Boston.
Gladstein, Mimi Reisling. "Hemingway, Faulkner, and Hawks: The Nexus of Creativity that Generated the Film *To Have and Have Not*." Curnutt and Sinclair 172–86.
Gott, Richard. *Cuba: A New History*. New Haven, CT: Yale UP, 2005.
Grant, Douglas. *Purpose and Place: Essays on American Writers*. New York: Macmillan, 1965.
Griffin, Peter. *Along with Youth: Hemingway, the Early Years*. New York: Oxford UP, 1987.
Green, Jonathan. *The Cassell's Dictionary of Slang*. 2nd ed. London: Weidenfeld & Nicolson, 2005.
Greene, Philip. *To Have and Have Another: A Hemingway Cocktail Companion*. New York: Penguin, 2012.
Grey, Zane. *Tales of Fishes*. New York: Harper & Brothers, 1919.

Grimes, Larry. "Introduction to 'The State of Things in Cuba: A Letter to Hemingway' by Richard Armstrong." Grimes and Sylvester 75–76.

Grimes, Larry, and Bickford Sylvester, eds. *Hemingway, Cuba, and the Cuban Works*. Kent, OH: Kent State UP, 2014.

Grissom, Candace Ursula. *Fitzgerald and Hemingway on Film: A Critical Study of the Adaptations, 1924–2013*. Jefferson, NC: McFarland, 2014.

A Guide to Key West, Compiled by Workers of the Writers' Program of the Work Projects Administration in the State of Florida. New York: Hastings House, 1941.

Guidry, Frank A. "'War on the Negro': Race and the Revolution of 1933." *Cuban Studies* 40 (2009): 49–73.

Hammett, Dashiell. *The Novels of Dashiell Hammett: Red Harvest, The Dain Curse, The Maltese Falcon, The Glass Key, and The Thin Man*. New York: Knopf, 1965.

Hanna, Alfred Jackson, and Kathryn Abbey Hanna. *Florida's Golden Sands*. Indianapolis: Bobbs-Merrill, 1950.

Hanneman, Audre. *Ernest Hemingway: A Comprehensive Bibliography*. Princeton, NJ: Princeton UP, 1967.

Hawkins, Ruth A. *Unbelievable Happiness and Final Sorrow: The Hemingway-Pfeiffer Marriage*. Fayetteville: U of Arkansas P, 2012.

Hemingway, Carol. "907 Whitehead Street." Curnutt and Sinclair 28–43.

"Hemingway Tells of War, New Play in Interview." *Key West Citizen* 1 February 1938: 1.

Hemingway, Ernest. "The Art of the Short Story." *New Critical Approaches to the Short Stories of Ernest Hemingway*. Ed. Jackson J. Benson. Durham, NC: Duke UP, 1990. 1–13.

———. *By-Line Ernest Hemingway: Selected Articles and Dispatches of Four Decades*. Ed. William White. New York: Scribner, 1967.

———. *Conversations with Ernest Hemingway*. Ed. Matthew J. Bruccoli. Oxford: UP of Mississippi, 1986.

———. *The Complete Short Stories of Ernest Hemingway: The Finca Vigía Edition*. Ed. John Hemingway, Patrick Hemingway, and Gregory Hemingway. New York: Scribner, 1987.

———. "Defense of Dirty Words: A Cuban Letter." *Esquire* September 1934: 19, 158.

———. *Ernest Hemingway: Selected Letters: 1917–1961*. Ed. Carlos Baker. New York: Scribner, 1981.

———. *A Farewell to Arms*. 1929. New York: Scribner, 2013.

———. *For Whom the Bell Tolls*. New York: Scribner, 1940.

———. *Green Hills of Africa*. New York: Scribner, 1935.

———. "He Who Gets Slap Happy: A Key West Letter." *Esquire* August 1935: 19, 182.

———. *Hemingway on Fishing*. Ed. Nick Lyons. New York: Scribner, 2002.

———. *Islands in the Stream*. New York: Scribner, 1970.

———. *A Moveable Feast*. New York: Scribner, 1964.

———. "Novel—Have Reached Chapter 20 Question." Unpublished fragment. MS 55, item 617, folder 34. Ernest Hemingway Collection. John F. Kennedy Presidential Library and Museum. Boston.

———. "One Trip Across." *Cosmopolitan* April 1934: 20–23, 108–22.

———. *The Only Thing That Counts: The Ernest Hemingway–Maxwell Perkins Correspondence*. Ed. Matthew J. Bruccoli. Columbia: U of South Carolina P, 1998.

———. "Sailfish Off Mombasa: A Key West Letter." *Esquire* March 1935: 21, 197.

———. *The Sun Also Rises*. New York: Scribner, 1926.

———. *To Have and Have Not*. New York: Scribner, 1937.

———. The *To Have and Have Not* manuscripts. Boxes 30–32, items 205–11. Ernest Hemingway Collection. John F. Kennedy Presidential Library and Museum. Boston.

———. *The Torrents of Spring*. New York: Scribner, 1926.

———. "The Tradesman's Return." *Esquire* February 1936: 27, 193–96.

———. "The President Vanquishes: A Bimini Letter." *Esquire* July 1935: 23, 167.

———. Unpublished letter to Jane Mason. 16 October 1933. Outgoing Correspondence, 1933. Ernest Hemingway Collection. John F. Kennedy Presidential Library and Museum. Boston.

———. Unpublished letter to Waldo Peirce. 27 July 1937. Outgoing Correspondence, 1937. Ernest Hemingway Collection. John F. Kennedy Presidential Library and Museum. Boston.

———. Unpublished letter to Maxwell Perkins. 15 December 1936. Outgoing Correspondence, 1936. The Ernest Hemingway Collection. John F. Kennedy Presidential Library and Museum. Boston.

———. Unpublished letter to Maxwell Perkins. 18 February 1937. Outgoing Correspondence, 1937. Ernest Hemingway Collection. John F. Kennedy Presidential Library and Museum. Boston.

———. "Who Murdered the Vets?" *New Masses* 17 September 1935: 9–10.

———. *Winner Take Nothing*. New York: Scribner, 1933.

Hemingway, Hilary, and Carlene Brennan. *Hemingway in Cuba*. New York: Rugged Land P, 2003.

Hemingway, Leicester. *My Brother, Ernest Hemingway*. Cleveland: World, 1962.

Hendrickson, Paul. *Hemingway's Boat: Everything He Loved in Life, and Lost*. New York: Knopf, 2011.

Hersey, John. *Key West Tales*. New York: Knopf, 1994.

Hily-Mane, Genevieve. "Point of View in Hemingway's Novels and Short Stories: A Study of the Manuscripts." *Hemingway Review* 5 (Spring 1986): 37–44.

"Hop Lee, the Chinese Slave Dealer; or, Old and Young King Brady and the Opium Fiends." *Secret Service Tales* 21 April 1899: 1–31.

Hotchner, A. E. *Papa Hemingway: A Personal Memoir*. New York: Random House, 1966.

Hovey, Richard B. *Hemingway: The Inward Terrain*. Seattle: U of Washington P, 1968.

Hunn, Max. "Octagon House—Its Roof Is a Concrete Piecrust." *Popular Mechanics* 112.1 (July 1959): 85–88.

Hurst, Carlton Bailey. *The Arms above the Door*. New York: Dodd, Mead, 1932.

Jenkins, Greg. *Florida's Ghostly Legends and Haunted Folklore: South and Central Florida*. Sarasota, FL: Pineapple P, 2005.

Jennings, John E. *Our American Tropics*. New York: Crowell, 1938.

Josephson, Matthew. *Infidel in the Temple: A Memoir of the Nineteen-Thirties*. New York: Knopf, 1967.

"Jury Acquits George Brooks: Verdict Returned at 4:20 O'Clock This Afternoon." *Key West Citizen* 12 July 1935: 1.

Kawin, Bruce. "Introduction: No Man Alone." *To Have and Have Not* by Jules Furthman, William Faulkner. Ed. Bruce Kawin. Madison: U of Wisconsin P, 1980. 9–54.

Karol, K. S. *Guerrillas in Power: The Course of the Cuban Revolution*. New York: Hill & Wang, 1970.

Kennedy, Stetson. *Grits and Grunts: Folkloric Key West.* Sarasota, FL: Pineapple P, 2008.
Kert, Bernice. *The Hemingway Women.* New York: Norton, 1983.
———. "Jane Mason and Ernest Hemingway: A Biographer Reviews Her Notes." *Hemingway Review* 21.2 (2002): 111–16.
Kerstein, Robert. *Key West on the Edge: Inventing the Conch Republic.* Gainesville: UP of Florida, 2012.
Key West in Transition: A Guide Book for Visitors. Key West: Key West Administration, 1934.
"Key West Sewerage Project Given Approval by Roosevelt and Various Agencies Operating under WPA." *Key West Citizen* 30 September 1935: 1.
King, Susan. "'The Breaking Point' Screens at L.A. Film Festival on Saturday." *Los Angeles Times* 12 June 2012.
Knott, Toni D. *One Man Alone: Hemingway and* To Have and Have Not. Lanham, MD: UP of America, 1999.
Knowles, Thomas Neil. *Category 5: The 1935 Labor Day Hurricane.* Gainesville: UP of Florida, 2009.
Koch, Stephen. *The Breaking Point: Hemingway, Dos Passos, and the Murder of Jose Robles.* New York: Counterpoint, 2005.
Kodat, Catherine Gunter. "*I'm Spartacus!*" *A Companion to Narrative Theory.* Ed. James Phelan and Peter J. Rabinowitz. Oxford: Blackwell, 2005. 484–98.
Kowalewski, Michael. *Deadly Musings: Violence and Verbal Form in American Fiction.* Princeton, NJ: Princeton UP, 1993.
Krutnik, Frank. *In a Lonely Street: Film Noir, Genre, Masculinity.* New York: Routledge, 1991.
Lanser, Susan Sniader. *The Narrative Act: Point of View in Prose Fiction.* Princeton, NJ: Princeton UP, 1981.
"Large Number Attend Strikers' Meeting at Park Last Evening." *Key West Citizen* 6 December 1935: 1.
Lewis, Robert W. *Hemingway on Love.* Austin: U of Texas P, 1965.
Long, Durward. "Key West and the New Deal, 1934–1936." *Florida Historical Quarterly* 46.3 (1968): 209–18.
———. "Workers on Relief, 1934–1938, in Key West." *Tequesta* 28 (1968): 53–61.
Lopez, Nilo C. *Magnolia Dairy: My Memories of Old Key West in the 20s and 30s.* Key West: Self-published, 1997.
Lynn, Andrea. *Shadow Lovers: The Last Affairs of H. G. Wells.* New York: Westview, 2001.
Lynn, Kenneth. *Hemingway.* New York: Simon & Schuster, 1987.
MacBride, Burton. Unpublished letter to Ernest Hemingway. May 1934. Ernest Hemingway Collection. John F. Kennedy Presidential Library and Museum. Boston.
Macdonald, Dwight. "Masscult and Midcult." *Masscult and Midcult: Essays against the American Grain.* 1962. Ed. John Summers. New York: New York Review of Books, 2011. 3–71.
Maier, Kevin. "'A Trick Men Learn in Paris': Hemingway, *Esquire*, and Mass Tourism." *Hemingway Review* 31.2 (2012): 65–83.
Mandel, Miriam B. *Reading Hemingway: The Facts in the Fictions.* Metuchen, NJ: Scarecrow, 1995.
Mason, Alane Salierno. "A Comedy with Animals: Ernest Hemingway, Jane Kendall Mason, and 'The Short Happy Life of Frances Macomber.'" *Boston Review* (February–March 2001): 23–26.
———. "To Love and Love Not." *Vanity Fair* July 1999: 108–18, 146–52.

McClintock, Scott O. "The 'Matter of Being Expatriots': Hemingway, Cuba, and Inter-American Literary Study." Grimes and Sylvester 102–22.
McCully, C. B. *The Language of Fly-Fishing*. Chicago: Fitzroy Dearborn, 2000.
McIver, Stuart. *Dreamers, Schemers, and Scalawags*. Sarasota, FL: Pineapple P, 1994.
———. *Hemingway's Key West*. 1993. Sarasota, FL: Pineapple P, 2002.
McLendon, James. *Papa: Hemingway in Key West*. Miami, FL: Seeman, 1972.
Meeks, Randall A. "Winner Takes Winner Takes Winner: Social Darwinism." Knott 81–89.
Mellow, James R. *Hemingway: A Life without Consequences*. Boston: Houghton Mifflin, 1992.
———. *Walker Evans*. New York: Basic Books, 2001.
Mencken, H. L. *The American Language: Supplement One*. New York: Knopf, 1945.
Meredith, James H. "Hemingway's Key West Band of Brothers: The World War I Veterans in 'Who Murdered the Vets?' and *To Have and Have Not*." Curnutt and Sinclair 241–66.
Meredith, Robert C. and John Dennis Fitzgerald. *The Professional Story Writer and His Art*. New York: Crowell, 1963.
Messenger, Christian K. *Sport and the Spirit of Play in American Fiction: Hawthorne to Faulkner*. New York: Columbia UP, 1981.
Meyers, Jeffrey. *Hemingway: A Biography*. New York: Harper & Row, 1985.
———. *Hemingway: The Critical Heritage*. London: Routledge, 1982.
Miller, Linda Patterson, ed. *Letters from the Lost Generation: Gerald and Sara Murphy and Friends*. New Brunswick, NJ: Rutgers UP, 1993.
Miller, Linda Patterson. "The Matrix of Hemingway's *Pilar* Log, 1934–1935." *North Dakota Quarterly* 64.3 (1997): 105–23.
Milton, Joyce. *The Yellow Kids: Foreign Correspondents in the Heyday of Yellow Journalism*. New York: Harper & Row, 1989.
Moddelmog, Debra A. *Reading Desire: In Pursuit of Ernest Hemingway*. Ithaca, NY: Cornell UP, 1999.
Moorehead, Caroline. *Gellhorn: A Twentieth-Century Life*. New York: Holt, 2003.
Monteiro, George. "The Writer on Vocation: 'Banal Story.'" *Hemingway's Neglected Short Fiction*. Ed. Susan F. Beegel. Ann Arbor: UMI Research P, 1989: 141–48.
Moreland, Kim. "To Have and Hold Not: Marie Morgan, Helen Gordon, and Dorothy Hollis." *Hemingway and Women: Female Critics and the Female Voice*. Ed. Lawrence Broer and Gloria Holland. Tuscaloosa: U of Alabama P, 2002. 81–92.
Morrison, Toni. *Playing in the Dark: Whiteness and the Literary Imagination*. New York: Random House, 1993.
Morton, Mark. *The Lover's Tongue: A Merry Romp through the Language of Love and Sex*. Toronto: Insomniac P, 2004.
Mort, Terry. *The Hemingway Patrols: Ernest Hemingway and His Hunt for U-Boats*. New York: Scribner, 2009.
Mount, Henry R. *Hemingway's Tribute to the Soil*. Lincoln, NE: iUniverse, 2005.
Murray, Albert. *The Blue Devils of Nada: A Contemporary American Approach to Aesthetic Statement*. New York: Pantheon, 1996.
———. *Conversations with Albert Murray*. Ed. Roberta S. Maguire. Jackson: UP of Mississippi, 1997.
Nagel, James. "Hemingway and the Italian Legacy." *Hemingway in Love and War: The Lost Diary of Agnes von Kurowsky*. Ed. Henry S. Villard and James Nagel. Boston: Northeastern UP, 1989. 197–269.

"Novel Is Barred from Shelves of Public Library." *Arkansas Catholic* 13 May 1938: 2.
Nyman, Jopi. *Men Alone: Masculinity, Individualism, and Hard-Boiled Fiction.* Netherlands: Rodopi, 1997.
O'Brien, Geoffrey. *Hardboiled America: Lurid Paperbacks and the Masters of Noir.* 1981. Exp. ed. New York: Da Capo, 1997.
Ogle, Maureen. *Key West: History of an Island of Dreams.* Gainesville: UP of Florida, 2006.
"Original Ernest Hemingway Signed Deed Key West 1937." Worthpoint.com. http://www.worthpoint.com/worthopedia/original-ernest-hemingway-signed-deed-key.
Ott, Mark P. *A Sea of Change: Ernest Hemingway and the Gulf Stream, A Contextual Biography.* Kent, OH: Kent State UP, 2008.
"Owner of Yacht Says Sub Base Fine Anchorage." *Key West Citizen* 29 January 1935: 1.
"Owner of Yacht Will Make Key West Port Home." *Key West Citizen* 14 January 1935: 1.
Palin, Michael. *Michael Palin's Hemingway Adventure.* New York: Macmillan, 2001.
Parker-Brady-Zimmerman Ancestor Tree. Ancestry.com
Partridge, Eric. *The New Partridge Dictionary of Slang and Unconventional English.* Ed. Tom Dalzell and Terry Victor. 2 vols. New York: Routledge, 2006.
Paul, Steve. "Tropical Iceberg: Cuban Turmoil in the 1930s and Hemingway's *To Have and Have Not.*" Curnutt and Sinclair 129–42.
Pearson, Michael. *Imagined Places: Journeys into Literary America.* Syracuse, NY: Syracuse UP, 1991.
Perkins, Maxwell. Unpublished letter to Ernest Hemingway. 7 February 1934. Ernest Hemingway Collection. John F. Kennedy Presidential Library and Museum. Boston.
Perrin, Thomas Gordon. "The Old Men and the 'Sea of Masscult'": T. S. Eliot, Ernest Hemingway, and Middlebrow Aesthetics." *American Literature* 84.1 (2012): 151–74.
Pero, Thomas. "Tom McGuane: 'A Passion for Tarpon.'" *Midcurrent.* http://midcurrent.com/books/tom-mcguane-a-passion-for-tarpon/. Excerpted from *A Passion for Tarpon.* Seattle: Wild River P, 2010.
Phelps, Henry C. "Literary History / Unsolved Mystery: *The Great Gatsby* and the Hall-Mills Murder Case." *American Notes and Queries* 14.3 (2001): 33–39.
Phillips, Gene D. *Fiction, Film, and Faulkner: The Art of Adaptation.* Knoxville: U of Tennessee P, 2001.
———. *Hemingway and Film.* New York: Ungar, 1980.
Phillips, J. D. "Batista Links His Destiny with Cuba's; The Ex-Sergeant Who Heads a Growing Army Says That He Is Guided to Do His Utmost for the Republic." *New York Times Magazine* 14 October 1934: 3–12.
Pizer, Donald. "The Hemingway–Dos Passos Relationship." *Journal of Modern Literature* 13.1 (1986): 111–28.
Pressman, Richard S. "Individualists or Collectivists? Steinbeck's *In Dubious Battle* and Hemingway's *To Have and Have Not.*" *Steinbeck Quarterly* 25.3–4 (1992): 119–33.
Pridemore, Adam. "Decolonizing the Native Conch in Ernest Hemingway's *To Have and Have Not*: Harry Morgan as a Cautionary Tale against Tourism." *Florida Studies: Proceedings of the 2006 Annual Meeting of the Florida College English Association.* Ed. Claudia Slate and Steve Glassman. Newcastle: Cambridge Scholars, 2006. 92–99.
Prince, Gerald. *A Dictionary of Narratology.* Rev. ed. Lincoln: U of Nebraska P, 2003.
Rao, P. G. Ramma. "Dynamics of Narration: Later Novels." *Ernest Hemingway's The Old Man and the Sea.* 2nd ed. Ed. Harold Bloom. New York: Infobase, 2008. 3–30.

Rastogi, Nina. "Wall Street Suicides: If We're in the Midst of a Financial Collapse, Why Aren't Executives Jumping Out of Office Buildings?" *Slate* 22 October 2008: http://www.slate.com/articles/news_and_politics/explainer/2008/09/wall_street_suicides.html.

Reynolds, Michael S. *Ernest Hemingway*. Detroit: Gale, 1999.

———. *Hemingway: The American Homecoming*. London: Blackwell, 1992.

———. *Hemingway: The Final Years*. London: Blackwell, 1999.

———. *Hemingway: The 1930s*. London: Blackwell, 1996.

Rintoul, M. C. *Dictionary of Real People and Places in Fiction*. 1993. New York: Routledge, 2014.

"Riverside Residents." *New Yorker* 7 October 1933: 18.

Rohmer, Sax. *The Hand of Fu Manchu: Being a New Phase in the Activities of Fu Manchu, the Evil Doctor*. New York: Burt, 1917.

———. *The Insidious Dr. Fu Manchu*. New York: McBride, Nast, 1913.

Romero, Robert Chao. *The Chinese in Mexico, 1882–1940*. Tucson: U of Arizona P, 2010.

Romney, John. "The Tracking Shot: Film-making Magic—or Stylistic Self-indulgence?" *Guardian* 4 December 2014.

Roosevelt, Franklin Delano. "Franklin D. Roosevelt's First Fireside Chat: March 12, 1933." *The Great Depression and New Deal: Documents Decoded*. Ed. Mario R. DiNunzio. Greenwood, CT: ABL-CIO, 2014. 102–07.

Roth, Clayton D., Jr. "150 Years of Defense Activity at Key West, 1820–1970." *Tequesta* 30 (1970): 33–51.

Rovner, Eduardo Sáenz. *Cuban Connection: Drug Trafficking, Smuggling, and Gambling in Cuba from the 1920s to the Revolution*. Chapel Hill: U of North Carolina P, 2008.

Ryan, William James. "Uses of Irony in *To Have and Have Not*." *Modern Fiction Studies* 14.3 (1968): 329–36.

Salinger, J. D. *The Catcher in the Rye*. 1951. New York: Little, Brown, 1991.

Samuelson, Arnold. *With Hemingway: A Year in Key West and Cuba*. New York: Holt, 1981.

Sanchez, Thomas. *King Bongo: A Novel of Havana*. New York: Knopf, 2003.

Scandura, Jani. *Down in the Dumps: Place, Modernity, American Depression*. Durham, NC: Duke UP, 2008.

Schaefer, Dave. *Sailing to Hemingway's Cuba*. Dobbs Ferry, NY: Sheridan House, 2000.

Schorcht, Blanca. *Storied Voices in Native American Texts: Harry Robinson, Thomas King, James Welch, and Leslie Marmon Silko*. New York: Routledge, 2003.

"Sewerage Project Approved." *Key West Citizen* 24 October 1935: 1.

Shakespeare, William. *The Tempest*. 1616. New York: Palgrave Macmillan, 2008.

"Shows Activities Thus Far in Sewerage and Water Projects." *Key West Citizen* 12 December 1935: 1.

Sinclair, May. "The Novels of Dorothy Richardson." *Egoist* 5 (April 1918): 57–59.

Sinclair, Upton. *A Prisoner of Morro; or, In the Hands of the Enemy*. New York: Street & Smith, 1898.

Skwiot, Christine. *The Purposes of Paradise: U.S. Tourism and Empire in Cuba and Hawai'i*. Philadelphia: U of Pennsylvania P, 2011.

Smith, Al. "Sound Money." *New Outlook* 162 (December 1933): 10.

Smith, Paul. *A Reader's Guide to the Short Stories of Ernest Hemingway*. Boston: G. K. Hall, 1989.

"Soldiers Rushed to Vets Camp." United Press. 1 March 1935: 1.

Spilka, Mark. *Eight Lessons in Love: A Domestic Violence Reader.* Columbia: U of Missouri P, 1997. 210–22.

———. *Hemingway's Quarrel with Androgyny.* Lincoln: U of Nebraska P, 1990.

Stanhope, Dorothy. "Havana Boatmen Smuggle Chinese; Carry Them across the Gulf to the Florida Coast." *New York Times* 30 November 1902: 28.

Staten, Clifford L. *A History of Cuba.* New York: Palgrave Macmillan, 2005.

Stephens, Robert O. Ed. *Hemingway: The Critical Reception.* Philadelphia: Burt Franklin, 1977.

Stewart, Donald Ogden. *By a Stroke of Luck: An Autobiography.* New York: Paddington P / Two Continents, 1975.

Strychacz, Thomas. *Hemingway's Theaters of Masculinity.* Baton Rouge: Louisiana State UP, 2004.

Stubbe, Henry. "Observations made on a Voyage from England to the Canbee Islands." *Philosophical Transactions* 2.27 (1667): 493–500.

Suchlicki, Jaime. *Cuba: From Columbus to Castro and Beyond.* Washington, DC: Potomac Books, 2002.

Swicegood, Tom. *The Submariner's Son: A Saga of Lust, Hurricanes and War at Sea.* Bloomington, IN: iUniverse, 2012.

Swift, Jonathan. *The Works of Jonathan Swift, D.D.: With Copious Notes and Additions, and a Memoir of the Author, by Thomas Roscoe.* Vols. 1–6. New York: Derby & Jackson, 1859.

Sylvester, Harry. "Hemingway: A Note." *Commonweal* 25 (30 October 1936): 10–11.

Szalay, Michael. *New Deal Modernism: American Literature and the Invention of the Welfare State.* Durham, NC: Duke UP, 2000.

Tone, Andrea. *Devices and Desires: A History of Contraceptives in America.* New York: Macmillan, 2002.

Tower, Wells. "Leopard." *Everything Ravaged, Everything Burned.* New York: Farrar, Straus & Giroux, 2009. 111–28.

Trogdon, Robert W. Ed. *Ernest Hemingway: A Literary Reference.* New York: Carroll & Graf, 2002.

———. *The Lousy Racket: Hemingway, Scribners, and the Business of Literature.* Kent, OH: Kent State UP, 2007.

Twain, Mark. *The Annotated Huckleberry Finn.* 1884. Ed. Michael Patrick Hearn. New York: Norton, 2001.

Tyler, Lisa. "'Women Have a Bad Time Really': Gender and Interpretation in *To Have and Have Not.*" *Marjorie Kinnan Rawlings Journal of Florida Literature* 7 (1996): 57–66.

Updike, John. *Conversations with John Updike.* Ed. James Plath. Jackson: UP of Mississippi, 1994.

U. S. Congress, House of Representatives, Subcommittee on Appropriations. *Investigation and Study of the Work Progress Administration (Formerly Works Progress Administration),* 76th Congress, 3rd Session, Parts 3–4. Washington, DC: Government Printing Office, 1940.

Valdez, Charlie g. "Racing *To Have and Have Not.*" *Film and Literary Modernism.* Ed. Robert P. McParland. Newcastle: Cambridge Scholars, 2013. 124–30.

Van Ash, Cay, and Elizabeth Sax Rohmer. *Master of Villainy: A Biography of Sax Rohmer.* London: Tom Stacey, 1972.

Van Vleck, Jennifer. *Empire of the Air: Aviation and the American Ascendancy.* Cambridge, MA: Harvard UP, 2013.

Vernon, Alex. *Hemingway's Second War: Bearing Witness to the Spanish Civil War.* Iowa City: U of Iowa P, 2011.

Wagman-Geller, Marlene. *Once Again to Zelda: The Stories behind Literature's Most Intriguing Dedications.* New York: Perigee, 2008.

Waldhorn, Arthur. *A Reader's Guide to Ernest Hemingway.* 1972. Syracuse, NY: Syracuse UP, 2002.

Walter, Ahto, and Tom Olsen. *Racing the Seas.* New York: Farrar & Rinehart, 1935.

Wells, Sharon. *Sloppy Joe's Bar: The First Fifty Years.* Key West: Key West Saloon, 1983.

White, E. B. "Across the Street and into the Grill." *New Yorker* 14 October, 1950: 28. Rpt. in *Fierce Pajamas: An Anthology of Humor Writing from the* New Yorker. Ed. David Remnick and Henry Finder. New York: Random House, 2002. 10–13.

———. "The Law of the Jungle." *New Yorker* 14 April 1934: 31.

Williams, Joy. *The Florida Keys: A History and Guide.* New York: Random House, 2003.

Wilson, Edmund. "The Literary Consequences of the Crash." *The Shores of Light: A Literary Chronicle of the Twenties and Thirties.* New York: Farrar, Strauss & Young, 1952. 496–97.

Woodrell, Daniel. *Tomato Red.* 1998. New York: Back Bay, 2012.

Wright, Richard. *The Outsider.* New York: Harper & Bros., 1953.

Wu, William F. *The Yellow Peril: Chinese Americans in American Fiction, 1850–1940.* Hamden, CT: Archon, 1982.

Vernon, Alex. *Hemingway's Second War: Bearing Witness to the Spanish Civil War.* Iowa City: U of Iowa P, 2011.

Yenne, Bill. *Tommy Gun: How General Thompson's Submachine Gun Wrote History.* New York: Thomas Dunne / St. Martin's, 2009.

Young, Elliot. *Alien Nation: Chinese Migration in the Americas from the Coolie Era through World War II.* Chapel Hill: U of North Carolina P, 2014.

Young, Philip. "To Have Not: Tough Luck." *American Fiction, American Myth: Essays by Philip Young.* Ed. David Morrell and Sandra Spanier. University Park: Penn State UP, 2008. 89–96.

INDEX

ABC Revolutionary Society (El ABC): Céspedes y Quesada and, 89; historical overview, 20–22, 148; threats to Harry Morgan by, 45, 53. *See also* Joven Cuba ("Young Cuba")
abortifacients, 128, 158–59
Across the River and into the Trees (Hemingway, novel), 7, 9, 111
Adams, Richard Hamilton "Saca Ham," 83
Adams, Willie, in *THHN*, 7, 69–70, 71, 75
Adderholt, O. F., 177–78
Adventures of Huckleberry Finn (Twain), 26–27
Afro-American (newspaper), 27
"After the Storm" (Hemingway, short story), 37, 63, 70
Ahto (sailboat), 193
Albrecht, H. O., 196
alcohol: "anaesthetic" of, 182; "carta del oro," 108; "Cuba libre," 117–18; Cuban customs on smuggling, 71; drunkenness, 55; Hatuey beer, 46; highball, 40; Key West dry era, 164; liquor trafficking, 67; ojen, 161, 165; rum-running, 43, 67, 68, 71, 78; self-discipline and, 146–47
Alice's (Key West brothel), 86
"alphabet man," 75
Alvo, Luis, 92
Alzira III (yacht), 192
American Language, The (Mencken), 115
American Mercury (magazine), 10
American Shoal Lighthouse, 67
Anderson, Sherwood, 6, 107, 147, 178, 188
Anita (fishing boat): cement factory and, 39; Hemingway's first extended stay in Cuba, 17–18; Jane Mason and, 129; Jig (black fisherman) and, 32–33; Kermath engine of, 50; in *THHN*, 28

Anticosti Flats/Anacostia Flats, 173–74
anti-Semitism, by Hemingway, 73
Appian of Alexandria, 174–76
Art and the Life of Action, with Other Essays (Eastman), 58
Atlantic Game Fishing (Farrington), 39
Aurura-Elgin train/tracks (Chicago), 191
Authentic Cuban Revolutionary Party, 95, 148
Autobiography of Alice B. Toklas, The (Stein), 22
Auto-Ordnance Company, 24–26

Bacardi, 117–18
Bacuranao, 51
Baker, Carlos, 4–5, 69–70, 107, 115–16, 118–22, 165
Baker, Milford, 56
Baldwin, Stanley, 192
"Ballad of Downsabel, The" (Drayton), 153
"balls," 151
"balls to you," 84
"Banal Story" (Hemingway, short story), 34
bank failures, of Great Depression, 179–80
Baracoa, 55, 57–58
barkentine (barquentine), 189
Barnum, P. T., 191
Batista, Fulgéncio, 89, 95, 148, 149–50
Battle of Waterloo, 172–73
"Battler, The" (Hemingway, short story), 107, 116
Beal, Fred, 178
Beals, Carleton, 18, 20
Beautiful and Damned, The (Fitzgerald), 4
Beegel, Susan F., 52–53, 84–85
Bender, Bert, 118–19, 204
Berg, A. Scott, 4
Beyond Desire (Anderson), 178
Big Annie's (Key West brothel), 85–86, 94, 164
"Bight, The" (Bishop), 78
Big Lucie in *THHN*, 85–86

Big Money, The (Dos Passos), 124–25
Big Rodger in *THHN*, 106, 107–8
"Big Two-Hearted River" (Hemingway, short story), 74
bilge, 154
binnacle lights, 61
Bird, Bill, 11n4
"this bird," 29–30
birth control, references to, 128, 158–59
Bishop, Elizabeth, 78, 164
"bitches," 130, 187, 195, 197
bitt, 77
Blanco Herrera, Julio, 26
Bland, John Otway Percy, 47
Blind Pig (Key West bar), 136
Blixen-Finecke, Bror von, 36
"blow," 191
Blue Heaven Billiard Parlor, 94
boats/ships: abeam, 69; barkentine (barquentine), 189; bilge, 154; bitt, 77; coaming, 198; engines, 50, 71; gimbals, 184; "house," 69; lighting on boats, 61; Marine Hardware (store), 134–35; "on the quarter," 38 (*see also individual names of boats*); rival party-boat captains and fishermen, 42; sculling, 61; scupper, 154; stuffing boxes, 147; vessel registration numbers, 71; "ways," 109; yawl-rigged, 193. *See also* fishing
Boca Chica Fish Camp, 108
Boca Grande Key, 78
bolita (lottery), 162–63
Boni & Liveright, 119–20
Bonus Expeditionary Force, 173–74
Bonus Marches (1932, 1933), 161
"boogie," 177
Borowski, Hulda, 190
Bradley, Helène, in *THHN*: characterization of, 128–31, 140–42; inspiration for character, 125, 128–31; introduction of, 114; Johnston's views of, 187; sexual aggression of, 41, 141–42, 156–57
Bradley, Tommy, in *THHN*, 29, 42, 141–42, 156–57, 159, 187
Braudy, Leo, 35
breakwaters, 196
Brennen, Carlene, 22
Brent, Loring, 48
Brest (France), 180
Brian, Denis, 130, 131
Brooks, George Gray, Jr., 88–89

Brooks, George Gray, Sr., 88
brothels: Alice's, 86; Big Annie's, 85–86, 94, 100; overview, 85–87, 100; prostitution fines, 87, 100; Square Roof, 164; women's portrayal as prostitutes, 112, 202
"brother," 37, 76
Brown, Sara Finch, 148
Bruce, Benjamin "Dink," 18–19
Bruce, Toby, 18
Budberg, Baroness Maura, 193–94
bullfights, Hemingway's early portraits of, 23
Burke, James Lee, 185
Burns, Harry H., 118–19
Bushwacked Piano, Ninety-Two in the Shade, and Panama, The (McGuane), 183
By a Stroke of Luck (Stewart), 119

Cabañas (Cuba), 95–96
Cabeza, Manolo, 199
Cabot, Eveillo, 115
Cain, James M., 138–39
Calabi, Silvio, 56
Calvino, Italo, 14
Calvo, Miguel, 25
Campbell, Donna M., 138–39
Camp Five (Lower Matecumbe Key), 168, 169
Camp Thomas Paine, 176
"canined," 197
Cap d'Antibes (France), 157
Capitolio, El, 54
"Cappy," 145
Careless People (Churchwell), 189
Caro, Robert A., 176
Carpender, Henry, 188
Carpenter, Henry, in *THHN*, 186–89
"carta del oro," 108
Casablanca docks, 52
Castro, Fidel, 73, 75, 95
Catcher in the Rye, The (Salinger), 15
"Cat in the Rain" (Hemingway, short story), 105
Cepero, Manuel, 20
Ceremony (Silko), 32
Céspedes y Quesada, Carlos Manuel de, 89
Chabas, Paul Emile, 113
Chatman, Seymour, 79
Chesterfields, 109
Chicago (Illinois), 190, 191
Chicago Tribune, 119
Chicha's (Key West), 163–64
Chinese Exclusion Act (1882), 47

INDEX · 245

Chinese immigrants: government monitoring of smuggling, 60; restrictions on women immigrants, 51; smuggling of, 21, 45; "yellow-peril" racism against, 46–50
Chinese Six Companies, 49
"Chink," 41
"chords," 198–99
Christmas Tree Island (Wisteria Island), 133–34
Christy, Bryan, 103
Churchill, Winstone, 191
Churchwell, Sarah, 189
cigar factories, 149
Cirino, Mark, 79
Civilization in the United States (Stearns), 62
Civil Wars (Appian of Alexandria), 174–76
Clemmer, William, 145
coaling docks (Garden Key), 63
coaming, 68, 198
Coast Guard: Dinner Key, 99, 143, 145; *Queen Conch* discovered by, 161, 183–85, 186–87
Cobbentz/Koblenz, 176
Coca-Cola, 117–18
Coccoloba uvifera, 60–61
Cojimar (Cuba), 54
cojones, 58–60, 93
Cold War, 175
Coles, Jack, 119
Comley, Nancy, 111–12
Communism themes: Cuba and Communist Party, 148; FBI file on Hemingway and, 171; "have nots" and, 171; Joven Cuba and Authentic Cuban Revolutionary Party, 148; Spartacus and, 175. *See also* Cuba
Comstock, Anthony, 113
"Conchs": "Conch Town," 162; defined, 42; "grits and grunts," 76, 162; Harry Morgan as native Key Wester, 55; as "have nots," 137; Key West tourism and culture of, 114–15; moral conservatism of, 73; poverty of, 139–40; Stone and, 92
Conrad, Barnaby, 17
Conrad, Joseph, 61
"cool," 171
Coolidge, Calvin, 130, 168
Cooper, Richard, 130
Cooperman, Stanley, 59–60
"coot," 104
Cowles, Alfred, 119
Cowles, John Cheney, 119–22
Cowley, Malcolm, 172, 185

Crack-Up, The (Fitzgerald), 189
Crawfish bar (sandbar), 144
Crime of Cuba, The (Beals), 18, 20
Crowley, Michael, 70
"crummy," 117
"crut," 116
Cruz, Mary, 9, 22, 41, 51, 52–53, 177
Cuba: airline service to, 41–42; Batista and, 89, 95, 148, 149–50; beer of, 26; *bolita*, 162–63; Cabañas, 95–96; Castro and, 73, 75, 95; cement factory in, 39; Chinese immigration restrictions, 51; Cojimar, 54; Communist Party, 148; Cuban quartet's (terrorists) identity in *THHN*, 94–95; Cuban Revolution of 1933, 29, 89, 150–51; Cuban Revolution of 1959, 75; El Mariel, 71; *guajiros*, 149; Guantánamo Province, 55; Havana, 14–19, 33, 52; as Hemingway's home, 17–19; Hotel Nacional de Cuba, 54; politics of, 18; Prado (Paseo del Prado), 202–3; Tampico, 155; violence in, 19, 27, 85. *See also* ABC Revolutionary Society (El ABC); Joven Cuba ("Young Cuba"); Machado, Gerardo
"Cuba libre," 117–18
Cuba y Hemingway en el gran rio azul (Cruz), 22
Cullen-Harrison Act (1933), 43
Cunard Bar (Havana), 26
Custer's Last Stand (print in Freddy's bar), 109
Customs House (Key West), 109, 145
Cutler, G. E., 190

Daily Telegraph, 191
Dain Curse, The (Hammett), 21, 30
Daly, Carroll John, 24
Dark Laughter (Anderson), 147
Darwin, Charles, 189–90
Dayspring (Sylvester), 165–66
"Dead Yellow Women" (Hammett), 48
Dealy Musings (Kowalewski), 24
Dearly Beloved (Sylvester), 165–66
Death in the Afternoon (Hemingway, nonfiction bullfighting study), 7, 9, 21, 58, 59–60, 79
Decker, George, 199
dedications, in Hemingway's books, 7–11
deep-sea fishing, in *THHN*, 14
"Defense of Dirty Words" (Hemingway, magazine article), 112
de Leon, Ponce, 30, 50
depth charge, 39–40
Derrick, Thomas, 40

Deutsche Waffen und Munitionsfabriken, 26
Devices and Desires (Tone), 158
Devotions upon Emergent Occasions (Donne), 6
DeVoto, Bernard, 58
Diario de la Marina, 46
Dickson, Eva, 36
Dictionary of Narratology, A (Prince), 43
Dinesen, Isak (Karen Blixen), 36
Dinner Key, 99, 145
direct address, second-person narration compared to, 14–17
Directorio Estudiantil, 22, 95, 148
Dixie Noir (Curnutt), 17
Donaldson, Scott, 140
Donne, John, 6
Donovan's (Havana), 41
Dorman-Smith, Edward "Chink," 11n4
Dos Passos, John: on Gattorno's work, 149; Hemingway's relationship with, 69–70, 124–28, 156, 159; homes of, 163; as inspiration for Gordon, 11, 124–26, 178; Laughton character's identity and, 119; wife of (*see* Smith, Katherine "Katy")
Down in the Dumps (Scandura), 114
drag, 37
Drayton, Michael, 153
Dry Banks, 185
Dry Tortugas, 50
Duffield, Marcus, 179
Duncombe, Helen, 118

Eastman, Max, 58, 127
Eby, Carl P., 80n1, 195–96
Ecclesiastes, 6
Eddie in *THHN*, 195
Eisenhower, Dwight D., 18
Eliot, T. S., 8
Ellis, Bret Easton, 8
Ellis, Havelock, 119
Ellsworth, Lumber Port (Peirce), 192
Emergency Banking Act, 179–80
Emilio (terrorist), 94–95, 143, 146, 147, 148, 149
epigraphs, of Hemingway's books, 5–7
Epitome of Roman History (Florus), 174–76
Ergoapiol, 158
Ernest Hemingway: Selected Letters, 1917–1961 (Baker), 119
Esquire (Hemingway's articles): articles about Gulf Stream, 30; columns of 1933–36, 16; *The Crack-Up*, 189; "Defense of Dirty Words," 112; Gingrich (*Esquire* editor) and, 118; "He Who Gets Slap Happy," 109, 169, 171–72; "Marlin Off the Morro," 38, 40, 46, 55, 135; "Night Before Battle," 107, 178–79; "Notes on the Next War," 37; "On Being Shot Again," 25–26; "On the Blue Water," 30, 35–36, 95–96; "Out in the Stream," 38; "Sailfish Off Mombasa," 135; "The President Vanquishes," 26, 83; "The Sights on Whitehead Street," 73, 93; "The Snows of Kilimanjaro," 120–21; "The Tradesman's Return," 66, 67–68, 71–72, 74, 75, 177
Esthonians, 193–94
Evans, Walker, 18–19, 20, 53
Everything Ravaged, Everything Burned (Tower), 14

"face like a ham," 123
Falla Bonet, Eutimio, 95, 101
Farewell to Arms, A (Hemingway, novel): British slang used in, 29–30; *cojones* reference, 59; dedication in, 9; First State Trust and Savings Bank reference in *THHN* and, 135–36; narrative style of, 17, 79; on rhetoric of glory, 172; title of, 3, 4; violence in, 62; women portrayed as androgynous in, 105
Farrington, S. Kip, 39
Fast, Howard, 176
Federal Bureau of Investigation (FBI), 74–75
Federal Deposit Insurance Corporation (FDIC), 171, 180
Federal Emergency Relief Administration (FERA) (U.S.), 72–73, 91–92, 108, 167–68, 171
Federal Writers guide (1941), 93
Fiedler, Leslie A., 102–3
Fielding, Henry, 6
fines, on prostitutes, 87, 100
First State Trust and Savings Bank, 133, 135–36, 143
fishing: deep-sea fishing, 14; feather squid, 38; grains pole, 63; "grunts," 133; Gulf Stream references and, 30–31; House of Hardy, 35; House of Hardy reel, 40; for jacks, 135; as "sloppy," 39; snapper lines, 63; still fishing, 40; for tarpon, 135; trolling, 37. *See also* individual names of boats; individual names of books about fishing
Fishing Voyage of the Good Ship Anita, The (movie), 32–33
Fishing Voyage of the Good Ship Anita, The (Sigman), 33

INDEX · 247

Fishing with Hemingway and Glassell (Farrington), 39
Fitzgerald, F. Scott: *The Beautiful and Damned*, 4; *Flappers and Philosophers*, 8; *The Great Gatsby*, 7, 8–9, 159, 188–89; Hemingway's views on, 121; Mizener and, 59; Perkins and, 58; "Sleeping and Waking," 196
Fitzgerald, Zelda, 8
Flagler, Henry, 44, 96
Flappers and Philosophers (Fitzgerald), 8
Fleming, Robert E., 125, 166
Flexner, Stuart Berg, 191
Florida College English Association, 29
Florida East Coast Railway, 31, 44
Florida Keys: Boca Grande Key, 78; Dinner Key, 99, 145; Garden Key, 50, 63; Matacumbe, Veterans Rehabilitation Camps, 168–69; Matecumbe, reference, 143, 144; Sand Key Lighthouse, 145; Sombrero Key, 185; Woman Key, 67, 77. See also Key West
Floridita (Havana), 19
Florus, 174–76
Foley, Barbara, 5
Fortaleza de San Carlos de la Cabaña (La Cabaña/Fort of Saint Charles), 33
For Whom the Bell Tolls (Hemingway, novel): backstories in, 138; *cojones* reference, 58; on Communist politics, 148; dedication in, 9; *gallegos* term in, 45–46; narrative style of, 16; narrative technique, 79; sea grape reference, 61; sexuality in, 103; "snotty," 107; title of, 6; women's portrayal in, 105, 111
Fountain, Gary, 164
Frankie in *THHN*, 14, 41, 42, 45, 51, 53
Freddy's (Freddie's) bar: "haves" introduced in novel at, 114; inspiration for, 83–84; "nickel-in-the-slot phonograph" at, 168–69; as setting for multiple chapters in *THHN*, 106; slot machines, 109
Frederichs, Herman, in *THHN*, 109
Frenzy of Renown, The (Braudy), 35
Frost, Robert, 114
Fuente de los Leones (Fountain of Lions), 19
Fuentes, Gregorio, 51, 54, 57
Fuentes, Norberto, 19, 26, 41

Gaginni, Giuseppe, 19
Gajdusek, Robert E., 116
Galápagos Islands, 189–90
Galbraith, John Kenneth, 190
gallegos, 45–46
gambling, in Key West, 162–64, 188
Garden Key, 50, 63
Garden of Eden, The (Hemingway, novel), 79, 105, 202
Garrison Bight (Key West), 77–78
gas, cost of, 31, 52
Gastonia (North Carolina), 177–78
Gattorno, Antonio, 149
Geary Act, 47
Gellhorn, Martha, 9, 18, 130, 134, 166, 193–94
Genette, Gerard, 7–8, 11, 82
Ghengis Khan, 122, 123
Gibbs, Arthur Hamilton, 34
"Gibraltar of America," Key West as, 122–23
Gilman, Charlotte Perkins, 47
gimbals, 184
Gingrich, Arnold, 118, 128–29, 130–31
Glassford, Pelham, 173
Glass-Steagall Banking Reform Act, 180
Gonzales, Francisco "Pancho Macaro," 162–63
González Rubiero, Juan Mariano, 20
"goofy," 35–36
Gordon, Helen, in *THHN*: breakup of marriage, 156–60; characterization of, 114, 118; inspiration for character, 124, 126–28; introduction of, 124; on Joven Cuba and bank robbery, 95, 120, 147–48; MacWalsey character and, 114, 131, 156; on "social phenomena," 131
Gordon, Richard, in *THHN*: book's title and, 4; Bradley and, 125; breakup of marriage, 156–60; characterization of, 114; "have not" characters and, 170, 176, 178; "haves" theme and, 161–62; inspiration for character, 124–26, 178; inspiration for character of Helen and, 126–28; introduction of, 95, 100, 120, 124; Key West bar/tourist district route of, 163–64; Marie as writing inspiration, 152, 198, 200
Gorky, Maxim, 193–94
Gorney, Jay, 37
Gorostiza, Paulino, Jr., 101
grains pole, 63
Grau, Ramón, 89
"Great Blue River, The" (Hemingway, essay), 30, 38, 135
Great Depression: bank failures, 179–80; effects on labor, 178; "Hoovervilles," 173–74, 176; Key West economy during, 43–44; "on the bum," 77; suicides during, 190–91; veterans during, 167–68. See also "have nots"

Great Gatsby, The (Fitzgerald), 7, 8–9, 159, 188–89
Greene, Philip, 117–18
Green Hills of Africa (Hemingway, nonfiction study of Africa), 7, 10, 30–31, 79, 135, 167, 204 Grey, Zane, 31, 35, 40
Grits and Grunts (Kennedy), 51, 86
"grits and grunts," 76, 162
"grunts," 133
guajiros, 149
Guantánamo Province (Cuba), 55
Guiteras, Antonio, 95, 101, 148
Gulf Stream, references to, 30–31

hair: of female characters, 105; Harry Morgan's name choice and, 52, 80n1
Hall, Mrs. Frances Stevens, 188
Hall, Rev. Edward, 188
Hammett, Dashiell, 21, 24, 30, 48, 49
Hand of Fu Manchu, The (Rohmer), 48
Harburg, Edgar "Yip," 37
Harrison, Frederick, in *THHN*, 69, 71–72, 76, 108
Harrow (London school), 192
"Harry and the Pirates" (Beegel), 52–53
"Harry Burns and Professor MacWalsey in Ernest Hemingway's *To Have and Have Not*" (Bender), 118–19
Hatuey beer, 46
Hauptmann, Richard Bruno, 35
Havana (Cuba): British-Spanish exchange for Florida, 33; customs, 52; Hemingway in, 17–19; Hotel Nacional de Cuba, 54; imagery of "bum-filled squares" in, 14–17; Pearl of San Francisco Café, 14
"have nots": Gastonia and labor struggles, 177–78; "Hoovervilles," 173–74, 176; hurricane victims as, 161–62, 167–68; overview, 161–62. *See also* "Conchs"
"haves": alcoholic drinks of, 118; introduction of, 114; privileges of, 156–60; symbols of luxury, 203–4; tourists as, 29, 114–15; women characters in *THHN* as, 123; yachts of, 186–87, 192, 193–94
Hawk, Howard, 32
Hawk Channel, 183
Hawkins, Ruth, 202
Hayward, Leland, 179
Hayzooz in *THHN*, 106, 107–8
Hearst, William Randolph, 46–47
Helsley, Steve, 56

Hemingway, Anson (grandfather), 191
Hemingway, Arabella (aunt), 33
Hemingway, Carol (sister), 152
Hemingway, Clarence (father), 191
Hemingway, Ernest: Brooks and, 88; Burns and, 118–19; Catholic conversion of, 128; charter-fishing business of, 31; children of, 9, 25, 111–12, 129, 131; as Cuba resident, 17–19; death of, 56, 75; Dos Passos and, 124–26, 124–28, 156; in Dry Tortugas, 50–51; FBI's investigation of, 74–75; injuries of, 57, 59; Jane Mason and, 128–31; journalism career of, 16, 18; Katy Smith and, 126–28; Kennedy Library collection of works by, 32–33; as Key West resident, 18–19, 42, 73, 87, 93, 152; on Key West tourism, 73, 114–15; marriages, overview, 9 (*see also* Hemingway, Pauline Pfeiffer [wife]); marriage to Hadley Richardson, 9, 127; marriage to Martha Gellhorn, 9, 18, 130, 134, 166, 193–94; marriage to Mary Welsh, 9, 134, 202; physical description of, 115, 202; profanity used by, 112–13; public release of correspondence by (1980s), 25; in Rincón and Baracoa, 57–58; sarcasm used by, 23–24; self-reference, as "Old Slob," 44; self-reference to, in *THHN*, 124; Sylvester and, 165–66; Thompson and, 134–35; views of laboring class, 139–40; weapons of, 55–56 (*see also* weapons); wives abused by, 134
Hemingway, Gregory (son), 111, 134
Hemingway, Hadley Richardson (wife), 9, 127
Hemingway, Hilary (niece), 22
Hemingway, John Hadley Nicanor (son), 9, 25, 131
Hemingway, Leicester (brother), 50, 71, 76
Hemingway, Marcelline (sister), 195–96
Hemingway, Martha Gellhorn (wife), 9, 18, 130, 134, 166, 193–94
Hemingway, Mary Welsh (wife), 9, 134, 202
Hemingway, Pauline Pfeiffer (wife): blonde hair of, 202; books read to husband by, 21; as character inspiration, 127, 128; death of, 134; friendship with Burns, 118–19; Hemingway's breakup with, 166; Hollis character in *THHN* and, 195–96; marriage to Hemingway, 9; *porra* attack witnessed by, 22; wealthy uncle(s) of, 9, 79, 192; Whitehead Street home of, 152
Hemingway, Tyler (uncle), 33

"Hemingway: A Note" (Sylvester), 165
Hemingway in Cuba (Fuentes), 19, 26
Hemingway in Cuba (Hemingway, Brennen), 22
Hemingway on Fishing (Lyon), 38
Hemingway on Love (Lewis), 204
Hemingway on the Great Blue River (Cruz), 52
Hemingway's Boat (Hendrickson), 91
Hemingway's Guns (Calabi, Helsley, Sanger), 56
"Hemingway's Key West Band of Brothers" (Meredith), 170
Hemingway's Quarrel with Androgyny (Spilka), 9
Hemingway's Tribute to the Soil (Mount), 74
Hemingway Women, The (Kert), 131
Hendrickson, Paul, 26, 35, 91
Henley, William, 85
Herbst, Josephine, 83
Hergesheimer, Joseph, 155
Herrera y Franchi, Alberto, 89
Herrmann, John, 50–51, 83
Hersey, John, 170
Hevia, Carlos, 89
"He Who Gets Slap Happy" (Hemingway, magazine article), 109, 169, 171–72
H. G. Wells in Love (Wells), 194
highball (alcoholic drink), 40
"high trucks," 108
Hillis, Marjorie, 195–96
"Hills Like White Elephants" (Hemingway, short story), 4, 103
Hollis, Dorothy, in *THHN*, 80, 187, 194–96
Hollywood Anti-Nazi League (HANL), 167
homosexual relationships, in *THHN*, 170
Hoover, Herbert, 75, 168, 173–74
Hoover, J. Edgar, 74–75
"Hoovervilles," 173–74, 176
Hopkins, Harry, 72, 92, 168
Hotchner, A. E., 34
Hotel Ambos Mundos (Havana), 18, 42
Hotel Nacional de Cuba, 54
House of Hardy, 35, 40
"House on Turk Street, The" (Hammett), 48, 49
House Un-American Activities Committee (HUAC), 175
Hudson, Elizabeth, 121
hurricane (Labor Day 1935), 97n1, 144, 145, 161–62, 167–68
hurricane (October 1926), 60

If on a winter's night a traveler (Calvino), 14
Imagined Places (Pearson), 94

"In Another Country" (Hemingway, short story), 17
influenza epidemic (1918), 181
informants (*lenguas largas*), 20
In Our Time (Hemingway, novel), 6, 9, 11n4, 23, 119–20
Insidious Fu Manchu, The (Rohmer), 48
interdit de sejour, 188
Internal Revenue Bureau, 189
International Hemingway Conference (1984), 33
Irish descendants, derogatory terms for, 159
Islanders, 199
Islands in the Stream (Hemingway, novel), 38, 74, 79, 171
Isleño (Islanders), 199
"Isle of Capri" (Williams, Kennedy), 168–69
Ivers, Joris, 167

jacks, 135
Jacks, Nelson, in *THHN*, 161–62, 170–71, 172, 176, 178
Jacksonville Journal, 92
James, William, 79
Japanese immigrants, "yellow-peril" racism against, 46, 47
Jig (black fisherman), 32–33
Joey (vet) in *THHN*, 170, 180
Johnson, Mr. (customer), in *THHN*, 14, 28–29, 35, 37, 39, 40, 44, 45
Johnson, Roger (sheriff), in *THHN*, 31, 101, 135, 167, 198
Johnston, Wallace, in *THHN*, 177, 186
"John Thomas" reference, 157–58
John W. Atkins (schooner), 101
Jordan, Robert, 146
Journal to Stella, The (Swift), 55
Joven Cuba ("Young Cuba"): Communism and, 147–48; Cuban quartet's identity, 94–95; Cuban quartet's shootout with Harry, 143–51, 198; Gorostiza and, 101; overview, 95, 146; relationship to Authentic Cuban Revolutionary Party, 148; robbery by, 85, 116, 120, 133, 135–36, 137, 143, 186, 198
Joyce, James, 79, 187, 194, 202
"Jungle Town," 94

Karol, K. S., 148
Kelly's Bar and Restaurant (Key West), 42
Kennedy, Jimmy, 168–69
Kennedy, Stetson, 51, 86

Kennedy Library, 32–33, 46
Kermath Manufacturing (Detroit), 50
Kert, Bernice, 111, 131
Key West: American Shoal Lighthouse, 67; bar/tourist district, 163–64 (*see also individual names of bars*); breakwaters, 196; brothels in, 85–87, 94, 100, 164; cigar factories, 149; Cuban airline service from, 42; Customs House, 109, 145; Dos Passos in, 124–26; Garrison Bight, 77–78; as "Gibraltar of America," 122–23; Great Depression in, 43–44; gritty view of, in *THHN*, 82; Gulf Stream and economy of, 31; "haves" of, 114 (*see also* "have nots"; "haves"); as Hemingway's home, 18–19, 42, 73, 87, 93, 152; Key West Administration (KWA), 72–74, 87, 90; Key West Art and Historical Society, 18–19; *Key West Citizen,* 86, 87, 88, 92, 108–9, 164, 192, 193; labor strike (Fall 1935), 91–92; Naval Station, 89–91; Rios reference, 76; Rocky Road, 124, 163, 181, 198; sub-base (Naval Station Key West), 187; tourism in, 73, 114–15; Trumbo Point, 78–79; Wisteria Island, 134; Works Progress Administration in, 72. *See also* "Conchs"
Key West Tales (Hersey), 170
kidnappings, 101
"Killers, The" (Hemingway, short story), 17
King Bongo (Sanchez), 19
Kingfish Shoals, 144
"Knights of the Open Palm" (Daly), 24
Knopp, Ray, 134
Kowalewski, Michael, 24
Krutnik, Frank, 23
Kubie, Lawrence, 130
Kubrick, Stanley, 175
Ku Klux Klan, 92, 199
Ku Klux Klan Kubano, 27

L (Chicago), 190
Labor Defender, 178
labor strikes, 91–92, 177–78
Lady Chatterley's Lover (Lawrence), 157–58
Lake Shore Drive, Austin (Chicago), 190
Language of Fly-Fishing, The (McCully), 37
Lanham, Charles T. "Buck," 177
Laughlin, James, 164
Laughton, James, in *THHN,* 114, 115, 118–22
Laughton, Mrs., in *THHN,* 114, 115–16, 118, 119, 122, 123

Lawrence, D. H., 157–58
Leddy, Raymond, 75
Leeds, Bill, Jr., 25, 26
Leftist National Workers Alliance, 92
"Leopard" (Tower), 14
Leroy, Richard, 86
Lewis, Robert W., 204
Lewis, Wyndham, 76n1
Life Magazine, 172
Life of Crassus (Plutarch), 174–76
"Light of the World, The" (Hemingway, short story), 202
lights, of boats, 61
Lilac Time (Key West bar), 161, 163–65, 188
Lindbergh, Charles, Jr., 35
Lindbergh, Charles, Sr., 34–35
Lippincott, J. P., 18
Listening to America (Flexner), 191
"Literary Consequences of the Crash, The" (Wilson), 178
"Literary History / Unsolved Mystery" (Phelps), 188–89
literary patronage, 140–42
Live Alone and Like It (Hillis), 195–96
Lizard King, The (Christy), 103
loggerheads, 103
Lopez, Lalo (pseudonymous rumrunner), 51–52
Lopez, Nilo C., 76
lottery (*bolita*), 162–63
Love and Death in the American Novel (Fiedler), 102–3
Lowe, Joe, 28, 68
Luger (gun), 26
Luger, George, 26
luminol, 196
Lynn, Andrea, 194
Lynn, Kenneth, 124, 126–27, 128
Lyon, Nick, 38
Lysol, 158

MaAlmon, Robert, 11n4
Machado, Gerardo: anti-Machado movement, 148 (*see also* ABC Revolutionary Society [El ABC]); *The Crime of Cuba* (Beals) on, 20; Cuban Revolution of 1933, 29, 89; as "El Supremo," 19; Mason and, 42; overview, 18; race issues and, 27; Tommy guns used by, 25; violence of, 85
MacLeish, Archibald, 9, 192

MacWalsey, John, in *THHN*: "have not" characters and, 179, 181–82; Helen Gordon and, 114, 131, 156; inspiration for character, 118–19; introduction of, 114; on Key West, 122; "nerts" reference by, 115; on "old rale," 180–81; Richard Gordon and, 162; as "twirp," 157
Magnolia Dairy (Lopez), 76
Maier, Keven, 28
male rape, references to, 170
Man Alone (Wright), 185
Mandel, Miriam B., 26, 45, 104, 183
Manuel (Cuban local), 19
Manuel Fernandez Company, 165
Mariel, El (Cuba), 71
Marine Hardware (Key West store), 134–35
marl, 74
"Marlin Off the Morro" (Hemingway, magazine article), 38, 40, 46, 55, 135
Márquez Sterling, Manuel, 89
Marshall, Eddy, in *THHN*: "Conchs" comment by, 55; drunkenness of, 55, 57; inspiration for character, 28–29; job request/as stowaway, 45, 54; mentions of, in Part Three, 98; overview, 14; replaced by Wesley character, 67–68
Marshall, S. L. A., 165
Martínez Sanz, Joaquin, 22
Marty, Andre, 146
Marx, Karl, 175
masculinity themes: "balls," 151; "boy," 116; *cojones*, 58–60; "John Thomas" reference, 157–58; "nerts," 115; power and privilege, 126; Skull and Bones (Yale University), 186, 192. *See also* sex themes; women, portrayal of
Mason, Alane Salierno, 130, 131
Mason, Grant, 11, 29, 42, 128, 130, 140, 159–60
Mason, Jane, 11, 29, 41, 118, 125, 128–31, 140
Matecumbe: camps, 168, 169, 171; reference to, 143, 144
Matinée de Septembre (Chabas), 113
Matthews, T. S., 194
Mavis Lee (prostitute), 94
McCarthy, Joseph, 175
McClintock, Scott O., 66
McCully, C. B., 37
McGillis, Kelly, 42
McGuane, Thomas, 183
McLendon, James, 83, 88, 94, 109, 162–63
McMorris, Herschel, 171

Meeks, Randall A., 189–90
Mellow, James R., 20–21, 53, 129, 131
Mencken, Henry Louis, 10, 115
Mendieta, Carlos, 89, 150
Menken, Solomon Stanwood, 10
Men Without Women (Hemingway, short story collection), 4
Meredith, James H., 170
Messenger, Christian K., 40
Metropolitan Museum of Art (New York), 18
Meyers, Jeffrey, 128, 166
Mianus (Connecticut) Electric Company, 71
Michael Palin's Hemingway Adventure (Palin), 41
"mick," 159
Mildred Pierce (Cain), 138–39
mill race, 38
Mills, Eleanor, 188
misogyny. *See* women, portrayal of
Mizener, Arthur, 59
"Mob, The," 69–70
Model T taxis, 181
Monteiro, George, 34
Moon Gaffney (Sylvester), 165–66
Morales, Albino "Pena," 164
Moreland, Kim, 104
Morgan, Harry, in *THHN*: ABC threat to, 45, 53; arm amputation of, 82, 84–85, 104, 105, 112, 139; backstory references about, 42, 55, 93, 104, 137–38, 149; book's title and, 4; characterization of, 52–53, 54, 68, 70, 137, 189–90; Coast Guard discovery of, 161, 183–85; daughters of, 111–12, 201; death of, 90, 198–200; derogatory epithets used by, 27; dying quote by, 184–85; Eddy and, 55, 57; fatal injury of, 143–51, 153, 198; first meeting with Cuban quartet, 94–95 (*see also* Joven Cuba ["Young Cuba"]); fishing references, 35–36, 40; "haves" and, 29, 114–15; Hemingway's sarcastic descriptions of, 23; interactions with officials by, 44, 69, 71, 78, 100, 106, 108; knowledge of Spanish by, 96, 98–99; liquor trafficking by, 67; Marie's reaction to death of, 198–200, 201–4; marriage of, 102–5, 111–12, 113, 201 (*see also* Morgan, Marie, in *THHN*); in Miami, 56; Mrs. Laughton and, 115–16, 122, 123; name of, 52, 80n1; as narrator, 14–17, 98; overview, 14; physical description of, 113; smuggling plans of, 116–17, 133, 134
Morgan, Marie, in *THHN*: characterization of, 80; daughters of, 111–12, 201; Gordon and,

152, 198, 200; Harry's death and, 198–200, 201–4; marriage of, 102–5, 111–12, 113, 201; as narrator, 79, 83, 201–2; New Orleans reference by, 118
Morgan, Sir Henry, 52–53, 85
Morrison, Toni, 27, 32, 36
Morro Castle, 33–34
Moses, Robert, 176
Motorboating (magazine), 90
Mount, Henry R., 74
"mouthed himself," 101
Moveable Feast, A (Hemingway, novel), 16, 126, 159, 170
Mudd, Samuel, 50
Murphy, Gerald, 125, 128
Murphy, Patrick, 83
Murphy, Sara, 25, 125, 128
Murray, Albert, 27

Nagel, James, 59
Napoleon Bonaparte, 172–73
narrative style, of *THHN*: complexity of Part Three, 81; detail used by Hemingway, 38; first-person devices, 82–83; "focalized" storytelling, 70; interior monologue, 77, 79, 98, 104, 147; introduction of Key West atmosphere as surreal, 106–7; narration/interior monologue by Marie, 79, 83, 201–2; second-person narration, 14–17, 53, 55; stream of consciousness, 79–80; tense, 31–33, 40, 41, 84; women's voices and *THHN* narrative, 199
National Origins Act (1924), 47
National Textile Workers Union, 177–78
Naval Station Key West, 89–91
"nerts," 115
New Republic, 178
New York Daily Mirror, 197
New Yorker, 14, 176
New York Times Magazine, 150
"nickel-in-the-slot phonograph," 168–69
"nigger," 26–27
"Night Before Battle" (Hemingway, short story), 107, 178–79
Nordquist L-T Ranch (Wyoming), 118
"Notes on the Next War" (Hemingway, magazine article), 37
"Novels of Dorothy Richardson, The" (Sinclair), 79
nurse sharks, 104
Nyman, Jopi, 62, 101

Ogle, Maureen, 44, 149
ojen (anisette), 161, 165
Old Man and the Sea, The (Hemingway, novel): Cabañas reference in, 95–96; Cojimar used in, 54; dedication in, 10; epigraphs and, 7; on Gulf Stream, 30; movie version, 179; Portugese men-of-war in, 155
"old rale," 180–81
"On Being Shot Again" (Hemingway, magazine article), 25–26
101 Best Scenes Ever Written (Conrad), 17
"one man alone" speech, in *THHN*, 184–85
"One Trip Across" (Hemingway, short story), 22, 43, 67–68, 90–91
"On the Blue Water" (Hemingway, magazine article), 30, 35–36, 95–96
"on the bum," 77
Origin of Species, The (Darwin), 189–90
Orteig Prize, 34
Ortiz, Arsenio, 20, 27
Ott, Mark P., 39
"Out in the Stream" (Hemingway, magazine article), 16, 38, 141
Out of Africa (film), 36
Overseas Highway, 161

Pacifico (Havana), 41
Palin, Michael, 41
Palmer, Frank, 71
Palmer, Ray, 71
Pamela, or Virtue Rewarded (Richardson), 6
Pan American Airways, 41–42
Pancho in *THHN*, 20, 21–22, 23, 26, 27, 45
Papa Hemingway (Hotchner), 34
Papa: Hemingway in Key West (McLendon), 83
Papy, Bernie C., 134
"party boats," 36
Paul, Steve, 94
Paula Louise (boat), 90
Peanuts (Schulz), 70
Pearl of San Francisco Café (Havana) in *THHN*, 14, 19
Pearson, Michael, 94
"peddle," 138–39
Pedro (terrorist), 94
Peele, George, 3
Pegler, Westbrook, 112
Peirce, Alzira, 192
Peirce, Waldo, 69–70, 85, 111, 169–70, 192
Percival, Philip, 36

Perdomo, Felipe, 28
Perkins, Maxwell, 3–4, 10, 22, 28, 44, 50, 58, 83
Pfeiffer, Gus (Pauline Pfeiffer Hemingway's uncle), 9, 79
Pfeiffer, Jinny (Pauline Pfeiffer Hemingway's sister), 22, 118
Pfeiffer, Pauline. *See* Hemingway, Pauline Pfeiffer (wife)
Phelps, Henry C., 188–89
Pilar (boat), 25–26, 51, 54, 70, 75, 83, 89–91
Pinder, Albert "Old Bread," 83, 108–9
Pinoy, Chin, 49
pirate references, in *THHN*, 53, 84–85
Pizer, Donald, 125
Playa Bacuranao, 51
Playa Baracoa, 55
"plugged," meanings of, 31, 53
Plutarch, 174–76
Pointed Roofs (Sinclair), 79
Poochy (vet) in *THHN*, 180
porra, 22
porristas, 23, 32
Porter, William R., 101, 136
Porter dock, 13, 101, 116
Porter Dock Company, 101
"Portrait of Mister Papa, A" (Cowley), 172
Portugese men-of-war, 154–55
postal savings system, 171, 180
Pound, Ezra, 8
Power Broker and the Fall of New York, The (Caro), 176
Prado (Paseo del Prado, Cuba), 202–3
prejudice. *See* racism and prejudice; women, portrayal of
"President Vanquishes, The" (Hemingway, magazine article), 26, 83
Pridemore, Adam, 29
Prince, Gerald, 43
Principles of Psychology (James), 79
profanity, 112–13
Prohibition, 68, 145
prostitution. *See* brothels
pulp fiction, 178–79
"Pulps, The" (Duffield), 179
pump guns, 55–56
Punch Magazine, 190
"punishment," fishing as, 40
"puss," 180
Putnam, G. P., 194

Queen Conch (boat), 153, 154, 161, 183–85
quinine, 158

Racing the Seas (Walter), 193
"Racing *To Have and Have Not*" (Valdez), 32
racism and prejudice: anti-Semitism by Hemingway, 73; "boogie," 177; "Chink," 41; "Conch Town," 162 (*see also* "Conchs"); "Jungle Town," 94; Ku Klux Klan, 92, 199; Ku Klux Klan Kubano, 27; labor strike (Key West, Fall 1935) and, 92; "mick," 159; Morrison's analysis of *THHN*, 32, 36; "nigger," 26–27; "nigger bartender," 169–70; sexual references, 104; "yellow peril," 46–50. *See also* women, portrayal of
"rale," 172, 180–81
Rao, P. G. Rama, 204
Raul's Club (Key West bar), 93, 114–15
"receiver," 133
Red Harvest (Hammett), 24
Red House (Key West), 163–64
Red (Joey) in *THHN*, 180
Red Rooster (Key West bar), 199
Reichenbach, Harry, 113
Remembering Elizabeth Bishop (Fountain), 164
"Revolutionist, The" (Hemingway, short story), 146
Reynolds, Michael S., 79, 134–35
Rhys, Jean, 153–54
Richard Hudnut Company, 192
Richardson, Hadley, 9, 127
Richardson, Samuel, 6
Rincon, El, 57–58
Rios (Key West), 76
Riverside Drive (New York City), 176
"Riverside Residents" (*New Yorker*), 176
Robby in *THHN*, 183
Roberto (terrorist), 94, 143, 145, 146–47, 151
Roberts, Samuel Winreal, 183
Roberts, Willy, 183
Robles, José, 126
Rocky Road (Key West), 124, 163, 181, 198
Rodriguez, Antonio "Kaiser Guillermo," 19
Rodriguez, Fausto, 117–18
Rodriguez, Juan, in *THHN*, 84
Rogers, Ginger, 179
Rohmer, Sax, 48
Romero, Robert Chao, 49
Roosevelt, Franklin D.: bank failures of Great Depression, 179–80; Cuban politics and,

18; Federal Deposit Insurance Corporation (FDIC), 171, 180; New Deal and, 108, 168; New Deal of, 72–73, 75; presidential election (1932), 174; Prohibition ended by, 43, 72–73; World War II and, 91
rumba (dance), 33
rum-running, 43, 67, 68, 71, 87
Ruskin, John, 5
Russell, Joe "Josie Grunts," 10, 17, 28, 31, 39, 83, 123

Sáenz Rovner, Eduardo, 71
"Sailfish Off Mombasa" (Hemingway, magazine article), 135
Sailing to Hemingway's Cuba (Schaefer), 19
Saladrigas Zayas, Carlos, 22
Salinger, J. D., 15
saltcellars, 177
Samuelson, Arnold, 39, 60, 90–91
Sanchez, Thomas, 19
Sand Key Lighthouse, 145
San Francisco wharf, 28
Sanger, Roger, 56
Santuario de San Lazaro (Sanctuary of St. Lazarus), 57
Sargasso weed, 153–54
Sartre, Jean-Paul, 60
Saturday Review of Literature, 130
Saunders, Berge 31
Saunders, Eddie "Bra," 31, 50, 69–70, 71, 195
"scab," 179
Scandura, Jani, 85, 110n1, 114, 203–4
Schaefer, Dave, 19
Schmidt, Dave, 73
Scholes, Robert, 111–12
Schruns (Switzerland), 147
Schulz, Charles M., 70
Scribner (publishing company): on character names, 11; *cojones* references in Hemingway's books, 58, 59; Eastman and Perkins, 58; Perkins (Hemingway's editor), 3–4, 10, 22, 28, 44, 50, 58, 83; on profanity, 112; *The Sun Also Rises* published by, 119; THHN title, 4
Scribner, Charles, III, 10, 172
sculling, 61
scupper, 154
Sea-Brothers (Bender), 204
"Sea Change, The" (Hemingway, short story), 105

sea grapes, 60–61
second-person narration, direct address compared to, 14–17
Secret History, The (Tartt), 8
"Secret Sharer, The" (Conrad), 61
Seeley, Coles Van Brunt, Jr., 167
September Morn (Chabas), 113
sewer system, of Key West, 87
sex themes: abortion/birth control, 128, 158–59; Bradley characters in THHN, 187 (*see also* Bradley, Hélène, in THHN; Bradley, Tommy, in THHN); Hollis character in THHN, 194–95; homosexuality, 186, 187–88; "John Thomas" reference, 157–58; Morgans' marriage and, 102–5, 111–12, 113
Shadow Lovers (Lynn), 194
Shakespeare, William, 55
sheriff in THHN, 167
ships. *See* boats/ships; *individual names of vessels*
Shipwreck at Night (Peirce), 192
Shoal Lighthouse, 67
"Short Happy Life of Francis Macomber, The" (Hemingway, short story), 3, 36, 56, 130, 160
Sidney, Sylvia, 167
"Sights on Whitehead Street, The" (Hemingway, magazine article), 73, 93
Sigman, Joseph, 33
Silko, Leslie Marmon, 32
Simmons, Robert "Bee-lips," in THHN: characterization of, 84, 101, 106; death of, 98, 120, 147; fee of, 114; Harry's smuggling plans, 116–17; Harry's suspicions about, 96; on "high trucks," 108; inspiration for character, 88–89; introduction of, 82, 167; introduction of character's name, 198
Sinclair, May, 79
Sinclair, Upton, 34
Sing, Mr., in THHN: characterization of, 21, 41; death of, 57, 61–63, 101, 117; Frankie and, 45, 51; Spanish spoken by, 50; "yellow-peril" racism and, 49–50
"skate," 70
Skinner, Alfred L., 169–70
Skull and Bones (Yale University), 186, 192
"slap happy," 169
"slappy," 171–72
Slate Magazine, 190–91
"Sleeping and Waking" (Fitzgerald), 196
Sloan's Liniment, 192
Sloppy Joe's (Key West), 83, 136, 169–70

Sloppy Joe's Bar (Wells), 170
slot machines, 109
"smack," 33
Smith, Al, 75
Smith, Bill, 69–70
Smith, Erik, 169–70
Smith, Katherine "Katy," 124, 125, 126–28, 163
snapper lines, 63
Snarl of the Beast, The (Daly), 24
"snotty," 107, 202
"Snows of Kilimanjaro, The" (Hemingway, short story), 79, 120–21, 128, 140–41
Sombrero Key, 185
"sounding," 34
Soundings (Gibbs), 34
South Florida (*THHN* boat), 69, 70
Spanish Earth, The (Hemingway, Ivers; film), 167
Spartacus (book character), 174–76
Spartacus (movie), 175
Spartacus League, 175
Spellman, Herbert, in *THHN*, 161, 165–66
Spilka, Mark, 9, 105, 134
Spirit of Romance, The (Pound), 8
Spirit of St. Louis (Lindbergh's plane), 35
Spirit of St. Louis, The (Lindbergh), 35
Springfield Republican, 112
Square Roof (Key West brothel), 164
Standard Oil, 52
Steadman, G. R., 101
Stearns, Harold E., 62
Stein, Gertrude, 6, 8–9, 22, 36, 170, 181
Stevens, Willie, 188
Stevenson, Robert Louis, 85
Stewart, Donald Ogden, 119, 167, 192
"stick her," 187
Stone, Julius F., Jr., 72–74, 87, 92, 114–15, 171
Strater, Henry "Mike," 26, 36, 69–70, 83, 182n1
Strychacz, Thomas, 60
Stubbe, Henry, 104
stuffing boxes, 147
sub-base (Naval Station Key West), 89–91, 187
Suchlicki, Jaime, 21
"suckers," 191
Suds (vet) in *THHN*, 180
suicides, of Great Depression/stock market crash, 190–91
Sullivan, James "Sully," 10
"Summer People" (Hemingway, short story), 127
Sun Also Rises, The (Hemingway, novel): British slang used in, 29–30; *cojones* reference, 59; dedication in, 9; epigraph of, 5–6; publishing of, 119; sexuality in, 103; "snotty," 107; title of, 3, 4; tourist characters of, 28–29
Swift, Jonathan, 55
Sylvester, Harry, 165–66
syphilis, as "rale," 172, 180–81
Szalay, Michael, 184

Tales of Fishes (Grey), 31
Tamerlane, reference to, 123
Tampico (Cuba), 155
Tampico (Hergesheimer), 155
tarpon, 135
Tartt, Donna, 8
Taylor, Ed, in *THHN*, 144
Tempest, The (Shakespeare), 55
tense, shifts in, 31–33, 40, 41, 84. *See also* narrative style, of *THHN*
termites, 152
Thompson, Charles, 10, 31, 88, 101, 134, 167
Thompson, John T., 24–26
Thompson, Karl, 31, 167
Thompson, Lorine, 134
Thompson guns (Tommy guns), 24–26, 144
Three Soldiers (Dos Passos), 124
Three Stories and Ten Poems (Hemingway, collection of short stories and poems), 9, 120, 122
"Tin Lizzie," 181
titles, of Hemingway's books, 3–5, 6
To Have and Have Another (Greene), 117–18
To Have and Have Not (Hemingway, novel): composition process, 185, 203; Cuban political history as backdrop for, 18; epigraph of, 5–7; *Esquire* articles incorporated in, 66, 67–68; as failed novel, 17; film adaptation, 32; Harry's dying quote, 184–85; lack of dedication in, 7–11; legacy of, 203–4; narrative style of, 14–17; "Note" in, 10–11; sarcasm in, 23; title of, 3–5; violence in, 61–63; "Winter" (Part Three), in novel form only, 81–204. *See also* alcohol; boats/ships; Cuba; fishing; Florida Keys; Hemingway, Ernest; Key West; masculinity themes; narrative style, of *THHN*; racism and prejudice; sex themes; violence; weapons; women, portrayal of; *individual names of characters*
Tomato Red (Woodrell), 17
Tone, Andrea, 158

Toronto Start Weekly, 16
Torrents of Spring, The (Hemingway, novel), 6, 9–10, 107, 147
Tortugas, 170–71
tourism, in Key West, 73, 114–15
Tower, Wells, 14
Tracy, Albert, in *THHN*: Cuban quartet and, 100; death of, 143, 144, 146; Harry's backstory revealed by, 93–94; hired by Harry, 133, 134; jacks reference, 135; labor strike and, 91–92; meeting with Cuban quartet, 94–95; as narrator, 82–83; wife of, 96, 198, 199; on WPA work, 108
"Tradesman's Return, The" (Hemingway, short story), 66, 67–68, 71–72, 74, 75, 177
Treasure Island (Stevenson), 85
Trippe, Juan, 42
Tropical Beer, 26
"Tropical Iceberg" (Paul), 94
True at First Light (Hemingway, nonfiction novel), 35, 56, 84, 172
True Gen, The (Brian), 130, 131
Truman, Harry S., 189
Trumbo, Howard, 78–79
Trumbo Point, 78–79
tuberculosis, 53
turtles, 103, 104
Twain, Mark, 26–27
"twirp," 157
Tyler, Lisa, 199

Ulysses (Joyce), 79, 187, 194, 202
Under Kilimanjaro (Hemingway, nonfiction novel), 35, 56, 84
unions, labor strikes and, 177–78
Updike, John, 5
"Up in Michigan" (Hemingway, short story), 103
U.S.A. (Dos Passos), 125
U.S. Postal Savings System, 171, 180

Valbenera (steamship), 70
Valdez, Charli g, 32
Van Brunt, Margaret, in *THHN*, 167
Vasquez, Raul, 93, 114–15
veterans, as "have nots," 161–62, 167–68, 169, 170–71, 172, 173–74
Veterans Rehabilitation Camps, 168
violence: abuse of wives, 134; of Cuban history, 19, 27, 85; male rape, 170; of Matecumbe camps, 169; in *THHN*, 61–63

Volunteer Works Corps, 73–74
von Kurowsky, Agnes, 126

Wagman-Geller, Marlene, 9
Waldhorn, Arthur, 184
Walker Evans: Cuba (Evans), 18
Wallace, Freddy, in *THHN*: bar of, 107, 114 (*see also* Freddy's [Freddie's] bar); boat of, 153; Gordon and, 120; Harry's disclosure about Cubans' bank robbery plans, 137; Harry's smuggling plans, 116–17; introduction of name, 167, 177; as narrator, 123
Wallace (bar employee) in *THHN*, 177
Walter, Ahto, 193
Walter, Kou, 193
Walton in *THHN*, 99, 144
War Aces, 178–79
Ward, Arthur Henry Sarsfield, 48
"War on Crime" campaign (FBI), 74–75
Waste Land, The (Eliot), 8
"ways," 109
"Way You'll Never Be, A" (Hemingway, short story), 130
weapons: *ametralladora* (machine gun), 146; depth charge, 39–40; Harry as gun runner, 138; Luger, 26; "plugged," 31, 53; "receiver," 133; shootout between Harry and Cubans, 143, 144, 151; suicide references, 191; Thompson guns (Tommy guns), 24–26, 144; Winchester pump gun, 55–56
Welles, Sumner, 18, 54
Wellesley, Arthur, 172–73
Wellington, Duke of (Wellesley), 172–73
Wells, H. G., 193–94
Wells, Sharon, 170
Welsh, Mary, 9, 134, 202
Wesley in *THHN*, 67–68, 71, 77, 78, 98
Western Story Magazine, 178–79
Western Union, 101
whetstones, 68
"whirling douches," 158
White, Raymond, 32
Whitehead Street (Key West), 42, 73, 87, 93, 152
"White Man, Black Man, Alphabet Man" (original title of "The Tradesman's Return") (Hemingway), 75
"Who Murdered the Vets" (Hemingway, essay), 161, 172
Wide Sargasso Sea, The (Rhys), 153–54
Wiggins, Ella May, 177–78

Williams, Hugh, 168–69
Williams, John, 49–50
Williams, Joy, 163
Williams, Tennessee, 164
Wilson, Edmund, 178
Winchell, Walter, 197
Winesburg, Ohio (Anderson), 188
Winner Take Nothing (Hemingway, short story collection), 4, 7, 9, 70, 76n1, 202
Wisteria Island (Christmas Tree Island), 133–34
With Hemingway (Samuelson), 91
Woman Key, 67, 77
women, portrayal of: abortion/birth control references and, 128, 158–59; abuse of wives, 134, 156, 159; in *Across the River and into the Trees* (Hemingway, novel), 111; alcoholic drinks of women, 118; androgyny, 105; as "bitches," 130, 187, 195, 197; Gordon's views of Marie, 152, 198, 200; insults to female characters, 115–16; Morgans' daughters, 111–12, 201; Morgans' daughters in *THHN*, 111–12; older women, 138–39; as prostitutes, 85–87, 94, 100, 112, 164, 202; sexual aggression of, 41, 141–42, 156–57; "social phenomena" reference, 131; *THHN* female characters as "haves," 123; women's voices and *THHN* narrative, 199. *See also individual names of female characters in* THHN
Woodrell, Daniel, 17
woodworms, 152
Woolf, Virginia, 106
Works Progress Administration, 72, 87, 91–92, 108–9, 161–62, 167–68, 192
World War Adjusted Compensation Act (1924), 173
Wright, Richard, 185
Wright Patman Bonus Bill, 174
Writer as Artist (Baker), 5

yachts, 192, 193–94
Yale University, 186, 192
yawl-rigged, 193
Yellow Claw, The (Brent), 48
"yellow journalism," 46–47
"yellow peril," 46–50
"Yellow Wallpaper, The" (Gilman), 47
"you," as narrative device, 14–17
Young, Elliot, 49
Young, Philip, 152, 157